THE ORIGIN AND EARLY HISTORY OF INSURANCE

INCLUDING THE CONTRACT OF BOTTOMRY

BY

C. F. TRENERRY, B.A., D.Sc., A.I.A.

THE LAWBOOK EXCHANGE, LTD.
Clark, New Jersey

ISBN-13: 9781584779322

Lawbook Exchange edition 2009, 2010

The quality of this reprint is equivalent to the quality of the original work.

THE LAWBOOK EXCHANGE, LTD.
33 Terminal Avenue
Clark, New Jersey 07066-1321

Please see our website for a selection of our other publications and fine facsimile reprints of classic works of legal history:
www.lawbookexchange.com

Library of Congress Cataloging-in-Publication Data

Trenerry, Charles Farley, d. 1911.
The origin and early history of insurance : including the contract of bottomry / by C.F. Trenerry.
p. cm.
Reprint. Originally published: London, P. S. King & Son,1926.
Includes bibliographical references.
ISBN-13: 978-1-58477-932-2 (cloth : alk. paper)
ISBN-10: 1-58477-932-2 (cloth : alk. paper)
1. Insurance--History. 2. Insurance, Marine. 3. Insurance, Life. 4. Bottomry and respondentia. I. Title.
HG8027.T7 2008
368.009--dc22

2008036928

Printed in the United States of America on acid-free paper

THE ORIGIN AND EARLY HISTORY OF INSURANCE

INCLUDING THE CONTRACT OF BOTTOMRY

BY

C. F. TRENERRY, B.A., D.Sc., A.I.A.

LONDON

P. S. KING & SON, LTD.

ORCHARD HOUSE, 14 GREAT SMITH STREET

WESTMINSTER

—

1926

FOREWORD

THE work which follows has been brought out under circumstances of special difficulty, for which the Editors would ask the indulgence of those who read it. It was, as will appear from its form, a thesis submitted to the University of London by the late Dr. C. F. Trenerry, whose intention was to recast it for publication, shortening and compressing it into a more compact form. After his death in 1911 the thesis was laid aside and subsequently during the years of war there was no thought given to the possibility of its publication. Now, however, it has been considered worth while to make available for a wider circle, even though in an unfinished state, a piece of work into which there was put much laborious research and intellectual power.

The Editors have therefore done their best; they are aware that much has been lost as regards literary form by repetition, but have felt that the attempt to cut down, without the technical knowledge of the author, might interfere with some essential factor, and that redundancy was to be preferred to this. The author's revision was to be directed mainly towards shortening, but he would without doubt have rearranged the chapters so as to give more even lengths, and would have almost certainly supplemented by an index.

In default of the latter, however, the chapter synopses and the very full marginal headings are a valuable aid to the mastering of the contents. The Editors would only add that in dealing with the many foreign languages and dialects, found mainly in footnotes, they have been careful to verify whatever came within the scope of their own knowledge, and their cordial thanks are due to the publishers for kind help in this and other respects; but the less familiar tongues have been left practically untouched, and there is accordingly very great possibility of mistake, for which they offer their regrets in anticipation.

They hope that in spite of its handicaps the book may succeed in reaching those who need its help, and that though the author's own work has so long been laid aside, others may still enter into the fruit of it.

E. L. G.
A. S. P.

CONTENTS

PAGE

CHAPTER VII

PART III

WHETHER LIFE ASSURANCE WAS KNOWN TO THE ANCIENTS

CHAPTER VIII

CHAPTER IX

CHAPTER X

CHAPTER XI

INTRODUCTION

THE Thesis which is presented herewith deals with the following:

(i) The origin and development of the contract of Bottomry and Respondentia down to the 11th century A.D.
(ii) The traces of methods of insurance other than life known to the Ancients.
(iii) The question whether life assurance was known and practised by the Romans or their predecessors.
(iv) The history of the development of mediæval insurance in the Low Countries from the family group system and of modern insurance therefrom.

In Part I the origin of the contract of Bottomry (or Respondentia) has been traced to the practice by the Babylonians of loans for trading purposes during and before the 3rd millennium B.C., and its development therefrom to the time of the later Roman Empire has been examined.

In Part II references to guarantees of indemnity against loss during transport by sea, to wager insurance, are discussed, and also a form of indemnity which might have been adapted to cover any class of risk. The examination has been confined to the practices of the Romans owing to the fact that no record could be traced of any such practices by any of the earlier peoples.

In Part III an examination has been made into the question as to whether life assurance was known to the ancients. This has, by the nature of the subject and the lack of evidence, been limited to an inquiry into the practices of the Greek religious societies, of the Roman religious and burial societies, military societies and veterans' societies, and to the examination of certain passages in the Roman Civil Law which appear to justify the belief that the Romans were in the habit of making non-mutual contracts of either term or whole-life assurance on their own lives or on the lives of other people.

In Part IV the discussion of the development of mediæval insurance from the family group system of the inhabitants of Flanders, etc., includes an examination of the communal system of the early Middle Ages under which a *quasi*-compulsory form of mutual fire, live-stock, etc., insurance was practised. Further evidence is produced which shows that life assurance was widely practised during and before the 16th century in Belgium. The development of the insurance idea from the primitive instinct of combination for mutual assistance underlying the family group system is demonstrated in this section.

The passages in early writings which afford the only direct knowledge of the existence of, and of the method of transacting, the special contracts which form the subject of this Thesis, are so disconnected and scanty as to necessitate the examination of a large amount of circumstantial and indirect evidence in order to bridge over the various *lacunæ* and thus complete the sequence of development of the various contracts. This accumulation of evidence has rendered the presentation of the several theories in a connected form difficult, and, at times, has tended to obscure the argument.

With a view, therefore, to placing the various points dealt with in the Thesis in their true perspective, the following summary has been inserted at this point.

SUMMARY

I

THE ORIGIN AND DEVELOPMENT OF THE CONTRACT OF LOAN ON BOTTOMRY AND RESPONDENTIA

(For definition of contracts see Chapter I.)

The order in which the early references to Bottomry are treated in the Thesis, and the scheme of development of contract, are mainly as follows :

A. BABYLONIAN.
- (i) System of trading through agent or borrower; *Commenda of Islam.*
- (ii) The contract as legislated for in the Code of Hammurabi.

B. PHŒNICIAN.
- (i) Probability that the Phœnicians acquired the practice from Babylonia.
- (ii) Changes which would have been made in contract.
- (iii) Probability that the Phœnicians transmitted the practice to Greece.

C. INDIAN.
- (i) Probability of introduction of the contract from Babylonia.
- (ii) The contract as legislated for in the *Mánava Dharma Sástra*: reference to, by modern writers.

D. GREEK.
- (i) Probability of introduction of the contract from Babylonia by the Phœnicians.
- (ii) Development and description of the contract.

E. ROMAN.
- (i) Question as to whether the contract was introduced by Greeks or by Rhodians.
- (ii) Description of the contract; references to, in Roman Civil Law.
- (iii) Development of the contract up to A.D. 1100.

GENEALOGICAL TREE OF CONTRACTS OF LOANS ON BOTTOMRY AND RESPONDENTIA

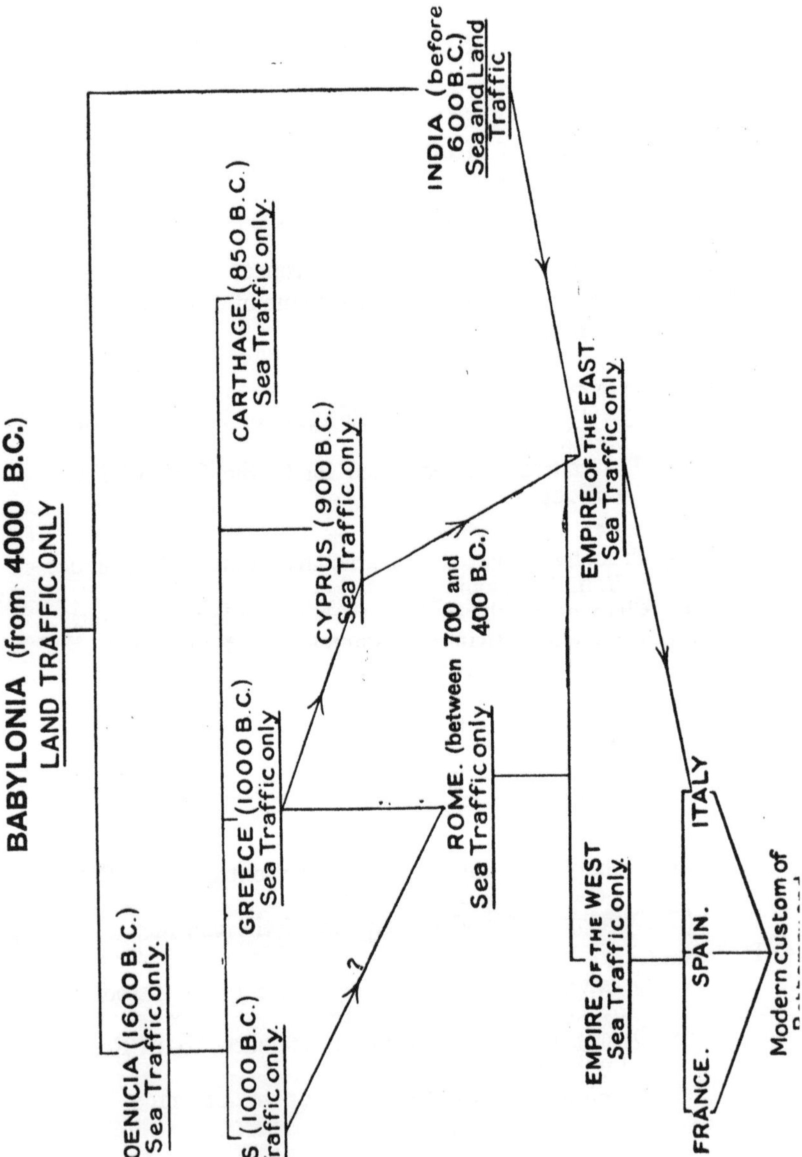

A. Babylonian.

The contract of Bottomry or Respondentia originated in a practice similar to that known as the *Commenda of Islam*, which was a development of the earliest form of trading by agents as practised in the Euphrates Valley. The Babylonians had at an early age (from 4000 to 3000 B.C.) developed their manufactures to an extent which far exceeded what they required for home consumption, and therefore were obliged to seek for foreign markets. In addition to this, Babylonia being naturally unprovided with building material, cotton, wool, silk, jewels, skins, etc., etc., all of which were essential to her manufactures, was forced to carry on a large import trade of raw material which she could use in the production of those manufactured goods. At first the manufacturers and big agricultural producers employed their slaves or relations to take their merchandise and make short trading trips as their representatives.

These employees were not partners with the employer, but simply his servants, incurring no liability and being entitled to no share in the profits. When, however, the output became more than enough to satisfy the wants of the home markets, it became necessary for the manufacturers to extend their operations and to search for more distant markets. In order to do this, they were obliged to use other means of sending their goods to foreign trading centres. Consequently, it became customary for the manufacturer or financier having large stocks of goods or money on hand, in addition to employing his own travelling salesmen or agents as described above, to find an equivalent to the modern commercial traveller. He did so by entering into a business relationship with a *Darmatha* (a sort of hawker or trader by caravan) and supplying him with goods (or money) with which the hawker might make a trade tour. This trader gave as security for the loan " himself, family and property, in town or country, on the road, or in stock." The interest or bonus he paid was either half his profits, if the said half exceeded 100 per cent. of the loan, if it did not he paid as a minimum interest 100 per cent. on the loan, or 100 per cent. of the loan only whatever his profit or loss might be, in addition in either case to refunding the capital value of the goods advanced. The rate of interest on any given transaction remained the same whatever the length of the period during which the trader was absent on his trading tour. This form of agreement apparently worked well in many cases, but involved great hardship on such traders as had the misfortune to lose their merchandise by an attack of robbers and through no fault or negligence of their own. This robbery of caravans must have happened frequently at a time when both brigandage and piracy were considered a far more honourable means of earning a livelihood than trading, and especially so when the trading journeys were carried on among the less civilized peoples.

The result was that many of these traders were unable to meet their engagements when due, and, consequently, they and their families became the absolute property of their principals, at whose discretion they could be kept or sold as slaves, or even killed.

This position becoming intolerable, the various parties interested gradually arrived at the following compromise.

The merchant advanced goods to the trader, who handed him in return a sealed memorandum or inventory containing the value, etc., of the goods, on the understanding that the security and the rate of interest payable were to be the same as those stated above; but that in the event of his being robbed on the journey, through no negligence or connivance on his part, on making a solemn declaration to that effect, he should be freed from the debt (both capital borrowed and interest).

This arrangement is referred to and given legal force in the Code of Hammurabi (2250 B.C.), wherein all the points raised above are dealt with.

This must be considered the earliest form of a contract containing the essentials of that of Bottomry which is known, viz. :—

(i) The contract was in some cases for a true loan and not a partnership, in others for a loan with limited partnership.

(ii) The merchandise or money advanced was under the custody of, and used by, the trader, not retained by the lender.

(iii) The trader was wholly free from liability for the debt on the happening of a contingency provided for in the contract.

(iv) The rate of interest was very much higher than that charged on an ordinary loan, which was at that time limited to 20 per cent.

B. Phœnician.

The origin of the Greek contract of Bottomry is a matter of conjecture, but it was probably due to the Babylonian practice referred to above. There is no reference to any such contract in Greek history prior to the 4th century B.C., at which date a contract is quoted which, as stated by Boucher in 1806, was practically identical with that used in France in his time, and which could, *mutatis mutandis*, be used for a similar contract to-day.

Since a complex business system such as is indicated by the existence of this contract must have been the result of many years' growth, it could hardly have originated in Greece, especially as the law was unfavourable to debtors before the time of Solon (*circa* 590 B.C.), who in his laws discouraged oversea traffic : whence it appears likely that the Greeks acquired a knowledge of this custom from some outside source. This source would most probably have been the same as that from which they derived their knowledge of mathematics, navigation, weights and measures, coinage, the alphabet, etc., and by the same channel, viz. from Babylonia by the Phœnicians.

Phœnicia was from 1600 to 1000 B.C. the great maritime power of the Mediterranean. In 1600 B.C. the six or seven towns composing Phœnicia, already enjoying a large and independent commerce for the sake of mutual assistance, joined themselves in a federation, with Sidon as the head, on somewhat similar lines to the Hanseatic League of 3000 years later. Her nature not only rendered it necessary for her to expand as a sea-trading nation and consequently to establish oversea marts and trade centres, but she also had the opportunity of doing so, with the result that she became a connecting link between the three continents of the then known world; and, as Maspero says, "Toutes les races du monde antique semblent s'être donné rendez-vous en Asie Mineure."

In order to develop her extensive and widespread trade, she was forced to found colonies and trading depôts for her merchandise in various countries bordering on the Mediterranean.

During the period of Greek maritime inactivity between the heroic age and the regeneration of commercial enterprise in the historic period, the Phœnician "ships were ever winding in and out of the Ægean Isles . . . and this constant commercial enterprise lasting for two centuries is amply sufficient to account for all the influence that Phœnicia exerted upon Greece." The Phœnicians themselves had for many centuries been learning business habits from the Babylonians, with whom they had the closest commercial relations; the Babylonians being the great land traders of Asia Minor, the Phœnicians the great oversea traders and carriers.

It becomes, therefore, almost a certainty that the Phœnicians, when they acquired from the Babylonians a knowledge of the contract of Bottomry as practised by them, should have submitted it to the Greeks, but in an altered form. As the Babylonian trade was a land traffic, their contract provided for losses by land journeys only. For a similar reason it is to be presumed that the Phœnician contract would have applied to marine risks alone, whence it would follow that the Greek contract derived from the Phœnicians would, at any rate, have started by being adapted to marine risks. This was the case, not only at the start but all through the history of the contract as confined to Greece, which tends to support the theory that the Greeks were indebted to the Phœnicians for the introduction to them of the Babylonian contract.

C. Indian.

It might perhaps be considered unlikely that the trading customs of one nation should have influenced other nations to the extent of communicating to them a small business custom. There is, however, another reference to the law of Bottomry which also was due to the Babylonians, viz. that in force among the Hindus from a date not later than 600 B.C. and probably much earlier. It is known that a large portion of the Babylonian trade was carried on with India, and, consequently, the Hindu and Babylonian traders must have been in continual business contact. During the early history of the country, at a time when the Babylonian civilization was approaching its zenith, the pursuits of the Hindus were, according to Max Müller, "patriarchal, their chief occupations being fighting and cultivating the soil." It is, therefore, probable that their interest in trade was, to a large extent, due to the example set them by the Babylonians, and that from them they gradually acquired their knowledge of business habits, including the laws relating to loans, rates of interest, contracts for trading purposes, etc., as set out in the Babylonian code. These laws would naturally have been amended and expanded to suit their own conditions, with the result that at some period anterior to the 6th century B.C. they were in possession of an elaborate form of contract of Bottomry of which the essential alterations from the Babylonian contract were as follows:—

(i) The contract applied to sea-borne as well as land-carried traffic.

(ii) The interest, instead of being 100 per cent. in all cases, was arranged with regard to the risks to be run and the length of time over which the money was required.

(iii) This rate of interest (or price of risk) was fixed by valuers skilled in sea voyages or journeys by land who were able to proportion the rate to the time required and to the risks to be incurred.

(iv) This rate of interest was specified in the contract.

(v) The borrower was excused payment, not only if he was robbed of his goods, but also if the goods did not arrive in good order, at the place and at the time agreed upon by the contracting parties.

From this, remembering that Babylonia was far in advance of any country of antiquity in respect of her knowledge of economics, finance and trade generally, it is reasonable to assume that the Phœnicians, who were second only to the Babylonians in their natural instinct for trade, would have been as likely to appreciate the benefits to be derived from the adoption, and when necessary the alteration of their trade customs, as were the Hindus. If this be granted, it must be admitted that in all probability the Phœnicians had a contract of Bottomry, and that they transmitted the knowledge of it to the Greeks.

D. Greek.

The contract as known to the Greeks in the time of Demosthenes (about 350 B.C.), which is the date of the earliest reference, had acquired a stable and highly complex form.

The chief points dealt with in making these loans by the Greeks were :—

(i) The agreement, which was practically the Bottomry bill or bond of Respondentia, stating the conditions of the loan, which was deposited at the bank.
(ii) The security, which was generally of at least twice the value of the sum advanced.
(iii) The period of the loan.
(iv) The rate of interest, which varied from 10 per cent. to 12 per cent. for outward voyages only and 22½ per cent. to 30 per cent. for the round voyage ; penal rates were charged if the conditions were broken.
(v) The risks provided against—which were total loss of principal and interest if the ship was lost or captured at sea ; loss of proportion of principal and interest in the event of some or all of the cargo being jettisoned or of a ransom being paid.
(vi) Representation of lender on voyage.
(vii) Obligations of borrowers—to take the most direct course ; to repay loan to lender, or his representative or assignee ; to declare if money had been borrowed already on the same goods ; not to give second mortgage on goods, as such action was held to be fraud by the first as well as the second mortgagee.
(viii) Captain's powers of borrowing.

It should be noted, however, that although the law was in favour of the lender, this class of investment was considered extremely hazardous, so much so that it was illegal to use the money of orphans in this way.

It has been suggested by certain authorities that the Greeks acquired a knowledge of this contract from the Rhodians. Even if this were granted, it would not vitiate the argument as to their having received a knowledge of the contract from the Babylonians through the Phœnicians, as the island had been colonized and civilized by the Phœnicians, who had introduced their own laws and trading customs.

E. ROMAN.

The Romans in their turn appear to have been indebted to the Greeks for a knowledge of this contract, either in the 7th century or later, when the Roman Commission on law went to Athens in the 5th century B.C. As shown by Professor Mommsen, the language and writing of Latium indicate that the early Latin commerce was confined almost exclusively to the inhabitants of the Greek colonies of Cumæ and Sicily. This introduction probably took place in or about the 7th century B.C. Pardessus suggested that the Romans owed their knowledge of this system and other maritime customs to the Rhodians, but if it be admitted that the Greeks were in possession of this system in an undeveloped form at the time when they founded the trading colonies in South Italy, it is probable that they would have communicated their knowledge to the Romans. This is rendered more probable by the fact that the contract as known to the Romans was always one of a loan of *pecunia trajectitia;* in other words, for a loan of money to be used in oversea trade.

As the trade of the Romans was confined at first almost entirely to land-carried goods, it is almost certain that if they had originated the practice, they would have started with a contract which, like that of the Babylonians, was intended to provide against the risks of land traffic, from which at a later date they would, perhaps, have developed one providing against risks either of land or of sea carriage similar to that of the Hindus. The legislation of the Romans in respect of the contract of the loans on Bottomry was practically identical with that of the Greeks. The chief differences were briefly :—

(i) The limitation of the cases in which the lender should be responsible for the loss.
(ii) The entire freedom from liability of the borrower in so far as any collateral security given by him was concerned in the event of the goods on which the loan was actually made having perished.
(iii) The inability of the lender to charge *fœnus nauticum* for the loan after the sea risk had ceased in case the borrower did not settle his account as soon as it became due, i.e. when the voyage was over.

This contract became exceedingly popular among the Romans, as it afforded wealthy gentlemen, who were not permitted to trade, a means of investing their money at a high rate of interest, and also gave the borrower an opportunity of increasing his trading capital and, at the same time, of insuring himself against total loss.

The extant references in the Roman Civil Law before the separation of the Empire dealing with this class of loan date from 100 B.C. to A.D. 300; but it is certain that the contract was known and used long before that date. During this period there was no legal restriction on the rate of interest, but it was left to the contracting parties to arrange what interest they considered mutually satisfactory. This was also permitted to the Western Empire and was, apparently, continued until a late period, since in the 11th century A.D. it was stated that 50 per cent. could be charged in a contract of this nature. In the Eastern Empire, however, Justinian in April A.D. 529 limited the rate of interest to 1 per cent. per month, which was found to be altogether too low, and consequently was repealed by him in Novel 106. Soon after, however, owing perhaps to pressure from the Church, the restriction to 1 per cent. per month was again imposed in Novel 110. Other reasons for this restrictions are suggested in the Thesis.

Comparing this rate of interest with the rates charged for insurance in the 14th century, it is seen that it was quite inadequate in proportion to the risk, and it is probable, therefore, that traders who had been in the habit of securing themselves by this contract had discovered some method of insurance which could be substituted for it. This appears to be supported by the wording of Novel 110. Whence it is likely that the contracts of Bottomry became less used as a means of obtaining a guarantee against loss of capital and were gradually supplanted by methods approximating more nearly to those of modern marine insurance.

II

TRACES OF INSURANCE (OTHER THAN LIFE) OCCURRING IN CLASSICAL ROMAN AUTHORS AND IN THE DIGEST

Owing to the exceedingly small amount of Roman classical literature dealing with business questions which has come down to us, the references to trade customs are but few. These, however, appear to show that the Romans understood and practised the following methods of providing against maritime and other risks:—

(i) Public indemnity to shippers against loss of ships or cargo from storm or attacks of enemies (215 B.C.).
(ii) Private guarantee for safe delivery of goods (50 B.C.).
(iii) Guarantee by the Emperor against the losses from storms incurred by shippers (A.D. 58).
(iv) Contracts for indemnification, which do not appear to have been confined to losses arising from sea-risks.
(v) Insurance by wager.

(i) In the case of the guarantee by the Republic against the risk incurred by certain trading companies who offered to supply goods to the army in Spain, Livy states that in about 215 B.C. there was an urgent demand from the Scipios, who were in Spain, for wages, clothes and food for the army, and also for all kinds of stores for the naval allies.

The Republic being heavily burdened by the expenses of an unsuccessful war, it was considered inadvisable to supply the above requirements from the public funds; consequently they offered terms to private trading companies who would undertake the risk of providing and shipping the stores to Spain. Three companies offered to do so, on two conditions, the second of which was the guarantee that all loss of the ships or of the shippers arising from the attacks of enemies or from storms should be borne by the State. This the Republic agreed to do.

It has long been a matter of debate whether this contract was a contract of insurance or not. The points on which the argument turns are :—

(*a*) As to the ownership of the supplies during the voyage.
(*b*) As to the liability of (i) the Government, and (ii) the shipper, for losses incurred in transit.
(*c*) As to whether the guarantee was (i) a voluntary promise of indemnification made by the Government for the benefit of its citizens, and not in return for a valuable consideration, or (ii) a contract of insurance against stipulated risks guaranteed by the Government in return for a valuable consideration paid or payable.

The points are considered fully in the accompanying Thesis, and the conclusion which has been there arrived at is that in 215 B.C. the Roman Government undertook in return for a valuable consideration (i.e. services to be rendered by the trading companies) to insure the safe arrival of certain shipments and supplies shipped by the three private trading companies who were the owners. These supplies were to be sent from Rome, and probably other centres, over the sea to Spain, where they would be sold by, and for the benefit of, the shippers.

(ii) About 150 years later Cicero, writing from Cilicia, stated that he expected to find guarantors at Laodicea for all the public money (or treasure) which he was sending to Rome, in order that both he and the State might be protected from danger of loss in transit. From this it appears that Cicero intended to send money (or treasure) from Laodicea to Rome, and had found men at Laodicea who were both able and willing to guarantee the safe arrival of its treasure.

In respect of this passage, two theories have been advanced: (*a*) that it refers to the remittance of money to Rome by the purchase at Laodicea of what were equivalent to modern bills of exchange payable in Rome, which argument is based on the hypothesis that Cicero did not intend to send the actual money or treasure to Rome; and (*b*) that Cicero did actually make arrangements to obtain guarantee of the safe arrival of certain definite sums of money and articles of value, including the spoils he had taken in his recent victorious campaigns in Cilicia, which he was sending to Rome; and that, consequently, the transaction was equivalent to obtaining a policy of marine insurance thereon.

There appears to be no particular reason for assuming that the first hypothesis is correct. Had Cicero meant bills of exchange, he would probably have referred to them in such a way as to admit no mistake in his meaning. Further, there is no reason why it should be taken for granted that Cicero was alluding to money only.

After his recent victory in Cilicia, he must have been in possession of a considerable amount of booty, and this he would be particularly anxious to send to Rome, as he was very desirous of receiving a triumph for his victories on his return, and in order to make the triumph as imposing as possible, he would have taken back to Rome as much of the actual spoils of the enemy as he could.

(iii) Suetonius states that in A.D. 58, in time of great famine in Rome, the Emperor Claudius offered to pay a fixed bounty on all corn imported, and further agreed to be responsible for all losses arising from storms.

This transaction clearly contains the essentials of insurance, for the following reasons: The property which the Emperor guaranteed was not his property nor that of the State, but belonged to the merchants who imported the corn, and on arrival at Rome was sold by them for their own benefit. There was no suggestion that the corn should be sold at a lower price, or that any restriction on the absolute ownership of the corn was placed on the merchants by their having received the bonus and the guarantee. It was the property of the importer only, who sold it to the people on its arrival. The risk is definitely stated to be that arising from storms. The premium, or consideration given in return for insurance, was the service rendered to Claudius by the merchants in importing corn at an unfavourable season of the year, whence it appears that Claudius was, in fact, a capitalist who guaranteed the owners of certain properties against certain specified marine risks, in return for a valuable consideration.

From these three instances which spread over 250 years, it appears highly probable that the Romans had for a long time been in the habit of using this method in their business.

This is especially likely to have been so as the merchants in the time of the Scipios demanded a guarantee against loss arising from attack by enemies or from storms as an important part of the consideration they expected to receive in return for the assistance they offered, whereas in the time of Claudius it was offered as part of the consideration to be paid for services which the Emperor asked the merchants to render.

(iv) In the Digest there are certain decisions which appear to refer to insurance, and show that contracts were made for the insurance of valuable property, quite apart from any question of marine risks. There is, for example, a statement by Ulpian that a contract based on the stipulation—

A. Do you promise that my £10,000 shall be safe?
B. I promise—

was valid.

As the force of this stipulation lies in the words *salva fore*, which appear to have no meaning excepting in so far as they refer to safety in respect of a possible loss arising from some anticipated risk, it is clear that a contract based on this stipulation must mean that B would indemnify A for any part of the £10,000 which might be lost.

Further, in order that the contract might be valid, it was necessary that specific performance could be enforced, which again proves that a payment must have been made by A to B in return for which B gives the desired guarantee. This follows from the fact that the contract could not be enforced unless valuable consideration had been paid for it, whence it is clear that in this contract are included all the essentials of the policy of insurance.

It should be noted that this class of contract differs from that to be examined in the next paragraph in the following important point: Under this contract A was guaranteed against a loss, but as the guarantee was a promise that the amount should be safe, it would follow that in no case could A force B to pay him more than the actual amount lost, i.e. sufficient to make the total amount £10,000; so that under no circumstances could A make a profit out of the contract.

(v) In addition to the methods suggested above, the Roman shipper had another means of protecting himself against loss.

In the Digest there are certain references to contracts which bear resemblance to a bet or wager, inasmuch as they are worded more or less in the following way:—

A asks B, "If my ship shall perish, will you pay me £10,000?" and on B's agreeing to do so, the contract was valid.

This species of contract cannot be considered parallel to a policy of marine insurance, inasmuch as it was not a contract of indemnity, since it is clear that a profit would have been made out of such a contract, if the value of the ship and the cargo did not amount to £10,000.

For reasons similar to those stated above, a premium or consideration must have been paid for the contract, and in all probability the contract applied during the duration of a certain voyage or during a specified period. There is direct proof that this contract was used constantly by merchants in the early Middle Ages in most of the leading seaport towns.

Gradually, however, it became recognized that such contracts were not contracts of true insurance, but were of an immoral nature, as they did not prevent a person from making a profit on the loss of his property, wherefore they were prohibited in most of the larger commercial centres.

There is, however, another possible explanation of this and similar passages dealing with two or more events, viz.

that they are counsels' opinions on the validity of certain contracts of contingent insurance. This suggestion has been examined below.

III

LIFE ASSURANCE AMONG THE ROMANS

This section deals with the following :—

(*a*) *Mutual Insurance*—as shown by the burial clubs and military societies which existed in large numbers during the first four centuries of our era. (In this connection is given a brief sketch of the Greek religious societies which provided funeral benefits for their members.)

(*b*) *Non-mutual Insurance.*—The data on which the hypothesis rests that this class of life assurance was known and practised by the Romans show that if they practised such insurance at all they were able to distinguish between whole-life, term, and contingent insurance.

The investigation of (*b*) is rendered difficult by the fact that the direct evidence on which the argument is based, although it may be considered to prove that contracts of life assurance would have been legal and enforceable by law, does not prove that such contracts were ever used. The presumption that they were used is, however, very strong, as in the event of their not having been used, it does not seem probable that the *responsa* referring to them would have been made. Whence, since it has been shown that the Romans had been in the habit of using other contracts dealing with risks, but not on lives, although their business and private requirements were such as to render it very desirable that they should be able to set up contracts of insurance on their own lives and on those of others, the presumption is that if they were aware of the advantages to be derived from insuring their lives, and were legally able to do so, they would have done so.

With reference to the means adopted by them for the calculation of the values of risks, premiums, etc., there is no evidence available, with the exception of the life-tables of Macer and Ulpian, the former of which was obviously not constructed from mortality experience, whereas the latter almost certainly was. Apart from these two tables, there is no record of the Romans having attempted to make any calculation based on experience of mortality.

There is also satisfactory proof that the Romans and other peoples of antiquity had noted the effect of increasing age on the power of living, that the knowledge of arithmetic and algebra possessed by the Romans in the 3rd century A.D. was very considerable, and, further, that they were versed in financial and business customs, such as the use of interest and discount, payments by instalments, of book-keeping, of banking, etc.

From an examination of these points it has been shown that the Romans were better qualified in the 2nd and 3rd centuries A.D. than the continental peoples of the 16th century to make the necessary calculations for carrying on life assurance business, in so far as they were better mathematicians, better business men, and had had their attention called to various problems arising out of the duration of life; moreover, they had long been, as stated in (*a*), in the habit of forming themselves into societies for the purpose of providing mutual benefits payable at death.

Another but less important point is that during the 2nd and 3rd centuries A.D. the Roman Empire was far richer and far more powerful than any mediæval continental nation. Her traders were, therefore, afforded the opportunity of carrying out their business in comparative safety. Again, the theory of probabilities and of the scientific treatment of insurance was at least as unknown to the French in 1650 as to the Romans in A.D. 250, but we know that policies of life assurance were declared illegal in France and other countries at that time, and at the same time were permitted in England and other countries. This being the case, it is clear that the fact that the Romans were ignorant of the scientific theory of Probabilities is no reason why they should not have practised life assurance as well as the equally ignorant mediæval peoples. The argument, therefore, may be stated thus:—

(i) That the business and private circumstances of a large number of the Roman people were such as to render them very likely to have adopted some form of life assurance, if it had been introduced to them.

(ii) That they had the necessary experience of census returns, of the record and experience of burial clubs, and sufficient knowledge of mathematics to enable them to deal with the various problems attached to life assurance in at least as scientific a way as was possible to the European nations in the 16th and 17th centuries.

(iii) That the Romans enjoyed a very extended knowledge of ordinary business transactions, such as those enumerated above, e.g., interest, discount, etc.

(iv) That the form of contract which they would have used if they wished to set up either a term or whole-life assurance policy was repeatedly stated in the *responsa* of the Jurisconsults of the 2nd and 3rd centuries A.D., in the Justinian Law and in the Basilicôn, to be not only legal but "utilis," i.e. of such a nature that specific performance of the contract could be enforced in the Pretorian Court.

(A) Mutual Insurance

The societies which practised an equivalent to mutual insurance may be divided into three classes, as follows :—

(i) Civilian.
(ii) Veterans'.
(iii) Military.

(i) Civilian Societies.

It is possible from the large amount of fragmentary evidence to evolve a fairly correct idea of the way in which these clubs were formed and carried on in respect of their

(1) Origin and Development.
(2) Membership.
(3) Government.
(4) Legal Position.
(5) Secretarial Department.
(6) Receipts.
(7) Objects.

(1) *Origin and Development.*—The burial societies of Rome were a development from the later phases of the religious

societies. These religious societies were in their turn most probably based on the Greek religious societies. The religious societies were, in the first place, a result of action on the part of those persons who, for some reason, did not belong to a *gens*, and consequently were unable to participate in any family group worship. They, desiring to take part in the worship of some divinity, formed themselves into societies each of which took as the object of its worship one or more divinities. Gradually, among other practices arising from the cult of the divinities, there arose the custom of conducting the funerals of members of the societies by and at the expense of the society, in order to ensure, not that the members should be properly buried, but that the divinities should be honoured by the due performance of the burial rites.

Later, as the religious feelings of the Romans became less strong, the advantages of ensuring that each member should be properly and decently buried became more apparent, and gradually the societies became burial societies proper, some of them having no patron divinity, others having one merely for the sake of respectability, or in order to obtain the advantage of being legally a religious society. So much was this the case that by the 2nd century A.D. all pretence of being combined for the purpose of worship was abandoned by most, if not all, of the societies in conducting their affairs, and they became, in so far as their internal economy was concerned, burial societies only.

It is also very probable, for the reasons given hereafter, that these burial clubs existed in many cases for what was practically mutual insurance business.

(2) *Membership.*—The membership of these societies was drawn from all grades, but as a rule each society was composed of members occupying more or less the same social position, though there are many instances of a mixed membership of slaves and free men. The only legal restriction of membership was an absolute veto against any person being a member of two or more societies. Women were admitted to membership. There appears to have been no qualification other than the payment of an entrance fee, appoint-

ment by the president, payment of a periodic subscription, and obedience to the rules of the general assembly, and the *decuria*.

There is no record of any examination of applicants such as is enforced in the case of entrance to the Greek societies. It is not certain whether there was an age limit for entrance; there is, however, an inscription which appears to limit the age of entrance to a particular society to such as had not arrived at the age of 30. Membership was terminated by being in arrears with the monthly subscription, by brawling, or by disobedience to the general assembly or officers of the society. Suicides were debarred from receiving the *funeraticium* or being buried at the cost of the society.

(3) *Government.*—The government of each society was vested in its members, who either met in a general assembly or elected a committee of management. Officers were elected by the members from among themselves. Women were eligible for some or all of the offices.

(4) *Legal Position.*

(*a*) In respect of their right of association. In the 2nd century A.D. societies were permitted to be formed provided that they could show that they were for public utility. Later, from the 3rd century onwards, the right of combination was limited to societies *causa religionis* and to *collegia tenuiorum*, with the result that, except in the case of the poor, when persons wished to join and form themselves into a society, they were obliged to have as their ostensible object the worship of a divinity or the burial of their members.

(*b*) In respect of their powers. Their legal powers were considerable, embracing *inter alia*:—

(i) The right to make and enforce their own by-laws, provided that the said by-laws were not in themselves illegal.

(ii) The appointment of treasurer, manager, etc., who could act as agents of the societies.

(iii) The keeping of a chest or treasury, the holding of and dealing in property, etc.

(5) *Secretarial Department.*—The secretarial work entailed the keeping of a register of members, of a register of monthly payments, minutes of the meeting of the general assembly or committee of management, correspondence, etc.

In some societies the registers were kept by the president, in others by the *arcarius*, etc. The financial methods varied accordingly in the different societies, and included looking after the investments of those societies, which consisted of land-owners, traders, slave-owners, etc. The valuation and change of officers took place every fifth year in the majority of cases; in a few cases at the end of every year, third year, or tenth year.

(6) *Receipts.*—The receipts of the societies included payments by members; interest from investments, etc.; and also donations, etc., from non-members.

The receipts from members consisted of—

(*a*) Entrance fees.
(*b*) Monthly subscriptions.
(*c*) Other subscriptions, donations, and fines.

(*a*) *Entrance fees*—payable in most, if not all of the societies—uncertain if used for part provision of funeral fund—small in proportion to funeral benefit.

(*b*) *Monthly subscription*—payable in all religious and burial societies—expressly permitted by law—strictly reserved in some, if not all, cases for the fund from which funeral expenses were paid—proportion of monthly subscription to benefits uncertain (in one case $\frac{5}{12}$ per cent. per mensem)—member failing to pay subscription when due forfeited right of membership.

(7) *Objects.*—The main object of the later religious societies or burial clubs was the provision of *funeraticium* on the death of each member.

This *funeraticium* has been understood to mean money for funeral expenses, and therefore it is claimed by Waltzing, Cagnat and others that the *funeraticium* was earmarked for the funeral expenses only. Their arguments, however, do not appear to be conclusive. In the first place, although *funeraticium* originally meant money for funeral expenses, it does not follow that it retains that meaning always. It is certain that the description *collegia causa religionis* had become in the early Empire a misdescription. This being admitted, there appears to be no valid reason why the term *funeraticium* should not also have expanded its meaning, and have come to mean money paid on the death of a deceased member for funeral expenses primarily, but not necessarily.

Further, the legislation against a man's belonging to two or more funeral societies would not have been necessary had the only benefit attaching to membership been the right to be buried, as no man wants to be buried more than once; whence the existence of this legal restriction implies that out of the several *funeraticia* payable on his death, some or all would have been used by his representatives for some other purpose than that of the burial of the deceased.

This question is discussed more fully below. The right of members to receive the *funeraticia* was invalidated by dismissal from the society and by suicide.

In this connection, I have added an appendix dealing at some length with the Greek religious societies, on which, it is probable, were based the Roman religious societies. In the Greek societies the members were entitled to be buried at the expense of the society, but this, as in the case of the early Roman societies, was done in order to ensure the due honouring of the divinity, and not with the object of benefiting the deceased member. In other respects, too, they closely resemble the earlier Roman religious societies.

(ii) Veterans' Societies.

These Societies, though composed of veterans, were really civilian societies in so far as their constitution and objects were concerned. The evidence with regard to them is scanty, but there is sufficient to show that their practices in respect of membership, management, subscriptions, etc., were very similar to those of the societies described above, excepting that their membership was limited to men who had received their discharge from the army as veterans. The *raison d'être* of these veterans' societies is not certain, but the following explanation is suggested:—

It was due, perhaps, to the recognition by the members of the ordinary civilian societies of the loss that they themselves would sustain by the admission to the society even at an advanced subscription of persons whose minimum age at entry was 46, and whose health was probably rather below the average. This loss would have been greater if the veterans had been admitted on the same terms in respect of entrance fees and monthly subscriptions as the other members, since, as pointed out above, in all probability persons who had passed a certain age were not admitted to membership of the civilian societies, and in one inscription, at least, this age appears to have been limited to 30. Whereas, if the entrance fee, which was required for incidental expenses, and the monthly subscriptions, which were accumulated for the purposes of providing the funeral fund, were so calculated as to be approximately correct for entrance at or below the age of 30, it follows that the same entrance fee and subscription would have been quite inadequate to meet the expenses and provide the funeral fund for a society which admitted members at or above the age of 46.

Further, it is not improbable that the formation of these societies was due also to the fact that the veterans, having spent nearly 30 years of their lives in the army, had broken away from the ties of early friendship and relations, and preferred to join a society where they would meet others who were interested in the same questions as they themselves, which would not have been the case in an ordinary civilian society.

These societies, after being pronounced illegal, were forbidden by Marcian.

(iii) Military Societies.

These societies, which were confined to military camps, differed in various ways from the civilian. In the first place they did not pretend to be religious societies, and further they do not appear to have been restricted in respect of their objects and of the benefits which they provided for their members. These benefits included :—

(1) Pecuniary assistance in the case of members being put to expense in the discharge of their professional duties.
(2) The payment of a certain sum to each member who died during his service with the colours.
(3) The payment of a smaller sum to members who were dismissed the service.
(4) The payment of a certain sum, *nomine annularium*, to members when they received their discharge from the service as veterans.

This last payment has hitherto been held by the great writers on this subject to have been the payment of an equivalent to the *funeraticium*, i.e. the veteran was supposed to have used the sum which he received on retiring for the purposes of obtaining membership in a veterans' society, in order that the society might provide him with a funeral when he died.

In opposition to this opinion, I venture to suggest that the benefit was not one payment, but an annual payment of the sum specified, being therefore an equivalent to an annuity. My reasons, which are given in detail below, are briefly as follows :—

(1) That the change from *annualis* to *annularis* is one which might easily have been made by a somewhat illiterate person, and once applied to a certain benefit, would have become permanently associated with that benefit.
(2) That, assuming a monthly subscription proportionate to that charged by the non-military societies, the funds of the society, if properly administered, would have been sufficient to meet the expenses of such payments.
(3) That these payments were made on January 1 only, and therefore were presumably of a different nature and requiring a different date of payment from the other payments provided for in the rules, which were paid, as far as is known, when they became due.
(4) That there is, apparently, no proof that the *annularia* had any connection with the *funeraticia*.
(5) That unless the *annularia* were used for club purposes other than those set out in the rules, there would have been a large surplus.

Even assuming that this hypothesis is not correct, and that the payment *nomine annularium* was a single payment made to the veteran on the 1st of January following the date of his retirement, there does not appear to be sufficient evidence to justify the assumption that the payment *nomine annularium* was intended to be used by the veteran as a means of joining a burial society. There is no reference to the subsequent use of this money in the rules of the society; it is therein stated that it would be paid to the veteran on retirement. Further, in the cases of a member who died during his period of service, and of a soldier who was dismissed the service, the rules as to the payments made to them are equally free from any allusion to the way in which the money should be used. It seems, therefore, that the writers who contend that these payments were used as *funeraticia* are biassed by their desire to make the military societies fall into line with their views in respect of the practices of the civilian societies. Even in the civilian societies, as is pointed out above, the evidence is not convincing that the payments made by these societies during the 3rd and 4th centuries to the representatives of the deceased members were made on the understanding that they would be devoted to the payment of the funeral expenses of the deceased.

The membership of each of these societies differed considerably in respect of the amount of the fees and subscriptions, and of the benefits; those of the junior ranks of the commissioned officers being necessarily composed of more wealthy men than those of the band or rank and file.

Certain of these societies, in addition to the admission of men who were fully qualified as private soldiers, bandsmen, etc., admitted *tirones* (recruits or students), and in this respect they resembled trade gilds (*collegia*), which also admitted apprentices. These students had certain privileges. They could pay the whole or part of their entrance fee, and begin the payment of a similar proportion of their monthly subscriptions when they chose, and were entitled to participate in the benefits attached to membership, *pro rata* with the amount of subscription paid by them;

their right of participation beginning on the day on which they completed their proportional payment.

Summing up, it may be considered—

(i) In respect of the civilian societies (including veterans' societies)—that there is a strong probability that from the religious societies providing for the burial of members as an incident in the worship of the divinity in whose honour they were established, were developed societies nominally *causa religionis*, whose object was the provision of burial funds for the members, and thence societies which provided for the payment of a sum of money on the death of each member, such sum of money being at the free disposal of his representatives.

(ii) In respect of military societies—that they provided payments to meet certain expenses which might or might not fall on members; payment of a certain sum on death if it occurred during their period of service; and of either a payment on a man's discharge as a veteran, or possibly an annuity beginning on the 1st of January next following his discharge. Whence it may be stated that the civilian societies had probably developed a system of mutual industrial insurance, and the military societies (*a*) term insurance against certain contingent expenses, (*b*) life insurance for a certain term, and (*c*) the payment of an endowment to members who survived the term, or if the hypothesis in respect of the meaning of the words *nomine annularium* be correct, the payment of a deferred annuity commencing on the retirement of the member.

(B) Non-mutual Life Assurance

The evidence on which is based my theory that the Romans were in possession of a limited form of life assurance dating from the 2nd century A.D. at latest, consists of certain *responsa* and imperial rulings contained in the Roman Civil Law, the earliest being that of Gaius written about A.D. 150, and the latest that of Basil or Leo of about A.D. 900. These *responsa* and rulings afford clear proof that certain contracts were valid, these contracts being of such a nature as to serve the purpose of a policy of life assurance; some of them, *mutatis mutandis,* would serve as a basis for a similar contract to-day.

It is, of course, possible that these contracts were not used for the purposes of life assurance, and that they may have referred to business of an entirely different nature; and with the very limited information which is given in respect of each contract, it is impossible to say that the business done under the contract was of the nature of a life assurance contract, but it is suggested that they appear more fitted to a contract for business of that nature than for any other, and, further, that there is no reason to suppose that they were required for other kinds of business. It has been suggested that they were used in connection with legacies, the return of a dowry on the death of a married daughter, etc., but these explanations are not satisfactory. In one case, for example, the translation of the *responsum* is "if anyone makes a stipulation 'for money to be paid to my daughter after my death,' or this, 'for money to be paid to me after the death of my daughter,' he will have made a stipulation in a valid manner." According to the explanations previously offered, the first of these would refer to the payment of a legacy to the daughter by the heir of the person making the contract, and the second to the return of a dowry to the father on the death of his daughter. These explanations do not seem to be mutually related, whereas in the *responsum* it is obvious that the two contracts are variations of the same form. Wherefore even if there were no collateral evidence on either side, it would be more reasonable to assume that they both referred to the insurance, in the first place of the father's life for the benefit of the daughter, and in the second place of the daughter's life for the benefit of the father.

This meaning is rendered more probable by the fact that the next sentence in the same *responsum* reads as follows :—

"Not only can we make a stipulation in this manner, 'when I shall die,' but also this, 'if I shall die,'" the natural meaning of which appears to be that it was legal for a person to make a contract for money payable to him at his death whenever it should occur, as well as at his death if it should occur at a certain time, or during exposure to a certain risk.

In the event of these contracts referring to a practice equivalent to life assurance, the first stipulation would have sanctioned the making of a contract for whole-life assurance, and the second for term insurance.

These notes quoted above are taken from the Digest, and are the *responsa* given by Ulpian (about A.D. 225), who was responsible for the table of annuity values known as Ulpian's Table, which, it is unanimously agreed, was constructed on experience derived from actual mortality. This fact, perhaps, renders it more probable that the business referred to is that of insurance, as, in the event of questions arising as to the validity of certain contracts of insurance, they would undoubtedly have been submitted to the *jurisconsult* who had made himself celebrated by the production of what was probably the first and only table based on mortality experience known to the Romans.

Further, in the Institutes of Justinian (published in the same month as the Digest, December A.D. 533) a ruling is added to the effect that a contract, based on the death of a third party, can be made correctly. There are several other references in Roman Law between the 2nd and 6th centuries A.D., including one contained in the Breviary of Alaric II, dealing with the same class of contract. From a comparison of the various references, it is seen that the contract could only be made in a very limited way in the time of Gaius, and that by the time of Justinian certain of the restrictions had been removed.

Passing on to the rulings contained in the *Basilikôn* (published by the Emperors Basil and Leo, A.D. 870–920) it is found that these contracts could be made with much greater freedom. One extract taken from Book 24 may be translated as follows :—

" In ancient times, stipulations, legacies and other contracts which matured after death (= at death) were set aside, but we for the sake of their general utility to mankind approve them ; as it has been agreed that that ruling which was in force in ancient days is amended by fixed custom."

From this extract are obtained several valuable hints with regard to the contracts referred to. In the first place it is clear that legacies formed a part only of the business done under these contracts. Secondly, it shows that the contract was of such importance as to render it advisable to set aside the legal restrictions in force in earlier times; and also that the contract had been sufficiently general and long-continued to justify itself by usage.

The first point mentioned is further strengthened by the ruling contained in Book 43, which states in reference to contracts based on death "that the stipulation is similarly valid whether it has been contained in a legacy or in another contract."

The extracts from the Roman Law to which I have referred briefly above, and which are stated in detail in the Thesis, can be shown to contain directly or indirectly all those essentials for the setting up of a contract of what is equivalent to life assurance, and in fact would be true life assurance, mentioning

i.e. (i) The life insured.
(ii) The person or company with whom the contract is made.
(iii) The duration of the risk.
(iv) The consideration in return for which the contract was made.
(v) The benefit.
(vi) The beneficiary.

(i), (iii), and (vi), i.e. the life insured, the duration of the risk, and the beneficiary, are directly referred to in the stipulation, e.g. ". . . to be paid to my daughter after my death" and "when I shall die" or "if I shall die."

(ii) i.e. the person or company with whom the contract is made. From the fact that the contract or stipulation was pronounced to be valid (*utilis*), i.e. it would support an action in the Pretorian Court for specific performance, it follows that the person or company granting the insurance must have been stated in the contract, since in order for an action for specific performance of a contract to be brought it would be necessary that the contract should state who was the person or company against whom the action would lie.

(iv) The consideration in return for which the contract was made. In order that the contract should be equivalent to a modern life assurance contract, the consideration or premium must have been (i) valuable and (ii) of less amount than the benefit. In addition it must have been payable either by a single payment or in instalments. For a contract to have been *utilis*, it was necessary that a valuable consideration should have been paid, as no contract could have been enforced which was based on a promise made voluntarily and not in return for a consideration. Wherefore it follows that these contracts must have been made in return for a valuable consideration, which consideration was in all probability set out in the actual contract, but if not could have been proved to have been paid. This question is dealt with fully below, and the lines on which the second problem is dealt with are, briefly, (*a*) the practices of the Romans in respect of their mutual societies, (*b*) money-lenders' methods in dealing with reversions, and (*c*) the practices in respect of wager and indemnity insurance. From these it will be seen that there is very strong probability that the Romans were in the habit of paying a small sum down or small periodic payments with a view to receiving a larger sum in the future at some date determinable upon the death of the person on whose life the contract was based.

(v) The benefit. Since the contract was *utilis*, it is clear that the amount or complete description of the benefit must have been attached to the contract.

To sum up, the following sets out briefly the reasons for the belief that the Romans were cognisant of and practised a non-mutual system of life assurance:—

(i) That the sale and purchase of reversions, etc., and life annuities were known in the earliest days of the Empire, if not before.

(ii) That the Romans had at least as good a knowledge of mathematics and finance as was possessed by the peoples of the 16th century who were acquainted with life assurance contracts.

(iii) That they had also noticed the effect of climate and race on longevity.
(iv) That, as is shown by Ulpian's Table, they had a rough knowledge of the features of a life table.
(v) That they had recognized the value of insurance in mercantile risks and were in possession of a form of contract, namely, the " wager " insurance, which may have been used as a means of setting up insurance on life.
(vi) That mutual combination for the purposes of providing funds payable at death was very generally practised by them.
(vii) That there is evidence that certain contracts bearing a distinct resemblance to contracts of modern life assurance were valid.

IV

THE SOURCES AND DEVELOPMENT OF INSURANCE, OTHER THAN LIFE, KNOWN AND PRACTISED IN THE MIDDLE AGES

In investigating the origin of insurance other than life, it has been customary to attempt to trace the connection between the methods adopted by the Romans and referred to in Part II, with the result that investigators have been able to find but two or three references, of which the earliest dates from the 14th century.

This want of evidence may be due to the fact that the disturbance caused by the separation of the Eastern and Western Empires, and the inroads of the barbarians, combined with the adverse influence of the Church, rendered it advisable for business men to keep their trade customs secret as far as possible. This secrecy, if it existed, was doubtless accentuated by the jealousies of the many competing seaport and trading towns on the Mediterranean.

There were, however, other sources from which the mediæval people may have derived insurance, namely, from a development of (A) the gilds of Mempisc, Flanders, etc., which were the outcome of the family group system of the Flemings and Germans, and (B) of certain forms of capitalist insurance practised by the Flemings as early as the 13th century.

That this line of descent was the true one is rendered more probable by the fact that the Roman system of insurance apparently ignored risks of loss arising from fire, illness, or other similar accident; whereas, the gilds provided against them.

(A) Development of Gilds from Family Group System.

The line of development of mediæval insurance from the family groups of the Germans and Flemings was as follows:—

(i) The "family group" of the Germans and Flemings.
(ii) The Gilds of Mempisc and Flanders, etc. (8th to 10th century A.D.).
(iii) Mutual insurance of the inhabitants of each village from 11th to 13th century A.D.
(iv) Communal insurance of groups of villages in a district, from the 14th century onwards.

The primitive tribes of Germany and Flanders regarded the family and not the individual as the unit. The collective rights and duties of the members of the family over and towards individual members were generally (i) mutual property in land belonging to the group, (ii) mutual right of succession to property of intestate member, (iii) mutual obligation to prosecute murderer of member of group, (iv) mutual liability to pay *wergild* for murder committed by member of group, (v) mutual obligation to assist fellow-members, (vi) mutual religious rites and burial. Thus each group formed in itself a "small combination for mutual assistance and support."

Subsequently, owing to reasons which are given in detail in Chapter XXIII, these families became of less importance, and were gradually superseded by gilds or a collection of individuals bound together by kindred tastes and pursuits, rather than by tie of blood or of religion. Owing to the fact that these collections of persons were of what may perhaps be called a progressive nature, they were regarded with suspicion both by the members of the families still in existence, and by the rulers of the land, whence these societies adopted a *quasi*-secret method of conducting their rites, meetings, etc., and being certain, as they were, that it would be bad policy for them to afford the Government any opportunity for supervising or interfering with them, they took care so to arrange their internal affairs as to render each member by the imposition of an oath personally liable to his fellow-members for the due observance of his duties towards the society.

These societies were known as gilds (or *geldonia*) and flourished chiefly in Flanders, Mempisc, etc. Among their other objects, they endeavoured to protect themselves against oppression by the great territorial lords, and also from losses by fire, shipwreck or other misfortune. They were, therefore, practically groups or societies formed for the purpose of mutual insurance of the members. Although little is known of the way in which they were formed and conducted, it is clear that they were originally organized as secret societies, and their members were required to take an oath of fealty to their gild and to their fellow-members.

In some ways these societies resembled closely the *collegia* of the Romans in so far as each was composed of men from much the same rank of life, and was supported by periodic subscriptions paid by the members. In their objects they were, however, very dissimilar. The Roman *collegia* were largely devoted to the cult of the respective patron divinities and, apart from the societies providing *funeraticia* and the military societies, provided no form of mutual insurance.

The gilds, however, were but little interested in religious observances, their chief object being the mutual welfare and insurance of their members. That these gilds were very numerous and that the mutual insurance side of their transactions was generally known and approved by the authorities, is clearly shown by the legislation of the Carlovingian Emperors, under which it was expressly stated that no one should dare to take an oath in respect of membership of such gilds. It is clearly indicated that no objections were taken to the gilds themselves or to their aims.

The first reference to these gilds is contained in the

Capitulare Francicum in a law, dated A.D. 779, which prohibits the combination of people bound together by an oath for the purpose of affording mutual protection against misfortune, fire or shipwreck, but the injunction is against the taking of the oath, not against the mutual insurance. This prohibition was repeatedly confirmed in later laws, showing that these gilds were numerous and consequently filled a definite want.

These gilds were gradually superseded by new combinations of the following nature: the inhabitants of many of the towns of Flanders, Mempisc, etc., began to form themselves into communities making their own laws, which the members obliged themselves to obey, although they had not legal sanction inasmuch as the overlords did not recognize them, and at first actively opposed them. Soon, however, the overlords found that it was practically useless to attempt to coerce these communities, and consequently making the best of the situation in which they found themselves, they gradually gave their sanction to them, generally in return for some favour which they received from the community, with the result that during the latter part of the 11th century, and subsequently, many of the village communities received charters from the overlords sanctioning their local customary law, giving them powers of punishment, and by the introduction of Roman Law gradually widening their scope and rendering them more efficient in the pursuit of their various functions. Among these combinations which received charters were the *Amitié d'Aire*, which was granted a charter in 1100 by Robert II and Clemence, his wife. This charter contained a clause dealing with the indemnification of a member whose house was burnt, or who, having fallen into captivity, had paid as his ransom the greater part of his property. To such an unfortunate member each of his fellow-members was obliged to pay one piece of silver.

Other village communities received charters of a similar nature about this time. Such were the charters of *Granmont* (about 1067–1070), *Minne* (Flemish for Amitié) of *Ghent* and of *Bruges*, etc. These charters or *keuren* gradually changed in character and became by the 13th century much more formal.

In the *keure* of *Veurnambacht*, for instance, it is stated that the person whose house was burnt down by a fire, *of which the origin was unknown*, was to be indemnified without delay by the whole village for his loss, and was to be paid by officers known as *ceurherrs* (or coratores) who were elected by the community. There is, as will be noticed, a marked change between this class and that of the earlier *keuren* such as the *Amitié d'Aire*, in which there was no mention as to the cause of the fire, and under which an equal amount was paid by each of the fellow-members, with the probable result that the total sum subscribed was considerably less than the loss incurred.

In the case of the later *keuren*, the overlords themselves recognized the advantages to be gained by this system of mutual insurance by fire, and, as is set out in the Chronicles of the Abbey of St. Nicolas of Furnes, dated December, 1241, they themselves were admitted to the benefits of this mutual insurance on the understanding that they should contribute *pro rata* with the value of their property which was at risk in the losses incurred by the other members through fires of unknown origin.

Whence it will be seen that by the middle of the 13th century a municipal system of fire insurance had arisen which was under the control of the *échevins* and the *ceurherrs*, and that the villages had learnt the necessity of stipulating that only losses arising from fire of unknown origin would be insured against and that each contributor was obliged to pay *pro rata* with the value of his own property in the indemnification of the losses of another; thus showing that the old idea of brotherhood had passed away and that the system had now become a matter of ordinary business.

A later development of this custom of village combination was the joining together of the villages in the district and the formation of the communal government of the entire district as in the case of *le Statut du Mont d'Hazebrouck*, dated 1340. In this statute, the fires insured against were required to be of external origin, and the demand for indemnification was required to be made "in accordance with the law of the country." The advantages attaching to this extension over a larger area in the case of fire is obvious, as the risks were spread over a greater number of houses, and, consequently, the amount that each individual had to subscribe towards any one fire became less.

In respect of indemnification against losses arising from shipwreck, it is found that this custom was, as might be expected, confined to the gilds composed of people living on the seashore, and was not carried on by the inland *keuren*; in fact, as will be shown, this class of insurance ceased, at an early period, to be run on mutual lines, and gradually was provided for by a species of proprietary insurance or of underwriting.

Returning now to the middle of the 13th century, it is found that another system of mutual insurance was also in vogue, namely that known as *Hamelinghe*. For instance, in Section No. 24 of the *keure* granted to the villages of Nord and Zud Schoöte (March 5, 1266) by their overlord, the Abbess of Messines, it is stated that the person who maliciously injures or kills the cattle of another, and thus permits him to claim *Hamelinghe*, is to be fined, etc. This *Hamelinghe* is the term applied to the indemnification of the loser of cattle, who, on making a claim in the manner prescribed by custom, was entitled to indemnification by his fellow-villagers. There are many other instances of this custom of *Hamelinghe*.

From this it follows that the custom of mutual combinations to insure against fire, shipwreck, loss of live stock, captivity, etc., were formed at a very early age in Flanders, and lasted in the form of *keuren* until the late Middle Ages.

(B) Forms of Capitalist Insurance practised by the Flemings.

Non-mutual or capitalist insurance can be traced as far as the middle of the 13th century A.D., at first as an indemnification granted against certain specified risks offered by an overlord in return for certain small payments, and later in the case of maritime risks by a corporation and by underwriters.

The earliest reference to any form of non-mutual guarantee against loss practised in Belgium is contained in certain letters from the *échevins* of Bruges and Ypres, dated A.D. 1227. In these documents, it provides that certain merchants attending a fair at Messines should pay two deniers more than others, and in return the "Abbesse prendra sous sa protection pendant toute la durée de la foire les marchands et les marchandises . . . et elle fera rendre justice à leurs réclamations," from which it appears that the Abbess in fact insured the merchants and their goods during the fair, and bound herself to meet, or to cause others to meet, their claims for losses, if any.

A more definite statement is contained in a letter of the Duke of Limbourg, dated January 12, 1248, wherein he states that merchants should pay certain rates for crossing his territory, and that in return, whatever loss happened either to their merchandise or to the men themselves, either in person or in goods, or in affairs, within thc said boundaries, should be made good.

A similar undertaking to that of the Abbess of Messines was imposed on Bruges on December 1, 1298.

Marine Insurance. There is found in the *Chronyke van Vlaenderen* a statement that—

> "at the request of the inhabitants of Bruges in the year 1310, he (Count Robert of Flanders) sanctioned the establishment in this town of a Chambcr of Insurance, wherein merchants might be able to insure their merchandise against risks, marine or otherwise, at a cost of a few deniers per cent., as is the practice to-day (1735). Moreover, lest the undertaking, of such value to merchants, should be dissolved as soon as it was established, he made various laws and forms which both the insurers (i.e. the company) and the merchants (i.e. the insured) were bound to observe."

This statement is supported by direct references in the *Jaer-Boecken van Brugge* and in the *Brugschen Koophandel.*

As all these references to the Chambers of Insurance were written in the 18th century and the charter has not been found, it has been doubted whether such a Chamber ever existed. The reasons for and against the accuracy of these statements are given below, and the conclusion arrived at is that the balance of evidence is in support of the statements, and that, consequently, there is a great probability that such a Chamber of Insurance was actually established in Bruges in 1310.

Apart from the reference to the Chamber of Insurance there is other evidence of undoubted authenticity of the existence of the practice of marine insurance in Bruges during the 14th century; for example, in the *Ouden Wittenbouc*, there is an entry dated December, 1377, giving the judgment of the *échevins* on an action under "Charter van Zecggerscepe" to recover the value of certain goods which had been lost and which were covered by the policy of insurance referred to. This judgment is entered as an ordinary item of the business of the College of Échevins and shows by its absence of comment or explanation that the business of insurance was understood clearly by all parties concerned. It should be noted that the contract was a contract for indemnity, non-mutual, and not partaking of the nature of a wager.

In the 15th century, the custom of marine insurance had become so general as to provide matter for continual lawsuits, the records of which have been preserved. The policy of insurance was known as a *Charter van Zecggerscepe*, and later as a *policie d'asseurance* which could be drawn up in the form of a simple "cédule" or note of hand by the parties, under their private seal or by the public notary or proctor, and made payable to order or not. Under all contracts of insurance, claims were payable immediately on proof of loss; counter-claims for rebate could only be made subsequently to the payment of the sum payable under the policy in respect of the claim.

The risks provided against were much the same as those of to-day, comprising capture, shipwreck, the unseaworthiness of the ship (if not known to the owner of the goods on which the policy had been taken out), etc. The policies do not cover *fraude de ribaudise* committed by the captain, although the owner of the policy had no share in or control over his action. They were also rendered void if the insurer could show that the insured had knowingly placed his merchandise on a ship which was unseaworthy.

The custom of " General Average " was understood, and, as is indicated in a case dated July 15, 1441, had been practised for many years, as it was therein prescribed that the goods should be computed according to the ancient custom.

When the policy-holder elected to claim the total sum covered by the policy, he was required to transfer his interest in the goods insured to the insurers. In the policy was a schedule setting out all the items of merchandise insured thereunder, and when the policy was signed and the contract of insurance completed, this schedule appears to have been held sufficient evidence as to the merchandise by risk, as in each record of an action arising out of marine insurance the claim is for the payment of the sum insured *selon le contenu des cédules*. Insurance was not confined to merchandise only, as ship-owners insured their ships also.

Policies of insurance were granted, as a rule, by merchants who guaranteed or underwrote the policy. The liability of these underwriters depended on the claims. In some cases the liability of each was limited to the amount of the risk which he had underwritten. In other cases all the signatories to a contract were jointly and severally liable for the total sum insured. There is a record, too, of a case in which the insurers are cited as " the Company of George Spingle," which may have been the company carrying on the insurance business only or, more probably, a trading company.

It must be remembered, as will be pointed out later, that these contracts of marine insurance were, generally speaking, not mutual, in that the large majority of them were either proprietary or underwritten.

Re-insurances were known at this time (1450) and were frequently made.

On examining the records of marine insurance, referred to above, it will be noted that many of the merchants mentioned therein, either as plaintiffs or defendants, were stated to belong to Italian, Spanish or other towns. From this it is clear that marine insurance must have been as well known and probably as much practised in the Latin as in the Low Countries during the 15th century and later.

Life Assurance. In the laws of Antwerp, dating from about 1550, there is a direct reference to the practice of insurance on lives, which was stated to have been customary from "all old times" and to be legal. In the later laws, dated 1581, this is reversed, as it states that an ordinance had been passed in 1571 which, although permitting the making of contracts of insurance on merchandise, ships, etc., forbade all insurances on lives. It is also stated that in 1544 the practice of making *wager insurances* on the lives of little boys and girls was prohibited. It is worthy of note that a distinction was drawn between *asseurantien* on the lives of persons and *weddinghen* on the lives of children, as it appears therefrom that the *asseurantien* were not wager insurances.

NOTE.—When the full title of a work referred to in the notes is not given, it will be found in the bibliography which follows the Appendices.

PART I

ORIGIN AND DEVELOPMENT OF CONTRACT OF BOTTOMRY AND RESPONDENTIA DOWN TO THE 11TH CENTURY A.D.

CHAPTER I

THE ORIGIN AND DEVELOPMENT OF THE CONTRACT OF BOTTOMRY

THE definition of Bottomry [1] and Respondentia [1] given in the *Encyclopædia Britannica* is as follows:—

Definition of Bottomry and Respondentia.

Bottomry, a maritime contract by which a ship (or bottom) is hypothecated in security for money borrowed for expenses incurred in the course of her voyage, under the condition that if she arrive at her destination the ship shall be liable for repayment of the loan, together with such premium thereon as may have been agreed for; but that if the ship be lost, the lender shall have no claim against the borrower either for the sum advanced or for the premium. The freight may be pledged as well as the ship, and, if necessary, the cargo also. In some cases the personal obligation of the ship-master is also included. When money is borrowed on the security of the cargo alone, it is said to be taken up at *respondentia*; but it is now only in rare and exceptional cases that it could be competent to the ship-master to pledge the cargo, except under a general bottomry obligation, along with the ship and freight. In consideration of the risks assumed by the lender, the bottomry premium (sometimes termed *maritime interest*) is usually high, varying of course with the nature of the risk and the difficulty of procuring funds.

Theory in respect of origin.

The origin and evolution of the contract of Bottomry are examined in this section of the Thesis, and the following theory in respect thereof is advanced:—

[1] For form of modern contracts see D. Owen, *Marine Insurance Notes and Clauses*, etc., 3rd edition, pp. 209–211.

(1) That the form of contract for loans was originated before 2250 B.C. by the Babylonians, who developed it from a trading custom similar to that known as the *Commenda of Islam.*

(2) That the Babylonians in the course of their trading introduced the contract to the Phœnicians and Hindus, by whom the contract was altered and amended in order to suit their respective requirements.

(3) That the Phœnicians handed on the contract as amended by them to the traders on the littoral of the Eastern Mediterranean, including the Greeks, Rhodians, etc., and that the Greeks, in whose case alone there is extant evidence, further amended the practice.

(4) That the Romans acquired their knowledge of the contract from the Greeks or, less probably, from the Rhodians.

(5) That the contract as known and used in the Middle Ages was the outcome, primarily, of the Roman contract, but ultimately of the Babylonian.

Direct evidence.

The direct evidence on which this theory is based consists of certain passages (i) in the Code of Hammurabi, King of Babylon, about 2250 B.C., (ii) in the Brahman Code known as the Mânava Dharma Sâstra, (iii) in Demosthenes and other Greek authors, (iv) in Roman Civil Law, etc., and (v) in the writings of later jurists.

From this it will be seen that there are certain *lacunæ* in the direct evidence which render it necessary to investigate such collateral evidence as exists of the trade intercourse between the various peoples referred to, and also of the influence exerted by the more businesslike of these peoples upon the trade and financial customs of the others.

The nation which was pre-eminent among the early races for its acumen and originality in business and trade was the Babylonian. As is shown in Appendix A, the Babylonians were the first and practically the only people in ancient times to evolve a theory of political economy, in addition to which Babylonia was for at least 2000 years the financial and trading centre of the eastern hemisphere. There are only, as far as we know, two other nations (of which we have records) the civilization of which dates from as early a period as that of the Babylonians. These are Egypt and China. But, as is shown below, there is no reference in the early writings of either of these peoples to any practice remotely approaching to that of the contract of Bottomry.

Babylonian.

It may, therefore, be assumed that the origin of the contract could not be traced back further than that suggested, viz. the practice of the Babylonians referred to in the Code of Hammurabi.

Indian.

The next direct reference is found in the writings of the Brahmans. It is probable, for the reasons stated in Chapter III, that the knowledge of the custom was introduced to the Hindus by the Babylonian traders, and that the custom as prescribed in the Institutes of *Menu* is an amended form of the earlier contract.

Greek.

Turning now to the writings of Demosthenes, it is seen that the Greeks by the middle of the 4th century B.C. had evolved a form of contract which was in essentials as perfect as that used in London to-day. If, as suggested, the Greeks were indebted to the Babylonians for the knowledge of the contract, it is clear, as they had little or no trade intercourse with the Babylonians, and the ex-territorial traffic of Greece was confined almost entirely to a coasting trade in the Ægean and Ionian Seas, that there must have been some connecting link between the great trading nations of the East and Greece.

Trade in Mediterranean, 1500–300 B.C.

This link is found in the Phœnicians, who had from 1500–300 B.C. almost a monopoly of the sea-borne trade of the Eastern Mediterranean other than that of the seas bordering on the Peloponnesos, which they shared with Greece. Unfortunately, there is no direct evidence extant that the Phœnician traders used this, or any, form of loan based on the sharing between the lender and the borrower of the risks incurred in voyages, but, as they were in continuous communication with the Babylonian traders, they could hardly have avoided learning the conditions on which they traded, and, similarly, would have passed them on to the Greeks. This appears to follow from conditions of trade which ruled about 1000 B.C.

Early civilization in Euphrates valley.

As will be shown below, in the valleys of the Tigris and of the Euphrates, there was a civilization dating from *circa* 5000 B.C., which from an early date carried on a very large and widely spread land-borne commerce based on extensive manufactures with Phœnicia and India. Later Phœnicia developed the largest sea-borne trade of antiquity; and shared, if not controlled, the trade of the Ægean Sea and of Greece for some 200 years. Her influence over the Greeks during the 10th and 9th centuries B.C. led them to adopt her system of navigation and her alphabet, weights and measures, etc., which she in her turn had acquired from the Babylonians. Further, Phœnicia met Babylonia as a country trading by sea as opposed to Babylonia whose trade was, practically, entirely carried on by land; if, therefore, she adopted the contract used by the Babylonians for purposes of land traffic, it is certain that she must have modified it so as to render it suitable for sea-borne trade, in which form it would have been introduced to the Greeks.

Introduction of Babylonian knowledge to Greeks by Phœnicians.

Roman.

Passing to the consideration of the contract as known to the Romans, a similar question as to the date of the introduction of the contract presents itself. That the contract was introduced by a seafaring nation follows from the fact that the use of it was confined to sea-borne trade, which would probably not have been the case if it had been originated by the Romans, as their trade was during the earlier part of their history confined almost entirely to that carried by land. The possible sources from which they derived their knowledge of the contract were (1) the Greek trading towns in Southern Italy founded about the 9th century B.C., (2) from Greece direct (cf. the case of the XII Tables), and (3) the Island of Rhodes.

Contract probably introduced to Romans by Greeks.

From this point the line of descent is easily seen. In the Roman Civil Law there are many references to the contract (the earliest extant being that of Scævola, which dates from 100 B.C.) down to the Laws of Basil in the Eastern

Empire, and in the Western Empire to the Breviary of Alaric, and subsequently in France and Spain. In Chapter V the history of the contract is brought down to the 11th century A.D.

For the purposes of the Thesis the cognate contracts of Bottomry and Respondentia are regarded as being similar, a method of treatment which has been adopted because the underlying principle of each contract is the same, namely, that the lender takes a certain risk of losing both the capital advanced and the interest thereon, in return for which he receives a higher rate of interest than that paid on ordinary loans, and the borrower is, under certain conditions, freed from all liability for the repayment of the capital borrowed and from the payment of the interest thereon.

CHAPTER II

THE ORIGIN OF THE CONTRACT OF BOTTOMRY, PRIOR TO 250 B.C.

Limits imposed on research as to origin and early history of contract of Bottomry.

THE necessary conditions for the investigation of the origin and development of the contract of loans on Bottomry or the contract of Respondentia are (1) the existence of intelligible records of contracts containing the fundamental ideas of the contract of Bottomry, (2) the lapse of sufficient time from the date of such evidence to that of similar contracts in the classical period to have permitted the gradual evolution of the system from the undeveloped and limited state in which it must have first appeared to the perfect form of the age of Demosthenes,[1] and (3) a connecting link by which the trade customs of the older people were transmitted to the Greeks. In addition, great assistance in tracing the growth of this contract is derived from a careful preliminary consideration of the comparative likelihood of the various nations satisfying conditions (2) and (3) above having been sufficiently interested in such forms of trade or finance as not only to evolve and use such a system in their everyday trading, but also to consider trade and financial operations of sufficient general importance to the country to necessitate direct legislation thereon. In this case the enquiry has been confined to the following nations of antiquity: peoples of India, Chinese, Egyptians, and Babylonians.[2] Examining the Indian records, nothing is found

[1] 350 B.C. See p. 75, below.

[2] The Hittite civilization, which was at its zenith about 1500 B.C., is omitted owing to the lack of intelligible records. (Cf. Prof. A. H. Sayce: *The Hittites, etc.*)

The Elamite and Akkadian civilizations were incorporated in that of Babylonia (see various text-books on Babylonia quoted in Bibliography).

bearing on the subject of earlier date than the *Mánava Dharma Sástra*,[1] in which the subject is referred to. The Chinese civilization, although of great antiquity, is yet of much inferior age to either the Babylonian or the Egyptian, and, as shown by the records, does not date from earlier than approximately 2500 B.C. Terrien de Lacouperie[2] is of opinion that China owed her civilization to an eastern movement of certain peoples from the Euphrates valley who took the early Babylonian civilization with them. Whence, if this somewhat extravagant theory be admitted, it follows that any record of the existence of any such system in Babylonia at, or before, 2500 B.C., would probably antedate any possible reference of Chinese origin. References to a similar contract of later date would, of course, assist in tracing the method and rate of evolution of the practice, but it would appear that there are none.[3]

Possible source of contract—Babylon, Egypt, China, and India.

No trace of contract in China.

The Egyptians, as shown by their early records, were, until they had mixed freely with the races of Asia Minor, devoted to pastoral and agricultural pursuits, and not interested in financial transactions, trading, or manufactures.[4] Their natural bent was artistic and philosophical rather than practical. Money-making and trade they regarded as fit for slaves and unsuited for the gentry, and, in addition to the sentiment of the people, the teaching of the priests was strongly opposed to the use of money as an interest-earning machine.[5] Such loans as were made in these early times were of an ordinary character, the most frequent being to small farmers and agriculturists. There being little trade, legislation was not

Trade not encouraged by Egyptians.

[1] See Chapter III, below.

[2] *Western Origin of Early Chinese Civilization—Babylon and China.*

[3] These remarks are based on a careful examination of the best translations procurable of the various Chinese classics, including the undermentioned, in which but one allusion is found (in the Sacred Edict) to the question of interest, and that referred to the rate of interest on a simple loan, and had no connection with the contract under discussion: *The Sacred Edict Yih-King, Divine Classic of Nan-Hua, Li Ki, Sze Shoo.*

[4] Cunningham, W.: *Western Civilization*, Vol. I, p. 18: "In Ancient Egypt, so far as we see . . . there was no speculation or money-grubbing on the part of individuals."

[5] See Appendix C.

provided to deal with loans made for trading purposes; money so used would have been cursed by the priests, and, consequently, if contracts of the nature of loans of Bottomry were in use among the Egyptians prior to the 15th or 16th century B.C., they must have been drawn up secretly and enforced by private sanctions, such as those by which members of the classical and mediæval trade gilds were controlled.[1]

No record of contracts of Bottomry in Egyptian writings.

The Babylonians, however, displayed in their view of financial matters a totally different national spirit. Being excellent business men[2] with a very clear idea of the nature of a contract and of the value of money as a means of earning more money[3] by loans on usury involving simple and compound interest,[4] and having no religious scruples of a nature to interfere with their financial systems, they evolved a series of laws at an early date, which dealt clearly and judicially with such points as would be likely to arise in trade.[5] That such laws were required and largely used is shown by the numerous[6] tablets found bearing details of contracts which were made not only by private people but also by the priests.[7] Occasionally two partners would finance one borrower,[8] or on the other hand several borrowers would

Great business capacity of Babylonians.

[1] See p. 249, below.

[2] " Ils avaient vu que toute obligation aboutit à un capital réclamable, à une créance, à une somme d'argent." E. Revillout: *La Créance*, etc., p. 79.

[3] " . . . sachant faire suer l'argent et par des prêts à intérêts . . . par des avances commerciales . . . arriver rapidement parfois à une fortune énorme avec un premier capital des plus restreints." E. Revillout: *La Créance*, etc., p. 240.

Cf. Rev. C. H. W. Johns: *Assyrian Deeds and Documents*, Vol. II, c. iv.

Cf. also Prof. Sayce: *Babylonians and Assyrians*, chaps. vi and vii *re* Banking and Finance in Babylonia.

[4] See Appendix A.

[5] " Quant au droit chaldéen, ce fut, depuis l'origine, un droit de banquiers, de commerçants, d'économistes, ayant pour principe fondamental l'évaluation de toute chose en argent." E. Revillout: *La Créance*, etc., p. 239.

[6] "C'est par dizaines de mille que l'on compte aujourd'hui les contrats de prêt, etc." Maspero: *Histoire Ancienne des peuples de l'Orient*, p. 156. Cf. Rev. C. H. W. Johns: *Assyrian Deeds*, etc., Vol. III, chap. iv.

[7] " La plupart des sacerdoces tenaient de véritables maisons de banque." Maspero: *Histoire Ancienne*, etc., p. 156.

[8] Rev. C. H. W. Johns: *Assyrian Deeds*, etc., Vol. II, p. 59.

join in borrowing a sum of money under such conditions that the combination of borrowers might "be considered as a sort of limited liability company, but only in a very vague way."[1] Finding, therefore, that this nation, which of all others of antiquity was the most business-like, the most practical, the inventor of political economy,[2] and the greatest commercial nation of the past,[3] has left records antedating all but those of Egypt, which, as stated above, contain no reference to such financial matters as contracts resembling that of Bottomry, etc., it would appear safe to state that the earliest mention of any method by which money or goods were advanced for trade purposes (either as true loans at a certain fixed rate of interest under which the lender had no right to any share in the proceeds of the trading venture or as mixed loans and partnerships which, in addition to the payment of a fixed minimum rate of interest to the lender, irrespective of the result of the trading, entitled him to receive a share of the profits if such profits exceeded a certain sum) on the understanding that the borrower should, in consideration of a high rate of interest, be freed from liability in the event of certain accidents happening, is found in the set of laws known as the *Code of Hammurabi.*

Earliest mention of contracts of Bottomry in *Code of Hammurabi.*

This Code is inscribed on a block of black diorite which was discovered at Susa in Elam by J. de Morgan in January, 1902. It consists of 282 clauses, (of which 34 from 66–99 inclusive have been erased from the stone), and was compiled by Hammurabi, King of Babylon, about 2250 B.C., being based on older laws, fragments of which have come down to us. The laws set out in the Code display a wonderful sense of proportion and deal in a clear and eminently judicial way with various questions as to the rights of individuals, real and personal property, contracts, etc., and are free

[1] Rev. C. H. W. Johns: *Assyrian Deeds*, etc., Vol. II, p. 59.

[2] "Les Babyloniens . . . de tous les peuples de l'antiquité, ont poussé le plus loin les notions vraies de l'économie politique." E. Revillout: *La Créance*, etc., p. 79.

[3] "Les Babyloniens étaient les hommes d'affaires les plus rusés, les plus retors, et les juristes pratiques les plus habiles de toute l'antiquité." E. Revillout: *La Créance*, etc., *Introduction*, p. ii.

from the religious element which is uniformly prevalent in Egyptian and Oriental collections of laws. There can have been little or no possibility of misconstruction as to the meaning of any clause, the language being clear and precise.

From the evidence afforded by fragments of other copies of the Code, it is known that some, if not most, of the missing laws dealt with the subject of loans,[1] as might have been inferred from the numberless records of contracts for loan[2]—of dates between *circa* 2500–500 B.C.—which have been preserved.

Clauses 100–107 of Code.

The requirements of this research are, fortunately, met by clauses 100–107, which legislate for a contract containing in an elementary form the characteristics of later contracts for loans on Bottomry. These clauses contain the two most important elements of such contracts, i.e., firstly, that the repayment of the loan was dependent on the safe arrival (as far as robbery was concerned) of the merchandise representing the advance, and, secondly, that the rate of interest charged for such loans was very much higher than that charged on ordinary loans. These laws (i.e. clauses 100–107) deal only with loans of merchandise or money for merchandise to be conveyed overland to a distance for trading purposes; they are translated by the Rev. C. H. W. Johns, as follows:—

100\. . . . the interests of the money as much as he took, he shall write down, and when he has numbered his days he shall answer his merchant.

101\. If where he has gone he has not seen prosperity he shall make up and return the money he took and the agent shall give to the merchant.

102\. If a merchant has given to the agent money as a favour and where he has seen loss the full amount of money he shall return to the trader.

103\. If while he goes on his journey the enemy has made him quit whatever he was carrying, the agent shall swear by the name of God and go free.

[1] Introduction to translations of Code by Father Scheil and others.
[2] Cf. Rev. C. H. W. Johns, *op. cit.*
Cf. Prof. A. H. Sayce: *Babylonians and Assyrians*, cc. vi–vii.
Cf. Maspero: *Histoire Ancienne*, etc., pp. 155 *et seq.*

104. If the merchant has given to the agent corn, wool, oil, or any sort of goods to traffic with, the agent shall write down the price and hand over to the merchant; the agent shall take a sealed memorandum of the price which he shall give to the merchant.

105. If an agent has forgotten and has not taken a sealed memorandum of the money he has given to the merchant, money that is not sealed for he shall not put in his account.

The two following sections state the penalties to be enforced against the agent for defrauding the merchant (106), and the merchant for defrauding the agent (107). In the former case the fine was three times the amount of the fraud, in the latter case six times.

For purposes of comparison other translations of 100, 101, and 103 are quoted in the footnotes,[1] from which it will be

[1] By Chilperic Edwards, 1904:—

100. . . . interest for the silver as much as he has received he shall write down; and on the day when he makes his account he shall pay to his trader.

101. If in the place where he has gone he has found no opportunity, the retailer shall give back in equal amount to the trader.

103. If the enemy has taken from him whatever he carries upon the road, the retailer shall swear by the name of God and be absolved.

By Prof. Harper, Chicago, 1904:—

100. . . . he shall write down the interest on the money, as much as he has obtained, and he shall make returns to his merchant.

101. If he do not meet with success where he goes the agent shall double the amount of money obtained and he shall pay it to the merchant.

103. If, when he goes on a journey, an enemy rob him of whatever he was carrying, the agent shall take an oath in the name of God and go free.

By V. Scheil, Paris, 1904:—

100. . . . Le commis marquera les intérêts de l'argent autant qu'il en a emporté et il comptera ses jours et payera le négociant.

101. Si là où il est allé, il n'a pas trouvé de profit, il égalera en quantité l'argent qu'il a pris, et le commis le rendra au négociant.

103. Si en route, pendant son excursion, l'ennemi lui a fait perdre ce qu'il portait, le commis en jurera par le nom de Dieu, et il sera quitte.

By Prof. Pietro Bonfanti, Milano, 1903:—

100. . . . gl' interessi del danaro nella misura della somma ricevuta, dovrà rimettere un' obbligazione per inscritto e pagare il negoziante nel giorno della scadenza.

101. Se nel luogo dove è andato non conchiude affari, il commissionario dovrà lasciare intatto il danaro che ha ricevuto e restituirlo al negoziante.

103. Se durante il viaggio il nemico gli porta via qualche cosa di ciò che egli reca con sè, il commissionario dovrà giurare nel nome di Dio, e andar libero.

By Dr. Francesco Mari, Roma, 1903:—

103. Si per la strada il nemico l'ha spagliato di tutto quello che portava, il commesso ne giurerà in nome di Dio, e andrà libero.

seen that, although there are certain small differences, yet in essentials the same ideas are displayed in all the readings. There is, however, one point, which will be dealt with below, which is of importance, and that is the actual meaning of the words "go free" in clause 103.

Forms of loan in Babylon, 2500 B.C.

At the time of the compilation of this Code there appear to have been two separate forms of loan in general vogue in Babylonia, one being that of an ordinary loan to a farmer, tradesman, etc., against good security which was pledged to, and, more or less, in control of, the lender, and at rate of interest of 20 per cent. per annum,[1] the second being that under discussion, which closely resembles that known as the *Commenda of Islam*,[2] and which was as follows.[3]

Commenda of Islam.

A capitalist, manufacturer, etc., having money, manufactures, produce, etc., on which he wished to make a profit by putting them into circulation, entered into business relations with a hawker or trader (*darmatha*) to whom he advanced money, manufactured goods, etc. (if money, it was on the understanding that it should be used to buy wares) on condition that he took the wares to other and distant markets with a view to trading with them to the best advantage. A list having been drawn up (as stated in 104 and 105 of Hammurabi's Code) setting out the quantities and values of all the money, jewellery, manufactured goods, or raw produce advanced to the trader, and approved, was sealed by both parties and handed to the lender as receipt. The security given by the trader for what was in some cases

[1] Revillout, in *La Créance*, etc., states that: "le taux légal de la Chaldée . . . à 20 pour 100," p. 62.

"Dans la vieille Chaldée, où le taux de l'intérêt était de 20 pour 100," p. 306, and cf. p. 282.

Also in *Obligations en Droit Egyptien*, p. 53: "Babylone où la limite était de vingt pour cent."

[2] "Il commercio in Oriente si svolgeva tutto fra grandi mercanti capitalisti e piccoli commercianti: i primi davano un capitale, i secondi lo dovevano negoziare. Cosi si spiega la parabola evangelica dei cinque talenti. In massima la regola è questa: se il commesso o piccolo mercante guadagna, restituisce il capitale e gl' interessi pattuiti, come nella parabola, se non fa affari, restituisce solo il capitale, se vien derubato per la strada giura davanti a Dio ed è libero." Dr. Francesco Mari: *Il Codice di Hammurabi*, etc., Roma, 1903, p. 19.

[3] For origin of this custom, see note at end of chapter.

a loan and not a partnership arrangement, in others a loan with certain contingent profit-sharing, was, firstly, his stock, and, ultimately, "himself, family, and property in town and country on the road or in stock," [1] as is definitely stated in contemporary agreements. The arrangement as to interest was generally one of the following, either that the trader should pay half the profit made by him on the venture subject to the minimum amount of interest payable being 100 per cent. of the value of the loan, or that he should pay 100 per cent. of the value of the loan only. This rate of interest, or consideration for the use of the money or goods advanced, was charged on all such loans irrespective of the journeys to be made by the borrower or of the length of time for which the loan was required. This interest was reduced under certain circumstances, as shown in the laws quoted, and remitted entirely (under law 103) when the trader had been robbed *en route*. In the event of such robbery, the trader was also freed from his liability under the contract to return the value of the principal sum borrowed. The exact meaning of this clause is not quite definite, as the translations are somewhat ambiguous. The phrase used by the Rev. C. H. W. Johns and Mr. Harper, "go free," that used by Professor P. Bonfanti, "andar libero," and by Dr. F. Mari,[2] "andrà libero," appear to mean that the trader, being ruined and having nothing left but his personal liberty, was permitted to retain that, whereas the phrase "be absolved" used by Chilperic Edwards, and that used by Father Scheil, "sera quitte," would imply that the trader was freed from his liability under that particular contract whatever his financial position might be. So that it might well happen, if the second interpretation be the correct one, that a trader might be quite solvent, even rich, yet under this clause would avoid all liability for merchandise of which he had been robbed. It would appear reasonable to assume that the second meaning must be the correct one, as otherwise the value of the indemnifi-

Security given by Darmatha.

Meaning of words "go free" in 103.

[1] My authority for this statement is the Rev. C. H. W. Johns.—C. F. T.

[2] See *Il Codice di Hammurabi*, Roma, 1903.

cation would not seem to have been sufficiently great to compensate for the enormous rise in the rate of interest,[1] from the 20 per cent. *per annum* charged on ordinary loans, to that chargeable on these trading loans. It is worthy of notice that the risk provided against, i.e., robbery under arms *en route*, was of a very limited nature, and that no provision was made for loss by accident, stress of weather, etc. This was probably due to the fact that at the early date to which reference is being made, the commerce of Babylonia was almost entirely land-borne, and that the merchant accompanied the caravan and took charge of the goods himself; that, consequently, the risk arising from accident to the caravan was but slight; that such accidents would nearly always be partial and, except on rare occasions, unlikely to cause a loss of the entire stock of the trader or of even an appreciable proportion thereof, and that, therefore, the risk of loss arising from such a cause was not sufficiently important to require, or sufficiently free from opportunity for fraud to justify, the protection by legislation of the trader against this class of risk. On the other hand, the risk actually provided against, i.e. that of robbery, was a very real and ever-present danger[2]; even at the present time small caravans are frequently attacked and pillaged, and occasionally large caravans even when protected by soldiers. In addition to the frequency of this danger there was also the likelihood that loss occurring under it would be "total." The salient points of resemblance between this contract of loan of money, or of goods, etc., for trading purposes and that of Bottomry are, then, as follows: (i) The contract was for a true loan in many cases; in others it provided for a sharing of profits over a certain minimum, but was never for a pure partnership; (ii) the merchandise or money lent was wholly or partially under the custody of, and used by, the trader, not retained

Risk run by Babylonian trader.

Points in which these contracts resemble contracts of Bottomry.

[1] Part of the extra rate is accounted for by the fact that the security was not retained by the lender. Cf. *Digest*, XXII, ii.

[2] Cf. Strabo, XVI, (i) 21, (ii) 15, (iii) 1.
Pliny: *Hist. Nat.* VI, cap. 26–28.
Diodorus Siculus, II, cap. 48.

by the capitalist or merchant; (iii) the trader was wholly freed from liability as to the debt on the happening of a contingency provided for in the contract; (iv) the rate of interest charged was very much higher than that charged on an ordinary loan. Hence, it is shown that in all essentials the idea of the contract of loans on Bottomry was present, *mutatis mutandis*, in the laws governing the loans for trading purposes made by the Babylonians from 4000–5000 years ago, as shown in the *Code of Hammurabi*, dating from *circa* 2250 B.C.

NOTE.—This very elementary form of the contract of Bottomry was the outcome of the special conditions under which Babylonia developed her manufactures and commerce. As stated in Appendix A, the Babylonians were renowned throughout the then known world for their manufactures, which were varied and extensive. Babylonia herself, however, being a country which produced little or no raw material, with the exception of agricultural produce generally, was forced to import the raw material necessary for her manufactures, and, in order to do so, was obliged to carry on a large trade with other countries. Although at first the manufacturers and agriculturists of Babylonia can have produced little more than was required for home consumption, and therefore bartered or sold their goods themselves, or by the agency of their relations or servants, yet, later, as their business increased, and it became necessary for them to go further afield both to obtain markets for their own goods and to acquire the raw material necessary for their manufactures, it became inconvenient or impossible for them to continue to rely on this domestic assistance, and they were compelled to find other agents. These agents, who resembled more or less the hawkers of to-day, made trading trips sometimes extending for months or even years on their own account, receiving on loan a certain amount of merchandise, etc., from the manufacturer or agriculturist, and on their return either paying a certain rate of interest for the goods advanced to them or sharing the profits acquired from their ventures. In every case the trader appears to have been obliged to repay the value of the goods advanced to him for which he had rendered himself, together with his family, personally liable, and, in the event of being unable to repay the capital, he, together with his family, became the property of the person who had financed him.

This system appears to have worked fairly well in all respects, excepting when the trader was robbed of his goods *en route*, and, consequently, through no fault of his own, was rendered unable to repay the capital advanced to him. In order to meet this difficulty, the system described in the *Code of Hammurabi* was introduced, under which, as stated above, the trader was freed from all liability under his contract if he made a solemn declaration that he had been robbed.

CHAPTER III

THE CONTRACT AS KNOWN TO THE HINDUS

Question whether modern contract is outcome of Babylonian.

A CONTRACT containing all the essential ideas of the contract of Bottomry, though in but a very primitive and limited measure, for which the Babylonians had legislated before 2250 B.C., having thus been found, the next question is how and to what extent was this early form the origin of that used in Greece 1,900 years later. Further, if it be granted that the circumstantial evidence to be examined as to the introduction of a more or less developed outcome of the custom to Greece by the Phœnicians,[1] who, in their turn, had acquired a knowledge of the advantages of the system from the Babylonians, justifies the belief that the classical form is the lineal descendant of that used by the Babylonians, the question arises as to the state of development of this custom at the time of its introduction to the Greeks. Was it in practically the same condition as that in which it appears in the *Code of Hammurabi*, or had it been gradually extended in its scope and changed to meet the requirements of Phœnician trade? The presumption, which is so borne out by collateral evidence as almost to amount to a certainty, is that the contract, if it was introduced to the Greeks by the Phœnicians, was transmitted to them (the Greeks) in a far

[1] Either directly or through the Phœnician settlement in Rhodes.

(NOTE.—It was stated by J. W. Gilbart, in his *Lectures on the History and Principles of Ancient Commerce*, p. 158, etc., that loans on Bottomry were known to, and very generally used by, the Carthaginians. If this statement is accurate, it follows that the Phœnicians must have known of the contract, as they were the founders of, and in continual trading intercourse with, Carthage. As, however, I have been unable to verify the statement, I have preferred to deal with the question of the Phœnician knowledge of the contract of Bottomry on the lines followed in the Thesis. —C. F. T.)

more elastic and generally useful form than that provided for under the laws quoted above.

From the evidence produced in Appendix B, it is clear that in many matters, especially in those relating to commerce, over-sea trading, finance, etc., Phœnicia transmitted to Greece the discoveries and practices of Babylonia. It must also be remembered that probably nearly every Babylonian trader who made a trade tour through Phœnicia was financed, and had protected himself against loss by the method described in the preceding chapter, whence it appears almost certain that these traders must have gradually brought this custom of theirs before the traders and merchants of Phœnicia,[1] by whom it would have been adopted.

Risks to which sea-traders were liable.

Further, their trade being confined to that borne by sea, they would have amended the contract to cover the risks to which they were exposed, namely, risk of loss arising from storms, etc., and also from piracy. This last risk was probably the most imminent, as, until quite a late date, piracy and brigandage were considered a more honourable means of earning a living than trading. The prevalence of the former in early classical times is proved by the repeated references to it in classical writers.[2]

In a similar way the contract would have been passed on by the Phœnicians to the Greeks, but as the Phœnicians were excellent practical business men, and had a far more widely extended commerce than the Greeks enjoyed, it is probable

[1] Probably at the period of the great expansion of Phœnicia as a commercial nation in the 16th century B.C.

See Appendix B.

[2] Odyssey, IV, 81, 90; IX, 40; XIV, 230, 245 *et seq.*; XXI, 397. Herodotus, I, 166; VI, 17.

Bury, *History of Greece*, p. 72, says: " Piracy was a common trade. . . . So many practised this means of livelihood that it bore no reproach; and when seamen landed on a strange strand the natural question to ask them was: 'Outlanders, whence come ye? Are ye robbers that rove the seas?' "

In a treaty made in 348 or 306 B.C. between Rome and Carthage, it was expressly stipulated that they should not permit their citizens to commit acts of piracy on each other. Polybius, III, 24, 4.

Also referred to by Livy, VII, 27, and IX, 43.

Cf. Strachan-Davidson, Polybius, Introd., p. 51, Mommsen, *History of Rome*, translated by Dickson, London, 1894, Appendix to Vol. II.

that it had been developed. There being no records extant of the trade customs of the Phœnicians, there is no actual evidence in the direct line of descent of such an extension of the original contract, but, turning the attention to other nations who were in constant trade relations with

References to similar contract in *Mánava Dharma Sástra.*

Babylonia from 2000–1000 B.C., there is found a most valuable reference to a similar contract in the ancient Sanskrit Code of Law known as the *Mánava Dharma Sástra*, which would point to the fact that the system had been introduced to the Hindus at an early date.[1] This stage in its growth, though not in the direct line of evolution of the classical contract, yet affords most valuable evidence of the steps by which it gradually reached its perfected form. That the Hindus were indebted to the Babylonians for their recognition of the necessity of such a form of contract is quasi-certain since the commercial relations of the two countries were important and continual.[2] Further, as the civilization of Babylonia had reached the stage when the codification of its laws had engaged the attention of its rulers before the growth of Indian civilization, the Hindus, being a newer people, would be more likely than the Babylonians to have

Probability that improvements in contract in *M.D.S.* were introduced by the Hindus.

developed further such a system, as they, having acquired the fundamental ideas from Babylonia worked out to the extent permitted by the Code, would have amended the conditions under which such contracts could be made so as to suit their own particular requirements. How marked the improvements introduced by the Hindus were will be shown below.

Probability that Phœnicians improved contract before introducing it to Greeks.

Assuming that this hypothesis as to the development of the system by the Hindus is correct, the probability is strongly in favour of the Phœnicians having made an equal or greater improvement in the contract after receiving it from the Babylonians before handing it on to the Greeks. The correctness of this assumption is rendered more certain by a comparison of the characteristic pro-

[1] Before 600 B.C. See p. 65, below.

[2] See Appendix A.

fessions, trades, etc., of the Aryans [1] as compared with those of the Phœnicians. By such comparison, it is found that the Phœnicians were more businesslike, more accustomed to undertake long voyages and to incur the consequent risks, and also, being more cosmopolitan, were probably much less conservative in their way of regarding the introduction of innovations into business contracts, etc., than the Hindus. Hence, it is reasonable to assume that the contract for Bottomry at the stage at which it had arrived immediately before it was transmitted to the Greeks by the Phœnicians was at least as highly developed and as suitable for the more advanced ideas of that date (*circa* 1000–800 B.C. ?) as that of the Hindus, and that at this time, as far as the Phœnicians were concerned, it had reached the period of its highest development and had attained to a position of stable equilibrium.

Babylonian contract for land-borne, Indian for land- and sea-borne, and Greek for sea-borne goods.

It should be noted in this connection that a very important difference had, presumably, been incorporated in the system: we know that the Babylonian form of contract provided for land traffic only, and that of the Hindus provided for land- and sea-borne trade; we are bound to assume that that of the Phœnicians would have been confined almost entirely to sea-borne goods, and, moreover, as the persons who would transmit this system to the Greeks must have been seafaring men or oversea merchants, it is almost certain that any such law, if introduced by them to Greece, would naturally be more adapted for sea than land traffic, whence we find the contract for journeys by land

[1] In the early stages of Hindu civilization, that is, in what might be named the Aryan or Vedic age, the social system of the Hindus was entirely different from those of the trading and manufacturing nations of Babylonia and Phœnicia. It was free from the system of castes in the ordinary sense of the word (Max Müller: *Hibbert Lectures*, p. 342), and was patriarchal, the chief occupations being fighting and cultivating the soil.

Kunti (*Vicissitudes of Aryan Civilization*, p. 191) states: "The patriarch and his sons and perhaps grandsons quietly cultivated their land, but when necessary they mounted their horses and sword in hand marched against their enemies."

The various manufactures, professions, trades, etc., of the Indian at this and a somewhat later age are enumerated in detail by Dr. Wilson: *India 3,000 Years Ago*, pp. 29–33.

among the Babylonians became adapted to journeys by sea among the Greeks. These changes in the nature of the risk covered by the contract as used by the Hindus are sufficient to show that the development of the custom was, partially at least, subsequent to the introduction of the contract to the Phœnicians and Hindus.

Mánava Dharma Sástra, origin of.

The evidence that the Hindus were in possession of a more developed form of the contract of Bottomry is contained in the *Mánava Dharma Sástra*; in which are found two sections which deal with a contract of a very much more advanced type than that provided for in the *Code of Hammurabi*. The *Mánava Dharma Sástra*, or the *Institutes of Menu*, was considered by Sir William Jones and other early writers to have been a Code of Hindu Law drawn up by the semi-divine hero "Manu"; later research has shown that this theory was incorrect.[1] In its present form the *Mánava Dharma Sástra* is a versified compilation, rather than a codification, of the precepts, known as *Mánava Dharma Sútra*, of a certain school of Brahmins.

The date[2] of the compilation is now considered to be

[1] Prof. Max Müller in a letter to Prof. H. M. Morley (see *Sacred Books of the East*, Vol. II, Introd. pp. ix–xi) advances the theory that the *Mánava Dharma Sástra* is the last redaction of the laws of the Mánavas. Prof. G. Bühler (*Sacred Books*, etc., Vol. XXV, Introd. p. 19) agrees with this theory and states that: "The *Mánava Dharma Sástra* may be considered to be a recast and versification of the *Dharma Sútra* of the *Mánava Sútrakarana*, a subdivision of the *Maitráyaniya* School, which adheres to a redaction of the *Black Yagur-veda*."

Sir Henry Maine (*Village Communities*, p. 52) says: "Indian Law may be in fact affirmed to consist of a very great number of local bodies of usage, and of one set of customs reduced to writing, pretending to a diviner authority than the rest," etc.

Sir M. Monier-Williams (*Indian Wisdom*, p. 205) states that the *Mánava Dharma Sástra* "represented certain rules and precepts (perhaps by different authors) current among a particular tribe, or rather school, of Brahmans, called Mánavas, who probably lived . . . not far from Delhi."

Dr. Beaman (*Monograph on Mānava Dharma Sāstra*) quotes a statement by Dr. Johaentgen (*Über das Gesetzbuch des Manu*, p. 100) to the effect that the name Mānava has not been derived from "Manu," the hero, but it has come directly from the school to which the original Sútra, which bore the name of Mānava, belonged.

[2] The following are the dates which have been suggested as being approximately probable:—

1280 B.C., by Sir William Jones (Preface to Translation of the *Institutes of Menu*).

1000 B.C., by G. Schlegel (quoted by Mayne, *Hindu Law and Usage*, s. 21).

between 200 B.C. and A.D. 200, but, as stated, the compilation is based on the *Mánava Dharma Sútra*, which date from at least 600 B.C. It is therefore reasonable to assume that the practice of the contract in its developed form for which this legislation was required must have considerably antedated 600 B.C., and, *a fortiori*, that its introduction in the less developed state of the Babylonian contract must have taken place at a very much earlier date. The two sections of the *Mánava Dharma Sástra* dealing with interest on loans on Bottomry are numbers 156 and 157 of Book VIII, which were translated by Sir William Jones, with the help of certain learned pundits, as follows :—

M.D.S., Date of.

> " 156. A lender at interest on *the risk of* safe carriage, who has agreed on the place and time, shall not receive such interest, if *by accident* the goods are not carried to the place or within the time."

Translation of *M.D.S.*, Book VIII, 156 and 157.

> " 157. Whatever interest, or *price of the risk*, shall be settled *between the parties*, by men well acquainted with sea-voyages or journeys by land, with times and with places, such interest shall have legal force."

Subsequently, various translations have appeared, of which

900 B.C., by Hon. Mountstuart Elphinstone (*History of India*, p. 227).

Not later than 500 B.C., by Sir M. Monier-Williams (*Indian Wisdom*, p. 207).

200 B.C., by Max Müller (*History of Ancient Sanskrit Literature*, pp. 64 and 244). This approximation was based on the hypothesis that during the Sútra period of 600–200 B.C. works in continuous epic verse were unknown in Sanskrit, which has since been shown to be untenable.

G. Bühler (*Sacred Books of the East*, XXV, p. xxii) states : " It seems no longer advisable to limit the production of Sútras to so short and so late a period as 600–200 B.C., and the existence of metrical school-manuals at a much earlier date has been clearly demonstrated (see Goldstücker, *Mánavakalpa-Sútra*, p. 78).

500–400 B.C. is the period from which Prof. J. Jolly considers that the Sútra Schools of the *Black Yagur-veda* date (*Sacred Books of the East*, VII, p. xvi).

Summing up, it would appear from G. Bühler's analysis of the dates of the various portions of the *Mánava Dharma Sástra* that the date of Sástra in its present form falls approximately between the limits of 200 B.C. and A.D. 200, but that the date of the Sútras and Slokas on which it was based is not later than 600 B.C. (see *Sacred Books of the East*, XXV, pp. lxv *et seq.*).

Dr. Beaman (*Monograph on Mānava Dharma Sāstra*) quotes from Prof. J. Jolly : " Practically speaking, as much of Manu's Laws as may be traced to the existing writings of the Sútra period, and a great deal more which appears to have been derived from Sútras now lost, is very old."

the best known are those by A. L. Deslongchamps,[1] by Dr. Burnell,[2] and by Professor Bühler.[3] The first of these evidently considers the benefit dealt with as being a high rate of interest, calculated on an abnormally high scale so as to compensate the lender for the risks he incurred. The two later translations, namely, those of Dr. Burnell and Professor Bühler, appear to regard the laws as applying to the fixing of a certain price at which the merchandise might be sold and thus limiting the rate of profit which the vendor could make. It is noticeable, however, that both of these translators in their notes admit the possibility of the other rendering being correct, i.e. that the word "vriddhi" is equivalent to "interest,"[4] rather than to "price" or

Its meaning.

[1] 157. Lorsque les hommes parfaitement au fait des traversées maritimes et des voyages par terre, et sachant proportionner le bénéfice à la distance des lieux et au temps, fixent un intérêt quelconque pour le transport des certains objets, cette décision a force légale relativement à l'intérêt déterminé. *Lois de Manou*, Paris, 1833.

[2] 156. He who has agreed upon a price to be paid on delivery * with a definite understanding in regard to the time and place, shall not receive the reward if he fails to keep the agreement in regard to time and place.

157. The price which men conversant with ocean travel and skilled in time, place, and goods set upon ware, this shall in that case be established as gain (allowed to seller).

To this translation of 156 and 157 Dr. Burnell has added the following:—"*Note.**—Perhaps better 'agreed upon compound interest.' So in verse 157 Nārada regards the *vriddhi* (price) as interest, the rate of which in cases of dangerous travel, etc., may be stipulated in each case."

[3] 156. He who has made a contract to carry goods by a wheeled carriage † for money and has agreed to a certain place or time, shall not reap that reward if he does not keep to the place and time (stipulated).

Note by Prof. Bühler.†—Nārada and Nandana both take *hahravriddhi* to mean "compound interest."

157. Whatever rate men fix who are experts in sea-voyages ‡ and able to calculate (the profit) according to the place, time, and the objects (carried) that (has legal force) in such cases with respect to the payment (to be made).

Note by Prof. Bühler.‡—The expression "in sea-voyages" is held by native commentators to include voyages by land and by Nārada to mean all voyages. The commentators who explain verse 156 as referring to compound interest explain verse 157 to mean that merchants trading by sea must pay any rate of interest for money borrowed which experts may fix.

The others, of course, understand by the rate (*vriddhi*) the carrier's or shipowner's wages.

[4] Cf. definition of compound interest by Nārada: "Interest upon interest is named Chakra-vriddhi." *Náradíya Dharma Sástra*, IV, v. 31, and cf. v. 29.

"wages." That the rendering "interest" is, *prima facie*, more likely to be correct would appear to the non-Sanskrit scholar a very reasonable assumption on account of the fact that the two sections 156 and 157 are preceded and followed by sections dealing with money lent at interest, with legal rates of interest, simple and compound, and fixing certain limits to which the unpaid interest might amount, whence, as the arrangement of the Code is very logical and the distinctions between the various subjects dealt with are clearly defined, it would seem more likely that these two sections would refer to loans rather than to other and entirely extraneous matters, such as fixing a maximum price for wares or prescribing the way in which a shipowner's or carrier's wages are to be calculated. In addition to this argument, there is the consensus of opinion of the Englishmen—Sir William Jones, who, in addition to being a profound Oriental scholar, had been peculiarly fitted to translate an Indian legal code by his own judicial experience in that country; Sir M. Monier-Williams;[1] the Hon. Mountstuart Elphinstone,[2] who says: "There are rules regarding interest on money lent on Bottomry *for sea-voyages*, and on similar risks by land." The same views as to the meaning of these sections are held by the great Indian commentator and code-maker of historic times, Nārada,[3] who holds that both sections refer to rates of interest only, and Nandana,[4] another native commentator who agrees with Nārada as to the meaning of 156; in modern times we have the testimony of Rameṣachandra Datta,[5] who, after a careful examination of the questions raised by various translators as to the exact meaning of the passages quoted, states that "special rates were allowed in the case of merchants going on sea-voyages, probably to cover the insurance on risks." Deslongchamps, in the section quoted,

[1] *Indian Wisdom*, London, 1893, p. 264.
[2] *History of India*, edited by Cowell, London, 1866, p. 34.
[3] See notes 2, 3, and 4, p. 67. Mayne (*Hindu Law*, p. 2) says: "The later commentators describe a state of things which, in its general features, though not in all its details, corresponds fairly enough with the broad parts of Hindu life."
[4] See note 3, p. 67.
[5] *History of Civilization in Ancient India*, Calcutta, 1899, p. 108.

clearly agrees with Sir William Jones, but his translation cannot be considered to have much weight in this argument as it was more than possible that he allowed himself to be unconsciously biassed by the translation of Sir William Jones, that being the only translation extant of the *Mánava Dharma Sástra*, at the time when he prepared his version from which the quotation is taken. Against this we have the more modern views expressed in the translations of Dr. Burnell [1] and Bühler,[2] both of whom are, without doubt, better and more reliable scholars of Sanskrit than was Sir William Jones, but who were perhaps less thoroughly in touch with Hindu legislation and trade customs than he; they, however, as pointed out above, admit the possibility of the older view as to the meaning of the passage being correct. Hence, it appears that the weight of the evidence tends to show that these sections do prescribe laws for dealing with a contract for loans on Bottomry. This granted, it is at once apparent, on comparing the form of contract which could be drawn up under these laws with that possible under the *Code of Hammurabi*, that the Indian system possessed great advantages which were missing in that of the Babylonians. It has been shown, too, that the Indian Code provided for a contract which was in no way foreign to that used by the Babylonians, but was a development of it. The various characteristic points of the Babylonian contract there enumerated are all contained in that of the Hindus. The main developments of the latter are as follows: (i) in place of the borrower being freed from his liability only in the event of his losing his merchandise, etc., by robbery *en route*, he was now absolved if, *by accident*, the goods were not delivered at the place and by the time stipulated; (ii) such risks were dealt with in contracts referring to sea-borne merchandise as well as to that which was land-carried; (iii) the interest varied with the place and the time, i.e. according to the nature of the risk to be incurred and the time during which the contract was to run; (iv) these rates were calculated by men who were

Development of Hindu contract compared with Babylonian.

[1] See note 2, p. 67. [2] See note 3, p. 67.

conversant with the dangers, etc., which would be encountered and with the length of time required for such a voyage or journey; and (v) that the rate of interest thus calculated had to be settled between the parties if the contract was to have legal force. Whence it is clear that the Greek law of Bottomry had been forestalled by a system in use in India which possessed almost as much elasticity and was almost as highly developed. Assuming that the hypothesis advanced above is correct, namely, that the Phœnicians and the Hindus derived a knowledge of this form of loan from Babylonia at about the same date, or possibly the Phœnicians at an earlier date than the Hindus, and that the Phœnicians amended and enlarged the scope of the contract they had acquired from Babylonia to at least as great an extent as the Hindus have been shown to have done and at the same date or earlier, it follows that the Phœnicians were in a position to bring before the notice of Greek traders considerably before the 7th century B.C. highly developed legislation for the contract for loans on Bottomry under which contracts could be drawn up with almost as much freedom as was possible under that of classical times. It has been shown,[1] moreover, that the Greeks were indebted to the learning and practical experience of Babylonia and Phœnicia for their weights, moneys, systems of arithmetic, alphabet, sailing charts, etc.; it would seem, therefore, that they could not have avoided knowing, and appreciating, so valuable a trade custom as that of loans on Bottomry, which, as shown, must have been constantly utilized by the Phœnician merchants and traders. Hence, it is suggested, it may fairly be assumed that the contract was brought before the Greeks by the Phœnicians, who in their turn had adopted it from the Babylonians.

Before proceeding to deal with the question during the classical period, it is necessary to recapitulate briefly the conclusions which, it is suggested, have been established by the arguments so far advanced. They are as follows:—

(i) That Hammurabi, King of Babylonia, *circa* 2250 B.C.,

[1] See Appendix B.

legislated for a contract which contained in a very elementary form the essential points of that of Bottomry or Respondentia.

(ii) That the Phœnicians and Hindus, *inter alios*, were in constant trade communications with Babylonia.

(iii) That the Phœnicians and Babylonians were much more advanced in matters relating to trade, finance, etc., than the Hindus.

(iv) That the Hindus, *circa* 1000–600 B.C., had a highly developed form of the Babylonian contract.

(v) That it is probable that the Phœnicians had acquired the same contract from the Babylonians, and had improved it to at least as great an extent as the Hindus had done.

(vi) That the Phœnicians were in constant communication with the Greek merchants and introduced much of the Babylonian civilization to them, and that, consequently, there is every probability that they introduced the custom of Bottomry also.

CHAPTER IV

THE CONTRACT AS KNOWN TO THE GREEKS

Date of introduction of loans on Bottomry by Phœnicians to Greeks.

IT having been shown that the Phœnicians were, most probably, the channel by which the knowledge of the Babylonian system of trading loans containing the essential characteristics of loans on Bottomry was transmitted to the Greeks, the next point to be determined is the approximate date at which the introduction of this system took place—probably during the 9th century B.C.

The commerce engaged in round the Ægean Sea by the Islanders, Cretans, etc., during the heroic age, i.e. from *circa* 1300–1000 B.C., was that of individuals making trading or piratical voyages, sufficiently powerful and numerous to prevent the Phœnicians acquiring the predominating influence or founding colonies or marts in that part of the Mediterranean, or establishing trading centres on the Greek shores, but not able, or possibly not desirous, to establish settlements in Phœnician territory. Such intercourse, which was more in the nature of an armed neutrality than of friendly trade relations, led to a limited mutual knowledge of the various nations and to the diffusion of certain information on nautical matters, but did not lend itself to the intimate and friendly intercourse of ideas, etc., which would have been necessary for the conveyance of the knowledge of the sciences, trade practices, and financial systems of the East from the Phœnicians to the Greeks. Subsequently to this period, during that of the Dorian expansion, the supremacy in the Ægean gradually deserted the Greeks, and the greater part of the commerce of that sea fell into the hands of the Phœnicians, who gradually monopolized the Eastern

Commerce in Ægean Sea monopolized by Phœnicians from 1000–800 B.C.

trade.[1] In addition, they succeeded in establishing a permanent settlement at Rhodes, marts in Cythera, Cos, Nisyrus, etc., and in developing and working the gold mines of Siphnos and Thasos and the silver mines of Attica.[2] The result of this occupation of Greek territory and of the stimulus given to trade generally by the energetic and businesslike Phœnician traders and merchants was the rapid absorption by the Greeks of the civilization of the East as exemplified by these settlers. What the Phœnicians could teach would, naturally, to a very large extent be confined to such subjects as were of necessity or of interest to them in their trade.

Introduction by Phœnicians to Greeks of alphabet, weights, monies, etc.

Of these the first and most important was the alphabet; of less importance, but, probably, of approximately the same date, were the weights, measures, and monies of the East (i.e. of Phœnicia and Babylonia).

It is known that the Phœnician trade expansion on the Greek littoral took place during the 10th and 9th centuries B.C., and that the introduction of the alphabet took place about the end of the 10th century, also that the Greeks acquired, during the 9th century,[3] the Babylonian and Phœnician weights, measures, etc., which they probably adopted as soon as they became accustomed to the written contracts of the Phœnicians. It follows, therefore, as a matter of great probability, that the introduction of the Babylonian and Phœnician theory and practice of finance, *lex mercatoria*, etc., took place at about the same time, i.e. during the 9th century B.C. This is seen to be even more probable when it is remembered how strongly the legal and trading practices of a race endowed with the wonderful business capacity of the Babylonians must have appealed to the judicially-minded Greeks. Such a contract as that of Bottomry, being necessarily of little practical use except to a certain class of traders, would have interested the Greeks but little

And, probably, of *lex mercatoria*, etc.

[1] See Bury: *History of Greece*, pp. 76 and 77.
[2] See Appendix B.
[3] See Bury, p. 77.

at first. Subsequently, the revival of trade and the consequent growth of commercial activity on the part of the Greeks and resumption of the maritime supremacy of the Ægean Sea by them in the 8th and 7th centuries[1] having removed the dominating influence of the Phœnicians from the Greek marts, the Greek traders in their turn began to establish a large oversea trade, and founded marts in Italy, Sicily, etc. This transfer of trade to the Greeks rendered it necessary for them to adopt such customs as tended to encourage trade. Hence, it is exceedingly probable that in the early days of this rejuvenescence of Greek trade, Greek traders, shippers, etc., eagerly adopted the trade customs of their Eastern rivals. As soon, however, as the Greeks had become fully *au fait* with these customs, they would, naturally, tend to adapt them to their own requirements and to amend them so as to render them more flexible. This was the more easily done, as, at first, there could have been no legislation on the subject, and the individuals making the contract could make any arrangements that were mutually convenient. That this gradual development of the contract lasted until the 6th century at least is probable from the fact that, until the time of Dracon's Code (*circa* 621 B.C.), there was little or no state legislation for private actions,[2] and, further, that even under this Code the laws of debtor and creditor were exceedingly harsh and such as to place the insolvent debtor absolutely in the power of his creditor.[3] As the law of contracts for Bottomry was especially designed to promote trade by facilitating the financing of travelling traders and by rendering (in the first instance at any rate) the results of failure caused by external influences less severe to the borrower, it is certain that, had there been any such law in the time of Dracon, it would have been remarkable for its

Growth of Greek commercial activity in Ægean Sea after 800 B.C.

Adoption by Greeks of trade customs of Eastern nations.

[1] See Bury, pp. 90 *et seq.*
[2] See Bury, p. 180.
[3] See Boeckh: *Public Economy of Athens*, chapters on Loans and on Bottomry.
Cf. Demosthenes, Orations *contra Apat.*, *pro Phorm.*, and Seneca, *De Beneficiis*, VII, c. 14.

dissimilarity to the rest of the law. Some thirty years later, in Solon's Laws, under which the position of debtors was greatly ameliorated, it is to be noted that the exportation of Attic products, except oil, was prohibited.[1] Such a measure as this would tend to limit the export trade of Athens, and shows clearly that the laws of that period were not intended to promote exterritorial commerce. From this it may be inferred that commercial legislation was at this period kept subservient to that for the amelioration of the oppressed lower classes; consequently, it appears probable that the laws relating to Bottomry, etc., were subsequent to this date. It is, however, certain that about this time commercial matters began to attract the attention of legislators, as it is found that during the next 200 years the trade of Athens increased very rapidly, and in the 4th century B.C. special tribunals were held for the prompt trial of mercantile actions in order that Athenian merchants might not be prejudiced by legal delays.[2] The law of Bottomry had also been developed to an almost perfect condition, as is shown by the fact that in the speech of Demosthenes against Lacritus there is quoted a contract of Bottomry[3] which, according to Boucher,[4] was almost the same as that in use in France in 1806, and which, as stated by Hendriks,[5] was so nearly identical in nature with that in vogue in London in 1862 that, *mutatis mutandis*, it could have been used at that date. The chief incongruities in fact arose, not from the nature of the contract, but from the different method of chartering ships and carrying merchandise in vogue in the 4th century B.C. and the 19th century A.D.[6]

Greek legislation on loans of Bottomry, subsequent to 550 B.C.

Tribunals for mercantile actions.

Contract of Bottomry given *in extenso* in speech of Demosthenes

[1] Bury, *op. cit.*, p. 182.
[2] Demosthenes, Oration *contra Zenoth.*
[3] For English translation, see *Assurance Magazine*, 1862, pp. 129–131.
[4] Boucher: *Droit Maritime*, Paris, 1803, p. 323. "... qui prouve avec la plus grande évidence que les Athéniens employoient, à bien peu de choses près, la même formule que nous dans le contrat à la grosse."
[5] *Assurance Magazine*, 1862, p. 131.
[6] See Appendix E.

Particulars of contract as practised by the Greeks.

The Athenian contract of Bottomry provided for the loan of money subject to risk of partial or entire loss to merchants or shippers at a high rate of interest [1] on security [2] which was not retained in the custody of the lender. The chief conditions on which such loans were made dealt with the following points :—

Agreements.

(1) Agreements, which were practically Bottomry bills or bonds of Respondentia stating conditions of loan, had to be drawn up and deposited with bankers.[3]

Security.

(2) Security [4] :—

(*a*) The ship and its rigging.[5]
(*b*) The rigging apart from the ship.[6]
(*c*) The merchandise or cargo.[7]
(*d*) The ship and the slaves attached to the ship.[8]
(*e*) Money to be received for freightage or passages.[9]
(*f*) Ship's furniture only.[10]
(*g*) Valuables carried, but not for sale.[11]
(*h*) In some cases all property of borrower was made answerable by a particular stipulation in contract.[12]

Period of loan.

(3) Period of loan :—

(*a*) For voyage outward only.[13]
(*b*) For voyage out and back.[14]
(*c*) For voyage back.[15]

[1] For rates of interest charged by Greeks on loans see Appendix D.
[2] See note 4 below.
[3] Demosthenes : *pro Phorm.*, p. 403, 6.
Note.—The references to the Orations of Demosthenes are taken from the edition published by Teubner at Leipzig in 1888.
[4] The security was required generally to be of at least twice the value of the sum advanced. See Demosthenes : *contra Lacrit.*, p. 421, 18.
[5] Demosthenes : *contra Polyclit.*
[6] Demosthenes : *contra Polyclit.*
[7] Demosthenes : *contra Lacrit.*, p. 419, 10.
[8] Demosthenes : *contra Apat.*, p. 391, 8.
[9] Boeckh : *Public Economy of Athens*, chap. xxiii.
[10] Demosthenes : *contra Polyclit.*
[11] Lysias, *pro bonis Aristoph.*, t. V, p. 630.
[12] Demosthenes : *contra Polyclit.*, and *contra Lacrit.*
[13] Rhod. Leg. : see *Digest*, Lib. XIV.
[14] Demosthenes : *contra Phorm.*, p. 403, 6.
[15] Cf. Demosthenes : *contra Lacrit.* and *Dionysodor.* Such loans for the return journey could only be made on goods which were to be taken back to Athens, not on goods which were to be dealt with *en route*.

(*d*) For fixed time only. Risk ceased on expiry of the period agreed on.[1]

Interest.

(4) Interest [2] :—

(*a*) Calculation of :—

(i) At so much per day or per month.[3]

(ii) At a certain round sum for the voyage, more or less great, depending on destination, season of year, direction of voyage, etc.[4]

(*b*) Rates of :

(i) For outward voyages only from 10–12 per cent.[5]

(ii) For outward and homeward voyages from 22½–30 per cent.[6]

(*c*) Penal rates of interest :—

(i) If borrower allowed security to become too small, did not repay entire loan plus interest on the due day, or failed to observe any of the conditions of the contract.[7]

(ii) If ship followed a more dangerous course than was originally intended, or sailed late in the year.[8]

Lender.

(5) Lender :

(*a*) Risks incurred by :—

(i) Total loss of principal advanced and interest if ship lost at sea from natural causes, or destroyed or captured by pirates, enemies, etc.[9]

(ii) Loss of proportion of principal and interest in the event of some or all of the cargo being jettisoned, or of ransom being paid to captors of ship.[10]

(*b*) Powers of :—

(i) Could place representative on board to guard

[1] Rhod. Leg. III, cap. xviii, see *Digest*, Lib. XIV.

[2] For rates of interest charged on loans in Greece at this period see Appendix D.

[3] Petitus (S.), Leges Atticæ, Lib. V, tit. iv.

[4] Demosthenes : *contra Lacrit.*, p. 419, 10.

[5] Salmasius : *De Usuris*, p. 35.

[6] Demosthenes : *contra Lacrit.*, p. 419, 6 ; *contra Phorm.*

[7] Demosthenes : *contra Phorm.*, p. 411, 33.
Cf. also Demosthenes : *contra Polyclit.*
(It will be seen on reference to p. 83 below that the later Roman custom differed from the above.)

[8] Demosthenes : *contra Lacrit.*, p. 419, 10.

[9] Rhod. Leg. c. xiv, see *Digest*, Lib. XIV.

[10] Demosthenes : *contra Lacrit.*, p. 419, 11. (Cf. Rhod. Leg. c. ix, see *Digest*, Lib. XIV.)

own interests and to receive money at end of outward voyage, if loan for outward voyage only.[1]

Borrower.

(6) Borrower :—

(*a*) Merchants or traders, obligations, etc., of :—

(i) To cause the ship to proceed to her destination by the course agreed on ; in the case quoted an alternative route was permitted subject to the payment of a higher rate of interest.[2]

(ii) If loan for voyage out only, money advanced had to be repaid to lender, to his assignee, or to his representative on board on arrival at destination specified.[3]

(iii) If loan for round voyage, out and home, money had to be repaid to lender or to his assignee immediately on return.[4]

(iv) In certain agreements the whole property of borrower was made liable for debt.[5]

(v) To ship goods of sufficient value to cover loan.[6]

(vi) If goods on which money was advanced were sold, borrower had to replace with goods of equal value.[7]

(vii) Goods could not be disembarked at places where Athenians had the right of reprisal.[8]

(viii) To declare if money had been already borrowed on goods.[9]

(ix) No second mortgage could be given on same goods, such action held to be fraud upon first as well as second mortgagee.[10]

(*b*) The captain of the ship :—

Could borrow on Bottomry on the ship and its cargo provided he owned not less than one-third of the lading.[11]

[1] Cf. case of Lampris in Demosthenes : *contra Phorm.*
[2] Demosthenes : *contra Lacrit.*, p. 423, 24.
[3] Demosthenes : *contra Lacrit.*, p. 423, 24.
[4] Demosthenes : *contra Lacrit.*, p. 423, 24.
[5] Demosthenes : *contra Lacrit.*, p. 420, 12.
[6] Demosthenes : *contra Lacrit.*, p. 403, 1.
[7] Demosthenes : *contra Phorm.*, p. 411, 33.
[8] Demosthenes : *contra Lacrit.*, p. 420, 13.
[9] Demosthenes : *contra Lacrit.*, p. 419, 11.
[10] Demosthenes : *contra Lacrit.*, p. 419, 11, and *contra Phorm.*, p. 403, 6.
[11] See fragments of spurious Rhodian Laws, quoted *in extenso* by Pardessus in *Us et Coutumes de la Mer*, and also Appendix F.

Loans regarded by Athenians as hazardous.

It should be noted that, although the law was practically entirely in favour of the lender, in accordance with the incorrect theory held at the time, this class of investment was regarded by the Athenians as extremely hazardous; so much so that it was entirely forbidden by law to lend the money of orphans on contracts of Bottomry.[1]

The influence, if any, of the practice of Rhodes on Greek legislation dealing generally with oversea commerce is incapable of calculation owing to the entire lack of reliable evidence. Since, however, the civilization of Rhodes was the outcome of the Phœnician settlements there, the Greeks would have been indebted to the Phœnicians, and thereby to the Babylonians, to almost the same extent, had they acquired their knowledge of maritime matters through the Rhodians, as they were if the hypothesis set out above is correct.[2]

[1] Boeckh: *Public Economy of Athens*, 2nd edition, 1842, quotes Lys. Frag., p. 37; and the case in Lysias: *contra Diognet.*, p. 908.

[2] See Appendix F.

CHAPTER V

THE CONTRACT AS KNOWN TO THE ROMANS

A.—Down to the End of the 3rd Century A.D.

Introduction of contract to Romans.

THE manner and date of the introduction of this contract to the Romans are difficult to determine, owing to the hazy and unhistorical accounts of the early periods of Roman history. Arguing along similar lines to those employed in considering the question of the introduction of the contract into Greece, it will be found that the very scanty evidence tends to show that the knowledge of this contract was transmitted to the Romans, or to their immediate forerunners, the Latins, by the Greeks who had established the trading town of Cumæ [1] and also those in Sicily. Professor Mommsen has shown that the language and writing of Latium indicate that early Latin commerce was confined almost exclusively to the Cumæans and Siceliots,[2] and Professor Bury states definitely that it is to the Greek colony at Cumæ that the inhabitants of Latium owed their knowledge of the alphabet.[3] Such close and continual intercourse with the young and progressive Greek colonies would lead to the gradual education of the Latin merchants and to the introduction of the trade customs, etc., of the more advanced to the less developed race. Whence, if the Cumæan traders knew of the contract of Bottomry, it is likely that they would have taught it to the Latins. It is known that the Romans had such a custom in later years; it is also practically certain that the custom

[1] Founded not later than 8th century B.C., Sicilian towns about 50 years later.

[2] Mommsen: *History of Rome*, Vol. I, p. 258.

[3] Bury: *History of Greece*, p. 77.

was not one which had originated in Rome, as in that case provision would have been made for land traffic as well as, if not rather in place of, that borne by sea. As pointed out above, it is most important to note the limitations of the contract as brought to Europe by the Phœnicians and developed further by the Greeks compared with that of the *Mánava Dharma Sástra.* There is no inherent reason why *fœnus nauticum* should not have been *fœnus terrestre*; that it was not was due to the system having been acquired from nations who used it only for oversea trade. In the case of the Romans, if they had evolved this system for themselves, being (as they were in the earlier period of their history) confined for the most part to land traffic, it would seem that the natural course would have been to have invented a system primarily suited for that sort of trade (as was done by the Babylonians), and later on to have extended that system so as to include land and sea traffic. It is remarkable that in every instance in which the system is alluded to by Latin authors, the interest is called "maritime interest," and the money lent "money sent over sea."

Knowledge of contract probably derived from nations having oversea trade.

The date of the introduction of the contract cannot be earlier than the 8th century B.C., and, seeing that it would require some considerable intercourse before sufficiently intimate trade relations between Greeks and Latins were established and also before the Latins had acquired sufficient commercial experience to enable them to appreciate the value of such a system, it is most probable that the introduction took place during the 7th or 6th centuries B.C. If such was the case, then all contracts of this nature must have been without legal sanction unless provided for by the private rules of the *Collegia*,[1] as in the XII Tables [2] interest was strictly limited to 12 per cent., and usury was punished; but *Collegia* were entitled to make their own private laws or rules, which were binding on their members as long as such private legislation

Date of introduction of contract.

[1] How and Leigh: *History of Rome*, p. 71.
[2] See Appendix G.

was not antagonistic to the laws of the State.[1] Pardessus[2] suggests that the introduction of the system of Bottomry and other customs, etc., dealing with maritime matters to Rome was the outcome of her friendship with Rhodes.[3] The effect of this intercourse was undoubtedly to stimulate the commercial activity of Rome as far as sea-borne trade was concerned, but, if it is admitted that the Greeks were in possession of the system in possibly a less developed form at the time of the foundation of Cumæ, then it would appear that, although the Rhodian laws may have developed the Roman practice, yet the true source of the Roman contract was Greece.

Suggestion of Pardessus that contract was introduced by Rhodians.

It is also possible that the knowledge of the contract may have been acquired at a later date directly from Greece, as it is known that the Greek legislation was held in high esteem by the Romans, and it was their boast that the Roman legal system was identical with that of Athens, and further that they had based their earliest code of laws on those of the Athenians.[4]

Roman legislation in respect of contract similar to Greek.

The actual legislation[5] of the Romans in respect of their loans on maritime risks was in the main identical with that of the Greeks. So much so that it is not necessary to enumerate the various forms of contract powers and limitations imposed by the legislation of the later Republic and earlier Empire. There are, however, several small points of difference which seem to show that the Roman contract was slightly more developed than that of the Greeks; though it is conjectural how far these apparent differences, apart from that marked (*c*), are real; they may be due to nothing more than the omission to refer to them by Greek writers. These points are, briefly, as follows:—

[1] Sanctioned by the XII Tables, 451 B.C.

[2] *Us et Coutumes de la Mer*, Paris, 1847.

[3] Which started about 305 B.C. (see Polybius, xxx, 5).

[4] Cf. Cicero: *De Republica*, III, c. 22, "Non erit alia lex Romæ, alia Athenis."

Cf. also the commission sent (455 B.C.) to Athens to study the Greek legal system preparatory to drawing up the XII Tables.

[5] Down to the beginning of the 6th century A.D.

Dissimilar in respect of— Responsibility of lender.

(*a*) In Roman Law it expressly provided that the lender should not be responsible for loss caused (i) by depreciation of goods, (ii) by the borrower having made no profit on the trade which he had carried on with the borrowed goods or capital, and (iii) by any loss arising through the confiscation of all or part of the goods covered by the contract if such confiscation should be due to the contravention (wilful or otherwise) of laws by the borrower.[1]

Collateral security.

(*b*) It was not unusual among the Greeks[2] for the lender to require other collateral security for the repayment of the sum advanced; this was also the case among the Romans, but it was expressly laid down that such collateral security could only apply to what may be called the true loan part of the contract, as the debtor was entirely freed[3] from all liability under the contract if the goods or money advanced perished, or were lost by reason of the occurrence of a disaster provided against in the contract *pecuniæ trajectitiæ*.

Penal interest for delay in payment.

(*c*) A more important difference is that of the way in which the borrower could be penalized if he was behindhand in repaying the capital together with the accrued interest when the loan period had expired by the termination of the voyage. The Greek capitalist could have allowed the loan to stand at the same rate of interest as that which had been in force during the voyage, or could have renewed the loan at any rate which the borrower was willing to pay.[4] The Roman capitalist, however, was in quite a different position.[5] As soon as the voyage was over the loan ceased to be one of *pecunia trajectitia*, and, consequently, ceased to bear *fœnus nauticum*, with the result that it came under the civil law as an ordinary business loan on which the interest was

[1] *Code*, IV, xxxiii, s. 3.
[2] See Demosthenes *contra Lacrit.*, p. 420, 12.
[3] *Digest*, XXII, 2.
[4] There being no restriction as to rate of interest payable on business loans. See Appendix D.
[5] This was prescribed in the *Responsum* of Papinianus (*circa* A.D. 200), which was confirmed by Justinian in the *Digest*, XXII, ii, 4.

limited.[1] He would, therefore, have been entitled to receive the capital plus the *fœnus nauticum* which had accrued during the voyage plus the interest at the rate payable on a business loan on the sum which he had advanced as *pecunia trajectitia*, subject to the condition that the interest could not accumulate to more than the amount of the capital.[2] Theoretically, therefore, the borrower could not be compelled to pay promptly by the imposition of a penal rate of interest. The creditor, however, could penalize the borrower in another way, namely, by charging for the services of the slave, whom, in order to protect his interests and act as his representative, he had sent with the borrower.

Investment of money of minors in such loans.

(*d*) In Athenian law it was expressly forbidden to invest the money of orphan minors in loans on Bottomry[3]; in Roman law this question does not appear to have been dealt with. There is, however, a passage which shows that minors could not have property in ships, etc., without the consent of their tutors, which may have been intended to cover the same case.[4]

References to contract in Roman Civil Law, before 4th century A.D.

Although there are no extant references in the *Corpus Juris Civilis* to the practice of loans on Bottomry in Rome of earlier date than the *Responsa* of Scævola in the *Digest* dating from (about) 100 B.C.,[5] yet there is every probability that the custom was of old standing and was continually in use among the Romans from a much earlier date. The laws dealing with the subject which are collected in the *Digest* and *Code* contain no reference to any legislation, with one exception, between the dates of Scævola (about 100 B.C.) and Pomponius (about A.D. 180), which tends to show that the practice was either considered to be adequately dealt

[1] See *Responsa* of Ulpian, *Digest*, LXXVII, and Papinianus, *Digest*, XXII, ii, 4.
Cf. *Code*, IV, xxxiii, 3 and 4.

[2] Probably the interest at the ordinary rate would have been payable on the original sum lent only and not on the original sum plus the *fœnus nauticum*, as compound interest was regarded unfavourably by the earlier jurists and forbidden altogether by Justinian. See Appendix G.

[3] See p. 79.

[4] See *Digest*, XIV, i, 1, s. 16.

[5] See p. 85, below.

with by local and trade customs or by-laws, and, therefore, not to require direct legislation, or was the subject of legislation which was superseded by that of the great school of jurists which flourished between (about) A.D. 180–240. This legislation, together with four constitutions of the Emperors Diocletian and Maximianus (about) A.D. 300, is all the ante-Justinian law on the matter which has survived, and consists of the following :—

Digest, XXII [1] (ii), *De nautico fœnore*, containing nine chapters, as follows :—

Cap. 1, 3,	by Modestinus	of	approximate	date	A.D. 240
„ 2,	by Pomponius	„	„	„	A.D. 175
„ 4,	by Papinianus	„	„	„	A.D. 200
„ 5,	by Scævola	„	„	„	100 B.C.
„ 6, 7,	by Paulus	„	„	„	A.D. 230
„ 8,	by Ulpian	„	„	„	A.D. 225
„ 9,	by Labeo	„	„	„	25 B.C.
Digest, XLV [1] (i), 122	by Scævola	„	„	„	100 B.C.

Code, IV (xxxiii), containing four laws all by Emperors Diocletian and Maximianus, about A.D. 300.

Subsequently to A.D. 300 there appears to have been no new legislation dealing with these contracts until about 100 years after the division of the Empire,[2] when the Breviary of Anianus[3] was published, in which is found a definition[4] of *pecunia trajectitia*, and under which the charging of as high a rate of interest as may be arranged between the parties is legalized. Up to this time the practice of contracts of Bottomry appears to have been the same in both Empires and remained so until Justinian, Emperor of the East,[5] imposed certain restrictions thereon.

[1] These *Responsa*, though taken from the *Digest*, were really given at the dates quoted. Their inclusion in the *Digest* merely confirms them.
[2] A.D. 395.
[3] End of 5th century A.D.
[4] See p. 90, below.
[5] *Code*, IV, xxxii, const. 26 (April A.D. 529). "In trajectitiis contractibus, vel specierum fœnori dationibus, usque ad centesimam tantummodo licere stipulari, nec eam excedere, licet veteribus legibus hoc erat concessum."

B.—In the Western Empire

Practice of contract in Western Empire.

With regard to the contract as known in the Western Empire, it is found that the direct references thereto are very few,[1] and, consequently, it is necessary to examine the indirect evidence.

It has been assumed that the contract of Bottomry was but seldom used or required during the later Empires because the trade of the Western Empire was (1) broken up and gradually destroyed by the barbarian occupations and the consequent insecurity of life and property arising therefrom, together with the want of a satisfactory legal system, or (2) prevented from recovering from such prostration by the restrictions imposed, and the enmity displayed, by the Church.

Two other suggestions have also been made, namely, that the greater proportion of the Italian trade that did exist was carried on by the trading towns of Genoa, Pisa, Venice, etc., and that the Saracens had acquired the mastery of the Mediterranean trade, which would appear to be exaggerated.

As to suspension of civil law during 4th century A.D.

(1) The effect of the barbarian occupation on the civil law and on the trade of Italy:—at the end of the 4th century A.D. the Western Empire was subdued and overrun by barbarians with the result that for a time there was no security for life or property, and no civil laws were enforced. Such a state of struggle and quasi-anarchy resulted in the complete dislocation of existing commercial enterprises and relations, and temporarily paralysed industrial pursuits of every description, but, although these social upheavals were exceedingly violent and disastrous, yet they were very spasmodic and of comparatively brief duration. History has proved that it is out of the power of the less civilized, but more robust, race, which has overcome by its fighting strength a highly civilized people, to destroy and do away with the legal and commercial systems of the conquered people; it can but

[1] See p. 90, below.

suppress them publicly, but these highly developed systems will continue to be those on which the members of the more civilized race rely when dealing between themselves. This was the case in the Western Empire. The inhabitants continued to regard the legal and industrial systems to which they were accustomed as the bases of their business and other relations between themselves. Gradually the invaders, as the immediate passions and excesses attending the raiding of the country quieted down, were led to recognize that the amount of comfort and luxury they could derive from their occupation of Italy very largely depended on the commercial activity and prosperity of the Italians, whose trade would be fostered by the perpetuation of the legal and commercial systems which had been evolved to meet the requirements of their social and commercial conditions, and to which they had been accustomed. Further, the rulers soon began to look on Italy with friendly eyes, and sought to help the recovery of trade, etc., by legislation on the lines of the older Roman laws. About the end of the 5th century Alaric II published the Breviary of Anianus,[1] which was compiled from the *Responsa*, etc., of Roman jurists.

Publication of Breviary of Anianus about A.D. 500.

In addition to this, and some fifty years later, Clotaire, son of Clovis, decreed that questions of private law arising between Romans were to be tried by Roman law.[2] This ruling was confirmed and made broader by that contained in the Code of the Visigoths, wherein it was provided that foreign merchants should be tried by foreign (i.e. their own) laws.[3] This legislation was followed (about

[1] In which Code the contract of *pecunia trajectitia* was defined and sanctioned. See p. 90, below.

[2] Gibbon: *Decline and Fall of the Roman Empire* (Bury), Vol. IV, p. 133, n. 75. "Inter Romanos negotia causarum Romanis legibus præcipimus terminari."

Cf. Pardessus, *op. cit.*, p. 135.

[3] *Ex Lege Wisigothorum*, Lib. XI, 3, 2. "Cum transmarini negotiatores inter se causam habuerint, nullus de sedibus nostris eos audire presumat; nisi tantummodo suis legibus audiantur apud telonarios suos." (Monumenta Germaniae Historica, Leg. Sect. 1.)

Cf. Hakluyt's *Voyages*, i, p. 135, where he alludes to the provision in the Act known as *Carta Mercatoria* (31, ed. 1) that in all cases in which foreigners were concerned half the jury should be foreigners.

A.D. 625) by an allusion to the use of the Rhodian law in respect of the merchant navy and business carried on by sea in the *Origines* of Isidore of Seville [1]; after which the next direct reference to *pecunia trajectitia* occurs in the compilation of laws published by Petrus [2] about the middle of the 11th century A.D. From these references it is evident that the barbarian incursions did not destroy permanently the old civil law of Rome. That the maritime trade of Rome and of Italy not only existed, but continued to be of great importance, is shown by the repeated legislation referring to trade, shipping, etc., contained in the Breviary of Anianus, the law of Majorian,[3] of Theodoric,[4] and by the references thereto in contemporary writings.[5] So far from being moribund and without commerce was Rome that she herself at the beginning of the Middle Ages absorbed by far the largest part of the products of the East,[6] and supported a strong merchant navy manned by very competent sailors.[7] Whence, in place of the assumption that the trade of Rome was broken up and her *corpus juris civilis* rendered of no effect by the barbarian invasion, it has been shown that such results were but temporary and that Rome regained her trade and her legal system.

References in later writers.

To come now to (2) The influence of the Church on the commerce of Rome. The effect of the Christianization of Rome on the trading and social systems was at first of a salutary nature, tending to exercise a restraining and purifying influence, but by the 4th century A.D. the growth of the ascetic movement had been

Influence of Church on commerce of Italy.

[1] See p. 91, below. [2] See p. 91, below.

[3] Nine laws by Majorian dating from A.D. 457–461 are extant—placed at end of *Theodosian Code* (January 15, A.D. 438).

[4] See Pardessus: *Us et Coutumes de la Mer*, pp. 135 *et seq.*

[5] See Letters of Symmachus.

[6] W. Heyd: *Histoire du Commerce du Levant au Moyen Age*, Vol. I, p. 93. "Aucun pays de l'Europe n'importait les produits de l'Orient en aussi grandes quantités et sous des formes aussi variées que l'Italie. . . . Au commencement du Moyen-Age, c'est *Rome* que reçoit et absorbe de beaucoup la plus grande quantité des produits de l'Orient."

[7] W. Heyd: *Histoire*, etc., Vol. I, p. 95. "L'Italie était aussi féconde en marins expérimentés qu'en marchands entreprenants et habiles: de tout temps, ils avaient été en relation avec les Grecs, mais ils ne se faisaient aucun scrupule d'entrer en contrat avec les Arabes mécréants."

the cause of the segregation of large numbers of the middle and upper classes who formed themselves into brotherhoods, etc., founding many monastic settlements and withdrawing themselves from all the business and interests of public life.[1] The result of this movement was to devitalize the Empire and to render it an easier prey to the barbarians.[2] It must be noted, however, that this ascetic movement had to a large extent died out before the end of the 5th century, and that so far from the Church acting as a deterrent to commerce in the 4th and later centuries the Popes themselves displayed a great interest in the commerce of Rome, as is shown in their biographies,[3] and when in the 7th century the competition of the seaport towns of Pisa, Genoa, Venice, etc., began seriously to affect the trade of Rome, they threw all their weight against the Lombards.[4] From this it is seen that after the 5th century A.D. the Church stimulated, rather than hindered, commerce in the Western Empire.

Ascetic movement, result of.

Commerce of Italy from 600–1000.

It has also been suggested that the trade of Rome was ruined by the competition of the trading Italian towns. This competition, though very keen in and after the 7th century, yet did not affect to any serious extent the commerce of Rome in the 5th and 6th centuries, during which time Rome had re-acquired her oversea trade. From this time on, until the early Middle Ages, these towns, though keen competitors, did not succeed in depriving Rome of her trade.

[1] Gibbon: *Decline and Fall*, etc. (Ed. by Bury), Vol. IV, 57, speaking of the ascetic Christians, says: "They seriously renounced the business . . . of the age."

[2] Gibbon: *Decline and Fall*, etc., Vol. IV, pp. 162 *et seq.* "The introduction, or at least the abuse, of Christianity had some influence on the decline and fall of the Roman Empire."

Cf. Bury, J. B.: *History of the Later Roman Empire*, I, i, p. 34, ii, chap. 9; II, vi, p. 47.

Crake, A. D.: *History of the Church under the Roman Empire*, pp. 80, 476.

Finlay, G.: *Greece under the Romans*, p. 158.

[3] W. Heyd: *Commerce du Levant*, etc., Vol. I, 94. "Les biographies des papes, surtout des papes du VIIIe et du IXe siècle, si avares de détails sur les événements historiques, abondent au contraire en renseignements du plus grand intérêt sur le sujet qui nous occupe."

[4] J. G. Sheppard: *Fall of Rome* (Lond. 1892), pp. 321 *et seq.*

The competition of the Saracens, too, has been mentioned in this connection, but the effect of that competition even in the case of the Eastern Empire, where, as will be shown, the merchants petitioned for protection against them, seems to have been greatly exaggerated.[1] In so far as the Western Empire was concerned, there does not seem to be any evidence of this competition having diminished the Italian trade.

To sum up, it appears that the commerce of the Western Empire did not, except during the 5th century, suffer very seriously from the barbarian inroads; that after the 5th century until the time of the Crusaders Italy was commercially very active; that the Roman law was preserved and used in all civil matters, to which Romans were parties, as is shown by the special legislation authorizing the use thereof; that the contract of Bottomry (or of *pecunia trajectitia*) was fully provided for before the division of the Empire; that it was defined by, and received legal sanction from, Alaric II, was probably dealt with in the Rhodian laws referred to by Isidore of Seville, and was directly legislated for, and a limit placed on the interest chargeable, in the book of Petrus. From this it follows that the custom of loans on Bottomry was generally and continually used from the time of Alaric II[2] down to the Middle Ages.

Extant legislation of Western Empire in respect of contract.

The extant legislation dealing with *pecunia trajectitia* which was published during the Western Empire is as follows:—

(1) By Alaric II. End 5th century.

Ex Aniani Interpretationibus ad Pauli receptas sententias, Lib. II, tit. xiv. *De Usuris.*[3]

Trajectitia pecunia dicitur quæ in navi ut ad transmarina deferatur, deponitur; quia maris periculo

[1] Cf. Finlay: *Greece under the Romans*, and Bury: *History of Greece*, p. 10.

[2] The law of Western Europe was, until the 12th century, based on the Breviary of Alaric. E. Caillemer in *Le droit civil dans les provinces Anglo-Normandes au XIIe siècle*, p. 10, says: " . . . En Angleterre, comme en France, les juristes étaient plus familiers avec le Bréviaire d'Alaric qu'avec les compilations de Justinien, promulguées à une époque où la Gaule était vraiment indépendante de l'Empire."

Towards the end of the 12th century the Justinian codes became better known and gradually took the place of the Breviary.

[3] See *Lex Romana Visigothorum*, p. 362, ed. Haenel, Leipsic, 1849.

committitur, in quantas convenerit usuras hanc pecuniam dare creditor potest.

(On the passage, "Trajectitia pecunia, propter periculum creditoris, quamdiu navigat navis, infinitas usuras recipere potest.")

Cf. *Digest*, XXII, II, fr. I. *De naut. fœn.*

(2) *Ex Isidori Hispalensis*[1] *Episcopi Originum Libro.* Ex Libro V, cap. xvii. *De Legibus Rhodiis.*

Rhodiæ leges navalium commerciorum sunt ab insula Rhodo cognominatæ, in quà antiquitus mercatorum fuit usus.

This extract does not explicitly refer to loans on Bottomry, but, as such loans were legislated for in the Rhodian Code,[2] it may be held to do so implicitly.

(3) From a book entitled *Exceptiones legum Romanorum, magistri Petri,*[3] *viri. sapientissimi.*

Sin autem detur mutuum ut ultra mare portetur, vel in aliquam partem longinquam, potest præstare per duplum, triplum.

This extract gives the only example of returning a fixed sum as bonus or interest for the loan irrespective of the period of the loan and of the nature of the risk in the history of the contract subsequent to the *Code of Hammurabi.*[4] Under that Code the debtor had to pay interest of 100 per cent. for the loan; in this contract he might be forced to borrow at 50 per cent.

C.—In the Eastern Empire

Eastern Empire.

Returning to the 5th century and proceeding to trace the subsequent development of the practice of Bottomry in the Eastern Empire, it is noticeable that the laws described above remained in

[1] Isidore of Seville, who died in A.D. 636.
[2] See Appendix F.
[3] Either Pierre de Chartres, who died in 1039, or Pierre de Damien, who died in A.D. 1072.
[4] See Chap. II.

force unaltered until the publication of the *Codex Justinianus* in April 529. In this Code [1] a restriction was placed on the contract which tended to render it entirely unsatisfactory as a business transaction, the rate of interest being limited to 1 per cent. per month. Subsequently,[2] Justinian repealed this law and again permitted interest to be agreed upon at any rate which was mutually satisfactory to the parties concerned. Shortly afterwards,[3] however, this law was annulled and the restriction to 1 per cent. per month again prescribed. Such a low rate of interest would appear to have been quite inadequate [4] to compensate the capitalist for the risk incurred in a loan which involved the possibility of loss arising from dangers of sea or from seizure by pirates, etc., and, consequently, if enforced, must have tended to the gradual suppression of the practice. That the practice did not die is shown by the repetition of similar restrictive legislation in A.D. 870, in the 11th century, and in the Laws in Cyprus in the 12th century A.D.[5] There must have been, therefore, some means by which the contract could be drawn up according to the law and yet so as to afford the lender a higher rate of interest for his money. This could have been done by the loan being nominally for X at the legal rate of 1 per cent. per month while the sum actually advanced was $X-x$, where x (payable at the same time and on the same terms as the repayment of the capital sum advanced, i.e. $X-x$) represents the premium or bonus charged for the loan, on which the true rate of interest was $\frac{X}{100(X-x)}$ per month.[6] That some such means of evading

Rate of interest on contract limited.

[1] *Code*, IV, xxxii, const. 26.

"In trajectitiis . . . contractibus, vel specierum fœnori dationibus, usque ad centesimam tantummodo licere stipulari, nec eam excedere, licet veteribus legibus hoc erat concessum."

[2] Novella 106.

[3] Novella 110.

[4] Pardessus: *Us et Coutumes de la Mer*. Hendriks: *Journal of Institute of Actuaries*, Vol. II, pp. 132 and 133.

Cf. rates for marine insurance in A.D. 1400, quoted by Uzzano, see Part IV, p. 279.

[5] See pp. 96–100, below.

[6] Cf. attempt to obtain illegal rate of interest by false discount referred to in Appendix G.

the law was adopted is obvious, or the practice, as stated above, must have been rendered useless. Granting that this, or a similar, method of evading the law was employed, it is still evident (*a*) that such a restrictive policy would not have been adopted without some excellent reason, and also (*b*) that the requirements of a very extensive trade could not have been generally met by the use of what would have been at the best a subterfuge. It follows, therefore, from (*a*) that the policy of Justinian must have been based on (1) a recognition of the inadvisability of encouraging this particular form of investment, (2) a desire to change radically the system of trading on borrowed capital, or (3) a desire to propitiate the religious party, and from (*b*) that either (1) merchants were content to forego the advantages of protection against loss of capital from sea risks, or (2) other means of acquiring security against trade risks existed which were substituted for loans on Bottomry. Assuming in the first place that the oversea commerce of the period other than that of merchants trading on their own capital was very largely carried on by means of loans on Bottomry, it follows that so drastic a measure as that of Justinian, if enforced, would have practically killed all such trade enterprise, as the rate of interest on such loans allowed thereunder would have been quite out of proportion to the value of the money [1] and the price of the risk.[2] That the trade was not seriously hampered is shown by the fact that from the 5th to the 9th centuries A.D. the Eastern Empire by its situation was natural heir to the commerce of the East,[3] and played the part of middleman,

Reason for limitation.

[1] At this time the legal rate of interest was 6 per cent.; but loans for commercial undertakings could be made at 8 per cent.

[2] Hendriks: *J. I. A.*, Vol. II, p. 136, quotes rates in latter part of 14th century of marine insurance from London to Pisa as being "always from 12 to 15 per cent. on the value and sometimes more, etc."; from Bruges to Pisa, 12 to 15 per cent., according to season. If this was so in A.D. 1400, it follows *a fortiori* that 12 per cent. *per annum* could not have adequately represented the value of the interest on the money plus the marine insurance thereof during the very unsettled period from A.D. 500–1000.

Cf. Duer, J.: *Law of Representations*, p. 12, *re* nature of risk incurred in sea trading.

[3] W. Heyd: *Hist. du Commerce du Levant*, etc., Vol. I, p. 2. "En effet, lorsque l'Empire s'était divisé en deux la monarchie byzantine avait,

or distributor, between the West and the East.[1] It controlled the coasts to which the trade routes of Asia descended, Egypt, whence was derived the trade of the Levant, Syria, Arabia, and the Red Sea.[2] This extensive commerce was retained by Byzantium,[3] unchallenged by the Western peoples, until in course of time the trading cities of Italy, France, Spain, etc., became sufficiently powerful to contest her trade supremacy. Whence it is clear that the Eastern Empire did not lose its trade by means of the restrictions imposed by Justinian, and also that the restrictions were not the result of an impoverished trade.[4] Again, it may be considered that the actions of the Emperors in regard to their legislation on this contract were not actuated by hostility to trade, as Justinian and his successors did all in their power to stimulate the commerce of the Empire.[5] Consequently, it is reasonable to assume that neither Justinian nor his successors anticipated a reduction of commercial activity from their legislation, and that they

naturellement, par l'effet de sa situation géographique, hérité du commerce de l' Orient."

Cf. Finlay: *Greece under Romans*, pp. 200, 511–516. Gibbon: *Decline and Fall*, etc., IV, 226–234 (speaking of silk trade especially).

[1] W. Heyd: *Hist. du Commerce du Levant*, etc., Vol. I, p. 2. "Ayant survécu aux invasions, elle joua dans les relations commerciales entre l'Occident et l'Orient un rôle intermédiaire."

Cf. Bury: *History of Greece*, II, p. 538.

[2] W. Heyd: *Hist. du Commerce du Levant*, etc., Vol. I, p. 24. "Les Byzantins conservaient donc dans la Méditerranée une suprématie que les Occidentaux ne songeaient les disputer. Ils étaient encore maîtres des côtes auxquelles venaient aboutir les routes commerciales de l'Asie; ils possédaient l'Égypte, où la mer Rouge amenait les marchandises du Levant, la Syrie . . . enfin . . . les points secondaires qu'intéressait le commerce du Levant."

[3] Finlay: *History of the Byzantine and Greek Empires*, Vol. I, p. 250, speaking of period A.D. 716–867, says: "Constantinople was as much superior to every city in the civilized world, in wealth and commerce, as London now is to the other European capitals."

[4] Hendriks: *J. I. A.*, II, p. 133, states that "in the Eastern Empire, during the dark ages, there was not much commerce which called for the contract against sea risk," but in this he appears to have been mistaken.

[5] W. Heyd: *Hist. du Commerce du Levant*, etc., Vol. I, p. 18. "Désireux d'avoir toujours à leur disposition assez d'étoffes pour satisfaire à leurs besoins et pour pouvoir en faire de fastueux cadeaux, les Empereurs de Byzance favorisaient de tous leurs efforts le commerce du Levant; dans les négociations avec les princes de Perse ou d'Éthiopie les intérêts du commerce n'étaient jamais oubliés; ils en étaient même le principal objet." (Quotes *Excerpta e Menandri hist.*, p. 361, and Theophanes, I, p. 377.) "Mais les Empereurs allaient encore plus loin; ils prenaient un intérêt direct au commerce et à l'industrie, etc."

did not act from caprice or without due consideration, but on the advice of the most skilled jurists and political economists of the day. It is difficult, owing to the want of evidence, to state definitely what were the causes which led to the limitation of the interest to 1 per cent. per month. All that can be done is to put forward tentatively certain probable causes and to examine the arguments for and against each, remembering that the change was based on reasoning which the continued prosperity of several hundred years after proved to be sound. The causes which may have influenced Justinian and his successors can be best learnt from a very brief survey of the state of commerce of the Empire at the date of his accession.[1]

State of commerce in Eastern Empire in 6th century A.D.

These were as follows :—

(1) There was a very extensive trade carried on by land and sea.[2]

(2) The sea-trade and matters pertaining to the mercantile marine were ruled by local laws, or by the private regulations of the *collegia*, etc., which are not set out, but only partially referred to, in the extant portion of the *Corpus Juris Civilis*.[3]

(3) Foreign merchants were continually using money for trading purposes which they had borrowed on contracts of Bottomry.[4]

(4) Enormous fortunes had been acquired by certain families who regarded loans on Bottomry as excellent, paying, and not over-risky investments.[5]

(5) Merchants and shippers had learnt from centuries of experience the value of protection against loss of their consignments, and this protection they had acquired from (*a*) contracts of Bottomry, (*b*) mutual insurance,[6] (*c*) capitalist insurance,[7] (*d*) wager insurance,[8] etc.

(6) There were in existence numerous gilds (*collegia*) and

[1] A.D. 527.
[2] See p. 93, above.
[3] Cf. reference to Rhodian Law in *Digest*, XIV, ii, 9.
J. M. Pardessus, *op. cit.*, pp. 194, 196, 205.
J. Duer: *Law of Representations*, Lecture I.
[4] See Duer, p. 25.
[5] See Hendriks: *J. I. A.*, Vol. II, p. 128.
[6] See Chap. VI, p. 105, below. [7] See Part II. [8] See Part II.

companies (*societates*) carrying out commercial and financial transactions on their own initiative and bound by their own by-laws as far as their own members were concerned.[1]

(7) A large portion of the commerce was carried on by foreign merchants, in foreign ships,[2] trading on capital borrowed on contracts from citizens of the Eastern Empire.

(8) The Church was opposed to high rates of interest.

Under these conditions it appears probable that Justinian was influenced by one or more of the following desires: (*a*) to obtain the approval and support of the Church; (*b*) to increase the resources of the Empire and to render it more powerful in the case of war by the reduction of the amount of Byzantine capital in the hands of foreigners and by the formation of a stronger mercantile marine; (*c*) to strengthen and increase the trading classes by forcing merchants to trade on their own capital and by inducing capitalists to use their money in commerce which they were personally conducting rather than leading unproductive lives; (*d*) to provide more employment for men of the lower classes; (*e*) to meet the request of Byzantine merchants who were suffering from external competition.

Influence of Church on trade in 7th century A.D.

Taking these possible reasons *seriatim*, it has been stated frequently that the reduction in the rate of interest chargeable for money lent as *pecunia trajectitia* was the outcome of a desire to propitiate the Christian party, and possibly this may have been the case, but, if so, it is difficult to understand why the Emperors of the Western Empire subsequently to the invasion of the Goths, influenced by a similar inducement, did not pass equally restrictive laws. If this change had been due to the clerical party in Byzantium, the clerical party in Rome must have heard of it and would in all probability have striven for a similar concession to their prejudices; and it must be remembered that the Church of Rome had attained to a high position and had acquired a considerable voice in public

[1] See Chap. VI, p. 105, below.

[2] W. Heyd: *Commerce du Levant*, etc., Vol. I, pp. 52–6, shows that Greeks did not interest themselves in trade—Léon V. (L'Arménien) *circ.* 820, "interdit à ses sujets de se rendre en Égypte et en Syrie."

matters by the end of the 6th century.[1] But in the Western Empire there was, as far as may be judged from extant records, no attempt to restrict the liberty of merchants and others to make contracts of loans on Bottomry, at any rate of interest that they considered suitable. Further, so far from viewing trade and trade practices with disapproval, the Popes themselves took great interest in the trade of the country, did all they could to protect and encourage it, and, apparently, entered the arena of commerce themselves, at least as sleeping partners.[2] Again, a large proportion of Justinian's subjects were non-Christian and the greater part of the trade of the Eastern Empire was with non-Christian countries,[3] by whom any such legislation would have been resented the more bitterly if they were of opinion that it was the result of religious pressure. Whence it appears unlikely that the change was made solely to satisfy the exigencies of the Church party, although, of course, the action of Justinian may have been partially due to this cause.

Necessity of forming a navy recognized.

The second reason is more likely to have been the origin of the change in the law. It is known that the Romans had recognized that the necessity of keeping a navy and a naval reserve was vital to the safety of the State,[4] also that the welfare of the merchant service and the quality of the *personnel* formed a very valuable adjunct to the navy. It is likely, therefore, that Justinian and his advisers were of opinion that a measure which practically prevented the loan of Byzantine capital for oversea trade would force the owners of such capital as would cease to be lent as *pecunia trajectitia*, and consequently be thrown on their hands, to furnish and man ships, with the result that there would be provided a very large trained mercantile marine which not only would give increased work to the Byzantines and afford the community greater profits on the trading, but also could be used by the

[1] But see references quoted and referred to on p. 89.
[2] See p. 89, above.
[3] Cf. W. Heyd: *Commerce du Levant*, etc., pp. 52–56.
[4] *Digest*, XIV, 1, 1, s. 20. "Quia ad summam rempublicam navium exercitio pertinet."

Government for the purposes of naval warfare, etc., if required. If this reasoning was the cause of his policy with regard to this legislation, it proves him to have been a very far-seeing and wise statesman, as it is historical that the navy of Byzantium, from being in the 5th century A.D. insignificant, became in the 8th century the finest in existence. It should be expressly noted that this legislation would not have prevented the employment of borrowed money by traders who had stock in Byzantium which they could hypothecate to the lender. They could, as will be shown,[1] protect themselves against the risk of loss when using this money for oversea trade by various methods of quasi- or real insurance. That this was actually done is suggested, if not proved, by the direct sanction given by Justinian[2] to the use of local customs in the very Novel which reimposed this restricted rate of interest. The statement that this Novel should not be held to supersede local customs connotes the existence of such customs as would be applicable to the matter and implies that there were other methods of procedure by which traders could protect themselves against *vecturæ periculum.*

The third and fourth reasons may have been of weight in influencing the action of Justinian and his successors. This is rendered the more likely by the fact that the larger part of the oversea trading of Byzantium was carried on by foreigners who at first obtained their capital from Byzantines on contracts of Bottomry and, with the Byzantine money thus acquired, were able, finally, to control the great part of the oversea trade. It is clear, however, that the legislation of Justinian, if directed against these foreign traders, was not very effective, since by the 9th century A.D. the Scandinavians had acquired very extended business rights, which the Byzantines protested against.[3]

The fifth reason is purely hypothetical, but is suggested by the fact that there exists a record of a complaint made by the Byzantine merchants against the facilities enjoyed by

[1] See Part II, below. [2] Novel 110.
[3] W. Heyd: *Commerce du Levant*, etc., Vol. I, pp. 52 *et seq.*

their foreign rivals, but this was of much later date.[1] It is, however, probable that the question had arisen before that date, possibly before the publication of the *Digest* or *Novellæ*. As shown in the discussion of the second reason, enforcing such a low rate of interest would have tended to reduce the foreign traders' working capital and, consequently, have improved the position of the Byzantine merchants. Summing up, it has been shown that although the contract of Bottomry was rendered practically useless as a paying investment, yet the commerce of the Eastern Empire did not appreciably suffer, that Byzantine merchants could obtain working capital in a way which would be difficult, if not impossible, to foreign traders (i.e. by hypothecating stock in Byzantium), that, probably, other means of insuring against total loss were in use, and, finally, that there was always a tendency to revert to loans on Bottomry which was kept in check by a repetition of the laws against unlimited interest.

Other methods of insurance provided in Justinian Law, but not in legislation of Western Empire.

In this connection it is of interest to note an important difference in the law of the two Empires which may, perhaps, have some bearing on the difference in their practice in respect of the rates of interest on loans of Bottomry. In the Eastern Empire: The *Digest* contains several allusions to contracts, other than those of Bottomry, by which a merchant could protect himself against loss arising from marine risk and would thus be independent of the contract of Bottomry in so far as indemnifying himself was concerned.[2] In the Western Empire: There is no

[1] *Early Voyages and Travels in the Levant.* Hakluyt Society, 1893. J. T. Bent says, in introduction, "As far back as the 9th and 10th centuries of our era, the Emperors of the East granted to the Warings or Varangians from Scandinavia capitulations or rights of exterritoriality, which gave them permission to own wharves, carry on trade, and govern themselves in the Eastern capital: these rights established numerous *imperia in imperio* during the succeeding centuries in Constantinople (Venet. 11th cent., Amalf. 1056, Genoese 1098, Pisa 1110), and then became so general that the Greeks of the later Empire complained that there were no wharves for themselves and that they could not compete with those indefatigable foreign traders."

Cf. Gibbon: *Decline and Fall*, etc., V, 23 *et seq.*

[2] See Chapter VII.

reference to any means of protection against marine or other risks, excepting that of Bottomry, which, although not proof that no methods were known, yet tends to show that they were not generally recognized, whence it follows that the contract of Bottomry would have been more necessary than was the case in the Eastern Empire.

Extant legislation of Eastern Empire in respect of contract.

Among the fragments of the legislation of the Eastern Empire dealing with *pecunia trajectitia* and *fœnus nauticum* are the following[1]:—

Digest, XXII (ii), and XLV (i), 122; and *Code*, IV, 33.

Code, IV, 32. Edict by Justinian limiting interest to 12 per cent. per annum.

Novel 106. Edict by Justinian re-admitting unlimited interest.

Novel 110. Edict by Justinian again limiting interest to 12 per cent. per annum.

Basilicôn, XXIII (iii), c. 67, 74. LIII (v), c. 1, 15, 16.

Harmenopoulos, manuale legum III, 7.

Greek Laws in Cyprus, (see Pardessus, *Lois Marit.*, Vol. I, 163).

Reasons for popularity of contract.

Before proceeding to investigate the question as to whether insurance *per se* was known to the Romans, it may be well to examine the reasons for the great popularity of the contract of Bottomry. Looked at merely as a loan, it would appear to have many inherent characteristics which would tend to render it inconvenient to the lender and to the borrower. From the lender's point of view there is the risk of loss of his capital, the removal of his security from his custody, and the uncertainty as to when his loan would be determined and the capital returned. The borrower, on the other hand, who was anxious to raise capital, might well object to being forced to pay a much larger rate of interest than a pure loan would demand; if the borrower possessed capital and merely required insurance or protection against the risk of loss of his invested capital, he would find the compulsory acceptance of money as a loan irksome, and would object to the trouble entailed in investing the money received, etc. The real reasons for the popularity of the contract would appear to have been as follows:—

[1] To economize space the text of the extracts is not quoted.

(i) It permitted the capitalist (who could not trade)[1] to enter into a quasi-partnership with a trader, assuming part of the risk and receiving a high rate of interest, which he could not do on a pure loan, as usury was strictly forbidden by law.[2]

(ii) It afforded the borrower who, though not requiring a loan for trading purposes, yet wished to ensure his invested capital, a certain guarantee that, in the event of his capital being lost, he would be indemnified, as he held the " insurance money " in his own control.

It is also of interest to consider the methods most probably used by those merchants and shippers who were in this position, especially as such consideration will show that the advantages of insurance without loans must have been brought to their notice and that, probably, insurance was practised by them. For them the best means of securing their object would, apparently, have been to have borrowed money on a contract of Bottomry on the security of the cargo and ship, then to have lent the money to a banker (*argentarius*) who, for the use of the money in his brokering and moneylending transactions, would have paid the market rate for money on a deposit account. The difference would have represented the premium for the insurance of the cargo, etc. In practice the result of this transaction would have differed from that of a modern insurance contract in the following respects only :—(i) The premium would have been paid, not as a fixed sum beforehand, but as interest on the sum advanced if and when the ship arrived safely, and, in the event of total loss, would not have been payable ;

[1] Boucher : *Institution au Droit Maritime*, p. 337, s. 1252, states : " Si les Romains n'ont pas assigné, dans leurs lois, aucune place distincte au contrat d'Assurance, c'est parceque ce peuple guerrier abandonnoit, aux esclaves et aux affranchis, le soin du commerce de mer et de terre."

Cf. Dionys. Halic., Lib. II, 28, and Lib. XI, 25.

Also *Digest*, XLIX, tit. 14, 31, and 61, 1.

Robiou and Delaunay, *Les Institutions de l'ancienne Rome*, Vol. III, p. 33, referring to Senators, state, " tous les profits compris sous les noms de *lucrum*, *quæstus* leur étaient interdits."

Cf. Philostratus : *Apollon. Vit.*, IV, 32.

[2] See Appendix G.

(ii) the lender could, in return for the guarantee, find a good speculative investment for his money. The first point of difference is, however, slight, as it is presumable that the merchant in taking stock of his assets and possible profits discounted this payment in some rough-and-ready way, and thus credited his account with the payment of the present value of the sum. The second is of little importance from the insurer's point of view, as it would not alter his action, but merely shows the consideration required by the lender. So far, it has been shown that by a somewhat circuitous method involving various financial operations, but which it is known did actually exist, a merchant could insure the safe arrival of his merchandise and ship by the contract to pay on her safe arrival a certain amount of money, representing the difference between the amount payable as *fœnus nauticum* or marine interest on the total sum advanced (the sum insured) and the interest which the sum advanced was earning when deposited at the bankers. Whence it appears reasonable to believe that the merchants living in a big trading centre would have formulated some system by which the loan and the deposit at the bankers could be done away with when not actually required; this, it is found, was customary in certain cases, as is shown in Chapters VI and VII below. Assuming, however, that it was necessary for a dissolution of partnership or other similar cause that a division of the capital of a partnership should be made and the book-keeper (*actuarius*) was ordered to make up the accounts and draw out a balance sheet (= *rationem conficere*), it would be necessary for him to be able to discount the amount payable under the contract *pecuniæ trajectitiæ* less the interest earned at the banker's; the value of the cargo, etc., being insured, could stand as it was in so far as the capital invested therein was concerned. Assuming this course of procedure to have been followed in any one instance, the convenience of such a system of payment in advance would have been immediately apparent to the supposititious wealthy merchant who did not require a loan. The strongest argument in favour of the loan system would appear to be that the loan was a guarantee of the payment of the money in the event of the ship's being destroyed, as the value of the goods insured was in the borrower's hands, but that argument would have applied in the 14th and 15th centuries equally well, and yet it is proved that the practice of insurance, as we understand it, was in general use then, although the system of loans on Bottomry was in force.

The reasons which would lead us to suppose that such insurances were known to the Romans and Greeks having been very briefly reviewed, the arguments that have been advanced against that supposition should be considered. They are, briefly, as follows: (i) That there is no mention in any authentic classical writing extant, with the exception of the references to be discussed presently,[1] of any contracts of Marine Insurance; (ii) that the contract *pecuniæ trajectitiæ* so completely met the requirements of the Roman merchant and capitalist that no other form of contract was necessary. To the former argument the reply would seem to be that the only two codes which have reached us in anything like a complete form are those of Gaius and Justinian, and these codes do not profess to touch on all points, and in fact expressly avoid dealing with local laws.[2] Marine Insurance, if it did exist among the Romans and Greeks, would probably have been a quasi-private arrangement among the merchants, shippers, and capitalists or bankers of the various important seaports, all of which had their own local laws, under which, in all probability, such matters as insurance would have been dealt with. This is rendered all the more probable as an explanation of the absence of mention by the Codes of such a contract, by the fact that practically all matters relating to the mercantile oversea traffic are dealt with in the *Digest* by a direct reference to the Rhodian laws,[3] which, unfortunately, have not been preserved. Whence it is clear that the non-mention of insurance in the *Digest* does not prove its non-existence any more than the non-mention of laws as regards the relations of captain and shipper to crew or the rights of ports to charge harbour dues, etc., prove that there were no

[1] See Chapters VI and VII, below.
[2] Cf. Novellæ 106 and 110.
[3] See Appendix F.

laws to meet such cases. The second point is, perhaps, more powerful as an argument that loan insurance was of very frequent occurrence rather than that insurance without loans did not exist. Mr. Hendriks has stated the case for the prevalence of loan insurance very fully in his article on the Treatise of De Wet, in Vol. II of the *Assurance Magazine*.

It must also be remembered that the oversea commerce of Rome in the classical period, and of both Rome and Byzantium from the 6th to the 12th centuries, was very widespread, and involved an enormous import and export trade.[1]

[1] J. B. Bury: *History of Greece*, I, p. 472.
Finlay: *Greece under the Romans*, I, 267–270; II, 62, 210, etc.
Gibbon: *Decline and Fall of the Roman Empire*, I, ch. 2.
Heyd: *Histoire du Commerce du Levant au Moyen Age* (F. Raymond, 1885), Vol. I.
Macpherson: *Annals of Commerce*, I, p. 56.
Pliny: *Hist. Nat.*, IV, c. 22; XII, c. 18; XIX, Proem.
Strabo: Lib. XVII.
Tacitus: *Annales*, III, 53.

PART II

TRACES OF METHODS OF INSURANCE OTHER THAN LIFE KNOWN TO THE ANCIENTS

CHAPTER VI

MARINE INSURANCE (OTHER THAN BOTTOMRY) PRACTISED BY THE ROMANS

Scarcity of classical references to trade customs.

THE satisfactory discussion of the question as to whether non-mutual insurance was practised in the classical period is rendered very difficult by the scarcity of reference to any trade customs by the classical authors, by the ambiguity of such references as exist, and finally by the difficulty of deciding how far the essentials of insurance were present in contracts which, while bearing a superficial resemblance to those of insurance, yet might easily be wanting in one or more of the necessary conditions.

Essentials of non-mutual insurance.

These conditions are: (i) That there is a risk to be insured against; (ii) that the property, etc., insured is of value; (iii) that the insurance is only to cover loss, and cannot honestly be made the means of acquiring a profit by the insured; (iv) that a valuable consideration (premium) is paid; and, in the case of non-mutual insurance, (v) that the insured does not act as an insurer of the person or persons who insure him.

Classical references to insurance.

As will be shown, there are certain references in Latin authors and in the Corpus Juris Civilis which, taken separately, would appear to point to the existence during the later classical period of (i) State insurance of certain merchandise against marine risks in return for services rendered to the State; (ii) a contract made by private individuals for insurance of safe arrival of goods; (iii) a guarantee by the Emperor of indemnity against marine risks, similar in some respects to (i); (iv) insurance depending on the happening or failure to happen of one or more contingencies; (v) insurances made by what has been called "wager"; (vi)[1] insurances on (*a*) the life of the insurer, (*b*) the life of a son or daughter, (*c*) of another person, either for the benefit of the insurer or of another person; there is also direct and reliable evidence that annuities[2] were dealt in and that they were calculated by means of a table of values based on a species of mortality table. It being admitted that any one or two of these references might be considered to afford far too slender proof of the existence of any such practices, it is contended that taken together (remembering how well known the contract of Bottomry[3] was) the evidence seems to be conclusive that some such system was thoroughly understood and continually employed by the commercial classes at least, in Rome during the period of, say, from 300 B.C. to A.D. 1000. Such of these references as have been discussed by writers on insurance have been held by some[4] to prove that insurance was both known and practised by the Romans, while others[5] have held the opinion that the references are to trading or other customs of quite a different nature.

Annuities dealt in by Romans.

The passages to be examined consist of (*a*) two from Livy referring to *circa* 215 B.C., (*b*) one from a private letter dated

[1] See Part III, especially Chapters XIX and XX.

[2] See Chapter XII.

[3] Cf. Hendriks, *op. cit.*, p. 127: "That the contract of nautical interest or loan on Bottomry, or Respondentia, was used from very remote ages by the Greeks, Romans, and other nations, as their ordinary insurance contract, which end it perfectly answered; and that eventually it formed the traditionary ground-work on which arose the superstructure of the insurance system of modern Europe."

[4] Cf. Émerignon, *Traité des Assurances*, Ch. I., p. 2, speaking of the practice of the ancients, which resembles that of insurance: "C'étoit un sauvageon non encore cultivé, auquel l'ésprit du commerce a donné le développement et la consistance dont il jouit aujourd'hui."

Hendriks: *Contributions to the History of Insurance*, etc., *J.I.A.*, II, p. 126: "The non-existence in ancient times of the theory of probabilities as a *science*, or as anything beyond a philosophical idea of the weight of testimony, cannot be accepted as a reason for the unlikelihood of the early practice of insurance . . . in early ages the numerical expression of chance was unknown, and then, as subsequently, the refinements of the science were, *from the nature of circumstances*, practically inapplicable to the estimate of sea risks, in which custom or observation of very rough average results was the basis of operations."

[5] Bynkershoek: *Quæst. Juris Publici*, I, 21: "Adeo tamen ille contractus olim fuit incognitus, ut nec nomen ejus, nec rem ipsam in jure Romano deprehendas."

49 B.C., written from Cilicia by Cicero to his friend Caninius in Rome, (*c*) one from Suctonius referring to A.D. 58, all four of which were first quoted by Henricus ab Aschen[1] in 1693 ; and others from the *Digest*, the *Code*, the *Institutes*, etc.

Reference by Livy to Government guarantee in 215 B.C.

Taking the passages in chronological order, the first to be examined is found in Livy (XXIII, 48 and 49), in which it is stated that in 215 B.C. P. and Cn. Scipio wrote from Spain, stating that there was a lack of money for wages, clothes, and food for the army, and of everything required by the naval allies. As to the money, that could be taken from the Spaniards, but the other things would have to be sent from Rome, as otherwise neither the army nor the province could be retained. On receipt of these letters, the question was discussed as to how the requirements of the army in Spain could be supplied. The Republic at that time being heavily burdened with the expenses of an unsuccessful war, which had drained its resources and necessitated heavy taxation, it was considered inadvisable to purchase and supply the necessaries for Spain with the proceeds of an increased tax. Consequently, the prætor Fulvius was instructed to go to the public assembly to explain the needs of the State and to urge the farmers of revenues to make loans to the Government and also to arrange contracts for the supply of what was wanting to the army in Spain, promising that they should be paid with the first funds which came into the Treasury.[2] This the prætor did, and arranged a day on which contracts would be entered into for the supply of clothes and food for the Spanish army and of whatever might be necessary for their naval allies. When the day came three companies

[1] Henricus ab Aschen: *Disputatio de Assecuratione*: "Licet vero ipsum vocabulum assecurationis vetustioribus JCtis incognitum fuerit, non tamen plane ignotam fuisse susceptionem periculi vel damni ex certa conventione, colligere est ex illo Livii lib. XXIII, c. 49 . . . Præcipue ex isto Suetonii *in Claudio*, cap. 18 . . . et Cicero cum Imperator esset prædam ex Parthis captam hoc genere securitatis servare voluit: ita enim ad Caninium scribit . . . quod est ipsum negotium assecurationis de quo agimus."

[2] Livy, XXIII, 48: "Quum pecunia in ærario esset, iis primis solveretur."

came forward and stated their willingness to supply the goods on the understanding that (1) they should be free from military service during such employment,[1] and (2) that all risk of loss, arising from the attacks of enemies or from storms, of the supplies which they placed in the ships should be borne by the State.[2] Both demands were agreed to[3] by the Republic and, as shown subsequently, the supplies were furnished to the army. We find, however, later (XXV, 3) that this Government guarantee was made the means of defrauding the State. Two of the *publicani* had been for some two years carrying on a system of fraudulent claims against the Republic. Their *modus operandi* was to make false statements as to wrecks which did not happen, and also to deliberately arrange for wrecks.[4] Livy states that they placed small amounts of supplies of little value in old and unseaworthy ships, and when they had sunk these ships at sea, they made false claims of many times their value.[5] This went on for some two years, during which the Senate did not interfere, so as not to incur the enmity of the order of *publicani*. Subsequently there was a popular riot, and Postumius was to be tried on a capital charge, but he forfeited his bail and was pronounced an exile if he did not surrender. It must be clearly noted that all through the case the liability of the Government was recognized, and also that there was no Government supervision of the goods which were placed on board these ships. It has been claimed by many writers on insurance that these passages, either taken with that from Suetonius, or by themselves, show that insurance was known to the ancients. Among those holding this

Guarantee of indemnity against risks required as part of consideration.

Opinions of writers *re* nature of transaction.

[1] Livy, XXIII, 49: "Unum, ut militia vacarent, dum in eo publico essent."

[2] Livy, *loc. cit.*: "Quæ in naves imposuissent, ab hostium tempestatisque vi publico periculo essent."

[3] Livy, *loc. cit.*: "Utroque impetrato."

[4] Livy, XXV, 3: "Ementiti erant falsa naufragia, et ea ipsa, quæ vera renuntiaverant, fraude ipsorum facta erant, non casu."

[5] Livy, *loc. cit.*: "In veteres quassasque naves paucis et parvi pretii rebus impositis, quum mersissent eas in alto . . . multiplices fuisse merces ementiebantur."

view are Aschen,[1] Loccenius,[2] Émérignon,[3] Pardessus,[4] and Duer[5]; against whom among others are Boucher,[6] Park[7] and Marshall.[8] These passages prove without doubt that one of the necessary factors in a contract for capitalist marine insurance was known to, and practised by the Romans, namely, that of the capitalist (in this case the Senate) guaranteeing the shipper against loss arising from *force majeure* or from storms, etc. The points on which the various schools of writers differ are (*a*) as to the ownership of the supplies during the voyage, (*b*) as to the liability of (i) the Government, and of (ii) the shipper for losses incurred in transit, (*c*) as to whether the guarantee was (i) a promise of indemnification made by the Government for the benefit

Argument as to nature of indemnification.

[1] See p. 109, above.

[2] Loccenius: *De Jure Maritimo*, p. 165: "Veteribus tamen non plane ignotam fuisse susceptionem periculi vel damni ex certa conventione constat ex illo . . ." (he quotes Livy and Suetonius).

[3] Émérignon: *Traité des Assurances*, Préface p. iv: "Je crois cependant apercevoir dans l'Histoire Romaine quelque trace de notre contrat d'Assurance."

[4] Pardessus: *Us et Coutumes de la Mer*, pp. 72–73: "Il semble qu'une telle convention est un véritable assurance, et a tous les caractères que nous reconnaisons à ce contrat . . ."

"Puisque ces entrepreneurs n'avaient pas vendu des corps certains, qui auroient alors voyagé aux risques de l'état acheteur, le droit commun les laissoit aux risques des vendeurs."

"C'étoit assurément être arrivé aussi près que possible du contrat d'assurance tel qu'il est connu. Cependant on ne peut se dissimuler que ces textes ne parlent point d'une convention principale par laquelle un des contractans, au moyen d'une prime, *pretium periculi*, qui lui est donnée ou promise par l'autre contractant, s'oblige à réparer le dommage que des événements de force majeure occasioneront à la propriété de ce dernier."

[5] Duer: *Law of Representations*, pp. 17–22: "Exhibit not merely traces of insurance, but the contract itself, in an unusual, it is true, yet in a perfect form," etc.

[6] Boucher: *Inst. du Droit Maritime*, p. 339, s. 1260: " . . . dans ce cas la Republique cautionnoit mais n'assuroit pas, puisqu'elle ne recevoit aucun prix pour l'assurance. Or, comme dans ce cas le contrat n'étoit pas interessé de part et d'autre, c'étoit donc un contrat de cautionnement, et non d'assurance . . ."

[7] Park: *Law of Marine Insurances*, Introduction, p. lix: " . . . this seems to bear no resemblance to the contract of insurance for it is nothing more than every well-regulated state is bound to do by the ties of natural justice."

[8] Marshall: *Law of Insurance*, I, 1, p. 7: "These instances only serve to show that the contractors were to transport the stores purchased of them to the places of their destination at the risk of the Republic. They have scarcely a resemblance in any one particular to the contract of insurance. . . ."

of its citizens, and not in return for a valuable consideration,[1] or (ii) contract of insurance against certain stipulated risks, granted by the Government in return for a valuable consideration, paid or to be paid.

Origin of State Indemnity.

Before taking the various points in detail, it is necessary first to examine the origin of the State Indemnity. This is clearly shown to have been the result of a demand[2] made by the shippers and regarded by them as part payment for the undertaking, and by the State as part of the price they would have to pay for the accommodation required. Against this view it has been urged (*a*) that it is the duty of a State to safeguard the interests of those working for it,[3] which, though true, would appear to be beside the point, and (*b*) that the supplies from the moment of embarkation were the property of the Government,[4] and that the stipulation was only effective to the extent of exonerating shipper and ship's captain if supplies were destroyed or lost *en voyage* ; this argument is apparently not only inconsistent with the sense of the passage, but also historically and legally incorrect.

Proof that Government were not owners of goods during transit.

In the first place, if the Roman Government had taken over ownership as soon as the supplies were placed on the ships there would have been :—
(*a*) no necessity for contract, because (i) the Government would not require to indemnify itself, and (ii) there was no liability on the part of either shipmaster or shipper for losses of supplies during the voyage, if such losses were due to *force majeure* or to unavoidable accident,[5] and (*b*) no advantage accruing to shippers

[1] This point was first raised by Curicke in his *Diatriba de Assecurationibus* : " Illud, etsi vim pacti habeat longe tamen ab assecuratione quæ hodie in usu est, discrepat, si quidem hic Respublica sola periculum in se recipit, cum tamen ex lege assecurationum, et assecurator ad damnum præstandum, et assecuratus ad periculi pretium, quod premium vocant, utrinque obligati sint."

[2] Livy, XXIII, 49 : " Quorum duo postulata fuere."

[3] Park : *Law of Marine Insurances,* Introduction.

[4] Marshall.

[5] *Digest,* Lib. IV, tit. ix, frag. 3 (Response by Ulpian) : " At hoc edicto omnimodo, qui recepit, tenetur, etiam si sine culpa ejus res periit, aut damnum datum est, nisi si quid damno fatali accidit, inde Labeo scribit si quid naufragio aut per vim piratarum perierit non esse iniquum exceptionem ei dari."

from their false claims, seeing that the indemnity in such a case could only have rendered them non-liable for goods shipped. Claims for indemnification against loss denote that the claimant is the sufferer, i.e. the owner.

Further, if the Government had been owner, the supplies would have been subjected to a rigid inspection by the officers of the Commissariat or their representatives in Rome; it was only owing to the fact that the goods might have been thrown back on the shipper at the time of delivery in Spain, that such an inspection, which would have led to the immediate condemnation of the supplies, was not held prior to shipment.

Risks of voyage on vendor.

Assuming, on the other hand, that the contract of purchase was not complete until the actual delivery of the goods, Duer states that the Roman Government was not bound either by positive law or by natural equity to sustain losses occurring in transportation. In such contracts the risks of voyage are on the vendor, and even if the purchaser of goods to be delivered at a foreign port agrees to assume some risks, the ownership of the goods does not change, but remains with the vendor until after delivery; the purchaser is the insurer and receives the actual compensation or premium for the risks incurred, in being able to purchase the goods at a lower price.[1]

That the merchants themselves recognized that the Government would not have been liable, *sine contractu*, is shown by the fact of their insisting on the guarantee,[2] which was evidently regarded by them as a valuable concession, as a necessary prelude to, and compensation for, the special service required from them in coming to the assistance of the State during a period of great financial depression.

This being so, the shippers must, necessarily, have regarded the assistance they were rendering to the State as being (*a*) the price of exemption from military duty at a time when every available male was being called out to protect the Republic against the victorious Hannibal, and also (*b*) the *pretium periculi* or premium for insurance against the risks they were incurring. Again, the Republic, having

[1] Duer. [2] See notes on p. 110.

asked for tenders, had shown itself willing to pay certain prices for the immediate supply of goods, etc., required in Spain. When the examination of the tenders took place, it was found that two valuable concessions were demanded by the companies submitting the tenders, and were granted by the State. It can scarcely be seriously contended that these concessions were not regarded by both parties to the agreement as valuable concessions to be paid for services to be rendered. The Latin *utroque impetrato* is absolutely clear, and it would appear that both parties recognized that the granting of these two demands formed an absolutely necessary preliminary to the whole matter.

Service rendered by shippers regarded by them as consideration in return for which Government granted indemnity.

From the arguments advanced, it is contended that the following points have been established, namely, that in 215 B.C. the Roman Government undertook, in return for a premium (i.e. the valuable services to be rendered by the *publicani*), to insure the safe arrival of certain shipments of supplies, shipped by the private trading companies who were the owners of these supplies, to be sent from Rome (and probably other centres) over the sea to Spain.

Even if it could be shown that there had been no such system in vogue before this date, and that up to this time no system of private (as opposed to Government) capitalist insurance had been practised, it would still be reasonable to assume that after this date a similar contract of capitalist insurance became an ingredient in everyday business. Seeing that it must have been more convenient to many persons than mutual insurance, it would be difficult to believe that so eminently practical a people as the Romans would have been blind to the many advantages arising to both the insurer and insured from a system of private capitalist insurance, especially as the swindling referred to by Livy[1] could have been guarded against easily by an inspection of the ship and her cargo.

The next reference to be examined is of about 160 years later date, and is found in the epistle of Cicero to Caninius

[1] XXV, ii, 3.

Sallust, wherein he, writing from Cilicia shortly after gaining a victory over the rebellious tribes there, states that he expects to receive guarantees at Laodicea for all the public money (or treasure) in order that both he and the State may be protected from danger of loss in transit.[1] From this passage it would appear clear that there were certain men at Laodicea who were both able and willing to guarantee the State and Cicero against the risk of loss of part or whole of the public money arising from the dangers to be encountered *en route*. That a premium was paid to them is also certain, since in Roman Law, just as in our own, in order that a compact might be binding, some valuable consideration must have been paid.[2] Assuming that Cicero intended to convey the actual money or treasure belonging to the State to Rome, it is seen that all the essentials of a contract of insurance are present, namely: (1) the property to be insured, i.e. *pecunia publica*, which obviously did not belong to the guarantors; (2) the risks to be incurred in transit, i.e. *vecturæ periculum*; and (3) the premium, which, as indicated above, must have been paid (or payable) to render the contract valid. The various writers on insurance have, in discussing this quotation, advanced one of two theories—either that (*a*) it was a remittance of money by the purchase at Laodicea of what were equivalent to the modern bills of exchange payable in Rome, based on the hypothesis that Cicero did not intend to send the actual money to Rome, and ignoring the fact that, as pointed out below, he may have wished to send some of the captured treasure too; or (*b*) that it was a true insurance for the

Reference by Cicero to private guarantors about 50 B.C. against loss in transit.

[1] *M. T. Ciceronis Epistolæ*—ed. Christianus Godofr. Schütz, Halæ, 1808, Vol. III, p. 287: "Laodiceæ me prædes accepturum arbitror omnis pecuniæ publicæ, ut et mihi, et populo cautum sit sine vecturæ periculo."

[2] *Digest*, II, cap. i: "Sine pretio, nulla venditio est."

Digest, II, cap. xiv, tit. 7, 4. Ulpian: "Sed cum nulla subest causa propter conventionem, hic constat non posse constitui obligationem. Igitur nuda pactio obligationem non parit."

And ss. 1 and 2, in which form is given as follows: "*Dedi tibi rem ut mihi aliam dares, dedi ut aliquid facias*, hoc συνάλλαγμα (id est contractum) esse, et hinc nasci civilem obligationem."

Paulus (J.): *Receptarum Sententiarum*, Lib. II, 14, 1, *De Usuris*: "Ex nudo enim pacto inter cives actio non nascitur."

safe transit of certain definite sums of bullion and articles of value from Laodicea to Rome. The former view is held by Heineccius,[1] Ayrer,[2] Marshall,[3] and Duer,[4] the latter being held by Aschen,[5] Boucher,[6] Émérignon[7] and Pardessus.[8]

Opinions of writers *re* nature of transaction.

Obvious meaning of phrase probably the correct one.

In considering the actual meaning which Cicero intended his words to convey to Caninius Sallust it would, it is contended, be quite reasonable to regard the obvious meaning as the correct one, and that would appear to be that Cicero hoped to be guaranteed (by the *prædes*) against loss (his own or that of the Republic) arising from an actual transmission of certain property. Had he intended to say that he had bought bills on Rome, he would, in all probability, have said so, as it would have been quite as simple to express in Latin that he hoped to make arrangements to have the money paid to him, or to his order, in Rome; whence it would

[1] Heineccius: Operum Tom. VII. *Elementa juris cambialis*, I, 7: "Talem enim pecuniæ permutationem sæpissime memorat Cicero."

[2] Ayrer: *De vestigiis cambii apud Romanos*, (see Bibliog.).

[3] Marshall: *Law of Insurance*, I, ch. i, p. 8: "It seems to bear a much stronger affinity to the practice of remitting money by means of bills of exchange than to that of insuring against the perils of the sea."

[4] J. Duer: *Law of Representations*, p. 35, note 4: "But I agree with Mr. Marshall, that the probable meaning of Cicero was, that he would deposit the money at Laodicea, and there take security for its being paid at Rome without any risk to himself or to the republic, and hence that the intended contract bears a much stronger affinity to the practice of remitting money by means of bills of exchange than to that of insurance."

[5] See note 1 on p. 109.

[6] Boucher: *Droit Maritime*, p. 336, s. 1250: "Qu'étoit ce que ces répondans, sinon des assureurs qui, pour un certain prix . . . que . . . nous appelons *prime*, s'engageoient à réparer toutes les pertes qui pourroient arriver? Il y a toute apparence qu'ils ne s'exposoient pas à courir des risques gratuitement: or, comme en de cas il y avoit assureur, assuré, risque, paiement du prix du risque, convention de dédommagement de perte, il y avoit donc assurance, contrat d'assurance."

[7] See note 3 on p. 111.

[8] Pardessus: *Us et Coutumes*, etc., p. 74: "Il annonce son intention d'envoyer à Rome les derniers publics et de les faire voyage par mer; il redoute les dangers de la navigation, *vecturæ periculum*; il désire que le peuple et lui soient garantis contre ce risque, *ut mihi et populo cautum sit*; il cherchera des garans, *prædes*: il y a donc une grande probabilité que sa lettre se réfère à une convention d'assurance plutôt qu'à une convention de change . . . c'est cependant ce (insurance against sea-risk) qu'il annonce bien clairement par les mots, *sine vecturæ periculo*, expression parfaitement en harmonie avec celles dont Tite-Live se sert dans les passages . . . en parlant des risques maritimes, et avec celles qu'on trouve dans les fragmens du Digeste relatifs au prêt à la grosse."

appear, at first sight, that he meant exactly what he said, namely, that he hoped to insure against loss on the journey by providing guarantors. Further, there is the question as to the actual nature of the treasure or money to which Cicero was referring and for the transport of which he was responsible. It may be urged that there are two possible translations of the words *pecuniæ publicæ* used in this passage, one of which leaves it quite open as to which of the two systems (specified as (*a*) and (*b*) above) Cicero referred to, the other showing clearly and beyond the possibility of argument that Pardessus, Émérignon and the others were right in their assumption that a contract of insurance had been entered into. The translation that first occurs to the reader is that of "money belonging to the State," i.e. money for the payment of the army and other officials in Cilicia, together with the receipts from the taxes, etc., and if this is the correct meaning, it is at least as likely (apart from the reason suggested above) that Cicero would have sent or brought home the actual money (it having been the custom for pro-consuls and generals to carry the war-chest with them on their journeys), in which case he would have been prudent in arranging for guarantors who would indemnify him and the Republic against loss if incurred *en route*, as that he would have purchased bills payable in Rome. The second, and perhaps equally possible translation, is "treasure belonging to the State," where "treasure" would denote not only the public money referred to above which was in his custody, but also the spoils of the Cilicians,[1] whom Cicero had reduced to submission a short time before the date of writing the letter. If this second rendering be the correct one, then the hypothesis that the transaction was merely the purchase of a bill of exchange on Rome is no longer tenable, the only possible meaning in such a case being that he hoped to obtain a guarantee, *prædes*, of the safe arrival of the treasure at Rome. From the grammatical point

Omnis pecuniæ publicæ probably included spoils captured from Cilicians.

[1] Cf. H. ab Aschen: "Prædam ex Parthis captam" quoted in note 1, p. 109, above.

of view there would appear to be no reason why *pecunia* should not be considered to imply (captured) "treasure" as well as "money," inasmuch as the meaning of the word was "treasure," "wealth," etc., before the introduction of money; and, moreover, the word is continually used by authors of the classical period, including Cicero, to signify "property," "wealth," etc., in a context which would not allow the meaning of "money" or "funds."[1] From the record of Cicero's actions in Cilicia, it appears more historically probable that he did intend to include captured treasure, etc., seeing that, having already been saluted as "Imperator" by his troops, he was most anxious, at the date of the letter, to be awarded a triumph for his victories in Cilicia, on his return to Rome; and with a view to receiving such an honour he would, naturally, have caused as much of the booty as possible to be conveyed to Rome in order that he might display it at the triumph which he hoped to enjoy. Hence, it appears almost certain that he did send the actual treasure, together with the balance of the public funds, to Rome, and that the passage refers to his intention to arrange a contract of insurance or guarantee of indemnification for any loss occasioned by risks to be incurred in the transit.

Transaction to which Cicero referred was probably well known.

If it be admitted that Cicero was referring to an arrangement of this sort, it follows that the custom of the shipper entering into a contract with guarantors for the safe delivery of his shipment was commonly practised and generally understood. Had it been otherwise, it is more than probable that Cicero would have explained to Caninius in more detail what his proposed mode of action would be; the casual manner in which the matter is alluded to shows that Caninius would have understood that Cicero was making an ordinary everyday contract with which Caninius was quite conversant. It should also be noted in this connection, that more than 150 years had elapsed since the State had

[1] Cicero: *De Divinatione ad M. Brutum,* 1, 49, 111; *Oratio pro Quinto Roscio Amerino,* 2, 6, and 3, 7.
Livy, XXIX, 31: "Familia aliquot cum mapalibus pecoribusque suis (ea pecunia illis est)," etc., etc.

guaranteed the safe arrival of merchant ships and their cargoes, and that, consequently, the practice of guaranteeing cargoes proceeding to foreign ports against losses arising from hostile attacks and storms had been familiar to the Romans for many years, at any rate as far as the State guarantee was concerned. It would, therefore, as suggested above, be quite in accordance with probability to accept the statement of Cicero as referring to direct capitalist marine insurance and not to regard it as an allusion to the purchase of bills on Rome.

Reference by Suetonius to personal guarantee by Emperor Claudius in A.D. 58.

The next instance of the practice of a custom which either was, or very closely resembled, a contract of insurance against marine risks, of which a historical record has come down to modern times, is that referred to by Suetonius in his life of the Emperor Claudius.[1] According to him, in A.D. 58 there was a severe famine in Rome due to the drought, which resulted in great distress and, consequently, popular demonstrations culminating in the Emperor being mobbed and pelted with dried crusts in the middle of the Forum to such an extent that he barely escaped to the Palace. This desperate conduct on the part of the people was due to the fact that no one expected any more food to be imported during the winter season. Claudius, then, in order to persuade the importers to render a most necessary service to the State, offered to pay a fixed bounty on all the corn they imported, and, further, agreed to be personally responsible for all losses arising from storms.[1] He also granted special facilities and bounties to shipbuilders for the encouragement of this winter sea-borne trade. This definite offer on the part of the Emperor, as soon as it was accepted by the importers, would have formed a contract, which it is contended is equivalent to that of marine insurance in its most modern and restricted sense. The essentials of insurance, namely, (*a*) ownership of insured property, (*b*) risk, and (*c*) premium, are all present.

[1] Suetonius: *De vita Cæsarum*, V, 18: "Nam et negotiatoribus certa lucra proposuit, suscepto in se damno, si cui quid per tempestates accidisset."

Taking the questions in order, (*a*) the ownership of the insured property—the Emperor did not propose that either he or the State should buy the corn; it was the property of the importer, who sold it to the people on arrival; (*b*) the risk—that arising from storms is specially mentioned as being the species of risk for which the Emperor's promise would hold; and (*c*) the premium—the question as to the valuable consideration to be given by the importer in return for the guarantee of indemnity depends, *mutatis mutandis*, on very much the same arguments as in the case quoted by Livy, namely, that the Emperor was anxious to buy a service from the merchants, and that in return for this desired service he offered certain inducements, one of which was a contract or guarantee against loss. It would appear clear that he regarded his offer as of value. Therefore he regarded what the merchants were to give, or do, in return as of value. That being admitted, as it is clear that their action was given and accepted as an equivalent for the bounty and the indemnity, it follows that both parties to the transaction regarded the services of the merchants as valuable and sufficient consideration for the grants of the Emperor. Whence, in modern language, these services were accepted as payment of, *inter alia*, the premium on the marine insurance policy covering the specific risk referred to. Whence it would seem that the contract made between Claudius and the importers was a contract of marine insurance in its purest form. It is of interest, and will tend to strengthen the contention that insurance was habitually practised among merchants and importers during the time of the Republic and of the Early Empire, to compare the three recorded instances dealt with in this section. In the first instance, the guarantee of indemnity was demanded by the contractors, whence it may perhaps be assumed that some such practice was used by them in their private (as opposed to State) contracts. In the third instance, it was offered by Claudius, thus showing that he and his advisers were of opinion that such a promise would prove an exceptional

Argument *re* nature of transaction.

Comparison of above three references.

inducement to the importers. Assuming that the first of these references refers to a contract which was practically an equivalent to an insurance of the goods by the State made at the request of the shippers, it is most likely that the shippers were obtaining, as part of the consideration for the services they rendered to Government, protection of a similar nature to that which they arranged for themselves in their ordinary trading, as it is unlikely that the idea of obtaining a guarantee against losses would have occurred to them then for the first time. It also seems probable that this guarantee was a special instance of a general practice of non-mutual contracts for indemnification which had been in vogue previously. Further, it is not unreasonable to assume that the origin of these equivalents to non-mutual contracts of insurance was either (i) the contract of Bottomry, or (ii) the practice of the *collegia* or gilds.

Origin of demand for indemnity by State.

(i) The contract of Bottomry.—As pointed out in Chapter V above, it is probable that the merchants who were not in need of money for the purposes of carrying on their trading borrowed money on a contract of Bottomry with a view to insuring themselves against the risk of losing the whole of the money at risk in that particular trade venture; and that if such merchants had been in the habit of borrowing money in this way simply for the sake of insurance, it is clear that sooner or later they would have appreciated the advantages of obtaining the guarantee at the cost of the difference between the *fœnus nauticum* and the rate of interest payable on ordinary business loans, without being burdened with the necessity of finding an investment for the sum of money which they did not require, and which was only of use to them in so far as it gave them the additional security of holding the money payable under the indemnity in their own hands; whence, especially when taken with the methods of obtaining guarantee against losses described in the following chapter, it is almost certain that a form of non-mutual guarantee against loss would have been originated by those merchants who were unwilling to borrow sums of money which they did not require.

(ii) The practice of the *collegia* or gilds.—It is stated [1] that Numa divided craftsmen by their callings into nine gilds, which probably means that he recognized combinations of men who had been attracted to each other by similarity of pursuits, and had formed themselves into a species of mutual society for the purpose of assistance in carrying out their craft, being permitted, under the law of the XII Tables, to associate and to make what rules they chose for their own Governments, provided that they did not interfere with the Civil Law.[2] These trade gilds, which were very numerous during the Republic, were formed and carried on for the mutual assistance of the members, and, almost certainly, had a system by which the losses of members were made good either wholly or partially.[3]

It is probable that at first these gilds met the requirements of their members and continued to do so as long as the members were men of more or less similar financial standing, carrying on similar business and mutually sharing risks of approximately the same nature and value, but later it must have happened that certain of the members of these groups found it advisable or necessary to protect themselves by means other than those afforded by the gild, perhaps on undertaking ventures of more than usual risk, or when acting in a way which was objected to by the majority of their fellow-members. When this occurred their only method of obtaining the guarantee against loss would have been by approaching some person or company, and effecting a contract of a non-mutual nature. It is also likely that, in the event of a member of a gild meeting with loss, his fellow-members did not indemnify him for the loss, but subscribed a small sum each for his relief,[4] and that, consequently, if he wished to be fully protected, it would be necessary for him to obtain a complete guarantee from some outside source. If either this hypothesis or

[1] How and Leigh: *History of Rome*, p. 24.
[2] See Chapter XXIII, below (p. 251).
[3], [4] Cf. Practice of Flemish Gilds and Village Communities, Chapter XXIII, below.

that based on the contract of Bottomry be correct, it is clear that by the date of the transaction referred to by Livy, the merchants, knowing the difficulty that they would have found in providing against the risk involved in complying with the requirements of the Government, naturally insisted on State guarantee as a necessary part of the consideration. These State guarantees, in return for services, soon became subject to fraud on the part of dishonest shippers; consequently, the State refused to carry on any such arrangements, with the result that merchants were compelled to resort again to private guarantors, such as those to whom allusion is made by Cicero in his letter from Cilicia. Finally, many years later, it is directly stated that the Empire, being desirous of buying the services of the importers, offered free State insurance as an inducement, which, as pointed out above, tends to show that it was considered by the Emperor and his advisers that the merchants would require some such guarantee before undertaking the exceedingly risky business of shipping corn at that time of the year, possibly because it was recognized that they could not obtain guarantees as in the ordinary way of business owing to the exceptional nature of the risk.

Long interval between first and last of these three references.

In the writer's opinion a correct appreciation of the evidence afforded by the quotations given has been rendered extremely difficult, if not impossible, by the want of discrimination on the part of earlier writers on marine insurance as to the dates of the various transactions in question. All three episodes are treated as of the same period, those recorded by Livy and Suetonius being usually dealt with as though they referred to quasi-simultaneous contracts. It should be carefully noted that these events did not happen simultaneously, but that between the dates of the episodes mentioned by Livy and Suetonius was an interval of 275 years, that is to say, an interval almost equivalent to that from the date of the first English statute on assurance (1601) to the present date. Admitting, then, that there may be some doubt as to the way in which the earlier contract was regarded by the *publicani* and the State lawyers, it is undeniable that the interval is sufficient to warrant the presumption that the custom was developed and understood by the later date.

CHAPTER VII

CONTRACTS OF INDEMNITY USED BY THE ROMANS

Contract referred to by Ulpian about A.D. 225.

IN addition to the passages discussed in the preceding chapter, there are certain decisions in the *Digest* which appear to refer to insurance,[1] and to show that not only were contracts made for the express purpose of insurance, but also that they were used for purposes in no way connected with marine risks. According to Ulpian,[2] whose judgment was incorporated in the *Digest* and confirmed in the *Basilicôn*, in a reply given by him on a point of law, the stipulation contained in the following formula was valid: A. "Do you promise that my ten thousand (pounds) shall be safe?" (B. "I promise.") As the essence of this stipulation is in the words (*salva fore*) "shall be safe," which in this connection have no force unless they imply a possible loss arising from anticipated risks,[3] there results a contract between A and B to the effect that B shall indemnify A for any part of the 10,000 (pounds) which may have been lost, which is practically the same as saying that A is insured by B in respect of his £10,000.

Agreement to indemnify in case of loss.

[1] Marshall: *Insurance Law*, p. 8: "There is, in the Pandects, an observation of Ulpian which affords greater colour for supposing that the contract of insurance was not altogether unknown to the Romans, than any of the passages above referred to."

"This passage shows, however, that the contract alluded to, whatever it might have been, was very little known at the time Ulpian wrote, since he thought it necessary to observe that *it was not illegal*."

[2] *Digest*, XLV, tit. I, frag. 67. Ulpian: *De verborum obligationibus*: "Illa stipulatio, *decem millia salva fore promittis?* valet."

Cf. *Basilikôn*, XLIII, i, 64.

[3] Pardessus: *Us et Coutumes de la Mer*, p. 75: "Il pourroit en résulter que l'assurance, comme stipulation principale, n'étoit pas inconnue aux Romains; les mots *salva fore* supposent un risque, et la promesse est précisément celle que, dans nos mœurs, fait celui qui assure une chose."

It may be considered that the reference is too short and too indefinite to afford sufficient evidence on which to base an argument as to the nature of the business contracted for under the stipulation, but on consideration it will be seen that the *responsum* contains everything which is necessary to prove that the contract was either one of insurance against loss or a third-party guarantee. The fact that the contract was valid means that specific performance could be enforced, which shows that, if the necessary technicalities imposed by law had been duly observed in making a contract based on the undertaking to make good any loss up to the limit set out in the instrument, the contract was legally enforceable.

It has, however, been suggested by Dr. Duer[1] that the phrase used in the agreement contained in the foregoing formula is merely the guarantee of a debt and is of the same nature as that used in the chapter of the *Digest*[2] entitled "*Rem pupilli salvam fore,*" in which case it would appear that the contract more closely resembles a guarantee or security given by a third party. In the case of the tutor or guardian he was required to find a surety for his behaviour towards the minor or ward and to furnish a guarantor that he was and would remain solvent. Even in such a case it may be contended that, if the party whose solvency was guaranteed paid (as premium) a consideration to the guarantor in return for his guarantee, such a guarantor would have been insuring the solvency of the tutor for the benefit of the pupil. In fragment 67, however, there is no mention of a third party or any suggestion, direct or implied by the context, that a third party was interested therein. The stipulation seems to have been made by some person who had money exposed to risk and who, being afraid of losing it, had transferred the risk of loss to the guarantor, with whom he had stipulated, in his own interest, that he should be guaranteed against any loss in respect thereof. If it

Not a third-party guarantee.

[1] Duer: *Law of Representations*, p. 33, note 1: "It is evident from the context of the law that the stipulation . . . had no relation to marine risks, but was simply the guaranty of a debt."

[2] *Digest*, XLVI, vi.

be admitted that this passage is intended to refer to a principal convention by which A obtains from B a promise to guarantee him against loss, then it follows, as a corollary, that the statements which have been made as to the entire absence of any mention of insurance in Roman Law are based on a misunderstanding of the passage referred to. That this response denotes a contract of guarantee against a risk is clear; it appears to be certain that the contract was made between A and B, as there is no allusion to any third party whatsoever; and, further, it follows that A paid B something (i.e. a premium) for the guarantee from the fact that the stipulation was valid, since, as shown above,[1] no contract could be valid in Roman Law unless a valuable consideration was paid or payable therefor. Hence, the whole question as to whether the reference is to a general contract applying to all kinds of risks or not depends on whether it is a contract between two interested parties or merely a third-party guarantee. Taken by itself, this passage may, perhaps, be read either way, but it is suggested that, taking into consideration the references to historical transactions and the certainty that they were agreements between two parties for an indemnity against risk (whether a premium is held to have been paid or not), and also the fact that wager insurances were known and used by the Romans, the probability is that the decision of Ulpian refers to a contract of insurance.[2]

Contract has all characteristics of true insurance.

Wager Insurance.

In addition to the above-described methods by which insurances could be, and most probably were, effected, there was the method known by mediæval and modern writers on the subject as that of "insurance by wager." The *Digest* contains replies[3] of

[1] See p. 115, n. 2, above.

[2] Pardessus: *Us et Coutumes*, etc., p. 75: "Or le contrat d'assurance tel que nous le connaissons est-il autre chose? N'est-ce pas la stipulation dans laquelle une personne dit à un autre, *rem salvam fore promittis?* et dans laquelle celle-ci répond *promitto*." "On pourroit donc en induire avec quelque fondement que le texte cité a tous les caractères d'une assurance."

[3] *Digest*, XLV, i, 63, Africanus, Lib. 6: "Si quis ita stipuletur, *Sive navis ex Asia venerit, sive Titius Consul factus fuerit*; utra prius conditio

jurisconsults on questions referred to them as to the legal result of certain agreements or stipulations which bear a resemblance to a bet or wager. The contention that such agreements were only wagers adapted to commercial ends is certainly supported by the fact that during the later Empire[1] and early Middle Ages such a system of insurance by wager was in constant use in the leading seaport towns,[2] such as Florence, Naples, Marseilles, etc., although it was recognized that such contracts were not contracts of true insurance,[3] but were of an immoral nature, as they lacked the necessary provisions for preventing the person insuring himself (to use the term "insuring" in a loose way) from making a profit on the loss of his property. This defect in the system resulted in a prohibition in most of the larger commercial centres. This was the case in Amsterdam,[4] Genoa,[5] England[6] and France,[7] where, on the grounds that insurance can only mean an indemnity, and cannot be utilized as a means of making a profit, special legislation was directed against this form of contract. Again, as shown

Similar contract in use at Florence, Naples, Marseilles, etc., in Middle Ages.

exstitisset, stipulatio committetur, et amplius committi non potest. Sed enim cum ex duabus disjunctivis conditionibus altera defecerit, necesse est, ut ea quæ exstiterit stipulationem committat."

Cf. Cujac, VI, ad Afric., p. 108: (i) Cf. *Digest*, XLV, i, 78.

Digest, XLV, i, 129. Scævola, 12.

"Si quis ita stipulatus fuerit, *decem aureos das, si navis venit, et Titius Consul factus est?* non alias dabitur, quam si utrumque factum sit."

"Idem in contrarium, *dare spondes si nec navis venit, nec Titius Consul factus sit?* exigendum erit ut neutrum factum sit. Huic *similis scriptura est, si neque navis venit, neque Titius Consul factus est?* At si sic: *Dabis, si navis venit, aut Titius Consul factus sit?* sufficit unum factum. Et contra, *dabis si navis non venit, aut Titius Consul factus non est?* sufficit unum non factum."

Cf. also *Digest*, XLV, i, 141, 7.

Émérignon: *Traité des Assurances*, ch. i, 1, says: "Cette espèce d'assurance n'étoit pas inconnue aux Romains. Si un tel navire arrive d'Asie je vous donnerai telle somme, *si navis ex Asia venerit*, Dig. 53 (D. *verb. oblig.*); s'il n'arrive pas vous me donnerez telle somme, *dare spondes si navis non venerit*. D. 129."

[1] See *Basilikôn*, XLIII, i, 138.

[2] See Rocius, resp. xxii, no. 9.

[3] Not true insurance to say "si merces meæ peribunt, dabis mille." Cf. Émérignon, cap. i, 2, and Straccha: *De Assecuratione*, vi, 4.

[4] See Règlement, Act. 1.

[5] See Straccha: *De Assecuratione*, Discourses vii and xv.

[6] See Act. 19, Geo. II., c. 37.

[7] See Ord. de la Marine.

above, as early as 215 B.C.[1] frauds on the Government by means of deliberate wrecking and misrepresentation of value of goods lost were carried on to a great extent; therefore the private individual or society which undertook capitalist insurance or underwriting must have been even more liable to fraud if wager insurance were in vogue. This system of fraud must have been known to every merchant of that date, whence it is likely, if not certain, that either such steps were taken to verify the value of the goods and ships at risk as to render the wager insurance a wager only in name—in essence a real insurance—or these references are to questions arising from true marine insurance of a somewhat crude form. That the law was strictly opposed to any form of contract or business transaction which would tend in any way to tempt the owner or master to wreck a ship is shown by the legislation on the subject. Both the individuals taking part in the contract as indemnifiers in the case of loss and the Government were keenly alive to the probability of fraudulent action on the part of the owner if an opportunity occurred; and, moreover, the Government had specially legislated to prevent the decay of the mercantile marine.[2] It cannot, therefore, be considered as probable that contracts which would render such fraud so easy and certain as to be irresistible to all but the most honourable members of trading communities, were not only tacitly permitted, but rendered specially powerful by being pronounced legal and binding. Whence it follows that these wager insurances were probably true insurances in so far as the value of the goods at risk were concerned.[3]

There is, it is suggested, another possible explanation of these passages, namely, that they are counsels' opinions on

[1] See Notes on pp. 109–10 *supra*.

[2] As anything tending to cause men wilfully to cast away ships is bad for the State.

Cf. *Digest*, XIV, i, 1, 20: "Quia ad summam rempublicam navium exercitio pertinet."

[3] Duer: *Law of Representations*, page 33, note 1, states that: "If insurance was practised in the form of a wager it adds great force to the presumption that it was also known as a contract of indemnity. Judging from the experience of Modern Europe it even seems probable that the legitimate use of the contract preceded the abuse."

contracts for contingent insurances. It is reasonable to assume that, if, as is almost certain, there were private associations conducting mutual insurance and also if, as is very probable, there were companies or money-lenders transacting capitalist insurance for their own profit, these associations, companies, etc. would have kept their affairs to themselves as much as possible, and, in the event of a dispute which could not be settled between the members of the gild, or the companies, etc. and their clients, a case would be stated for legal opinion, similar in form and presenting the point legally doubtful, but so arranged as to conceal as far as possible the true nature of the business transactions involved. If this view be granted, it follows immediately that, in the event of there having been a dispute as to the legality of, or as to the due observance of the necessary conditions for performance of, a contract of contingent insurance, the case would have been stated in some such form as those quoted. That the particular risks in the cases quoted are not intended to be anything more than hypothetical would appear certain, as the same two contingencies are regarded in their relationship to the maturing of the contract, from every possible point of view, and are apparently chosen as being quite independent of each other.

Probability that passages are counsels' opinions on contracts for contingent insurances.

It is, therefore, submitted that insurance other than life insurance was known and practised by the Romans, in support of which there is evidence of the following:—

Summary of Chapters VI and VII.

(*a*) 215 B.C. Contract whereby the Government insures merchants. In this contract are shown (i) the existence of a guarantee against loss arising from certain causes; (ii) the equivalence of services rendered to the *premium*; and (iii) the ownership of the cargoes.

(*b*) 49 B.C. Contract between Cicero and *private* persons who guaranteed safe arrival of all the treasure he was sending to Rome.

(*c*) A.D. 58. Contract whereby Emperor Claudius undertook to indemnify shippers against risk of loss from storms.

(*d*) In *Digest.* Response by Ulpian stating that contracts guaranteeing something of value should be safe.

(*e*) In *Digest.* Wager Insurance, including, perhaps, contingent insurance.

NOTE.—The practice of mutual sharing of loss incurred at sea for mutual benefit, i.e. "General Average," has not been discussed. It is not a form of insurance in the strict sense of the word, and is too wide a subject to be treated in this Thesis. It may be mentioned that it was well known to, and generally practised by, the Romans, who based their later law dealing with the subject on the Rhodian Law *De Jactu.*[1]

[1] See Appendix F.
Cf. the references to the practice in Belgium in the 15th century in Chapter XXIV, below.

PART III

WHETHER LIFE ASSURANCE WAS KNOWN TO THE ANCIENTS

CHAPTER VIII

LIFE ASSURANCE AS KNOWN TO THE ROMANS

THE question as to whether contracts for the payment of certain sums of money on the death or deaths of a specified person or persons, if within a certain term or whenever occurring, and resembling in essentials the modern contracts of life assurance, were made by the Romans is investigated in this and the following chapters.

The direct evidence of such contracts to be examined comprises numerous records of a widely extended system of mutual insurance as carried on by the burial clubs and, possibly, of societies for ordinary insurance; in addition to which there are certain passages in the Roman Civil Law which, when taken in connection with the circumstantial evidence to be adduced, justify the belief that the Romans were cognisant of, and practised, life assurance. The question as to the data on which they calculated the risks involved and the payments required to be made for such contracts (i.e. premiums) is, unfortunately, rendered almost unanswerable owing to the want of direct evidence in respect thereof, but it is highly probable that calculations based indirectly on an (imperfect) mortality (or subscription) experience were made, and that, consequently, the premium, etc., bore a reasonable proportion to the amount of the benefit and to the class of risk.

Difficulty in examining data on which calculations were based.

A careful examination of the legal codes, etc., of Babylonia, Egypt,[1] India and Greece[2] has revealed no trace of the

[1] There was a very rudimentary form of life annuity—cf. *Zeitschrift für ägyptische Spräche und Altertumskunde*, 1882, p. 159, wherein is mentioned the purchase of an annuity by Hepd'efæ (a prince ruling in Sint in Middle Empire).

[2] There was, however, a very limited form of mutual insurance practised in the religious societies (see Chapter XVII below, and Appendix J).

existence of any such contracts[1] or customs among those peoples. It has, therefore, been impossible to find any forerunner whence the Romans could have acquired their knowledge and appreciation of these contracts of proprietary life insurance. In addition to the want of definite knowledge as to the origin of the practice,[2] another serious difficulty confronts the investigator when examining the evidence of the existence thereof, due to the fact that the only direct evidence bearing on these stipulations or contracts is that which is found in the extant portions of the Roman Civil Law. This evidence, which is confined to the *responsa* of various jurisconsults on the legal points arising from these contracts, and to the rulings of certain emperors in regard thereto, shows that they would have been legal if used, but does not prove that they were used. Moreover, direct information in respect of the business, financial, or mathematical details of these contracts is wanting. There is, however, collateral evidence that the Romans and their predecessors had observed the effect of mortality; that they (the Romans) had the material and skill necessary for the construction of annuity tables, one of which, though rough, shows distinct signs of being based on actual mortality experience; that they understood thoroughly the system of life annuities; and that they had experience of a class of business which involves a practical example of the incidence and effect of mortality on the funds of societies which disbursed money on the deaths of their members. It is, therefore, proposed to examine the question as to the existence of contracts of life assurance among the Romans under the following heads:—

No trace of similar contracts in laws of other ancient peoples.

Paucity of evidence bearing on these contracts.

Order of points to be examined.

(1) The probability that the business and private requirements of the Romans and their knowledge of insurance other than life would have suggested, and have led them to devise,

[1] Of non-mutual life assurance.
[2] These remarks do not apply to the Roman mutual insurance societies, etc., in respect of which there is considerable information. See Chapters XVI–XVIII, below.

some means by which loss arising through death might be reduced or nullified.

(2) The proof that the attention of Roman and earlier authors had been called to the probable duration of life, etc., as shown by their allusions to longevity, etc.

(3) The knowledge of mathematics and of finance possessed by the Romans.

(4) The tables of values of a_x or e_x which were sanctioned by Roman Law as bases for calculation of annuity values.

(5) The possibility of carrying on insurance business without actuarial knowledge.

(6) The formulas and procedure which the Romans would have used in making contracts of life insurance if they were cognisant of and used such contracts.

(7) The nature and essentials of a policy of life assurance.

(8) The early mutual societies which provided sickness and burial, etc., benefits for their members.

(9) Analysis of *Responsum* of Ulpian.

(10) Examination of other extracts from Roman Law dealing with similar contracts.

Object of the investigation.

The object of the present investigation is to show :—

(1) That in and after the 1st century A.D. there were very numerous mutual societies or clubs which accumulated funds for (*a*) the provision of funeral expenses, or of a sum of money payable at death of members or on their attaining a certain age ; (*b*) the payment of expenses incurred in profession ; and, perhaps, (*c*) of deferred annuities or pensions, etc.

(2) That from the 3rd century contracts could be made within certain very defined and restricted limits which could have been used as equivalent to modern contracts of non-mutual, term and whole-life assurance, and that these limitations and restrictions were gradually removed until, in the 9th century A.D., the contracts could be made as freely as in modern times.

(3) That the Romans in the 2nd and 3rd centuries A.D. were as competent as the peoples of Western Europe in the 16th and 17th centuries to calculate roughly the values required for setting up these contracts.

(4) That the use of some such means of protecting them-

selves against death was almost as necessary in their business and financial transactions as in those of modern times.

If, then, the evidence to be presented in support of each of these points be held to be satisfactory, it follows that contracts equivalent to those of modern life assurances were used by them from the 1st to the 12th centuries A.D.

CHAPTER IX

PROBABILITY THAT THE ROMANS HAD SOME MEANS BY WHICH LOSS ARISING THROUGH DEATH MIGHT BE REDUCED OR NULLIFIED

Large credit business of Rome and of Eastern Empire.

THE business of the Romans during the later days of the Republic and during the first ten centuries of our era was largely based on credit, that is to say, the early systems of barter had become obsolete, and, owing to the development of banking and the accumulation of capital by patrician families and those of senatorial rank, who were not permitted to enter into trade,[1] large sums of money were advanced to merchants for trading purposes. Some of these loan transactions were practically partnerships in which the capitalist was a sleeping partner; others were contracts of Bottomry; others loans to merchants on security which was subjected to no especial risk.

Loans for trading purposes.

Contract of Bottomry safeguards borrower but not lender.

As shown above, the loan on Bottomry,[2] which was very commonly made, provided, under certain conditions, for the indemnification of the borrower from whose point of view it was, doubtless, satisfactory. The lender, however, was liable to lose all or part of his money in the event not only of the occurrence of the accidents specified in the contract *pecuniæ trajectitiæ* [3] but also of the death of the merchant during the trading voyage or journey, if, as was very often the case, the merchant made a round, taking his merchandise with him. Whence it might be assumed that the capitalist, seeing that the merchant had thought it advisable to protect

[1] Cf. Livy, XXI, 43. *Digest*, XLIX, xiv, 31, 61, s. 1. Robiou and Delaunay: *Les Institutions de l'ancienne Rome*, p. 33. Chapter V, *ad fin*.
[2] See Part I, Chapter V. [3] See Part I, Chapter V.

himself against loss, would have followed his example and have entered into some contract, such as a wager insurance,[1] to cover his risk of loss under the contract of Bottomry, and also to recoup him in the event of his being damnified by the death of the trader. If such contracts were in use, they would in every case have been for the temporary insurance of the life of the trader while subjected to a certain risk or series of risks.

Loans on reversions, etc.

Another form of moneylending, namely, advancing money against absolute and contingent reversions, was also widely practised, and would have required, if made on lines similar to those on which transactions of such nature would be made to-day, a knowledge of, and facilities for setting up, contracts of (1) whole-life assurance and (2) contingent assurance.

Legal restraints on money-lending.

Owing to the excessive extravagance[2] which was prevalent in the early Empire, this custom was carried on to such an extent that, as both Tacitus[3] and Suetonius[4] have left on record, legislation was required to check the evil, with the result that reversions to a father's estate could not be hypothecated and money-lenders were deprived of any legal claim for repayment of money advanced against such reversions. The existence of very numerous transactions of this nature during the later days of the Republic, and during the earlier Empire, tends to the belief that, since the idea of obtaining a guarantee of indemnity against risk incurred in business transactions had occurred to the Romans, as evidenced in a limited sense in the contracts of loans on Bottomry,[5] etc., and in other transactions more closely resembling true insurance,[6] moneylenders

[1] See Part II, Chapter VII.

[2] Cf. Juvenal, XI, 46–48 :—

" Hi plerumque gradus : conducta pecunia Romæ
Et coram dominis consumitur ; inde ubi paullum
Nescio quid superest et pallet fenoris auctor."

[3] Tacitus, Ann. XI, 13, 5 : " Et lege lata sævitiam creditorum coercuit, ne in mortem parentum pecunias filiis familiarum fænori darent."

[4] Suetonius : *De Vita Cæsarum*, VIII, Div. Vesp., 11 : " Neve filiorum familiarum fœneratoribus exigendi crediti jus unquam esset, hoc est ne post patrum quidem mortem."

[5] See Part I, Chapter V.

[6] See Part II.

would have evolved some means of protecting themselves against the certain loss which would devolve on them in the case of their clients dying before succeeding to their share of their fathers' estates. It is not, of course, contended that this class of moneylending could not have been carried on without any system of life assurance; the proposition is that such loans could have been made with much greater certainty as to their values if the lender could have insured himself against loss caused by the death of the person to whom he had granted the loan, and that, if the financiers and moneylenders adopted some system of mutual sharing of losses on their investments, there is great probability that the practice would have become general in a form more adapted to public requirements. Further, every purchase or sale of a reversion involves calculations of a similar nature to those on which single premium whole-life or contingent insurances are based.

Advantages afforded to private individuals by assurance.

In addition to the advantages which would have been afforded to capitalists and moneylenders by the practice of life assurance there are those which would have been enjoyed by private individuals. In the case of professional men, of those receiving annuities, of merchants about to make trading voyages, etc., it is clear that insurance, or an equivalent, would have been of great service in providing for persons depending on them. The Romans having become acquainted with "wager insurances"[1] in the case of goods, etc., exposed for a limited time or to a certain risk or series of risks, it would not have required any great power of invention on the part of merchants and others for them to have extended this class of contract so as to include the insurance of themselves against death arising from certain risks or against death by accident during certain specified periods. Assuming that they had arrived at this state of development, it would probably have occurred to them to include death arising from natural causes in the risks covered by such an equivalent to a term insurance. This development

Wager insurance may have been extended to cover term insurance against accidents

[1] See Part II, Chapter VII.

is not of such a nature as to render it unlikely that the practice of wage insurance on goods, etc., had been expanded and amended so as to cover policies of term insurance on human life.

and, possibly, to term-life assurance.

There is, perhaps, more inherent difficulty in passing from "wager insurances" covering certain periods or risks to contracts of whole-life assurance, as the fundamental ideas are dissimilar. In the case of the term insurance the policy may or may not mature, in that of a whole-life policy it must mature, for which reason the question of a "wager" cannot be considered to enter into the contract of whole-life assurance.[1] The only connection between the two classes of policy appears to be the fact that they are both payable on the death of a certain specified person or persons. This analogy, however, could not be considered sufficient to form the basis of any argument in favour of the existence of proprietary life assurance among the Romans, were it not that there is direct and definite evidence [2] that the difference between "if he shall die" and "when he shall die" was understood and appreciated by the jurisconsults. Whence it appears probable that the Romans had extended their system of "wager" insurance so as to cover term insurance on lives; and so were acquainted with a rough form of whole-life insurance.

Passing from term- to whole-life assurance.

Difference between whole-life and term insurance understood by Roman jurists.

Moreover, in the Burial Clubs a species of limited [3] mutual whole-life assurance was carried on, which may have suggested non-mutual life assurance.

[1] But see Chapter XV, p. 164, below.
[2] See Chapters XIX and XX, below.
[3] See Chapters XVI–XVIII, below. The insurance benefits provided by these clubs were so limited both in amount and by the restrictions imposed by the nature of the business that they would have served merely to indicate the advantages of insurance.

CHAPTER X

ALLUSIONS TO LONGEVITY, MORTALITY, ETC., BY EARLY WRITERS

ALTHOUGH there is no direct evidence that vital statistics were observed and used by the peoples of antiquity for commercial purposes, yet there are many interesting references to the various periods in the life of man, to the age at which he might expect to die, and to the fact that a man's power of living is finite. These references show that the problems connected with the duration of human life had received careful consideration.

References in—(1) Old Testament. The earliest of these references are contained in the Old Testament. In the Book of Job,[1] there are repeated allusions to the limited or appointed term of a man's life. In Psalm xc.,[2] there is a direct statement that "the days of our years are threescore years and ten, and if by reason of strength they be fourscore years, yet is their strength labour and sorrow, for it is soon cut off and wc fly away." When it is considered that this statement was made possibly some 3000 years ago, and when the age 70 is compared with the age of most probable death,[3] 73, given in the mortality table contained in the *Institute of Actuaries Text Book*,[4] and the latter part of the verse compared with the values l_x and p_x for ages 80 and upwards, it will be admitted that the author of this psalm was accurate and must have based his statement either on the careful

[1] vii. 1: "Is there not an appointed time to man to enter upon the earth?"
Cf. xiv. 5 and 14.

[2] v. 10.

[3] After the age of 3, as there are more deaths in that year than in any other.

[4] Vol. II. p. 496, of first edition.

observation of a not inconsiderable mortality experience, or on the observations of others. Again, there occur repeated injunctions to lead a religious life in order that "thou mayest prolong thy days upon the earth,"[1] which, as the religion of the Old Testament contained much hygienic and sanitary teaching, was probably intended to be taken in the strictest and most literal sense. Referring to the age at death, it is interesting to note that Caleb,[2] when applying for an allotment of land, considered it sufficiently unusual for a man to be sound at 85 to require him to call the attention of Joshua to his physical condition and age; also that David, who came to the throne at the age of 30, after reigning 40 years,[3] died at the age of 70, "being old and full of days."[4] Leaving Biblical history, and turning to later Jewish writers, there is found in the *Pirqē Abōth*[5] the following passage: "At 5 years (the age is reached) for the study of the Scripture, at 10 for (the study of) the Mishrab, at 13 for (the fulfilment of) Commandments, at 15 for (the study of) the Talmud, at 18 for marriage, at 20 for pursuing (a calling? or the enemy?), at 30 for entering into (one's full) strength, at 40 for understanding, at 50 for counsel, at 60 (a man attains) old age, at 70 the hoary head, at 80 the special strength (gebūrāh, as in Ps. xc. 10), at 90 bending (beneath the weight of years), at 100 as if one were already dead and now passed away from the world."

(2) *Pirqē Abōth.*

(3) Greek authors.

The early Greek authors have also left evidence to show that the question had come under their notice and that they had arrived at the same opinion as that held by the author of the ninetieth Psalm: among whom were Solon of Athens, who (*circa* 600 B.C.) divided the duration of human life, in so far as men are concerned, into ten stages, each of which lasted seven years. Shortly after (*circa* 580 B.C.), Pythagoras stated that human life contained four periods of twenty years each. Plato[6]

[1] Deut. iv. 40. Cf. also xxii. 7, and Exod. xx. 12.
[2] Josh. xiv. 10.
[3] 2 Sam. v. 4.
[4] 1 Chron. xxiii. 1 and xxix. 28.
[5] Ch. iv, 24, etc.
[6] Plato: *Timæus.*

(*circa* 400 B.C.) noted the effect of the equable climate in Syria and Egypt on the health, and pointed out that residents in those countries frequently attained to a great age. Eusebius [1] (*circa* A.D. 300), referring to these statements of Plato, adds that they are not altogether to be relied upon, as a re-examination of the effect of the climate of those countries had been made and had resulted in a more correct analysis.

(4) Roman authors.

Among the Roman writers Pliny [2] (A.D. 80), in his observations on the census of Vespasian, calls special attention to the number of persons living who had passed the age of 100. In his Natural History he alludes to the longevity of the inhabitants of Ceylon,[3] " who look upon 100 years as a short life." Later, in the same work,[4] he again refers to length of life. Macrobius (*circa* [5] A.D. 390) adopted a division of human life similar to, and based on, that of Solon. He describes at considerable length the various characteristics of the different septennial periods from birth to the end of the tenth, and says that the allotted duration of human life is finished with the completion of the seventieth year of age.[6]

(5) In the Koran.

In the Koran,[7] there is a reference to the periods of weaning, puberty, etc., and in the commentary by the great jurist, Al Shafii (*circa* A.D. 800), on the last verse of Sūra 63 (" Allah will never respite a soul when its appointed time has come "), it is stated that the appointed age was 63 years.

Comparison of classical with Jewish references.

It is interesting to note that in all the classical references to greater or less longevity the question is dealt with as being the direct result of climate or of racial conditions, whereas the Biblical references to length of life treated it as either a reward to be looked forward to because of, or the outcome of, a strict conformity with the religious requirements of the Jews, irrespective of

[1] Quoted by Hendriks, *Journal Instit. Act.*, Vol. 2, p. 223.
[2] Quoted by Hendriks, *J.I.A.*, Vol. 2, p. 223.
[3] Book VI, Ch. 24.
[4] Book VII, Ch. 49.
[5] Macrobius : *Comment. in Somn. Scrip.*, Lib. I, Ch. vi, 45–77.
[6] " . . . et hoc vitæ humanæ perfectum spatium terminatur."
[7] Sūra 46, v. 14.

climate—race not entering into the question, as the Old Testament Law was intended for Jews alone.

Mediæval reference.

Later, about A.D. 1600, Hippolytus Guarino,[1] the town physician of Speyer, asserted, giving good reasons for his assertion, that a man of the most delicate constitution, if he come into the world without any deformity, possesses enough vitality to carry him on to his sixtieth year; while a very strong man should attain to his hundredth year. "If any die before this age . . . they are themselves to blame, since by excesses, or by neglect of the natural demands of life, they have undermined their own health and that of their children, and have hastened their death."

NOTE.—Wiedemann (*The Ancient Egyptian Doctrine of the Immortality of the Soul*, p. 6) tells us that the age to which the Egyptians hoped to attain was 110 years, but there is nothing to show that the Egyptians looked upon that age as being the age to which the ordinary man might reasonably hope to attain.

[1] Referred to by Comenius: *The Great Didactic*, ch. xv, 3.

CHAPTER XI

THE SUFFICIENCY OF THE KNOWLEDGE OF MATHEMATICS AND OF FINANCE POSSESSED BY THE ROMANS DURING THE EARLY EMPIRE FOR THE CALCULATIONS REQUIRED

Financial and mathematical knowledge of Romans.

IT may be urged that the calculations required for arriving at the values of annuities, subscriptions to burial funds and to clubs in which members mutually insured each other, and *a fortiori* the single or periodical payments for sums of money payable at death, or during a term of years on a certain risk whenever it should occur, would require a greater knowledge of mathematics and of finance than could have been possessed by the Romans during the third century of our era. It is known, however, that by that date they and certain other races of antiquity had acquired sufficient knowledge of financial[1] methods to deal with such problems, not with the scientific exactitude of modern actuaries, but very roughly, and also that they either had reached a state of mathematical,[2] or rather arithmetical, skill which afforded them the necessary knowledge for calculating such tables of values as those referred to, or were in a position to employ Greek or Alexandrine mathematicians to do so for them. This follows from the fact that about the end of the 1st century A.D. arithmetic had become of sufficient importance to require that a text-book should be published. Consequently, at Alexandria about A.D. 100, Nicomachus published a treatise on arithmetic, which was followed in A.D. 300 by the Algebra of Diophantus. These two works were of such excellence and so advanced as to retain their position as the standard books on the subject until the 12th and 16th centuries

Arithmetic of Nicomachus published about A.D. 100.

Algebra of Diophantus published about A.D. 300.

[1] See Appendix G. [2] See Appendix H.

respectively. Further, in addition to their knowledge of arithmetic and algebra, the Romans had long been accustomed to use the abacus, with the help of which they worked out intricate arithmetical calculations.

Abacus used by Romans.

In addition to their arithmetical and algebraical knowledge, they were acquainted with the elements of the theory of finance; that is to say, they understood, and continually employed, the following [1] financial methods of using money and of recording their transactions:—

Financial knowledge of Romans.

(1) *Interest.* Simple and compound, including discount and present values. To such an extent had the practices of lending money at interest, buying reversions, etc., become general that legal restrictions had been repeatedly imposed on such transactions.

(2) *Banking.* Current and deposit accounts, loans, securities, bills of exchange, etc., repayments by instalments, etc., foreign exchanges, etc.

(3) *Trading.* Correspondents and agents, travellers on commission, partnership, division of profits, liability of partners, etc.

(4) *Book-keeping,* including the keeping of separate books for receipts, payments, loans, etc., which books were received as evidence in lawsuits—preparation of balance sheets, valuations for dissolution of partnerships, etc.

Roman qualifications for carrying on life assurance business as great as those of European nations of 16th century, by whom such business was largely carried on.

It follows, therefore, that the business and scientific attainments of the Romans were at least as highly developed by A.D. 200, and, probably, long before, as those of Europe in the 16th century, that is to say, at the time of the publication of *Le Guidon,* wherein it was stated that policies of life assurance were made freely in some countries and forbidden by law in others. Whence, arguing from the respective fitness of the business men of the two periods to see the advantages of, and to inaugurate and carry on, life assurance, it may be urged fairly that, other things being equal, the probability that the Romans initiated

[1] See Appendix G.

non-mutual life assurance during some 700 years of great prosperity is greater than that the mediæval peoples did so during 400 or 500 years of disturbance and fighting. As far as actuarial knowledge is concerned, it must be admitted that, as life assurance was carried on by certain of the European nations although their knowledge of mathematics, etc., was extremely limited, it could have been transacted equally well by the Romans, who, as pointed out above, possessed at least equal knowledge. (See also Ch. XIII.)

CHAPTER XII

TABLES OF ANNUITY VALUES WHICH WERE SANCTIONED BY THE ROMAN LAW FOR THE PURPOSES OF THE LEX FALCIDIA

No trace of tables of premiums, etc., used by Romans.

ALTHOUGH there is no trace of any attempt on the part of the Romans to construct a table of mortality or rates of subscriptions payable by members of burial clubs, yet there are records of two tables which were sanctioned by the civil law for the capitalization of annuities. The necessity for such tables arose from the provisions of the

Lex Falcidia.

Lex Falcidia,[1] by which it was ruled that the heir or heirs to an estate should receive not less than one-quarter of the total property left by the testator. As it frequently happened that the will was made when the testator was in better circumstances than at the time of his death, it became necessary in such cases for the values of the various legacies to be proportionately reduced in order that the total value should not exceed three-quarters of the estate. In the case of the ordinary legacy, this reduction presented no difficulty, but when the testator had left a life annuity to one or more legatees, the question arose as to the basis of reduction of the values of such annuities.

Two tables of annuity values authorized.

In order to meet this requirement, it was necessary to capitalize the annuities, and, in order to permit of this being done, a table of annuity values, known subsequently as "Macer's Table," was used. This table was, as will be seen from the quotation below, authorized in a *responsum* of the jurisconsult Macer, who, at the same time, sanctioned the use of another and more correct table, the authorship of which he

[1] Passed 40 B.C. See *Digest,* XXXV, ii, 1.

attributed to Ulpian.[1] In the case of the first table, it is clear on inspection that the values are arbitrary, and in no way based on a mortality experience. Ulpian's Table, however, shows distinct signs of an attempt to represent more nearly the actual values of annuities.

Construction of Macer's Table quite arbitrary.

Ulpian's Table based on life experience.

It has been held by various writers[2] that the values given by Ulpian are those of the expectation of life rather than those of annuities, and the reason put forward for this assumption is that the Romans were unlikely to have used the factor of interest when compiling the table. There seems, however, to be no particular justification for this assumption. It is generally admitted that the table of Ulpian shows signs of having been calculated with direct reference to either a mortality or a subscription experience, but, so far, no satisfactory suggestion has been made of the way in which the table was constructed. On inspection it will be seen that, if the values of the table be taken as representing the expectation of life at the respective ages, the rate of mortality in Rome was much higher than that of modern times, and, further, that the table itself includes a sequence of values which cannot possibly represent true values of either e_x or a_x. This is also the case if it be assumed that the factor of interest was included in the computation of the values

Table of Ulpian probably table of values of a_x, not of e_x

[1] *Digest*, XXXV, ii, 68. Æmilius Macer, Lib. 2, ad legem vicesimam hereditatium. "Computationi in alimentis faciendæ hanc formam esse Ulpianus scribit, ut a prima ætate usque ad annum vicesimum quantitas alimentorum triginta annorum computetur, ejusque quantitatis Falcidia præstetur: ab annis vero viginti usque ad annum vicesimum-quintum annorum viginti octo: ab annis vigintiquinque usque ad annos triginta, annorum vigintiquinque: ab annis triginta usque ad annos trigintaquinque, annorum vigintiduo: ab annis trigintaquinque usque ad annos quadraginta, annorum viginti: ab annis quadraginta usque ad annos quinquaginta, (tot) annorum computatio fit, quot ætati ejus ad annum sexagesimum deerit, remisso uno anno: ab anno vero quinquagesimo usque ad annum quinquagesimum quintum, annorum novem: ab annis quinquagentaquinque usque ad annum sexagesimum annorum septem: ab annis sexaginta cujuscunque ætatis sit, annorum quinque. . . . Solitum est tamen a prima ætate usque ad annum trigesimum computationem annorum triginta fieri, ab annis vero triginta, tot annorum computationem inire, quot ad annum sexagesimum deesse videntur, nunquam ergo amplius quam triginta annorum computatio initur."

[2] Cf. Hendriks, *J.I.A.*, VI, p. 313.

given in the table, and that, consequently, they represent annuity values and not values of expectation of life. But the series of values answering to the expectation of life which is obtained on this assumption by the inclusion of interest, although obviously impossible, suggests that this impossibility is the direct outcome of an error in calculation of such a nature as to have been most likely to have occurred in the calculation of a table of values of expectation of life based on a subscription experience when made by a clever person unskilled in actuarial work.

Macer's Table more popular.

Although Macer's Table was so obviously incorrect and inferior to Ulpian's, yet it appears to have been more generally used, possibly because it was easier to remember and also because it gave smaller values for all ages above 50. As is shown by the reference to the table in the *Basilikôn*, an amendment had been introduced which tended to render the table less unfair in respect of the values at the later ages. In the original form, as given by Macer, the value of an annuity to a person aged 60 or over was nil, whereas in that given in the *Basilikôn* the value at 60 or over was 5 times the yearly payment. It appears that this later table is incorrect, as it does not seem probable that a person aged 59 would have received one year's payment, whereas a person aged, say, 61 would have been entitled to a 5 years' payment. It is more probable, therefore, that all persons above 55 would have received 5 years' payments as the capitalized values of their annuities.

Amended in the *Basilikôn*.

Ulpian's Table authorized in Middle Ages in Italy.

Although, as Macer said, it was customary to use the simpler table, yet it is clear that Ulpian's Table was also in general use from the fact that it continued to be used as the official annuity table in Northern Italy until the end of the 18th century.

CHAPTER XIII

ACTUARIAL KNOWLEDGE NOT ESSENTIAL FOR TRANSACTION OF LIFE ASSURANCE BUSINESS

Theory of probabilities unknown to Romans,

As there is nothing in the early history of mathematics to suggest that the theory of probabilities was known prior to the 17th century, it is clear that the Romans cannot be considered to have had any of the scientific knowledge of the modern actuary, but it is submitted that, although they had no such theoretical knowledge, they had some elementary ideas on the question of chance. Common sense, although in no way an equivalent to scientific training, would have enabled business men and financiers to see that in ordinary series of events certain things had been in the habit of occurring more frequently than others in the past, and would have led them to believe that, under similar conditions, those things would be more likely to occur than the others, and, consequently, that it would be safer to risk money on their occurrence than on the occurrence of the alternatives. It follows, therefore, that they were in a position to make a *rough* calculation of the value of the risk they were incurring in undertaking, or in guaranteeing another person against the possible loss involved in, any transaction involving uncertainty. That they did allow for such risks is conclusively proved by the numerous references to the excess in the legal rate of interest on contracts of Bottomry [1] over that of ordinary loans *because of the risk* involved, and to wager insurance, etc.[2] Whence, assuming that Mr. Hendriks [3] was absolutely correct in his

who had elementary ideas of chance.

Made rough calculations of values of risks.

[1] See Chapter V, above. [2] See Part II, above.

[3] *J.I.A.*, Vol. II, p. 126: "The non-existence in ancient times of the theory of probabilities as a *science* . . ."

contention that the Romans had no scientific knowledge of mathematical probability and, also, that their ideas as to the effect of the increase of age, etc., on mortality were limited to those suggested by Ulpian's Table,[1] or even that they did not in any way derive the monetary arrangements involved in the contracts made by them for the payment of money "when I shall die"[2] or "if I shall die"[2] from the values of a_x (or e_x) given in that table, it does not follow from such an assumption that the transactions of that nature were not made with the object of setting up a contract which answered the purpose of the modern policy of life assurance and which contained all the necessary attributes of the modern policy.[3] As is shown by the direct references to, and prohibitions of, all kinds of insurances on life contained in various ordinances, etc., of the 16th to 17th centuries,[4] the making of such insurances was common in certain of the European nations and absolutely forbidden in others at that time; consequently, the practice must have been general for some considerable period prior thereto. In discussing these references to insurance, Mr. Hendriks[5] stated that: "Temporary insurances *on lives* were clearly not unfrequently effected about this time, or previous to it, to provide against hazards of a definite duration, and, like the contract of marine insurance, were doubtless little better than rough estimates of odds; but laboured under a disadvantage which was never the fate of marine policy, viz. of being considered reprehensible and illegal." As this statement is, perhaps, somewhat misleading, and as a correct appreciation of the nature and legal position of these contracts will assist the present argument, a brief examination thereof is advisable.

Assurances on lives made in 16th and 17th centuries.

In the first place, "temporary insurances on lives" are spoken of as being "little better than rough estimates of odds." Granting that this description is correct, it does not appear to affect the question as to whether insurance on

[1] See Chapter XII, above.
[2] See Chapters XX and XXI, below.
[3] See Chapter XV, below.
[4] See pp. 277 and 278, below.
[5] *J.I.A.*, Vol. II, p. 227.

lives could be, and was, set up without the use of actuarial science, at least as far as temporary exposure to risk was concerned. The accuracy of the data on which, and the adequacy of the method by which, a policy of assurance is calculated cannot decide the nature of the contract. If the contract contains the necessary characteristics of a true policy of assurance, it is no less a contract of assurance when calculated on " rough estimates of odds " than when calculated by a modern actuary on the latest mortality table. It is not, however, in any way certain, or even very probable, that these insurances were against temporary risks only; it is more than possible that some, if not many, were " whole-life." In the case of the Roman contracts it is clear, from the distinction drawn between the formulas " if I shall die "[1] and " when I shall die "[1] on which they were based, that, if the former phrase was used as a means of contracting against temporary risks, the latter must have been the basis of a " whole-life " policy.

Romans distinguished between term and whole-life assurance.

Life assurances in 16th century forbidden in France, Holland, etc.

Returning to Mr. Hendrik's statement, it may be pointed out that the insurances to which he refers were not "considered reprehensible and illegal" everywhere.[2] The extracts quoted below show that they were so considered in Belgium,[3] France,[4]

[1] See Chapters XX and XXI, below.

[2] Émérignon: *Traité des Assurances*, Ch. 8, 1: " A Naples, à Florence, en Angleterre, et en divers autres endroits, il est permis de faire des assurances sur la vie des hommes. Mais ces sortes d'assurances ne sont pas des Assurances proprement dites, ce sont de véritables gageures. . . . Ces gageures . . . sont prohibées en Hollande, et en plusieurs autres pays. Depuis longtemps elles avoient été prohibées en France. Cette prohibition a été renouvelée par l'Ordonnance de la Marine. L'homme est hors de prix. La vie de l'homme n'est pas un objet de commerce; et il est odieux que sa mort devienne la matière d'une spéculation mercantile. Ces espèces de gageures sont de triste augure et peuvent occasionner des crimes. Pareilles Assurances sont donc absolument nulles. La prime stipulée n'en est pas due. Si elle a été payée, on peut la répéter *condictione sine causâ*."

[3] After A.D. 1571.

[4] *Le Guidon de la Mer*, XVI, 5: " Autre sorte d'asseurance est faite par les autres nations sur la vie des hommes . . . qui sont toutes pactions reprouvées contre les bonnes mœurs . . . qui sera aussi prohibé et défendu en ce pays." (Pardessus: *Lois Maritimes*, Tom. II, p. 422.)

Marine Ordinance of Louis XIV, dated 1681. III, vi, 10: " Défendons de faire aucune assûrance sur la vie des personnes." III, vi, 11: " Pourront neantmoins ceux qui racheteront les Captifs faire assûrer sur les personnes

Holland,[1] and, probably, Spain.[1] In Belgium life assurance was in common use from an early period, as is shown by the reference to it in the local laws of the Antwerp quarter of the Duchy of Brabant.[2] In the compilation called "In Antiquis" it is stated that "contracts of insurance have been made from all old times on ships, on merchandise sent by land and sea, and also on the lives of persons," and that such contracts could be made.

Again, by the Ordinance of Charles V,[2] although life assurance was permitted, yet it was forbidden to make *weddinghen* (= wager insurances) on the lives of little boys and little girls. Later, by the laws of Antwerp[2] known as "Impressæ" (dated 1581), all insurances on the lives of persons are stated to "have been prohibited by the Ordinance of 20th January, 1571."

Permitted in England, Italy, etc.

In Italy[3] the right to make such insurances was dependent on the approval of the Senate in so far as the lives insured were of ecclesiastics or of high temporal dignitaries; there is, however, no reference to insurances on the lives of the middle or lower classes. In other countries[4] they could be made without contravention of the law, whence, as at the date of the Guidon, i.e. between A.D. 1556 and 1584,[5] and even a hundred years later,

qu'ils tireront d'esclavage le prix du rachapt; que les assûreurs seront tenus de payer, si le racheptė, faisant son retour, est repris, tué, noyé; ou s'il perit par autre voye que par la mort naturelle." (*Ib.*, Tom. IV, p. 371.)

[1] *Netherlands Ordinance* of Philip II, dated 1570. XXXII: "Ende om te verhorden de abuysen, fraulden, bedrogh ende crymen die ghecommitteert zyn gheweest inde assuerancien ende versekerynghen op t' leuen vaude lieden ende persoonen . . . hebben wy alle die selue gheprohibeert ende verboden . . ." (*Ib.*, Tom. IV, p. 116.)

Amsterdam Ordinance, dated 1598. XXIV: "Oock en sullen geene assuerantie mogen gedaen worden op't leven van eenige luyden ofte persoonen . . ." (*Ib.*, Tom. IV, p. 131.)

Cf. *Rotterdam Ordinances*, dated 1604 and 1655.

[2] For fuller particulars and quotations, see Part IV, pp. 276–278, below.

[3] Genoa: *Statut. Civil.* of December 16, 1588. V, 17: Sine licentia "Senatus non possint fieri securitates . . . super vita Pontificis, neque super vita . . . aliorum dominorum, aut personarum ecclesiasticarum . . ." (*Ib.*, Tom. IV, p. 533.)

[4] See notes 2 and 4 on p. 155, above.

[5] Pardessus: *Us et Coutumes de la Mer*, Vol. II, pp. 371–3, discusses the date of *Le Guidon* at length and states that "il ne seroit pas impossible que le Guidon de la mer eût été rédigé entre 1556 et 1584."

actuarial science, including the Theory of Probabilities,[1] was as unknown as in the time of the Romans, and, as far as is known, no table based directly or indirectly on mortality experience other than Ulpian's Table had been constructed; it is evident that insurances on lives could be, and were, made without such scientific aids. Hence, it follows that the Romans, although they too were quite ignorant of the scientific side of life insurance, could have set up contracts of a similar nature. Further, it is more probable that a highly civilized people, such as the Romans undoubtedly were, enjoying all the accumulated mathematical and business knowledge of the great nations of antiquity, should, in the course of a prosperous career extending over more than fifteen centuries, have evolved and developed this system of protection against loss caused by death, than that the European nations of the early Middle Ages, who were not only less advanced in business capacity and even civilization, but also laboured under the disadvantage of being restricted in their financial operations[2] by their governments or by religious or other principles,[3] should have done so in the comparatively short and very unsettled period from, say, the 12th to the 16th centuries. It is therefore clear that, even if it be admitted that the Romans had little or no actuarial knowledge, the argument is not affected thereby, since it is historically certain that the practice under discussion was carried on extensively by other nations who were, at best, no better equipped with such knowledge than the Romans.

Admitted that the mediæval peoples made contracts for life assurance; probability that Romans did so during the Empire.

[1] First investigated by Pascal, 1674–7.
[2] See notes on pp. 155–6, above.
[3] See notes on pp. 155–6, above.

CHAPTER XIV

THE MANNER OF MAKING CONTRACTS OF NON-MUTUAL LIFE ASSURANCE AND OF TRANSACTING THE LEGAL PART OF THE BUSINESS

Contracts would have been between individuals.

IF the Romans made contracts or stipulations, equivalent to insurance policies, which matured at the death of a person or terminated at the end of a certain period, provided the life survived that period, they would have done so as follows: (1) Between A and B payable at the death of A, B, or C, whichever was specified in the contract, where A and B were two individuals, or (2) with a gild or company in preference to an individual on the ground that the permanent financial stability of the gild or company would be better guaranteed than that of any individual, however rich and powerful. From the later Republic until the last days of the Eastern Empire gilds (*collegia*)[1] were very numerous, and, being in possession of large funds which they could use in any financial or commercial transaction, not in itself illegal, would probably have carried on a similar business to that done by the numerous partnerships or companies[1] formed for trading or other purposes.[2] Many of these companies, which were very similar to companies of to-day in their methods of transacting their partnership business and in the legal abilities and disabilities attaching to them, carried on business of a financial nature, such as farming the taxes, banking, moneylending, buying reversions, etc. If, as suggested above, a form of life insurance had been developed

[1] Better "corporations," as they were said "corpus habere." See *Digest*, XVII, ii, 59; 63, 8; and 65, 15.

[2] Working gold and silver mines, salt deposits, etc., and even purely industrial companies, such as bakers, etc.

to cover moneylending and trading risks, it is probable that a large proportion of the life assurance business of Rome would have fallen to them. Whence it would appear likely that, if the Romans made such contracts, the insurer would have done so, generally speaking, with an individual in a small proportion of cases, and more often with a gild or with a company. The form in which such contracts or stipulations would have been made, however, would have been very similar in all three cases. In the first place, the parties to the contract, A and B, would represent individuals in almost every case, firstly, because A was an individual; secondly, because all gilds [1] and corporations [2] for trade purposes were permitted and accustomed to act through an officer, generally known as the *curator, syndicus*, or *actor*,[3] who signed all agreements and made all stipulations for and on behalf of the gild, was the legal representative of the gild, and could receive or pay away money or property on behalf of the gild; in the third case, a partnership could, if legally authorized, be represented by, and act through, one or other of the members of the firm or company.[4] Consequently, in almost all cases the parties to the contract or stipulation would be A and B, two individuals. Further B could be taken to represent the name of the firm and thus include all the partners, in cases where the firm was not entitled to act through a representative.

Wording of any contract.

Stipulations were made, in the majority of cases, orally before witnesses, occasionally in writing, and consisted of a definitely worded question and answer. The form most generally employed was " . . . $\left\{\begin{matrix} \textit{dare} \\ \textit{facere} \end{matrix}\right\}$ *spondes?* Spondeo," but other words were frequently used. The object of this form of question and answer was to make it clear that a com-

[1] *Corpus Inscr. Lat.*, VI, 671 (and note), 10232, 10234.

[2] *Digest*, III, iv, 1, and II, xiv, 14, and numerous other records; also p. 184, below.

[3] In the case of the tax-farming *collegia* the representative was known as "magister."

[4] See *Digest*, XVII, ii, 1, s. 1–3; 68; 74 and 82; and XLVII, ii, 52, s. 18.

plete understanding had been arrived at between the two parties to the contract.[1] The conditions of validity were :—

Conditions of validity of any contract.

(1) That the stipulation was not of such a nature as to require an illegality to be committed if it were specifically performed.[1,2]

(2) That the answer must follow the question without any considerable interval and without the interpolation of any other business.[3]

(3) That the answer must fit the question and be a direct reply to it.[4]

Performance of the action stipulated for could only be enforced by those who had a direct valuable interest in the stipulation and were parties to it.[5] No one outside the actual parties to the stipulation could begin obligation; whence obligation could not begin with heir[6] of any party, as he was outside the actual parties to the stipulation at the time when it was made.

Formulas of contracts which would have been equivalent to contracts of life assurance.

In the event of an individual A desiring to make a stipulation with B for the term insurance of C, the formula would have been the following, or its equivalent : "*si morietur C antequam . . . mihi X* $\left\{\begin{matrix}\textit{dari}\\\textit{dare}\end{matrix}\right\}$ *spondes?*" and on B replying "*Spondeo,*" the contract or stipulation would have been complete. If, however, A wished to make a contract with a gild for the payment of X to be made to his daughter (say), after his own death whenever it might occur, i.e. the parallel to an ordinary policy of whole-life assurance, he would have made a contract or stipulation with B (the *syndicus* or *actor* of the gild) in the following or equivalent

[1] See Gaius, *Commentaries*, III, 92 and 93.
Digest, XLV, tit. I, fr. 1, s. 6, and fr. 134, s. 2.
Code VIII, 37, frr. 1 and 14.
[2] See Gaius, *Commentaries*, III, 102.
Digest, XLV, tit. I, fr. 1, s. 34, fr. 83, s. 1–4, and fr. 137, s. 1.
[3] See *Digest*, XLV, tit. I, fr. 1, s. 1, 2, and 12.
[4] See p. 159, above.
[5] See *Digest*, XL, tit. 7, fr. 9, s. 2 : "Ea in obligatione consistere quæ pecunia lui præstarique possunt."
[6] See Chapter XXI, pp. 228 and 229, below.

words: { "*Post mortem meam* / *Cum moriar* } *filiæ meæ X* { *dari* / *dare* } *spondes?*" and on B replying "*Spondeo*," the contract would have been complete. If, however, he wished to insure his life for her benefit for a term only, e.g. to cover the risks attendant on a voyage, etc., he would have worded his proposal somewhat as follows: "*Si moriar antequam . . . filiæ meæ X* { *dari* / *dare* } *spondes?*" and B would have accepted as before.

Conditions of validity of contracts.

In considering these suggested cases and forms of stipulation or contract, it must be remembered that by Roman Civil Law there were three qualifications necessary to render them legally valid (*utilis*). These were (1) the observation of the prescribed procedure when making the contract, (2) the sanction of the law to the business dealt with under the contract,[1] and (3) the payment of a valuable consideration.[2] Whence, if a contract drawn up in one of the forms indicated above had survived, all that could be assumed therefrom would be that a contract had been made between two, or more, individuals with a view to providing for a money payment in case of death; failing additional evidence to show that such contracts were legal, it would be impossible to state definitely that they were valid. If, on the other hand, there is evidence to prove that contracts so worded were not only legal in form, but also valid and capable of being enforced by the Prætorian Court, it will be evident that the practice of making such contracts was sufficiently developed, valuable, and frequent to have attracted the attention and received the approval of the jurisconsults and of the Emperors of Rome and Byzantium. As will be shown below,[3] such evidence does exist, not merely in one or two isolated references to contracts of this kind, but in repeated passages, showing that the limitations

Evidence as to importance of practice of assurance.

[1] See Gaius, *Commentaries*, III, 92 and 93.
Digest, XLV, I, fr. 1, s. 6, and fr. 134, s. 2.
Code, VIII, 37, frr. 1 and 14.

[2] *Digest*, II, xiv, 7, s. 1.
Cf. *Digest*, II, xiv, 7, s. 2–4; XLV, i, 17; 46, fr. 3; 108, fr. 2.

[3] See Chapters XX and XXI, below.

and restrictions imposed by the early jurisconsults were gradually removed, and, therefore, that the practice had become of sufficient importance to render it advisable that the strict law should be set aside in favour of this practice when the two came into conflict. Whence it will be seen that the Romans had the legal power required for the making of contracts which *prima facie* appear to have been equivalent to modern policies of life assurance.

CHAPTER XV

THE NATURE AND ESSENTIAL PARTS OF A CONTRACT OF LIFE ASSURANCE

In discussing the nature and essentials of a contract for a payment to be made if and when a certain life or lives are terminated, the distinction must be carefully observed between what is absolutely necessary for making such a contract and what is included in a scientifically drawn-up contract of life assurance of to-day. It is not intended to represent that the points to be discussed would cover the very specialized and highly scientific method of treatment that is necessary for the satisfactory transaction of modern business of life assurance; but only that they are sufficient to prove that the essential parts of the contract itself, in the absence of which the contract would not be one of insurance, were present in the stipulation or contract used by the Romans and legalized by direct reference in the *Corpus Juris Civilis*.

Life assurance among Romans may have been carried on by companies or individuals.

Whether the contracts, although they must have been very numerous to have required repeated specific legislation, were the outcome of an extensive practice carried on by companies who dealt chiefly, or entirely, in this class of business, or were merely independent contracts made fortuitously, is uncertain. If the former, such a business could not have been carried on successfully without a rough-and-ready equivalent to actuarial knowledge, but if the latter, such contracts could have been made on any terms as to premium, etc., which were approved by both the parties thereto. Whence, if it can be shown that certain of the contracts or stipulations made by the Romans were based on the fundamental idea underlying the modern contract for temporary, contingent, or whole-life assurance, and that, in addition, they contained the essential features of the modern contract, it follows that the Romans were cognisant of, and accustomed to deal in, true policies of life assurance. The contract of life assurance as used in modern times is one in which one party agrees to pay to the other party or to his representatives, a given sum if or when a particular event contingent upon the duration of human life shall happen in consideration of the immediate payment of a smaller sum or of certain periodical payments equivalent thereto by the other party. A policy of whole-life assurance is a *chose in action* under which certain benefits are payable on the failure of a specified life or of specified lives. As every life must terminate sooner or later, it is clear that such a policy must mature at some future time and, as the date of death is uncertain, the time of the maturing of the policy must also be uncertain.[1] The contract or policy of temporary or contingent life assurance is, on the other hand, a contract which matures only in the event of death occurring within a specified time or during the exposure of the life to a certain risk or risks. Consequently, the period within which the policy can become a claim is limited, and, also, the contract may be determined without the occurrence of a claim. The difference between the two forms of contract is shown in the following formulas which might be used:—in the first case: " . . . payable when A shall die " (whenever that may occur), and in the second: " . . . payable if A shall die " (during or before . . .). The necessary [2] parts

[1] Bunyon: *Law of Life Assurance*, 3rd edition, pp. 6 and 7, states that the contract of life assurance is really a wager or, rather, equivalent to a series of wagers. This, from the point of view of the probabilities involved in the calculations of tables of A_x, is doubtless true in a sense, but to the layman there would appear to be little, if any, of the nature of a wager in a contract of whole-life assurance, whereas that of temporary or of contingent life assurance is obviously more or less of a wager.

Cf. Émérignon: *Traité des Assurances*, ch. 8, s. 1: " . . . assurances sur la vie des hommes. . . . Mais ces sortes d'assurances ne sont pas des assurances proprement dites; ces sont de véritables gageures."

Pardessus, in discussing this statement, points out that Emérignon overlooked the fact that a man's death may, and frequently does, involve actual pecuniary loss in many cases.

This contract is known as aleatory or of the nature of a wager.

[2] The proposal, declaration, etc., are omitted. It is to be presumed that the Romans, if they made such contracts, would have made some enquiries

of a contract for the payment of money (etc.) payable if or when A shall die are, briefly, the following: (1) The life insured; (2) the person or company with whom the contract was made; (3) the risk during a fixed period or, in the case of whole-life assurance, the undeterminable duration of the life of the assured on which the policy is set up, known respectively as temporary or whole-life; (4) the consideration in return for which the company or individual undertakes to pay the claim if, or when, such claim occurs; (5) the benefit[1] provided by the policy, i.e. the sum payable in case of, or at, death; (6) the beneficiaries under the policy; and (7) in the event of the policy not being taken out by the assured, the insurable interest of the person taking out the policy. Of these, the first six are essential to the existence of the contract or policy, the seventh has been made necessary by the Gambling Act.[2] For none of these is actuarial science an absolute necessity; it has become a practical necessity in the calculation of the value of (3) the risk and of (4) the premium, and also, for the purposes of valuation, etc., connected with the modern practice of insurance, but a contract would be no less a true policy of insurance or assurance if the premium was inadequate or excessive for the risk covered by the contract provided that it was not equal to, or greater than, the sum assured. This being so, the question as to whether the Romans were cognisant of, and accustomed to deal in, contracts of insurance does not depend on their having had or not having had a knowledge of actuarial science, but on their having been accustomed to make contracts under which certain benefits were provided for on the determination of the contract by the failure of a certain life or lives. It is, therefore, necessary to enquire into the practice of the Romans with regard to

Necessary parts of a contract of life assurance.

or have obtained some particulars in respect of the risk that was involved in each contract. Misrepresentation on the part of either of the contracting parties would have invalidated the contract. See *Digest*, XLV, i, 1, s. 6 and 134, s. 2; also *Code*, VIII, xxxvii, 1 and 14.

[1] The benefit differs from that of marine, fire, etc., insurance in that it is not, in any sense, an indemnity. Cf. Bunyon, p. 8.

[2] Gambling Act, A.D. 1774 (14 Geo. 3, c. 48).

the way in which the first six points mentioned above were involved in the contracts made by them. As the questions in respect of (1) the life insured, (3) the risk (temporary or whole-life), (5) the benefit, and (6) the beneficiaries are directly and conclusively answered in the extracts from the *Corpus Juris Civilis* to be examined below, it is unnecessary to discuss these points here. (2) The person or company with whom the contract was made must have been stated in the contract, inasmuch as the contracts were *utiles*, which could not have been the case had there been no person or persons definitely liable for the due observance of the terms thereof. (7) The insurable interest of the person taking out the policy is a modern and artificial restriction which did not appear in the Roman contracts; there was, however, a limitation of a similarly arbitrary nature imposed by the earlier Roman Law.[1] The question of (4) the consideration in return for which the contract was granted must be investigated carefully, as the argument in favour of the life-policy nature of these contracts depends largely thereon. This question involves two independent points—first as to whether valuable consideration was paid in the case of these contracts, and second whether the consideration was a true premium, that is to say, was less than the sum accruing under the contract (the sum assured), which consideration might be payable at one time (a single premium) or in periodic instalments (annual or other premiums).

Risk, benefit, and beneficiaries described in contract.

The first of these problems, i.e. that as to whether a consideration was paid, or payable, in the case of the transactions to be discussed, is capable of solution by indirect evidence, as follows: In the event of A undertaking to pay B a sum of money at a time depending on the death of A or B or C, it is certain that he must have done so in one of the following ways: (i) As a free promise and in return for no valuable consideration, direct or indirect; (ii) with a view to (*a*) making B his heir or (*b*) leaving him a legacy instead of doing so; (iii) on account of natural love,

Nature of consideration paid under contract.

[1] See p. 170, below.

as in the case of a father and daughter; (iv) in return for a valuable consideration paid or payable. It must be noted that in the responses of the jurisconsults it is expressly stated that the agreements (*stipulationes*) were valid,[1] i.e. would support an action[2] in the prætorian court, whence, if any of the considerations given above would have rendered the agreements ineffective, they may be assumed to be entirely foreign to these agreements. With regard to the first, that is, to the stipulation which is based on a promise made freely and in return for no consideration, it is found that all such agreements had no force,[3] and that no action could arise from,[4] or obligation[5] attach to, an agreement based on such a promise. Therefore reason (i) may be ruled out as being inadmissible. The second reason is equally untenable as far as making B his heir is concerned, as any agreement based on a promise to constitute a person the heir of another person was held to be invalid[6] and to afford no ground of action because all such agreements were held to be immoral (*contra bonos mores*). As to (iii), an agreement based on such a consideration as the natural love existing between near relatives, it does not seem quite certain how such an agreement would be regarded, but it would probably be considered valid, in so far as it was not opposed to the laws regarding the disposal of property by will. In any case, it appears most unlikely that the majority of cases with reference to which these jurisconsults' responses had been obtained were based on such a consideration. Wherefore, by a process of elimination, it is shown that most, if not all, of the agreements dependent on life contingencies must have

If not valuable the contract was invalid.

[1] See ch. xxi, below.

[2] *Actio utilis*, see p. 161, above.

[3] See note 2, p. 161, above.

[4] See *Digest*, II, xiv, 7.

[5] *Digest*, II, xiv, 7, s. 4. *Ulpian*: "... Igitur nuda pactio obligationem non parit."

Cf. ss. 1 and 2.

[6] *Code*, II, iv, 34, Impp. Dioclet et Maximian. VIId. Novembr. A.D. 294: "Nec ad implendum promissum hereditatis propriæ pollicitatione quisquam adstringitur."

Cf. *Digest*, XLV, i, 61. *Julianus*, Lib. 2, ad Urseium Ferocem: "Stipulatio hoc modo concepta, *si heredem me* non feceris, tantum *dare spondes*? Inutilis est; quia contra bonos mores est (hæc stipulatio)."

been made on the payment, or undertaking to pay, of such valuable consideration as was held by the two parties concerned to be a fair price for the future payment which must mature in the event of a promise to pay "when X shall die" (*cum morietur*), and which might, or might not, become payable in the case of an agreement to pay "if X shall die" (*si morietur*). Hence, it may be stated that these contracts were made for valuable consideration in almost every case.

Proportion of consideration to benefit and method of payment.

The second problem, i.e. as to the proportion of the consideration paid for the contract to the benefit thereunder and as to whether such consideration was payable in one payment or by periodic instalments is, from the nature of the evidence, capable of less absolute solution. As shown in Part I, the Romans were thoroughly acquainted with the practice of paying much higher interest on money lent on Bottomry, recognizing, as stated in the law thereon, that the difference between the rate of interest on ordinary loans involving no risk and that on loans of Bottomry was due to the risk—or that the risk involved had a value which could be paid for by a sum of money, i.e. the excess of interest over that of ordinary loans. This excess varied with the class of risk and with the duration thereof and was the equivalent to a premium paid by the borrower or lender. Again, in the contracts of indemnity described in Part II, Chapter VII, above, the consideration paid was, it is certain, of much less value than the sum of money, etc., at risk, otherwise no one would have made such a contract. Similarly in the "Wager Policy," which remained in use until it was pronounced illegal in the later Middle Ages. In the latter case there is ample proof that the sum paid for the wager contract was, generally speaking, very small in proportion to the value of the money or goods at risk. These last two methods of providing a guarantee against loss may have been, and probably were, extended to cover the trader himself against personal danger on his trip, at first possibly because, if he were incapacitated, his trading venture would have been rendered more likely to fail.

Turning to the societies which provided funeral benefits, it is found that the entrance fees were much smaller than the *funeraticia* and, therefore, that the greater part of these *funeraticia* were paid out of the accumulated monthly subscriptions of the members. In fact, it is very doubtful if the entrance fees were used for the funeral benefits ; it is known that, in many societies, the accumulated subscriptions formed the only fund from which the *funeraticia* were paid. Consequently, it follows that the Romans were quite used to the provision of funds to meet claims payable at death either wholly or partially from accumulations of periodic subscriptions. If, therefore, the custom of mutual insurance had been developed into non-mutual insurance, i.e. a person or company receiving subscriptions and becoming liable for payments on death of each subscriber, in all probability the custom of making monthly payments would have been continued. In the case of single payments—these would have originated, probably, in the practices of the moneylenders when advancing money against reversions. In the first place A would have borrowed the sum of Y on his absolute reversion to property worth, say, X and have paid iY every year until the reversion came into his possession and he could repay the loan. As the moneylender could not be sure of receiving all or any of the interest, when due, he would have had to calculate the amount he could lend (i.e. Y) on basis Y plus interest payable during life of present holder as equal to or less than X. This, if age of holder be taken as x at date of loan, he could have done by finding in Macer's or Ulpian's Table the value of an annuity on life aged x and calculating X to be equal to, or greater than, $Y(l + ia_x)$,[1] from which he would have found that the amount he could afford to lend was equal to, or less than, $\frac{X}{l + ia_x}$. If, therefore, the person or company transacting business in contracts for payments at death knew of the practices of these moneylenders, it might follow that they calculated the single premiums in a similar way, though, of

[1] This would be strictly Macer's or Ulpian's a_{x+1} as the values in those tables are those of immediate annuities.

course, at a much lower rate of interest. Whence, if the Romans had made contracts based on the stipulations found in the Civil Law, they would have made payments which would in all probability have been equivalent to single and periodic premiums. This follows since the contracts by their nature show that a consideration must have been paid in each case, which consideration would have been less than the sum at risk and also would have been payable either in one payment or by periodic instalments.

Insurable interest not referred to. The question of insurable interest appears to have received no attention in the development of the legal aspect of the Roman practice. In the earlier period of the Empire no one could make a contract for the payment of money on the death of a third person, it must have been payable on the death of A or B, the parties to the contract[1]; therefore, in this class of contract one of the persons making the contract must have had an insurable interest, i.e. in his own life. Later, however, it was within the power of A to make a contract with B for money to be paid on the death of a third party, or parties, in which case there appears to have been no restriction as to the insurable interest owned by A. The only limitation imposed was one which has been referred to above, namely, the inability of persons other than those having a valuable interest in any contract to enforce the performance of the contract,[2] and this, being common to all contracts or stipulations, cannot be considered to have been directed specially at the contracts under discussion. This ruling was observed strictly at first, but as time went on the demand for greater freedom in the making of such contracts became so urgent that the law was ignored and this restriction treated as non-existent, with the result that Basil,[3] about A.D. 870, removed the restriction on the ground that " the ruling which was in force in ancient days is amended by fixed custom."

[1] But see Ulpian's decision as to insuring life of daughter, Chapter XX, p. 233, below.

[2] *Digest*, XL, vii, 9, s. 2 : " Ea enim in obligatione consistere quæ pecunia lui præstarique possunt."

[3] *Basilikôn*, XXIV, iii, 19.

CHAPTER XVI

SOCIETIES AMONG THE GREEKS AND ROMANS WHICH PROVIDED FUNDS AT DEATH OF MEMBERS FOR BURIAL OR OTHER PURPOSES, WITH OR WITHOUT OTHER BENEFITS

THE foregoing sections having served to show that the practice of life insurance would have been of great service to the Romans in carrying on their financial transactions; that they had the mathematical knowledge necessary for the calculation of values of interest, etc.; that a table of annuity values which appears to be based on mortality experience had been constructed and was in general use; and that they, and other nations of antiquity, had noticed the effect of climate, etc., on longevity, the next step in the investigation of the question is the consideration of such means as they are known to have had for the provision of benefits, the payment of which was contingent on the death of persons. These benefits may be divided broadly into two classes: (i) mutual and (ii) non-mutual or proprietary, the former class being of much older date than, and probably the direct ancestor of, the latter. The earliest form of mutual benefit depending on the death of the beneficiary, of which evidence is extant, is the right to be buried at the expense of the society to which the deceased belonged and to which he had subscribed. From these societies which were constituted, primarily, for the carrying on of religious exercises and the worship of a divinity, and which included in their rules provision for the burial of members, were derived the societies which were purely burial clubs, except, perhaps, in name. These burial clubs appear to have suggested the addition to the benefits provided for their members when living of

Earliest form of mutual benefit at death found in religious societies.

Which afterwards became burial clubs.

And, probably, mutual life assurance—which suggested non-mutual life assurance.

Term-life assurance probably suggested by wager insurance.

the payment to the representatives of each member who died of a sum of money, destined at first probably for the provision of a funeral for the deceased, but afterwards apparently not earmarked for that purpose. From such societies to mutual societies for a limited form of life assurance would be but a small advance; and again the transition from the provision of simple life assurance benefits by mutual subscription to the purchase of the equivalent of a whole-life assurance policy from a capitalist or from a company would have been easy and natural. The commercial custom of arranging for the indemnification of the owner or shipper of merchandise in case of loss during exposure to a particular risk or during a specified period probably suggested term-life assurance.

In early religious societies, burial of members was a minor incident in worship of divinity.

Became main object of later Roman societies.

Origin of Roman societies uncertain.

If the above hypothesis as to the evolution of proprietary life assurance be correct, then proprietary whole-life assurance, if known to the Romans, was the outcome of a series of developments of the early religious society, which provided a funeral for each member at death. In the case of these societies,[1] this provision for the burial of members had no connection with mutual insurance, but was due to the desire of the members to ensure that the prescribed rites attaching to the worship of their particular divinity should be observed at their funerals, not, apparently, for the sake of the persons buried, but in order that the divinity for whose worship they had combined should be duly honoured. Later this point of view was reversed, and, as the religious beliefs and rites became of less value, owing to the growing indifference to the ancient religion, so the provision of the burial expenses became more important, until, finally, the societies existed for that purpose and were religious in name only. The origin of the Roman religious societies

[1] Cf. the Greek religious societies.

is uncertain. It is, however, probable that the Romans were indebted to Greece for these societies.

Owing to the paucity of the evidence as to the objects other than religious of the Greek societies, it is not possible to estimate the value to members of the burial benefit as compared with the value of the other objects of these societies. All that can be stated definitely is that the burial of members was always very subsidiary to the main object, namely, the building and preservation of the temple of, and the performance of the sacrificial and other rites attaching to the worship of, the society's tutelary deity, whereas in the Roman societies the burial of the members became, in the large majority of cases, the main or sole object. As the Greek societies of which we have records are of older date than the Roman, and as there is a great probability that the Romans derived some of the main features of their early societies from the Greek, it is necessary to consider very briefly the nature and working of the Greek societies.[1]

Greek Societies Providing Funeral Benefits

The societies in Greece which provided for the burial of members were, as far as the evidence which is extant permits us to judge, confined to three classes of religious societies, namely, the Thiasoi, Orgeones, and Eranoi—the first two being strictly religious in their objects, and the third combining with its religious observances the provision of loans for members on exceptionally favourable terms. These societies, although receiving considerable assistance from donations, etc., were established and carried on by mutual co-operation and subscriptions.

The government of the society was vested in an assembly elected by the members from among themselves, which had supreme control; it was legally competent to make by-laws for the society, to hold money or property, to sell, lend, mortgage, and generally to deal in property, and had also the sole right of appointing the officers and servants, both religious and lay, of the society.

[1] For more detailed account see Appendix J, p. 307.

The legal status of a society in Greece was the same as that of a private citizen. There appears to have been no restriction in Greek law on the formation and carrying on of societies, provided that in doing so nothing was done which was contrary to the law.

No restriction on membership excepting moral fitness.

The membership of these societies was democratic in the extreme. Any person, native or foreign, of either sex, of any class of society, was eligible for membership provided that the intending member could pass the prescribed examination as to his moral fitness. Every member whose subscriptions were paid up to date was eligible for any office in the society and could remain a member unless he rendered himself liable to expulsion for continued non-payment of his subscription or for brawling or riotous behaviour.

The receipts of the societies consisted of the money received from members in payment of entrance fees; monthly subscriptions; subscriptions for expenses incurred in religious observances; fines; interest, etc., from loans; profits from investments; donations from non-members, etc. Of these, the entrance fees, monthly subscriptions, and fines bear directly on the present investigation, and, consequently, require rather more detailed consideration. The entrance fee, which was payable by each member on joining, was small in proportion to the monthly subscription. In the society of Heroistes, for example, the entrance fee was equal to ten monthly subscriptions only. It may therefore be assumed that the entrance fees were regarded as being more of the nature of registration fees than as an important part of the payments to be received from members. The monthly subscriptions were, apparently, applied to meet the office expenses of the society, including the burial of members, as further subscriptions were payable to defray the costs of religious practices. Fines were charged to all such members as were in arrears with their monthly subscriptions.

The benefits provided by these societies included the burial of members, provided that these members had not been deprived of the right of burial on account of being in arrears with their subscriptions. This benefit was granted to all members irrespective of the length of their membership or of their age, and was, in short, mutual insurance of funeral expenses. In the case of the Eranoi, members were entitled to loans of money on favourable terms. Although certain writers have been of opinion that these societies provided sickness and other benefits in addition, there is no conclusive evidence that this was so. Summing up, it may be stated that in the Greek societies burial benefits were provided in return for a small monthly subscription, but only as a subsidiary object of the society, and that the *raison d'être* of the Greek societies was always religious. These societies cannot, therefore, be regarded as having been formed or carried on for the purposes of mutual insurance; such insurance as there was, was the outcome of a religious instinct or desire which manifested itself in a form which resembled that of mutual life insurance. Were these societies the only ones under discussion, this point would be comparatively unimportant, but for the purposes of this argument it is of great interest, suggesting, as it does, the origin of the Roman religious society, whence were developed the burial club and, probably, proprietary life assurance among the Romans.

In Greek societies: burial fund supported by monthly subscriptions always very subsidiary to religious object of societies.

Roman Societies Providing Funeral Benefits

Gilds and trading, etc., societies of Romans.

The question of the growth and development of these societies among the Romans, from gilds or brotherhoods established and, at first, carried on for the mutual protection and assistance of persons of the same social status engaged in the same or similar trades, and from societies whose *raison d'être* was the worship of a particular divinity or the inculcation and preservation of the practices and rites of a certain cult, has been investigated fully by various writers. It is not therefore necessary to examine here in detail the causes which led to their formation or the various steps by which these societies reached their later development; it will be sufficient for the purpose of the present argument to describe the way in which societies came to be formed for the provision of funds to meet the funeral expenses of members when they died and, in certain cases, to pay sums of money on the death of members; the membership of such societies; their mode of government and the means by which they carried on their business; and their legal position and powers. From these it will be found that these societies not only resembled in many of their characteristics the burial clubs of modern times, but also that they were, in fact, a species of mutual insurance societies in that they provided benefits payable at death in return for a periodical subscription. It has been stated that these societies, or certain of them, fulfilled the functions of Friendly Societies in that they provided for the relief of such members as had become destitute through misfortune or sickness, but this, as shown below, does not appear to have been a specific object of these bodies.

Roman religious societies, their origin and objects.

In the early days of the Republic there were formed by persons who, being foreigners, freedmen, slaves, or expelled from their family, did not belong to any recognized *gens*, numerous societies, each with the object of carrying on the worship of a particular divinity in honour of whom festivals were held, to whom sacrifices were made, and for whom, in many cases, a temple or shrine was built and supported by the society.

Their internal economy.

In order to provide the necessary money for the expenses incurred in carrying out this worship, the members of the society, following the practice of the earlier societies of the East, paid into a common fund subscriptions from time to time, to which were added donations from rich patrons, who were, generally, not members of the society. Later, these subscriptions became payable monthly. At first the money thus collected was expended only on the worship of the divinity in whose honour the society was founded, but it soon became recognized that the due worship of the divinity necessitated the possession of a common burial place for the members of the society and that each member should receive the funeral rites prescribed in such worship. Consequently, the attention of the society was turned to the provision of such a burial ground, etc., and the funds of the society began to be shared between the two objects, namely, the worship of the divinity and the provision of the funeral expenses of, and burial ground for, the members. Subsequently, as the Romans gradually drifted away from the religious beliefs of early days and became more or less indifferent to the performance of rites, these societies, while retaining the names of the various divinities, became almost purely burial societies, and new ones were formed in large numbers which, although choosing divinities either as patrons or merely for purposes of avoiding legal restraints, confined themselves entirely to the provision of funeral expenses. At first, in the majority of such cases, each society provided for its members a common burial ground or *columbarium*, and carried out the burials of the members, thus insuring the correct observance of all the religious rites attaching thereto. When, however, the due performance of such rites became of little or no consequence, a later development which brings these societies more into line with mutual non-profit assurance companies was introduced, namely, the custom of paying to the relations of the deceased member a sum of money known as the *funeraticium*, instead of providing him with a funeral. This method was first adopted when members died abroad, or under circumstances which rendered it impossible for the society to bury them in the common burial ground, and each such payment was earmarked for the purpose of providing a funeral elsewhere. Subsequently, this method of payment appears to have become more general, and in the case of many societies, in the 2nd, 3rd and 4th centuries A.D., to have been the only one employed; further, these payments do not appear to have been more than nominally, if that, for the purpose of providing funeral expenses, but to have been made unconditionally to the representatives of the deceased member. A still further development was the custom of certain of the later societies

Reasons for introducing custom of providing funerals for members.

Societies gradually became burial clubs.

Provided common burial ground or *columbarium*.

Later, paid *funeraticium* to relations.

of receiving subscriptions of different amounts from different members and of making the payment depend, to a certain extent, on the amount of the subscription received from the individual member. Whether the amount depended on the age at which the member joined the society is undecided; the direct evidence on the point is too limited and too doubtful to support an authoritative statement.

Amount of benefit varying *pro rata* with subscriptions.

Societies were not Friendly Societies.

The question as to whether these societies acted as Friendly Societies in providing sickness benefits and in assisting members who were destitute has been dealt with at length by the various writers on the subject. Marquardt and Herzog are of opinion that in the case of certain of these societies the provision of funds out of which such benefits could be paid was an integral part of the purpose for which these societies were formed and that these benefits were paid in return for, and out of, subscriptions received from the members. Waltzing and G. Boissier, however, maintain that not only did the societies not undertake such business, but also that in no case could any society have used the subscriptions received from its members for the purpose. All that could have been, and was, done was the distribution of the donations made to the society by non-members which was carried out by the society at the request of, and in accordance with, the wishes of the donors. It is clear from the investigations of Waltzing that the latter view is the correct one, and that the societies of which records are extant only acted as distributing agents for the external donors and not in any way as insurance societies in so far as this class of benefit was concerned.[1]

Military societies provided benefits other than *funeraticia*.

There were, it is true, societies which provided certain financial benefits in addition to benefits payable at death, but not as a means of assisting poor or needy members. These benefits were, in a sense, mutual insurances against sudden demands which might come on individual members. As far as is known, such societies were confined to military camps,

[1] But see correspondence between Pliny and Trajan *re* formation of a (Friendly ?) Society by the Amiseni, quoted in note 4, p. 185, below.

and existed during the 2nd and 3rd centuries of our era only. As the information in respect of their composition, etc., is much less satisfactory than that about the civilian societies, the consideration of their objects may be postponed until after the investigation into the civilian societies; the great value that they have for the student is due to the light they throw on what may have been the private practice of the civilian societies—the word private being used to show that, as such practices would have been illegal in the civilian societies, it would have been necessary for them to be kept in the background—the ostensible object of the society being the performance of its religious duties and the supervision of the burial of its members. It must be remembered that the evidence we have as to the objects and practices of the civilian societies refers to the legally authorized objects only, and can, consequently, serve to show the minimum work done by them, and that, had they carried on any other form of insurance, etc., they would have avoided any exposure thereof as far as was in their power.

NOTE.—In this connection mention should be made of what appears to have been a society providing funeral benefits, established in Egypt nearly 4,500 years ago.

In a well-preserved list of the household of a soldier Senefru, son of Hera, discovered some years ago by Professor Petrie at Kahun, is found a noteworthy mention of a gild of necropolis stone-masons. Senefru was a soldier in the army of Sekhem-ka-Ra,[1] the second king of the 13th Dynasty according to the Turin Papyrus, and seems to have been without rank or wealth. His grandmother and three aunts are spoken of as

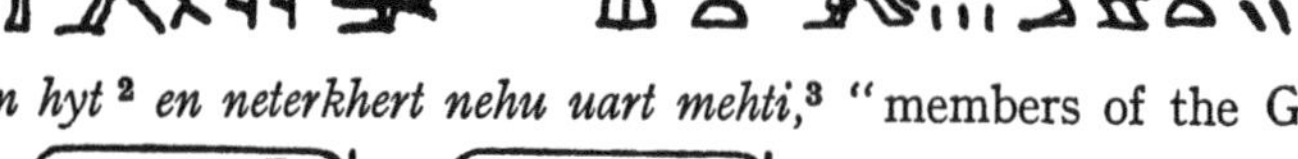

nem hyt[2] *en neterkhert nehu uart mehti*,[3] "members of the Gild

[1] 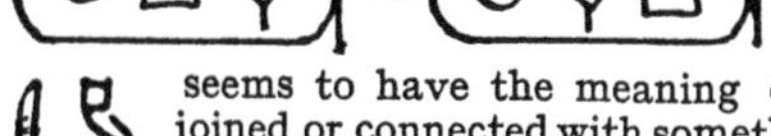 about 2500 B.C., according to Petrie.

[2]  seems to have the meaning of a person who seems to be joined or connected with something—an associate or member of a society.

(Cf. 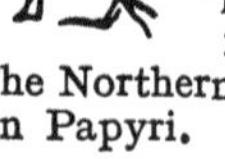 in Pierret: *Vocabulaire Hiéroglyphique*, 267.) Griffith renders the following word Gild (see his article on "Wills in Ancient Egypt" in the *Law Quarterly Review*, January, 1898).

[3] The Northern Division, i.e. of Lower Egypt, is often mentioned in the Kahun Papyri.

of Necropolis stone-masons of the Northern Division." (See Kahun Papyri, legal documents, Plate IX.) As women could not have worked as stone-masons and, consequently, would not have joined the gild for the special professional advantages which membership conferred on stone-masons, it is probable that their connection with the gild of necropolis stone-masons was made with the intent to provide suitable burial for themselves at death. We know what great importance the Egyptians attached to their tombs and burial, and we learn from Diodorus that "the Egyptians call their houses hostelries on account of the short time during which they inhabit them, but their tombs they call eternal dwelling-places." It would have been beyond the power of the less wealthy members of the community to make adequate provision for their entombment without some association of the kind alluded to in this passage.

CHAPTER XVII

THE ROMAN CIVILIAN (I.E. NON-MILITARY) SOCIETIES[1]

Origin of societies uncertain.

THE origin and development of these societies has been discussed above. It is uncertain whether they were introduced directly from the East, or by the Greeks, or whether they were originated by the Romans. The gradual change of character of such societies from religious to burial societies may be considered to afford an argument for their having been introduced as religious societies and, in consequence of their religious objects not appealing to the practical minds of the Romans to the extent in which it had appealed to the peoples of Asia Minor and Greece, of their having been changed to what would be known now as burial clubs. This hypothesis as to their origin is strengthened by the similarity of the practices of the Greek and Roman societies.

MEMBERSHIP

Drawn from all classes, including slaves.

The membership of these societies was drawn from all grades excepting the aristocracy; but in the majority of cases each society was composed of persons of, more or less, the same social standing. In certain societies the membership was confined to free men, slaves being specifically debarred therefrom;[2] in others it was limited to slaves[3]; but there are many

[1] The references given are not intended to be exhaustive. Those quoted are chosen as having the most direct bearing on the points under consideration. Quotations from the *Corpus Inscriptionum Latinarum* are given thus—VI, 10234. The Laws of the College of Æsculapius and Hygeia (VI, 10234) are quoted in full, and a selection of those of the College Cultorum Dianæ et Antinoi at Lanuvium (XIV, 2112) are quoted in a note at the end of this chapter.

[2] VI, 10234. [3] III, 5657.

examples of societies with mixed membership,[1] whence it follows that, while certain of them must have been made up of very illiterate members, others must have numbered among their members many of the shrewdest and most businesslike of the tradesmen and smaller merchants. The number of members varied greatly in the various societies; in some it was limited,[2] in others there appears to have been no limit.

The *social conditions of entry* were remarkably free from limitations. In the majority of the societies any person seems to have been eligible for membership; but in some it appears to have been a matter of some difficulty to become a member, so much so that a member desiring to nominate a relation to succeed himself on his death was obliged to grant the society the right to retain a moiety[3] of the *funeraticium* which would come to his heirs at his decease. There was no disqualification on social or other similar grounds; but yet it appears that the membership was confined, to a great extent, to the lower middle classes and to the poorer people, who, generally speaking, joined societies wherein the bulk of members belonged to their own class or business. Persons wishing to become members submitted their names to the assembly or to the *Magister* (*Quinquennalis*), by whom they were admitted or refused; in some societies they were admitted by the *curator* or *adlector*. There appears to have been no qualification necessary for membership other than the payment of the entrance fee and periodic subscriptions, and good behaviour. Women[4] were admitted to many of the societies, and slaves also,[5] provided that their owners gave their consent.[6] There is no record of any examination of applicants as was enforced

Method of becoming members.

Women as members.

[1] III, 5196. 14 slaves, 6 freedmen. III, 6150. 109 names, including several slaves.
[2] VI, 10234: "Ut ne plures adlegantur quam numerus s(upra) s(criptus)" (i.e. 60).
[3] See p. 197, below.
[4] To religious societies—III, 870; VI, 261.
To burial societies—VI, 23328, 4420, 27779.
[5] See note 1, above.
[6] *Digest*, XLVII, 22, 3, s. 2.

in the case of entrants to the Greek societies,[1] but, as the societies were self-supporting and it was of direct interest to each member that *funeraticia* should not be paid too often, it is reasonable to assume that a delicate person and *a fortiori* one at the point of death would not be enrolled as a member. The question as to whether persons could become members at any age or were obliged to be under a fixed age at joining is undecided. It is clear from numerous records that there was no lower limit, as the deaths of infants are recorded.[2] There is one inscription[3] which refers to the age of a member or members, and is explained by Schiess as limiting the age at entry to that society to those under 30. This explanation is not altogether convincing, as the evidence on which it is based is too fragmentary to warrant a general statement on the subject. As there is no allusion to the age of applicants for membership in any other inscription referring to these societies, this extract may be held to refer to a particular case and not to a general practice.[4] Membership was terminated by being six months in arrears with the monthly subscription,[5] and, probably, by brawling or disobedience to the general assembly or officers of the society.[6]

Limiting age of entry.

The *legal restriction*[7] *on membership*, apart from the necessity of a slave's obtaining the permission of his master before joining, was confined to an absolute veto against a member of one society becoming a member of another. Any person who had joined two or more societies had the right to select which of the societies he preferred in which to retain his membership, and on retiring from the other or others was entitled to receive his share of the accumulated funds and

No person could belong to more than one society.

[1] See Appendix J.
[2] VI, 9884: "... qui vixit annis II m. VII di(ebus) XV."
X, 8099: "... qui vicsit annis II m. XI d. XXIII ... pater fecit ex col(latione) collegium."
VI, 6222: "... qui v(ixit) a(nnis) XIII."
[3] VI, 5179: "placuit ... annos XXX."
[4] But see p. 205, below, *re* Veterans' Societies.
[5] XIV, 2112, I, 22, see p. 198.
[6] Cf. ruling on this point in Society of Heroistes (Fourmont: *Corpus inscrip. Græc.*, 126, 11, 40–42).
[7] *Digest*, XLVII, xxii, 1, 2.

property of the society or societies in which he ceased to be a member.

Government

Vested in general assembly or elected committee of management.

The government of each society was vested in its members, who either met in a general assembly[1] and voted on the matters laid before them or elected a committee of management by whom the affairs of the society were conducted. The practice in regard to the appointment of, and nature of, the officers varied somewhat in different societies, but, in general, was somewhat as follows: The members from among themselves elected a president (*magister* or *quinquennalis*),[2] administrators or directors (*curatores*),[3] a managing director or agent (*syndicus* or *actor*),[4] a treasurer (*curator arcæ* [5] or *thesaurius*), who had charge of the treasury or chest (*arca*);[6] in addition to these they nominated as patrons (*patres*,[7] *matres* [8]) those persons who, not being members, made donations to their funds, and also appointed privileged members (*immunes* [9]), who were not required to pay subscriptions. The functions and privileges of these officers and honorary members were clearly defined and understood, which is evidence that in many of the societies the members were practical and well-trained business men. In some societies, if not in most, women were eligible for some or all of the offices.[10]

Officers.

Women eligible to be officers.

[1] *Decuria*, see p. 189.
[2] VI, 10234, 1920; XIV, 2112.
Occasionally *perpetual*. VI, 10234, 1, 10: "qq. p(er)p(etuus) vel qui tunc erit."
[3] VI, 10234, 10232.
[4] VI, 671, and note.
[5] V, 5738.
[6] *Digest*, XLVII, 22, 4.
[7] XIV, 2112, i, 9, and of College of Veterans, V, 784.
[8] II, 5812; VI, 10346.
[9] VI, 10302 ("*perpetui*," VI, 541).
[10] *Magistra*, VI, 8639.
Quinquennales, VI, 10309.
Curator, VI, 10331.
Quæstor, VI, 10342.
Immunis, VI, 10363.
Women as ordinary members in very many, see VI, 10331, 10332, and, with few exceptions, 10351–10394.

LEGAL POSITION

(i) In respect of their right of association:—

No legal opposition to societies in early Republic.

There appears to have been no legal opposition to the formation of societies of any kind in the early Republic. The quotation from the XII Tables [1] prohibits nocturnal assemblies, and the *Lex Gabinia* clandestine meetings only. During the early parts of the 1st century B.C. societies of all kinds were very numerous, and many of them, being carried on purely for political or for unworthy purposes, had shown themselves to be a source of danger to the State. The Senate, therefore, in 64 B.C., decreed that societies were to be suppressed, but this ruling became a dead letter under Clodius, who, as tribune, in 58 B.C., encouraged the formation of societies and used them politically for his personal ends. So great was the scandal and danger caused by these societies that the Senate two years later again ordered the suppression of all societies excepting those only which were of public utility and of old standing, which order was carried into effect by Julius Cæsar,[2] whose action was repeated by Augustus.[3] Subsequently, under the earlier Empire, the emperors permitted certain societies to be formed, which societies were obliged to obtain permission before they could begin their operations. This permission seems, at the beginning of the 2nd century A.D., to have been given very sparingly (cf.[4] Pliny's letter to

Suppressed by Julius Cæsar and Augustus.

[1] Latro (M. Porcius): *Decl. in Catilinam*, XIX: "Primum XII tab. cautum esse cognoscimus, ne quis in urbe cœtus nocturnos agitaret, deinde lege Gabinia promulgatum, qui coitiones ullas clandestinas in urbe conflaverit, more majorum capitali supplicio multetur."

[2] Suetonius: *Jul. Cæs.*, c. 42: "Cuncta collegia, præter antiquitus constituta, distraxit."

[3] Suetonius: *Oct. Aug.*, c. 32: "Collegia, præter antiqua et legitima, dissolvit."

[4] C. Plini Cæcili Secundi epistularum ad Traianum liber.

XCII. C. Plinius Trajano Imperatori: "Amisenorum civitas libera et fœderata beneficio indulgentiæ tuæ legibus suis utitur. In hac datum mihi libellum ad eranos pertinentem his litteris subjeci, ut tu, domine, dispiceres quid et quatenus aut permittendum aut prohibendum putares."

XCIII. Trajanus Plinio S.: "Amisenos, quorum libellum epistulæ tuæ junxeras, si legibus istorum, quibus de officio fœderis utuntur, concessum est eranum habere, possumus quo minus habeant non impedire, eo

Trajan and the reply). Under the Antonines the law was relaxed in favour of the societies, and certain financial privileges were permitted to corporations which were working in the public interest. The ruling of Gaius[1] gave them large powers, and Justinian quoting from Marcianus (1, s. 1), approves the formation of religious societies, but (3) orders the disbanding of the illicit *collegia* and the division of the property, money, etc., between the members. Some 350 years later Basil[2] repeated the limited permission afforded by the *Digest* in an almost verbatim translation. From this, it is seen that from the time of Marcian (A.D. 220) the only societies which could be legally constituted were the *collegia tenuiorum*[3] and those formed *causa religionis*,[3] and that, therefore, in the event of any persons desiring to form themselves into a society other than a *collegium tenuiorum*, they were obliged to have as their ostensible objects the worship of a divinity or the burial of their members. Whence it follows that if the Romans had had numerous mutual insurance societies they would have represented them as being religious in their objects.[4]

Permitted under Antonines.

Permission limited to *collegia tenuiorum* and those formed *causa religionis*.

Mutual insurance societies, if any existed, must have masqueraded as *causa religionis*.

(ii) In respect of their powers :—

The legal powers conferred on these societies were considerable, embracing, *inter alia*, the power of[5] (*a*) drawing up and enforcing their

Societies could make own by-laws.

facilius, si tali conlatione non ad turbas et ad inlicitos coetus sed ad sustinendam tenuiorum inopiam utuntur. In ceteris civitatibus, quæ nostro jure obstrictæ sunt, res hujusmodi prohibenda est."

[1] For text see note 5, below.

[2] *Basilikôn*, VIII, 11, and XL, xxxii, 1–4.

[3] *Digest*, XLVII, 22, 1, and 1, s. 1. But cf. *Digest*, XLVII, 11, 2.

[4] Cf. Waltzing : *Corporations professionels*, etc., I, p. 79.
Bouché-Leclercq : *Manuel des institutions romaines*, p. 473.
Robiou-Delaunay : *Les Institutions*, etc., III, 10.
Mommsen, T. : *De Collegiis*, etc., p. 36, 84–101.

[5] *Digest*, III, iv, 1, 1 : "Collegia Romæ certa sunt quorum corpus senatus consultis et constitutionibus principalibus confirmatum est, . . . quibus autem permissum est corpus habere collegii vel societatis, eorum proprium est, ad exemplum reipublicæ, habere res communes, arcam communem et actorem, sive syndicum, per quem, tanquam in republica, quod communiter agi, fierique oporteat, agatur, fiat."
Digest, XLVII, 22.

own by-laws if, and as long as, the said by-laws did not conflict with the laws of the Empire; (*b*) appointing the officers mentioned above, who could act for the society; and (*c*) keeping a chest or treasury, and holding or dealing in property of every description, including land and slaves. They had also certain financial privileges. The way in which these societies carried on their business is difficult of investigation owing to the want of evidence. This lack of evidence is due chiefly to the fact that these societies could make and enforce the observance of their own by-laws,[1] and, consequently, did not require to make any appeal to the law courts, whence the only references to them in the *Corpus Juris Civilis* deal with the rights, etc., of the society as a society, and scarcely touch on the internal arrangements which were made between the society and its members.[2]

Secretarial Department

Album and register of subscriptions.

The secretarial work attaching to the upkeep of these societies was considerable, and entailed keeping the *Album* or register of members,[3] in which the names of members were enrolled when they joined the society, the register of the monthly subscriptions made by members, notes of the proceedings of the assembly, correspondence, etc. The *Album* and subscription register were kept by the president in some societies, in others by the *arcarius*, *scriba*, or *tabularius*.[4] The *scriba* also had charge of the correspondence and was the secretary of the assembly.

[1] By expulsion of offending members.
[2] But see *Digest*, XLVII, 1, ss. 2 and 3, and 3, s. 2.
[3] XIV, 2112, ii, 8, " . . . ex ordine al(bi) . . ."
In many societies the *Album* served both as *Album* and subscription register.
In the 4th century, and probably long before, the colleges were obliged to submit the names of those enrolled as members and entered in the *Album* to the government.
Cf. Waltzing, 1, c. II, 362, 344–5, 350.
[4] VI, 1959, 868; XIV, 2112, ii, 1, 19 and 20.

Financial Methods

Reason for variation in financial methods of different societies.

The financial methods of the Roman societies varied greatly in the different societies. It is evident that a combination of tradesmen would conduct their co-operative investments, etc., in a different way from that adopted by a society of agricultural labourers, and so on. In some respects, however, there was a similarity of method in all of the Roman societies. As far as can be judged, in every society there was the *arca*, or chest, into which the receipts were paid, and one or more officers (*curatores*), whose duties were to act as treasurers. In some societies there was also a factor, or syndic, who was the financial representative of the society, to whom was entrusted all the business connected with the investments and interest-earning portion of the funds of the society. Evidence as to the actual system on which the books were kept is wanting, but, remembering how advanced the Greeks and Romans were in book-keeping and accounts generally, it is clear that they had the necessary knowledge, and it is, therefore, to be presumed that they developed a system which was sufficient for their purpose.

Probably accounts of larger and richer societies were kept most carefully.

Probably, as in the Greek societies, a system of accounts was adopted, in the better societies at any rate, involving the use of books and of such a nature as to show the financial position of the society. Since something of the nature of a valuation would have been necessary in order to calculate the share due to a retiring member,[1] it follows that the books of the society must have been of such a nature as to afford means of finding out the amount due to him. Again, as in some, if not all, societies members became liable to expulsion if their subscriptions were six months in arrears,[2] it is clear that a close record of the members' payments was kept. In some of the larger and more wealthy societies there must have been a comparatively large number of accounts to be dealt with, seeing that, in

[1] See p. 183, above.
[2] Cf. XIV, 2112, i, 11, 22 and 23 (see p. 183).

addition to collecting subscriptions and paying for burials, etc., these societies were land-owners, capitalists, traders, slave-owners, etc., and, consequently, must have kept records of how their funds were invested and of the income derived therefrom. This would have been the case more especially in those societies in which the subscriptions of members were kept for the burial expenses,[1] the provision of the feasts, etc., being met partly out of the receipts from donors and patrons and partly by the contributions in money or kind from the members. In short, it is not unlikely that the records and books of some of these societies were kept at least as strictly as those of many burial clubs of modern times.

Normal valuation period of societies was 5 years.

The majority of the societies, not only those granting funeral benefits, but also the trade gilds, took as their valuation period five years.[2] Their officers-in-chief, i.e. the *magistri, patres, or quinquennales*, were elected for that period and were eligible for re-appointment for a second or subsequent term. The word *quinquennalis* in itself explains the time for which the president was appointed. There are a few instances in which the election was made annually, triennially and decennially respectively. It is a fair assumption to make that, if the societies considered it necessary to re-arrange the *personnel* of their higher officers at fixed periods, they would have looked into their financial position more carefully at those times than at the usual meetings of the assembly or decuria.

Occasionally 1, 3, or 10 years.

Method of calculation of monthly subscription unknown.

The method of calculation of the monthly contributions, which were equal for all ages in each society, is unknown, but it is probable that it was based on actual experience of either mortality or of expenditure, and was calculated on the assumption of an average age[3] of entry. These

[1] Cf. XIV, 2112.

[2] Cf. the *Lustrum*, or five-yearly interval between taking census in Rome.

[3] Possibly taken as age 30, which may have been the limit of age at which persons could become members. Cf. p. 183, above.

monthly contributions may have been generally, and certainly were in at least one instance, used only for the provision of *funeraticia*. There is one inscription which points to a practice of re-insurance of risks among several colleges, but, as the exact meaning of it is uncertain, and as such an arrangement would not have been of any particular use to burial clubs having very small claims to meet, it is not advisable to press this point.[1]

Case of re-insurance (?).

Receipts

The receipts of the societies may be classified as follows: Those received from (i) members; (ii) investments, trading, etc.; (iii) non-members; and (iv) legacies, etc.

Receipts from members.

(i) *Members.* The payments made by members consisted of (*a*) entrance fees, (*b*) monthly subscriptions, (*c*) subscriptions to pay cost of funerals of fellow-members, (*d*) subscriptions other than (*b*) and (*c*), (*e*) donations, and (*f*) fines, of which the monthly subscription and, possibly, the entrance fee were compulsorily payable in every society.

Entrance fee.

(*a*) The entrance fee,[2] which appears to have been charged by most, if not all societies, was required by the by-laws of the society and was, presumably, a matter which was decided by the society itself as being within their legal powers, as there is no reference to it in the laws relating to societies. It is not certain whether the entrance fees were used by the society for the provision of part of the cost of funerals, or for the maintenance of the secretarial, convivial, and incidental expenses attached to the carrying on of the society.[3] It should be noted, however, that in all the societies in respect

[1] X, 8099: "(Illi) pater fecit ex col(latione) collegium."

[2] The fee was payable *Kapitulari nomine*, i.e. for registration of the newly admitted member in the *Album* (= Register) of the society. (XIV, 2112, see p. 187, note 3.)

[3] Most probably *not* used for funeral expenses, as the monthly subscriptions would have been ample for that purpose and, in one case at least, were stated to be earmarked strictly for the provision of the *funeraticia* (see p. 196, below).

of which we have sufficient evidence to afford a means of comparison, the entrance fees are much smaller than the *funeraticia*, and that, consequently, the expenses of members who died soon after admission must have been met from the accumulated monthly subscription ; i.e. that the members acquired a right to a benefit greatly in excess of their entrance fees. In the case of the *collegium salutare cultorum Dianæ et Antinoi* at Lanuvium [1] the funeral benefit amounted to 300 HS., whereas the entrance fee was 100 HS.

Fund for payment of *funeraticia* provided out of monthly subscriptions, not entrance fees.

(*b*) The monthly subscriptions, which were payable in all the religious societies, were expressly permitted by Marcian (about A.D. 220) and, subsequently, by Justinian (A.D. 540) and by Basil (about A.D. 870).[2] These subscriptions [3] formed the fund from which the *funeraticia* were paid, and are a parallel to the contributions or premiums now payable by members of burial clubs or Friendly Societies and by holders of industrial insurance policies. Failure to pay subscriptions when due was punished by the loss of all rights to the *funeraticium* by any member who was six months in arrears. The basis on which these subscriptions were calculated is unknown, but an idea of the rate in one society may be obtained from the laws of the *Cultores Dianæ et Antinoi*, where it is seen that a yearly scale of 15 HS. (payable monthly) ensured a *funeraticium* of 300 HS. (or, in modern language, that the monthly premium was $\frac{5}{12}$ per cent. of the sum assured). It is interesting to note that if the average age at entry was taken as being 40, instead of 30, as suggested on p. 183 above, this premium of 5 per cent. per annum would have been the correct one according to the annuity tables of Macer and Ulpian, if interest on the accumulated premiums be disregarded.

Monthly subscriptions permitted by law.

Members whose subscriptions were six months in arrears lost right to receive *funeraticia*.

[1] For text, see p. 202.
[2] *Digest*, XLVII, 22, 1.
[3] It must be remembered that the cost of collection of the monthly subscriptions was *nil*, as the members had to bring or send them when due. Cf. practice in Greek societies, Appendix J.

Collection from surviving members to defray cost of burial (?).

(*c*) It has been stated that in certain societies the members paid a further subscription on the death of a member. That this was the case is extremely probable, but the evidence on which the statement has been based is not conclusive, consisting, as it does, of one record [1] only. This record of the *Collegium Silvani* at Philippi reads: "*Sacerd(os), item vivus (singulos) mortis causae sui remisit,*" which Schiess explains by saying that in this society the total expense of the burial of the deceased member was not met from the treasury of the society, but only a part, the balance being paid by the surviving members, each of whom subscribed one denarius for that purpose. Waltzing [2] considers this explanation to be the most satisfactory; certainly it is quite in accordance with what would be likely to have happened, as, in the event of the funds of any society proving inadequate, the most natural means of obtaining the required balance would have been by a further subscription of this kind. It must, however, be remembered that the extract on which the hypothesis is based refers to an action of the society, which may have been resorted to on one occasion only,[3] in respect of the expenses incurred by the erection of the particular monument on which the inscription is found. It is, therefore, quite uncertain whether the modern "assessment" or "natural premium" system had been anticipated by the Romans or, in the particular case referred to, the society had adopted the method which seemed to them the most equitable of supplying an unexpected deficit.

(*d*) Occasional contributions.—Cf. VI, 10,234, where a member desiring to be succeeded on his death in his place in the society by his son, brother, or freed man was requested to leave half the *funeraticium* to the society. This particular form of subscription shows clearly that the whole of the *funeraticium* was not necessary to provide a suitable funeral for a deceased member.

[1] III, 633.

[2] *Corporations professionels*, etc., Vol. I, p. 272.

[3] The fact that particular mention was made of this method of raising the required sum appears to show that it was not usual.

(*e*) Donations and legacies of members, being uncertain both in amount and incidence, need not be considered in relation to the burial fund and may be considered as being of similar character to those of non-members.

(*f*) Fines received from officers of the society for neglect of duty, such as malversation of funds,[1] not carrying out funeral,[2] not announcing death of members.[3] Also from members who had allowed their monthly subscription to fall in arrears and who wished to continue their membership.[4]

Societies had legal right to own property and deal with their own funds.

(ii) *Investments, trading, etc.* As stated above, the Roman societies which were legally entitled to exist and carry on the business of burial clubs were authorized to deal with their funds, for the purpose of rendering them interest-earning, by investment in mortgages, etc., by financing and becoming partners in business or agricultural enterprises, by the purchase and employment of slaves, and by many other similar methods. In respect of the way in which the funds were employed, the powers of the societies were unlimited, provided that they did not act in a manner which would have been illegal in the case of any other corporation or partnership. It follows, therefore, that the only guarantee which the members had as to the soundness of their investments was the supervision of the officers exercised by the members through the assembly. This supervision was probably stringent, especially in the case of societies whose membership was derived from the lower commercial and agricultural classes, who would, naturally, have regarded the safety of their capital as being of more importance than the gaining of a high rate of interest. If this were so, it follows that the rate of interest would have been little, if any, higher than that earned to-day, since the interest derivable from really sound investments appears to have been from 4 per cent. to 5 per cent.[5] during the first five centuries of the Christian era.

[1] VI, 10234.
[2] XIV, 2112, II, I, 29. [3] VIII, 14685.
[4] Cf. Practice in Greek Societies, Appendix J.
[5] See Appendix G.

Another means of obtaining money practised by certain societies was the sale of places in the society's burial ground or *columbarium* to non-members.[1]

(iii) *Non-members.* Donations from non-members when not earmarked by the donors were generally applied to the purposes of the society other than the burial fund. They might have been, and probably were, used as a means of supplementing that fund, if it was inadequate, but from the records it appears that there was, not infrequently, a surplus on that fund, in which case the donations would certainly have been applied to the maintenance of the society or to building or acquiring new *columbaria*, etc.

Donations of non-members distributed by societies, which gave rise to statement that societies were Friendly Societies.

Many of these donations were earmarked for the provision of benefits to members of the society who were sick or had fallen on evil days, and, although administered by the society, were not applicable to the purposes thereof. It is on the record of the presentation or administration of donations thus allocated by the donors that Marquardt, Wescher and others based their hypothesis as to the similarity of the business of these societies to that of the Friendly Societies of to-day. It may, therefore, be stated that the donations of non-members were not regarded as contributions to the burial fund, and that when used to supplement that fund, they were so used because the fund was found to be inadequate owing either to the subscription of members being too small, or to an unforeseen increased mortality.

A further source of income was the damages obtained by the societies against such persons as violated the tombs of the members.[2]

(iv) *Legacies* were very frequently left to societies both by members and non-members, and formed a not inconsiderable portion of their receipts.[3]

[1] VI, 6150; X, 1746: "Locum emit ab ordine . . ." X, 7803, etc.
[2] *Digest,* XLVII, xii, 1, *Sepulchri violati actio.*
[3] *Digest,* XL, iii, 1, 2 (Ulpian).
Code, VI, lxii, 1, 5.
Nov. Val. III, tit. xxviii, 1.
Nov. Theod. II, tit. iv, 3.

It is necessary to recall here that as explained at the beginning of Chapter XVI, the main object of the religious societies was originally the maintenance of a particular cult and, incidentally, the burial of members. Subsequently, the relative importance of the two branches became reversed and it may be said that ultimately the *raison d'être* of the society was the burial of its members. This the societies performed in various ways. In some the practice was to bury the members in a burial ground acquired by and reserved for the sole use of the society; in others, the ashes of members after cremation were preserved in urns which were placed in the *columbarium*, i.e. the common mausoleum of the society; others paid the stipulated *funeraticium* to the representative of the deceased member in order that he might pay the expenses of the funeral therewith; others paid a certain portion of the funeral expenses only, and so on.

Ultimate object of societies to provide burial funds for members.

The purpose and nature of payments known as *funeraticia*.

It is held by modern writers[1] that the *funeraticia* were paid on the distinct understanding that the money was to be entirely devoted to the funeral expenses, and they base their opinions on the fact that the word *funeraticium* can only apply to money payable on account of such expenses, on the statement contained in the rules of the *Colleg. Antinoi et Dianæ* that the monthly contributions could only be spent in that way, and on the extract from the *Digest.*

These arguments do not, however, appear to be conclusive. In the first place, it may be granted that *funeraticium* meant originally "money for funeral expenses," but it does not follow that it always retained that meaning[2] only. It is a matter of common knowledge that the description *religious societies* had become in the early empire a misdescription, and that the adoption of a patron divinity was a mere formality in order to comply nominally with the law. Since this is admitted, there appears to be no valid

[1] See Cagnat, Waltzing, Mommsen, etc.

[2] Cf. III, 925, 11, 16 and 17: "Convenire voluerint aut conferre funeraticia sive munera." In this inscription *funeraticia* is used as the exact equivalent of *stips*.

reason why the term *funeraticium* should not also have been retained in order that the society might appear to be carrying on the business of a burial club only; although it may have acquired a broader significance than that of money to meet funeral expenses and have come to mean money paid on the death of a deceased member for funeral expenses primarily, but not necessarily. This supposition is greatly strengthened by the fact that the practice of belonging to more than one[1] such society had become so common as to necessitate direct legislation,[2] which, as no man required more than one funeral, implies that one or more of the *funeraticia* which his representatives would have received would have been regarded and used in a similar way to that in which the sum assured under an industrial life policy is to-day. Secondly, if the *funeraticium* had acquired this broader meaning and was generally understood to mean a payment at death, then the legal restriction as to the appropriation of the monthly contributions would have resolved itself into a statement that money subscribed for the payment of industrial life insurance could not have been used for any other purpose. This would, perhaps, also apply to the extract from the rules of the *Colleg. Dianæ et Antinoi*, or it may have been that in that society the allocation of the *funeraticia* to payment of funeral expenses was strictly observed. The natural inference from this extract is not that the strict reservation of the contributions for the provision of funeral expenses was normal, but the contrary, and that that society was anxious to inform intending applicants for membership that in their case the subscriptions would be used in a certain way. That this latter reason is the more probable is shown by the care taken by the assembly in drawing up their rules to provide for the correct use of the *funeraticium* in every case, e.g. in the provision for the burial of a member dying intestate.[3]

Probable expansion of meaning of word *funeraticium*.

Reason for by-law of *Colleg. Dianæ et Antinoi* earmarking monthly subscriptions.

[1] Cf. III, 5657, etc.
[2] *Digest*, XLVII, 22, 1, s. 1.
[3] XIV, 2112, II, 1, 2: "Si quis intestatus decesserit, is arbitrio quinq(uennalis) et populi funerabitur" (see p. 203).

Surplus after payment of burial expenses.

Even if it be assumed that the word *funeraticium* always retained its original meaning, it does not follow that the representatives of the late member were required to expend the whole of the *funeraticium* on the burial of the deceased; in fact, there is evidence [1] as to the use of the balance of the *funeraticium* after paying for the funeral expenses by the societies themselves in cases where they superintended the burial of the member. If the society, which, presumably, would have conducted the funeral in as correct a way as was possible, found that there was a surplus, it seems likely that the possibly needy relatives of the deceased would have so arranged matters as to have a surplus which they would have converted to their own use. Again, as stated above, in certain societies,[2] if a member wished to obtain for his son, brother, or freedman, the right to succeed him in the society on his death, he was obliged to authorize the society to retain a moiety of the *funeraticium*, which would otherwise have been paid in full to his representatives. It is assumed by Waltzing and others that the *funeraticium* was intended to provide a necessary and fitting funeral; consequently, if the entire *funeraticium* was required for that purpose, it follows that a half of the sum would have been insufficient. But a half was considered sufficient to enable the funeral of the deceased member to be duly conducted, whence it is clear that, when the entire sum was paid, there was a surplus, or a surplus could easily have been arranged by his relatives. Certainly, if they wished to do so, there appears to have been no legal restriction. Ulpian prescribed that the cost of burial should be defrayed by the heir, but it does not follow that the recipients of the *funeraticium* could be legally forced by the society to spend the whole, or even a considerable portion, on the burial. In short, there appears to be absolutely no evidence of supervision by the society of the expenditure by relatives. In any case, the operation of the society's by-laws was

[1] VI, 10322: "Quot ex funere ejus superfuit."
XI, 286 add: "Ex pecunia quæ funere su(per) fuit."
[2] VI, 10234.

restricted to the members, and would have afforded no power to interfere with the action of the representatives of the deceased member when they had received the *funeraticium*; all the society could have done would have been to demand a guarantee that the money would be used for a certain purpose, but of any such a guarantee having been required or given there is no record whatever.

Forfeiture of rights by members.

The right of members to the *funeraticium* was invalidated by (i) failing to pay the subscriptions as they were due and becoming more than six months in arrears [1]; (ii) brawling, creating a disturbance, or disobeying by-laws of the society [2]; and (iii) suicide.[3]

This system of providing *funeraticia* for members was not far removed from that of mutual industrial insurance (even if *funeraticia* be taken in its strictest sense), as the practice was that each member should contribute so much per month, which money, with the addition of any donations which may have been received (less working expenses, presumably), was devoted to meeting the burial expenses of the members when such burials took place or to paying sums of money on the death of members. As these societies were in most cases composed of business men, small traders, workmen, or even slaves (in later times), and were managed by the members themselves through officers chosen by them from their fellow-members, it is but reasonable to assume that many, if not the majority, were conducted honestly, and were solvent. This is also probable because, such institutions being very closely watched by the government, only those societies which could show that they were well conducted, of public utility, and strictly non-political, were permitted to be formed and to carry on their existence.[4] It follows, therefore, that the officers or members must have been able to calculate roughly the monthly payment (or premium) which would suffice for (*a*) working expenses, (*b*) current or burial ex-

Societies were probably well and honestly managed.

[1] XIV, 2112, i, 11, 22, 23 (see p. 183).
[2] See p. 183, note 6, above.
[3] XIV, 2112, ii, 11, 5, 6.
[4] See pp. 185, 186, above.

penses claims, and (*c*) a reserve to meet future expenses for burials (or claims). The tendency in such mutual societies limited in their membership, and, as the great majority of these were, strictly local, is for the claims to increase in number as the society becomes older and the average age of the members increases; consequently, as the premiums must have been adequate to meet these charges, it follows that the various officers of these clubs must have been able to form an opinion as to the minimum rate that could be charged safely. The question which now arises is, by what means did they acquire this information? Unfortunately, there is no evidence dealing with this point—in all probability the earlier clubs charged too much and accumulated a large surplus, or too little and became insolvent. The clubs of later date, basing their calculations on the experience (not necessarily the *mortality* experience, but the *adequacy of the monthly subscription* experience) of their predecessors, were enabled to make an approximate calculation as to the amount of subscription necessary to be charged. It is, of course, possible that some rough-and-ready calculation based on the mortality experience was made; if it could be shown that this was so, it would practically settle the question as to the data on which Ulpian[1] constructed his table. It seems more in accordance with probability to assume that, in one or more of these very numerous clubs, some persons with a mathematical bias and possessing enquiring minds should have had their attention called to, and should have considered, the experience of their own and of other kindred societies, than to assume that no ideas as to the incidence of mortality occurred to them. As pointed out above, there is little written evidence extant in reference to any of the business customs, or of the technical and professional work done by the Romans during more than 1,000 years, but it is known from indirect evidence that such customs and such work in the Rome of 1,800 years ago were in a highly developed state. Judging by the same standards, it is exceedingly probable that exact methods of

And monthly subscriptions calculated with care.

[1] See Chapter XII.

trade and finance and a sufficient empirical science (taking the place of modern actuarial science) for the due calculation of the subscriptions to these burial clubs had, too, been acquired by the Romans.

Probable that subscriptions were approximately correct, in later societies, at any rate.

It may be objected that, although these societies existed for the provision of funds to provide burial expenses, there is nothing in the records of these societies to show that the Romans ever regarded them as being for any other purpose or that the idea of mutual insurance to provide against possible contingencies ever occurred to them. The reply is simple and conclusive. Legally these societies could not exist for any other purpose than that of carrying on religious observances or the provision of *funeraticia* in the strictest sense (either in cash for funeral expenses or in a common burial-place, *columbarium*, etc.), and, therefore, they could not betray themselves by appearing to transact any other business. Wherefore, they left no record of having done anything but what was strictly within their powers. The idea of mutual combination for the purpose of providing against risks of certain kinds and for the provision of funds to meet professional and other charges which might be incurred, and for mutual endowment insurance and, perhaps, term insurance with deferred annuities, had suggested itself in the second century of our era, and probably long before, as is shown by the practice of the Military Societies, which provided all these benefits.

NOTE.—

Lex collegi Æsculapi et Hygiæ. |

Salvia C. F. Marcellina ob memoriam Fl(avi) Apolloni proc(uratoris) Aug(usti), qui fuit a pinacothecis, et Capitonis Aug(usti) l(iberti) adiutoris | eius, mariti sui optimi piissimi, donum dedit collegio Æsculapi et Hygiæ locum ædiculæ cum pergula et signum marmoreum Æsculapi et solarium tectum iunctum, in | quo populus collegi s(upra) s(cripti) epuletur, quod est via Appia ad Martis intra milliarium (primum) et (secundum) ab urbe euntibus parte læva inter adfines Vibium Calocærum et populum. Item | eadem Marcellina collegio s(upra) s(cripto) dedit donavitque (sestertium quinquaginta) m(ilia) n(ummum) hominibus n(umero sexaginta) sub hac condicione, ut ne plures adlegantur quam numerus s(upra) s(criptus), et ut in locum defunctorum loca veniant et liberi adlegantur, vel si quis locum suum legare volet filio vel fratri vel liberto dumtaxat, ut inferat arkæ n(ostræ) partem | dimidiam funeratici, et ne eam pecuniam s(upra) s(criptam) velint in alios usus convertere, sed ut ex usuris eius summæ diebus infra scriptis locum confrequentarent. | Ex reditu eius summæ si quod comparaverint, sportulas hominib(us) n(umero LX) ex decreto universorum, quod gestum est in templo divorum in æde divi Titi con | ventu pleno, qui dies fuit V id(us) Mart(ias) Bruttio Præsente et Iunio Rufino co(n)-s(ulibus), uti XIII k(alendas) Oct(obres) die felicissimo n(atali) Antonini Aug(usti) n(ostri) Pii p(atris) p(atriæ) sportulas dividerent: in | templo divorum in æde divi Titi C. Ofilio Hermeti q(uin) q(uennali) p(er) p(etuo) vel qui tunc erit, (denarios) III, Ælio Zenoni patri collegi (denarios) III, Salviæ Marcellinæ matri collegi (denarios) III, imm(unibus) | sing(ulis denarios binos), cur(atoribus) sing(ulis denarios binos), populo sing(ulis denarios singulos). Item pl(acuit) pr(idie) non(as) Nov(embres) n(atali) collegi dividerent ex reditu s(upra) s(cripto) ad Martis in scholam n(ostram) præsentibus q(uin)q(uennali denarios sex), patri colleg(i denarios sex), matri collegi (denarios sex), imm(unibus) sing(ulis denarios quaternos) cur(atoribus) sing(ulis denarios quaternos), panem [a(ssium) III]; vinum mensuras q(uin) q(uennali) s(extariorum novem), patr(i) coll(egi) s(extariorum novem), imm(unibus) sing(ulis sextariorum senatorum,) cur (atoribus singulis sextariorum senorum) populo sing(ulis sextariorum ternorum). Item pr(idie) non(as) Ian(uarias) | strenuas dividerent, sicut s(upra) s(criptum) est XIII k(alendas) Oct (obres). Item VIII k(alendas) Mart(ias) die karæ cognationis ad Martis eodem loco dividerent sportulas pane(m) et vinum, sicut s(upra) s(criptum) est | pr(idie) non(as) Nov(embres). Item pr(idie) id(us) Mart(ias) eodem loco cenam, quam Ofilius Hermes q(uin) q(uennalis) omnib(us) annis dandam præsentibus promisit, vel sportulas, sicut solitus est dare. Item | XI k(alendas) Apr(iles) die violari eodem loco præsentibus dividerentur sportulæ vinu pane sicut diebus s(upra) s(criptis). Item V id(us) Mai(as) die rosæ eodem loco præsentib(us) dividerentur spor | tulæ vinu et pane sicut diebus s(upra) s(criptis), ea condicione qua in conventu placuit universis, ut diebus s(upra) s(criptis) ii qui ad epulandum non convenissent, sportulæ et pane et vinu | eorum venirent et præsentibus divideretur excepto eorum qui trans mare erunt vel qui perpetua valetudine detinetur. Item P. Ælius Aug(usti) lib(ertus) Zenon | eidem collegio s(upra) s(cripto) ob memoriam M. Ulpi Aug(usti) lib(erti) Capitonis fratris sui piissimi dedit donavitque (sestertium decem) m(ilia) n(ummum), uti ex reditu eius summæ in contri- | butione sportularum dividerentur.

Quodsi ea pecunia omnis, quæ s(upra) s(cripta) est, quam dedit donavit collegio s(upra) s(cripto) Salvia C. F. Marcellina et P. Ælius Aug(usti) lib(ertus) Zeno, in alios usus convertere voluerint, quam in eos usus qui s(upra) s(cripti) s(unt), quos ordo collegi n(ostri) decrevit, et uti | hæc omnia, quæ s(upra) s(cripta) s(unt), suis diebus ut ita fiant dividantque, quod si adversus ea quid fecerint, sive quid ita non fecerint, tunc q(uin) q(uennalis) vel curato|res eiusdem collegi qui tunc erunt, si adversus ea quid fecerint, q(uin) q(uennalis) et curatores s(upra) s(cripti) uti pœnæ nomine arkæ n(ostræ) inferant (sestertium viginti) m(ilia) n(ummum). |

Hoc decretum ordini n(ostro) placuit in conventu pleno, quod gestum est in templo divorum in æde divi Titi V id(us) Mart(ias) C. Bruttio Præ | sente A. Iunio Rufino co(n)s(ulibus), q(uin) q(uennali) C. Ofilio Hermete, curatorib(us) P. Ælio Aug(usti) lib(erto) Onesimo et C. Salvio Seleuco.

(*Corpus Inscriptionum Latinarum*, Vol. VI, 10234.)

Extract from Laws of Collegium Cultorum Dianæ et Antinoi at Lanuvium

I. 10. Kaput ex s(enatus) c(onsulto) p(opuli) R(omani).

11. Quib[us coire co]nvenire collegiumq(ue) habere liceat.

12. Qui stipem menstruam conferre volen[t in fun]era, in it collegium coeant, neq(ue) sub specie eius collegi nisi semel in mense c(oeant co)nferendi causa, unde defuncti sepeliantur.

18. Tu qui novos in hoc collegio |

19. intrare vole[s, p]rius legem perlege et sic intra, ne postmodum queraris aut heredi tuo controver[si] am relinquas.

Leges collegi.

20. [Plac]uit universis, ut, quisquis in hoc collegium intrare voluerit,

21. dabit kapitulari nomine | (sestertios centum) n(ummos) et vi[ni] boni amphoram, item in menses sing(ulos) a(sses quinos).

22. Item placuit, ut quisquis mensib(us) contin[uis se]x ? non pariaverit et ei humanitus acciderit, eius ratio funeris non habebitur,

23. etiamsi [tes]tamentum factum habuerit.

24. Item placuit: quisquis ex hoc corpo | re n(ostro) pariatu[s] decesserit, eum sequentur ex arca (sestertii trecenti) n(ummi), ex qua

25. summa decedent exe|quiari nomine (quinquaginta) n(ummi), qui ad rogum dividentur; exequiæ autem pedibus fungentur. |

26. Item placuit: quisquis a municipio ultra milliar(ium vicesimum)
27. decesserit, et nuntiatum fuerit, eo exire debebunt | electi ex corpore n(ostro) homines tres, qui funeris eius curam agant, et rationem
28. populo reddere debebunt | sine dolo m[alo]: et si quit in eis fraudis
29. causa inventum fuerit, eis multa esto quadruplum. Quibus | [funeraticium] eius dabitur, hoc amplius viatici nomine ultro citro sing(ulis)
30. (viceni) n(ummi). Quodsi longius | [a municipio su]pra mill(iarium vicesimum) decesserit et nuntiari non potuerit, tum is qui eum fune-
31. raverit, testa|[tor rem tabu]lis signatis sigillis civium Romanor(um
32. septem), et probata causa funeraticium eius, sa | [tis dato ampli]us
33. neminem petiturum, deductis commodis et exequiario, e lege collegi dari [ei debebit]. [A n(ostro) co]llegio dolus malus abesto. Neque patrono neque

II. 1. patronæ neque d[omino] | neque dominæ neque creditori ex hoc
2. collegio ulla petitio esto, nisi si quis testamento heres | nomina[tu]s erit. Si quis intestatus decesserit, is arbitrio quinq(uennalis) et populi funerabitur.|
3. Item placuit: q[ui]squis ex hoc collegio servus defunctus fuerit et
4. corpus eius a domino dominav[e] iniquitatæ [scr. iniquitate] sepulturæ datum non fuerit neque tabellas fecerit, ei funus imag[ina]—
5. rium fiet.
Item placuit: quisquis ex quacumque causa mortem sibi adscive-
6. ri[t] | , eius ratio funeris non habebitur.|

(*Corpus Inscriptionum Latinarum*, XIV, 2112.)

CHAPTER XVIII

THE ROMAN VETERANS' SOCIETIES

Nature of veterans' societies.

In addition to the civilian societies, there were also societies which resembled these in respect of their internal economy composed of veterans who had received their discharge from the army. These veterans' societies were very numerous and were apparently permitted by law until the time of Marcian,[1] who stated that it was illegal for veterans to form societies either under the pretext of religion or on the pretence that it was for the carrying out of a vow. This ruling was confirmed by Justinian in the *Digest.*[1]

Permitted until time of Marcian, by whom they were prohibited.

Reasons for formation.

As the veterans on leaving the army reverted practically to the status of civilians, it might appear that there was no reason why they should not have become members of the ordinary civilian societies, but on consideration it will be found that there are several reasons which may have tended to render it more convenient and more agreeable to them to form societies for themselves in which their fellow-members would also be veterans; and further, as will be shown, it is probable that they were not welcomed as members by many of the civilian societies. In the first place, it must be remembered that the veteran would have served in the army for some 30 years, during which time he would in all probability have been on service away from home. Consequently on his return to his native parish it is likely that he would have found himself practically a stranger[2] to

[1] *Digest,* XLVII, xi, 2: "Sub prætextu religionis vel sub specie solvendi voti cœtus illicitos nec a veteranis tentari oportet."

[2] G. Boissier: *La Religion Romaine,* etc., 2nd edition, Vol. II, p. 258.

his neighbours and relations. If, therefore, he became a member of a civilian society, he would have found himself debarred from participating in the social intercourse attaching thereto, except as a stranger, and also would be cut off from any real share in local concerns and interests. This reason alone would probably have been a strong factor in forcing the veteran back to the society of his fellow-veterans with whom he had community of interest.

Want of community of interest between the civilians and veterans.

Strain on funds of civilian burial clubs consequent on admission of veterans.

A second, and, perhaps, even stronger reason was the recognition by the members of the ordinary civilian societies of the loss that they themselves would sustain by admitting to their society persons whose minimum age at entry was 46, and whose life was probably rather below the average duration. As there is no evidence of a higher subscription being payable in a civilian burial society by a member joining at an advanced age, it is probable that the veterans, if admitted to the society, would have been required to pay the same entrance fee and monthly subscriptions as the other members. This would naturally have meant a considerable loss to those who were already members of the society, as in all probability the greater number of them joined at a comparatively early age. Possibly, as suggested above,[1] in certain societies, the age at entry for ordinary members was limited to 30, in which case, if veterans were admitted on the same terms in respect of entrance fees (which were required for incidental expenses) and monthly subscriptions (which were accumulated for the purpose of paying the *funeraticia*), but at the advanced age of 46, it follows that if the entrance fee and subscription had been calculated so as to be approximately correct for entrance at or below the age of 30, the fees and subscriptions would have proved to be quite inadequate. In certain societies, for example, it is probable that subscriptions were calculated for the admission of members at a higher age than 30. In the case of one important society the subscription, as shown above,[2] would, on the basis of either Macer's or

[1] Chapter XVII, p. 183, above. [2] Chapter XVII, p. 183, above.

Ulpian's annuity table, have been the correct premium for age 40, in which case there would have been a margin which would have covered the extra risk involved by the admission of veterans, provided that the number of veterans so admitted was not excessive. Although in this case, and perhaps in others, a fairly high subscription was required from the members, yet it appears probable that in the majority of cases the subscription payable was not calculated on the assumption that persons would become members at an advanced age, and it is fair, therefore, to assume that the admission of any large number of veterans would have resulted in the financial position of the ordinary civilian societies becoming unsound. Whence it follows that the civilian members would probably have objected to the unfair strain thrown on their resources by the admission of veterans.

Further, the argument as to the want of similar interests would have almost as much force in leading the civilians to object to veterans as fellow-members, as it would in keeping the veterans from wishing to join such societies. If the objection to the admission of veterans on the ground that they would not subscribe their share to the common fund had occurred to the civilian members as being serious, it follows that the veterans, if they desired to provide *funeraticia* for themselves, must have formed their own societies for that purpose,[1] as, being barred from the civilian societies, they would have been unable to do so otherwise. There are, however, inscriptions which show that these societies resembled the civilian burial societies in many points, such as the method of government and election of officers of the society, the payment of a monthly subscription, the register of members,[2] the possession of a common burial ground,[3] etc. They appear to have varied considerably in number of members, but were, generally

Points of resemblance between veterans' and civilian societies.

[1] Cf. G. Boissier: *La Religion Romaine*, 2nd edition, Vol. II, p. 300.
[2] VIII, 2626: "Alb(um) vet(eranorum)."
[3] V, 884. Collegia Aquileiæ: "locus sepultura(e) gentilium veteranor(um)."

speaking, small. In one register there are 12 names,[1] in another 47.[2]

Veterans admitted to certain professional societies.

Although the veterans do not appear to have been welcomed as members of the civilian societies providing financial benefits, yet there is evidence to show that in certain of the professional *collegia*, veterans were admitted to membership and were also elected to hold office therein.

More especially was this the case in the societies of the Centonarii and Fabri.[3] There appears to be considerable difference of opinion as to why veterans were received as members of these societies, and it has been suggested that veterans were admitted on the strength of the technical knowledge they had acquired as armourers, etc., during their period of service.

There is, however, but little evidence on which to base any direct statement, but it may possibly have been due to a desire on the part of the members of the society to confer some mark of their appreciation of the career of the veteran. This is rendered more likely as it was customary in civilian societies to elect a person who had conferred some benefit on the society, or to whom the society desired to show honour, to the position of an *immunis*, i.e. a member enjoying all the rights attaching to membership without the obligation to pay any subscription to the society.[4]

Veterans' societies apparently not very numerous.

Although, as stated above, there is every reason to believe that veterans would have been induced to form separate societies, yet those societies do not appear to have been very numerous. Professor Halkin gives a list of 16, 8 of which were in Italy and 8 abroad [5]; this does not of course prove that there were not many others, yet when this small number of records is compared with the very numerous records of the civilian societies, the natural inference is that,

[1] VIII, 2618. [2] VIII, 2626.

[3] III, 3554, 3569; V, 908; IX, 3843, 3923.

[4] See Chapter XVII, p. 184.

[5] Léon Halkin: "Les Collèges de Vétérans dans l'Empire Romain," in *Revue de l'Instruction Publique*, XXXVIII, p. 369.

comparatively speaking, the veterans' societies were but few in number.

As the examination of these societies does not throw any additional light on the insurance side of the internal economy of Roman burial societies, it is perhaps unnecessary to enter into further details here. Full information is given in the article by Professor Halkin to which reference has been made.

CHAPTER XIX

THE ROMAN MILITARY SOCIETIES

Military societies: range of objects wider than in civilian societies.

IN addition to the burial societies composed of civilians and of veterans, which were so restricted in their operations as to have been unable to appropriate any part of their funds to the payment of sickness benefits or of benefits other than the provision of funeral rites, etc., or for money actually or nominally to defray the cost thereof, on the death of their members, there were numerous societies which did not pretend to be religious societies, possessing the power of accumulating funds for the purpose of defraying expenses which might be incurred by members during a certain limited period in addition to the provision of a cash payment at death if death occurred during the same period, and, in the event of the member surviving that period, of a single cash payment[1]; possibly also of a deferred annuity.[2]

Confined to military camps.

These societies, as far as can be determined, were confined to the various military camps, and were composed exclusively of soldiers on active service. They were, in effect, mutual societies which, though not providing sickness benefits,[3] yet had as their objects the provision of pecuniary assistance in the case of members being put to expense in the discharge of their professional duties, and the payment at death of a certain sum to such members as died during their time with the colours; and to such members as became veterans[4] or

[1] Resembling endowment insurances of to-day.
[2] See pp. 216–219, below.
[3] Except in the case of members who left the service through ill-health or wounds.
[4] But see pp. 216–219, below.

were dismissed the service,[1] a certain payment was made and their membership determined.

Rules of society of Cornicines at Lambæsa, A.D. 203.

The benefits granted by, and the subscriptions payable to, these military societies varied in the different societies in amount and in incidence, but were similar in nature; it will, therefore, serve the purpose of this enquiry if the rules of the society of *Cornicines* at Lambæsa[2] be examined in detail. This society, which consisted of 36 members, was conducted on the following lines:—

Subscription.—On entry each full member was required to pay an entrance fee of 750 denarii. (Each recruit a smaller sum. Probably a further monthly payment was required from every member.)

Benefits. (i) A member of the society, if, on being transferred to another legion, obliged to cross the sea, to receive, if a foot soldier, 200 denarii, if a trooper, 500 denarii.[3]

(ii) Veterans, i.e. members when they became veterans, to receive 500 denarii (*nomine anularium*).[4]

(iii) Any member promoted to a superior rank to receive 500 denarii.

[1] On account of ill-health, wounds or other causes.

[2] VIII, 2557. The text is as follows:—

College of Cornicines at Lambæsa.

Scamnarii n(omine) dabunt col(legæ) qui fac(ti) fuer(int) denarios DCCL.

Si qui d(e) col(legis) tram(are) pro(ficiscetur) cum pr(omotus) s(it), acc(ipiet) viat(icum) pro(cessus) m(iles) denarios CC, eq(ues) * a(utem) D.

It(e)m vet(e)ranis anularium nomine denarii D.

Item, si qui ex coll(egio) amplio(re) grad(u) prof(iciscetur), accip(iet) denarios D.

Si qui obitum naturæ red(diderit), acc(ipiet) her(es) ips(ius) sive proc(urator) denarios quingentos.

Item quod abom(inamur), si q(ui) locu(m) su(um) amis(erit), accipiet denarios CCL.

† (I)t(e)m qui arc(a) solut(i) sunt et si quis de tironib(us) ab hac die satis arcæ fec(erit), accipiet quitquit debet(ur).

Lex fact(a) XI Kal(endas) sep(tembres) (Plautiano) II et Geta II cos.

[3] If the reading suggested by Renierus be adopted, this rule would prescribe that each member should receive 200 denarii, and that a similar amount would be payable to such members as were brought back again after absence.

[4] See pp. 216–219, below.

---

* Renierus reads—eq(ue) a(bsentia) r(egressi).

† Mommsen reads—ei s(cilicet) t(antum) m(odo) qui arca soluti. . . .

(iv) On the death of a member his heir or agent[1] to receive 500 denarii.

(v) Any member dismissed the service to receive 250 denarii.

Moreover, those who were exempt from (further?) contribution to the funds to receive what was due to them, and also such of the recruits as had contributed their prescribed quota from the day when they paid the necessary subscription to the funds calculated *pro rata* with the amount they had paid.

Scamnarium.

From the first paragraph it is clear that the *scamnarium* included an entrance fee of 750 denarii. It is doubtful whether this entrance fee covered the entire payment of members or whether they were required to pay periodic subscriptions in addition. It is certain that the custom of most, if not all, of the civilian societies was to charge a monthly subscription, in many cases, in addition to an entrance fee, and to terminate the membership of those who were in arrears. Further, the reference in the last paragraph of the rules appears to be to payments to the funds (*arca*) other than the entrance fee. René Cagnat,[2] basing his argument on the variant reading suggested by Mommsen,[3] is of opinion that the *scamnarium* consisted of two parts, (i) an entrance fee and (ii) the monthly subscriptions. Waltzing considers that the reading generally adopted is practically equivalent to that of Mommsen and agrees with Cagnat as to its meaning. It is, however, possible that this sentence does not refer to the payment of periodic subscriptions, but refers to such members as were not expected to have paid the full entrance fee, having been exempted from the payment of part, or all thereof, in return for services rendered to the society

Was periodic subscription payable?

Opinions of Mommsen, Cagnat and Waltzing.

Possible that reference is to *immunes.*

[1] *Digest*, III, iii, 1 (Ulpian): "Procurator est qui aliena negotia mandatu domini administrat. Procurator autem vel omnium rerum vel unius rei esse potest constitutus" (but cf. Mommsen, T., *De collegiis*, etc., pp. 36 and 37).

[2] *L'Armée romaine d'Afrique*, p. 470.

[3] See p. 210, note 2.(†)

or as a mark of the society's appreciation, as was the case with *immunes* in the civilian societies.

Was *funeraticium* earmarked for funeral expenses in military societies?

The rules relating to the benefits provided are almost self-explanatory; it is, however, worthy of note that the payment of the sum of 500 denarii on the death of a member was to be made to his heir or agent, and that no reference is made as to the manner in which this money was to be employed. It is considered by Boissier, Cagnat, Marquardt, Mommsen, Waltzing and other writers that these payments were in (almost) every case made on the distinct and explicit understanding that they were to be used to defray the expenses of burial of the outgoing member. Waltzing is also of opinion that the sum payable to veterans on retiring was necessarily to be used in payment of the fees for becoming members of burial clubs composed either of civilians or of veterans. This appears to be straining the point, as although there is evidence that there were certain burial societies composed wholly or partly of veterans, yet there is in the rules of these military societies no allusion to any such earmarking of these payments or mention of any legal or moral obligation on the part of the veteran to do so. It is unlikely that the common soldier, who received a comparatively large sum of ready money to use as he thought fit, would have applied it to the provision of a funeral which he might not require for many years, when spending the money would have afforded him self-gratification or have assisted him in earning a living. Waltzing based his opinion on the requirements of the law as to burial, on the direct statements of some of the *collegia*, on the inscriptions on tombs, etc., on the name *funeraticium* which was applied in many cases to the payments, and on the fact that the funeral societies were the outcome of the religious societies and were permitted to exist because they served a public need in providing for the due interment and sepulchral rites on the decease of their members. The question whether these arguments are in the main correct and applicable to the civilian societies in the latter part of the Republic and the earlier part of the Empire has been considered above; it is suggested that they limit too strictly the practice of the military societies, if not of the civilian also.

If the sum provided in § iv of the rules under consideration was to be used in that way only, it follows that this would have been stated in the rules and the payment would have been referred to as a *funeraticium* of 500 denarii; instead of which the destination of the money is left absolutely unspecified. Again, if it be admitted that this payment was intended for the defraying of funeral expenses, it is to be assumed that the sum of 250 denarii payable under § v to any member who was dismissed the service was also intended as a *funeraticium* or that the payment was made without restriction. It certainly seems more likely that in both cases the money was paid over without any limitations in respect of its use.

Further, it must be remembered that the law regarded more favourably the property and rights of soldiers when in camp than those of civilians. Remembering that the soldier passed from active service into the reserve at the age of 46 and would in the majority of cases require to supplement his income or to earn his living, it would seem more probable that the money received by the veterans would frequently have been invested in some business or property which would have afforded some opportunity of earning a livelihood than that it should have been devoted to the payment of the entry fee to a burial club.

As, however, there were societies whose membership was partly or wholly confined to veterans, it must be admitted that in many cases the retired soldier did actually join a burial society and presumably paid the sum he received on retirement, if it was a single payment,[1] to the society on admission. It is clear from the above-mentioned age of veterans that a fairly heavy payment must have been made.

Position of *tirones* in military societies.

The position of the *tirones* (the recruits), which is defined in the last paragraph of the rules, is interesting. They were entitled to participate in the benefits attaching to membership when they had paid the amount due from them to the

[1] But see pp. 216–219 below.

treasury; their right of participation beginning on the day on which they had completed their payment. It is uncertain from this by-law whether they were called upon to pay an entrance fee or only the periodic subscriptions. In another inscription is found the phrase *item discentib(us) pro proport(ione) scamnari sui (sestertios) m(ille) n(ummos)*,[1] which shows that recruits might pay either a proportion of the entrance fee (or a proportion of the total subscription, i.e. entrance fee and periodical subscription, depending on the meaning of the word *scamnarium*) and were entitled to receive benefits attaching to membership in proportion to the amount they had subscribed.

Entitled to subscribe a portion of ordinary fees and receive a benefit *pro rata* with their subscription.

Returning to the question of the payments made to veterans retiring from active service, it is found that they were to receive 500 denarii *nomine anularium.*[2] Similar payments, but for 6,000 denarii instead of 500, were made by the quæstor on January 1, according to the regulations of the College of *Optiones*,[3] to the veterans retiring from that society. The meaning of the phrase *nomine anularium* is not entirely clear. It has been explained that the word *anularium* refers to the right of the equites to wear rings and suggested that the veterans on retirement acquired a similar right, whence a payment made to a veteran would be known as a payment made *nomine anularium.* In view of the comparative rarity of the word it is difficult to decide as to the correct meaning. It may have been quite different from that given hitherto, and perhaps have meant that each veteran received an *annual* payment of the sum mentioned; the first payment being made on January 1 next following the date of his discharge: in which case the main object of these societies was the provision of a pension fund for veterans.

Payments *nomine anularium*: were they deferred annuities?

[1] VIII, 2553.
[2] VIII, 2552 and 2553: " . . . decreverunt ut veterani qui ex eo collegio dimittentur singuli anularium accipiant." Cf. VIII, 2554.
[3] VIII, 2554: " . . . veter(ani) quoque missi accipiant Kal(endis) Jan(uariis) anularium singuli sestertium sex mil(ium) num(mum), quæ anularia sua die quæstor sine dilatione adnumerare curabit."

As this hypothesis presents the question of these payments in an entirely new light it is necessary to examine in detail the reasons on which it is based. They are (1) that the change from *annualis* to *anularis* is one which might easily have been made by a somewhat illiterate person, and once applied to a certain benefit may have become identified with the benefit; (2) that, assuming a monthly subscription bearing the same proportion to the entrance fee as that charged by the non-military societies, the funds of the society, if properly administered, would have been sufficient to meet the expenses of such payments; (3) that these payments were made on January 1 only, and therefore presumably differed in respect of their nature and of the necessary manner and date of payment from other payments provided for in the rules, which were paid, as far as is known, when they became due; (4) that there is apparently no direct or indirect proof that the *anularia* had any connection with the *funeraticia*; (5) that, unless the subscriptions were used for club purposes other than those set out in the rules, there would have been a large surplus.

Reasons for suggestion.

Possible confusion of *annualium* with *anularium*.

(1) The transposition, omission and insertion of letters and syllables was very common not only in the writings of the Latin poets, but also in those of the prose authors. As shown in great detail by Mr. Housman,[1] the orthography of even the educated writers of the most correctly classic period was very varied. Although the word under discussion is not quoted in his list of examples, many words and phrases are quoted therein which exhibit more radical and violent changes than that of *annualium* to *anularium*. Further, it must be recollected that the bandsman or ranker of the Roman army was not at all likely to have been an educated man, and, probably, was quite the reverse. Whence, as *anularium* is easier to pronounce than, and both when spoken and written bears a certain resemblance to, *annualium*, it is probable that the change was made. Again, if such a

[1] Housman, A. E.: *M. Manilii Astronomicon*, Lib. I . . . London, 1903, Intro., pp. liv–lix.

change was made, the most probable time for it to have been made was when the benefit described as being *nomine anularium* was first introduced, as at that time the word *annualium*, being unusual, would not have been so well known to the common soldier as it became when many soldiers were interested in the benefit thus described. The change is rendered more probable owing to the fact that the men were acquainted with the right of the *equites* (or gentlemen of the cavalry) to wear rings and, consequently, had become accustomed to the word *anularium*. Assuming that the confusion between the two words had taken place and become general on the introduction of a new and popular deferred annuity scheme (or pension fund), as suggested, it is certain that the popular name would have been applied to the benefit, however unsuitable it may have been.

Adequacy of accumulated subscriptions of members for provision of deferred annuities.

(2) The question of the proportion borne by the benefits granted to the subscriptions received. In the College of *Cornicines* the entrance fee was 750 denarii, and the benefits (other than those paid to veterans) varied from 200 to 500 denarii, whence it may be inferred that probably the entrance fee sufficed to meet those payments. But, as suggested by Cagnat and Mommsen and approved by Waltzing, it is exceedingly probable that a monthly subscription was also payable by each member. Assuming that this monthly subscription bore a similar proportion to the entrance fee to that borne by the respective fees of the civilian societies, and taking that of the society of Diana and Antinous at Lanuvium[1] as an average rate, i.e. 1·25 per cent., the monthly subscription of the College of Cornicines would have been 9 denarii for each member. As men entered the army at 16,[2] were full soldiers at 19, and became veterans at 46, it follows that each member who survived to become a pensioner would have subscribed 108 denarii per annum for some 27 years, and of the non-survivors it is to be assumed that each member who died or left the society

[1] See Chapter XVII, p. 202.
[2] See Livy, XXII, 57; XXV, 5; and XXVII, 11.

would on the average have contributed, say, 16 years' subscriptions, and that, the bulk of their subscriptions being received in the early part of their membership, in the seventh year after joining, they would on the average have paid in half of their total contributions to the society's funds. On Macer's or Ulpian's Tables, which were in use in Rome at the date of this society, the value of an immediate annuity of 500 denarii per annum payable yearly at age 46 was 7,000 denarii, the suggested annuity or pension was payable on January 1, i.e. deferred on an average six months —therefore the value may be taken at 6,750 denarii. But, on the assumption that 60 per cent. of the soldiers who at age 19 became full soldiers were discharged as veterans and that the society earned 5 per cent. simple interest on its funds, the share of the accumulated funds standing to the credit of each veteran was 7,232 denarii, made up as follows :—

Subscriptions paid by veteran	= 108 × 27 plus simple interest at 5 per cent. for 14 years.
	= 2,916 × (1·70)
	= 4,957 denarii.
Share of subscriptions paid by non-veteran	= ⅔ × 108 × 16 plus simple interest at 5 per cent. for 19½ years.
	= 1,152 × (1·975)
	= 2,275 denarii.

From this approximate calculation it follows that if the funds had been accumulated and administrated with care, they would have been more than sufficient to provide for the annuity or pension when due. The inclusion of the factor of interest is justified by the fact that not only are there many records of societies which invested their funds in loans on mortgage, etc., but also by the legal sanction which provided that societies could use their money in this way. One other point bearing on the subscriptions should be remembered, namely, that they were practically net premiums, as there was no cost of collection, and in certain civilian societies it is stated distinctly that these subscriptions were retained in full for the provision of *funeraticia.*

Reason for special date for payments *nomine anularium.*

(3) The date of payment of this class of benefit. As far as is known, this payment alone of all the payments made by civil and military societies was made on January 1—all the others were made as, and when, they became due. It is probable that there was some important reason for this differentiation between the various payments. Such a reason would be found in the necessity of avoiding complications or mistakes in the payment of annuities, as it is clear that such payments could have been made with much greater chance of accuracy if made once a year on a fixed date, than if paid on each anniversary of the day on which the veteran ex-member of the society received his discharge.

Payments *nomine anularium* not equivalent to *funeraticia.*

(4) Cagnat is of opinion that the "nomine anularium" payment was the payment of the *funeraticium* in advance to a person who could not remain in the society to receive it when it became due on his death. Waltzing holds the same opinion. There is, however, no evidence to show that these benefits did bear that relationship to each other. Further, as *funeraticium* was the name of a benefit known to most persons in the lower classes, whilst *anularium* was a very rare and unusual word, it seems almost certain that the benefit would have been known as a *funeraticium* if it was the equivalent to that payment in civilian societies. Whence it follows that the *anularium* did not mean a *funeraticium* but something different.

(5) This follows from § (2).

If equivalent, there would have been large surplus.

This hypothesis is, however, not pressed, but merely suggested. Should it be correct, it follows that these military societies, instead of having as their *raison d'être* the provision of funds to meet certain emergencies in the career of the members, would have had as their chief aim the provision of a pension fund, and, as a secondary and minor object, the provision of certain small benefits, such as those set out in the rules under discussion.

Military societies provided, in addition to smaller benefits, either mutual "endowment assurances" or mutual "term assurance combined with deferred annuity."

In any case the military societies provided, in addition to certain mutual aids and benefits payable in the event of certain occurrences, for the payment of a certain sum when the member died, if he died within a certain period, and in the event of his surviving that period, either for the payment of a fixed sum down or for the payment of an annuity until the death of the beneficiary. The first case would be a parallel to an endowment assurance granted by a mutual company of to-day, and in the second to a combined term assurance to age 46 and an annuity of which the first payment was made at the average age of 46 years and 6 months.

Did civilian societies provide similar benefits?

It is, of course, impossible to state definitely that no civilian societies existed providing similar benefits *mutatis mutandis* for their members; it appears much more probable that many of them did afford some such benefits. As, however, in the 3rd century A.D. the government ruled that military societies were illegal although the army was regarded with a much more lenient eye than civilians, it is clear that if any of the civilian societies were in the habit of granting similar benefits to their members they would have done so in such a way as to prevent their actions becoming known to the authorities. Whence it follows that there could have been no reference to such benefits in the published rules of these societies, nor in the inscriptions which were open to the general public, and that, therefore, there is no direct evidence thereof. It is, however, submitted that the probability that the civilian societies did follow the example of the military societies and grant similar benefits is very strong.

If so, they must have done so surreptitiously.

CHAPTER XX

NON-MUTUAL CONTRACTS FOR PAYMENTS ON DEATH OF A PERSON OR PERSONS AS KNOWN TO THE ROMANS

In the preceding section it has been shown that the Romans were fully aware of the advantages to be derived from mutual accumulations of funds for the purposes of providing funeral benefits; that, probably, mutual life assurance (or, better, mutual industrial insurance) had been developed from the payments for funeral expenses and was largely practised under the cloak of those payments. Whence it may be urged that if the Romans had learnt the value of life assurance the burial or religious societies would have supplied their requirements and would have rendered it unnecessary for them to have developed further the business of insurance by evolving a system of non-mutual life assurance. This objection is, however, invalidated by the following considerations:—

Roman mutual life assurance of limited value.

(*a*) In the case of a person insuring his own life the disadvantages of these club insurances were:—
  (1) the limitation to a very small sum of the amount which could be obtained in a mutual society;
  (2) the nominal object for which the money was paid by the society;
  (3) the actual illegality of such payments;
  (4) the difficulty of insisting on the payment of the *funeraticium* to any particular individual; and
  (5) the fact that the insurance was limited practically to whole-life.

(*b*) In the case of a person wishing to buy or sell a reversion or to use the insurance contract for the purposes of lending or borrowing money, this class of insurance was almost useless.

(c) In the case of a person wishing to insure the life of some other person, this form of mutual insurance was not available except under certain very restricted conditions.

From a consideration of the various limitations and disadvantages attaching to club insurance it is seen that this class of insurance was not adapted to meet the requirements of anyone other than the person who wished to secure the payment of a small sum to his representatives at his death. That persons had repeatedly attempted to obtain from these clubs larger sums is clear from the fact that membership had been restricted to one society only,[1] thereby limiting the amount of the benefit a man could obtain. Again, that which was illegal as between a society and its members owing to the strict definition of their powers and disabilities, would have been perfectly legal if duly set out in a proper contract between two individuals, or between an individual and a company or society. Further, if a man wished to insure himself for a term only, the only way in which he could have done so in a burial club would have been to become an ordinary member by paying the entrance fee and, subsequently, the monthly subscriptions for as long as the risk lasted. In this way he would have paid "whole life" rates for a term—probably a short-term—insurance, in addition to a heavy entrance fee. For these reasons it follows that mutual insurance of this nature can have been of little general use and that a person desiring to insure himself or another would have been obliged to seek some other method. The only method which would have been available was the "Wager Method,"[2] and this only for term insurance against certain risks. As the idea of whole-life assurance had been made general by the burial societies, and that of insurance of property against marine and other risks by the practices described in Part II, it is likely that the person who desired to protect himself against a term risk would have done so by a "wager," and, by an extension of the "wager" system, could, in the event of his desiring to set up a contract for the payment of a sum of money at his death, whenever it might happen, have

[1] See *Digest*.

[2] See Chapter VII.

approached the person or company with whom he had made the " wager policy " and have negotiated with him a contract to that effect.

Contracts for such payments at death appear to have been made very generally, as there are several references to them in the Roman Civil Law. Further, these contracts do not appear to have been connected with wills or legacies, as in the Justinian and ante-Justinian collections of laws they are not placed in juxtaposition with the laws referring to wills, etc. As the order of the subjects dealt with is strictly logical and accurate it is most likely that these contracts do not refer to wills but to a totally different class of business. A stronger argument is the statement in the Institutes that contracts could be made for payments due on the death of third parties, which must have been for sale, etc., of reversions, or the equivalent to an insurance contract; they could not in any case refer to the making of a person heir or legatee to a third party.

It will be noted that the opinions of the jurisconsults and the rulings of the Emperors with regard to contracts for payments to be made at the death of a specified person contained in the extracts discussed below are given in clear and definite words and that the contracts are referred to in terms which show that they were numerous and important.

Limited nature of *Responsa* in Roman Civil Law referring to these contracts.

In considering the references about to be examined, it is necessary to remember that, as shown above,[1] the *Corpus Juris Civilis* was not, nor was intended to be, a complete body of all the local and private laws in use in the Roman Empire. For example, it is very expressly stated that questions arising from matters connected with the sea are to be dealt with under the law of Rhodes,[2] and rights of private legislation are explicitly and implicitly permitted to companies.[3] Whence it is not to be expected that the replies of the jurists (answering almost to the opinion of counsel) would give detailed accounts of the contracts of insurance or of the manner in which such contracts were to be drawn up and enforced. All that can be looked for

[1] See Chapter V. [2] See Appendix F. [3] Cf. Chapter V.

in each case is the reply of the jurist to the question or questions submitted to him. As will be shown, these replies recognize the validity of stipulations which provide for the payment of money on the death of the stipulator or of some person nominated by him.

Most exhaustive *Responsa* those of Ulpian, who prescribed improved table of annuity values.

It is perhaps something more than a coincidence that the most detailed replies dealing with questions which arose from a contract of, or resembling that of, insurance in the Roman Law, are those of Ulpian, who is responsible for the table discussed in Chapter XII.

Examining these "responses" (of Ulpian to Sabinus)[1] first, as they afford more detailed information with regard to these agreements than those in the *Institutes* and in the *Code*, it is found that the following would form the basis of a valid agreement (*utilis actio*) which could be enforced by an action before the Prætor:—

Responsa of Ulpian.

I (*a*) A man could stipulate "when he shall die."
(*b*) Those in the power of others (such as *filiifamiliæ* etc.), could stipulate "when they shall die."

II (*c*) A man could stipulate for "money to be paid to my daughter after my death."
(*d*) A man could stipulate for "money to be paid to me after the death of my daughter."

III (*e*) Further an agreement could be made not only "when you shall die," but also "if you shall die."

Examining each of these conditions in turn we find with regard to (*a*) that an agreement could be made determinable at the moment of death of the person proposing the

[1] *Digest*, XLV, i, 45. Ulpian, Lib. 50, ad Sabinum. De stipulatione collata in tempus mortis, vel post mortem.

§ 1. Sicuti, *cum morietur*, quis, stipulari potest: id etiam hi qui subjecti sunt alienæ potestati, *cum morientur*, stipulari possunt.

§ 2. Si quis ita stipulatus sit, *post mortem meam filiæ meæ dari*; vel ita, *post mortem filiæ meæ mihi dari*? Utiliter erit stipulatus: sed primo casu filiæ utilis actio competit, licet heres ei non existat.

§ 3. Non solum ita stipulari possumus *cum morieris*; sed etiam, *si morieris*. Nam sicuti inter hæc nihil interest, *cum veneris*, aut *si veneris*: ita nec ibi interest, *si morieris*, et *cum morieris*.

conditions on which it was to be based. This would have been either a contract to provide for the payment of a sum at his death, in which case it may have referred to—

(i) either a legacy or the sale of a property, the ownership of which would have remained with him during his life and have been transferred at his death, or some similar transaction, or

(ii) the payment of a sum of money to his representatives when he died, in which case it would have contained all the essentials for a contract for an own-life assurance, i.e. the person assured, the determination of the risk and the maturing of his policy at the moment of his death, and the payment of a valuable consideration.

Contract equivalent to whole-life assurance.

Price or premium was paid.

As shown above, a price or premium must have been paid, or was payable, by the person who was going to benefit by the action of the other party to the agreement, and the benefit did not mature until the moment of his death (*cum morietur*). Under (*b*) it is found that this privilege was not only permitted to persons holding the full status of citizenship and under their own control, but also to persons subject to the control of others. In order to appreciate the full value of this concession and the great bearing it has on the question under discussion, it must be remembered that, until late in Roman history, the head of the family (*paterfamilias*) exercised quasiplenary jurisdiction over his descendants,[1] other than married daughters, and over their wives, children, and property; also that it was customary for fathers to waive these rights over their sons, especially if their sons were married. The advantages conferred by this clause were, therefore, very valuable. For example, a man *subjectus patris potestati* might have wished to take out a whole-life policy, but he could not have done so without the powers given thereunder.

Subjecti alienæ potestati able to make these contracts.

[1] *Digest*, I, vi, 3; Ulpian, V, 1: "In potestate sunt liberi parentum ex justo matrimonio nati," and see *Digest*, XXXIII, ii, 2, 4; *Code*, V, iv, 27; Ulpian, V, 3–6.

Assurance of father's life for benefit of daughter.

Under (*a*) it seems to be implied that a man could insure his own life, presumably for the benefit of a third person; in the decision actually given in (*c*) it is definitely stated that he could do so as far as his daughter was concerned; but it is quite open to doubt as to whether this form of contract was valid only in the case of a man insuring for the benefit of his daughter. It appears more than probable that such a contract would have been equally good (*utilis*) if the beneficiary had been his wife or his son; possibly it was extended to more distant relations and even to non-relations. Section (*d*) gives legal sanction to the contract for payment on the death of his daughter for the benefit of the assurer. Here, again, the question would appear to arise as to the extent of the assurer's right to insure the life of a third party, and it might, from the passage under consideration, be held that this right extended to near relations only. That this was not so is shown by a passage in the *Institutes*[1] which states definitely that an agreement depending on the death of another person (*post mortem alterius*) could be made validly.

Assurance of daughter's life for benefit of father.

Reasons why this was not a contract for return of dowry.

This contract for payment to a person on the death of his daughter has been explained as being a contract for the return of her dowry in the event of her death. Had the contract been in the section on dowry, or had it stood alone, that explanation would have been very plausible. In this connection, however, it does not appear to be applicable, as the contract is obviously a variant of the other in the same clause from which it is separated by the words "vel ita." Since the first contract clearly has no connection with the refund of a dowry it follows that the second cannot have, unless it be advanced that Ulpian placed in juxtaposition as part of the same sentence two contracts dealing with entirely different matters.

[1] *Institutions of Justinian*, III, xix, 16: "Item post mortem alterius recte stipulamur." Cf. *Code*, VIII (xxxviii), 11 (quoted in note on p. 233).

Term and whole life assurance contracts equally valid.

From (*e*) it is seen that by the admission of stipulations based on the phrase "if you shall die" the person who was contracting to pay money on the death of another or to receive money on his own death was enabled to set up—

(*a*) a term insurance in the ordinary sense, and
(*b*) an insurance during the continuance of certain risks.

That this form of stipulation not only would, but must, imply a term insurance is clear, since, owing to the fact that every one must die, the words bear no meaning, unless the period during which the life is insured is limited, otherwise the life could not survive, and, consequently, the stipulation would be for the certain payment of the sum agreed upon. From this then, as stated, the insured could set up a term insurance; he could, if he survived the period, presumably do this a second time on the expiry of the first term, and so for a third term, at probably an increasing price each time. Whence it follows that, in the event of his finding an individual or company willing to continue to reinsure him he could obtain a life policy for consecutive periods which would correspond to a policy with an annual (or other period) premium of the present day, except that the premiums would not be level, presumably, and that he would be liable to find that his policy would not be renewed. It is, however, quite possible that in making such agreements it was customary to stipulate for the right to extend the period of risk on payment of a further premium. Again, such a condition might be used to set up a contingent insurance payable if A died during the lifetime of B. That such a contract is not referred to is, of course, a strong argument against the existence of such contracts, but, though strong, it is in no sense conclusive. From the above it has been shown that a contract of this nature could be legally made.

CHAPTER XXI

EXAMINATION OF OTHER EXTRACTS FROM ROMAN LAW WHICH DEAL WITH CONTRACTS OF A SIMILAR NATURE

References in Roman Civil Law to these contracts.

THE references in Roman Law to stipulations based on the death of either of the stipulators or on that of a third party are as follows :—

I Before separation of Eastern and Western Empires.
  A. Gaius : *Commentaries*, I, iii, 100, *circa* A.D. 150.
    (Gaius incorporated in *Breviary* of Alaric II, ix, §§ 7 and 8, *circa* A.D. 150.)
    (Ulpian incorporated in *Digest*, XLV, i, 45, *circa* A.D. 225.)
II Western Empire.
  B. (Gaius) *Breviary* of Alaric II, II, ix, §§ 7 and 8, *circa* A.D. 500.
III Eastern Empire.
  C. *Codex Justinianus*, VIII, xxxviii, §§ 11 and 15. April 529.
    Digest, XLV, i, 45 (Ulpian). Dec. 533 } Justinian.
    Institutes, III, 20, §§ 13, 15, 16 and 17. Dec. 533 } Justinian.
  D. *Basilikôn*, XXIV, iii, 19 } Basil and Leo.
    „ XLIII, i, 42 } Basil and Leo.
    „ XLIII, v, 11 } Basil and Leo.

From this table it is obvious that, if the references are to a practice of a nature resembling that of life assurance, the practice must have existed from not later than early in the 2nd century of our era down to the 10th century at least. Hence it may be suggested that although at first the contract may have been of a very rough nature and based on mere guesswork as to the value of the benefit, yet the changing conditions under which such contracts were made and the increasing familiarity in dealing with them would have tended to improve the form in which they were made and would have led to the adoption of some less rough-and-ready system of calculating the values of such contracts than that in use at first.

Commentaries of Gaius.

Taking the extracts set out above in their chronological order, the first to be considered is that taken from the *Commentaries* of Gaius [1] (about A.D. 150). At the time when Gaius was compiling these *Commentaries* the Roman Empire was at its zenith. Under the beneficent rule of the Antonines commercial and professional interests in Rome had been studied and fostered with as much assiduity as those of a literary nature. It is, therefore, reasonable to assume that in business circles it had been found necessary by this time to devise some means by which a man could make a contract under which he would pay or receive a sum of money at his own death or at the death of another.[2] This being so, cases would have arisen necessitating a reference to counsel or an action at law. The jurisconsults, to whom such questions were submitted, would have treated the matter laid before them in respect of their legal aspect only, as it is clear that they could have known little or nothing of the mathematical or business side of the transaction. Whence the investigator would anticipate finding in the Roman Civil Law :—

References to jurisconsults on legal points only.

(*a*) no references to these contracts, or
(*b*) a general reference to local laws deciding such questions,[3] or
(*c*) a concise opinion on the purely legal questions raised.

[1] Gaius : *Commentaries*, III, 100.
Denique inutilis est talis stipulatio, si quis ita dari stipuletur : *post mortem meam dari spondes ?* vel ita (*post mortem tuam dari spondes ?* Valet autem, si quis ita dari stipuletur *cum moriar dari spondes ?* vel ita) *cum morieris dari spondes ?* id est ut in novissimum vitæ tempus stipulatoris aut promissoris obligatio conferatur. Nam inelegans esse visum est ex heredis persona incipere obligationem. Rursus ita stipulari non possumus, *pridie quam moriar*, aut, *pridie quam morieris, dari spondes ?* quia non potest aliter intellegi *pridie* quam aliquis morietur, quam si mors secuta sit, rursus morte secuta in præteritum redducitur stipulatio et quodammodo talis est *heredi meo dari spondes ?* quæ sane inutilis est.

[2] See Chapter IX.

[3] Cf. reference to Rhodian Law as deciding questions raised in respect of marine cases. *Digest*, XIV, ii, 9. See also Novel 110.

The third point (*c*), namely, the statement as to the forms of sound and unsound contracts or stipulations depending for their determination on the death of a person, is that found both in the *Responsa* of the jurisconsults and in the constitutions or laws of Alaric II., of Justinian and of Basil. In the first extract it is seen that although Gaius held no hostile opinion to such contracts *per se* he based his ruling on the opinion that all such contracts were invalid if they interfered with the status of the heir or heirs of either party to the contract. He stated therein that all stipulations made in the form: "Do you promise that —— shall be paid after my death?" or "Do you promise that —— shall be paid after your death?" were invalid on the ground that it was unfitting that the obligation should begin in the person of the heir. Also he considered that such stipulations as "Do you promise that —— shall be paid on the day before I shall die?" or "on the day before you shall die?" were invalid because in this case the date on which the payment would become due could only become known by the fact of death having ensued, in which event the stipulation was held to be equivalent to "Do you promise that —— shall be paid to my heir?" which was pronounced to be "clearly invalid." At the same time Gaius ruled that contracts based on the forms "Do you promise that —— shall be paid when I shall die?" or "Do you promise that —— shall be paid when you shall die?" were valid, since in these cases the obligation matured at the very last moment of the life of the stipulator or of the promissor. Although the opinion given by Gaius is restricted and shows a certain objection to this species of contract, the fact that the question as to the legality of such contracts was of sufficient importance to have been referred to a jurist of his eminence, indicates clearly that the right to make such contracts was considered to be of great importance. It may be mentioned here that this minute differentiation, which had so much legal importance in the time of Gaius, was held to be of little or no importance by later jurists and emperors.[1]

[1] Cf. Extract from the *Code*, p. 233, footnote 1.

Gaius quoted in *Breviary* of Alaric.

The next extract in chronological order is that from Gaius, incorporated by Alaric II in his *Breviary*. This, although taken from the writings of Gaius, appears to have been considerably altered and restricted by Alaric; it is, therefore, more correctly a part of the legislation of the Western Empire and will be discussed later.

The next great jurist to deal with this form of stipulation was Ulpian, who, about A.D. 225, published his *Responsa* on the points in question, some or all of which were incorporated by Justinian in the *Digest*. The extract from his writings which has been considered above[1] shows that in the time of Justinian a much greater freedom was allowed in these stipulations. It cannot be stated definitely whether Ulpian himself intended to give such an entirely favourable opinion in reference to this matter; it is possible that his original *Responsa* contained limitations and restrictions comparable to those imposed by Gaius, but there is no evidence as to this point. All that can be said is that if Ulpian did differentiate between various forms of stipulation in the same way as Gaius had done, Justinian ignored these limitations and used such of the *Responsa* of Ulpian as dealt with the general recognition of such stipulations.

Doubtful if Justinian adopted *Responsa* of Ulpian in their entirety.

No reference in Roman Law to these contracts between A.D. 250 and 500.

From the time of Ulpian to that of Alaric II nothing was said on this subject of sufficient importance to merit recognition by Alaric II in his *Breviary* or by Justinian in his *Corpus Juris Civilis*. If any jurist of minor importance recorded his opinions in regard to stipulations of this nature no trace thereof has been handed down. The next evidence as to the legal position of these stipulations, found in the *Breviary* of Alaric, is, as will be seen from the text,[2]

[1] See p. 223, above.

[2] Gaius: Ex *Breviario Alariciano*,* Lib. II, ix, §§ 7 and 8.

§ 7. Præterea inutilis est et interrogatio et promissio, si ita aliquis interroget debitorem: *Post mortem meam* vel *tuam illud dari spondes?* . . .

§ 8. Item inutilis est obligatio, si dicat creditor, *pridie quam moriar dare spondes?* (vel interroget debitorem) *pridie quam moriaris?* Similiter et hæc stipulatio inutilis judicatur, quia non potest scire quando sit pridie quam aliquis moriatur, nisi postquam mortuus fuerit.

* See Gaius' Institutes, *Lex Romana Visigothorum*, p. 334, ed. Hänel, Leipsic, 1849.

an excerpt from the portion of the *Commentaries* of Gaius dealt with above.

The Western Empire

Breviary of Alaric.

Alaric II, Emperor of the Western Empire, in his ruling[1] on the subject endorsed the opinion of Gaius as to the invalidity of stipulations for money payable *post mortem meam* vel *tuam* or *pridie quam moriar* vel *moriaris*, but did not give as his reason for doing so that such stipulations would interfere with the obligations and rights of the heir. It should be noted that in this extract the person who stipulated for the payment of the money is referred to as the creditor, the other party to the contract who promised to pay being called the debtor. Whence it would appear that the ruling of Alaric was expressly directed against the moneylenders, as this law made contracts for the sale of reversions useless. It is possible, however, that the terms are used in a book-keeping sense, and that *debitor* means the person who has received the consideration (premium) in return for which he undertakes to pay the money stipulated for, and, similarly, that *creditor* means the person who paid that consideration. This manner of referring to the parties to the stipulation is used in this instance alone; in all the other extracts the parties being undescribed. The other form (i.e. *cum moriar* vel *moriaris*) which Gaius pronounced to be valid is not alluded to in the *Breviary*. This omission may have been either due to the fact that the last form was in such constant use as to require no further legal sanction or to a feeling that all contracts depending on the death of human beings were contrary to good morals and to the welfare of the Empire. As the existence of the custom cannot be doubted, seeing that the necessity for laws (either permissive or restrictive) referring to any practice could only have arisen from the existence of the practice, and as Alaric would have found it as easy to

Use of terms *creditor* and *debitor*.

Contracts "cum moriar vel moriaris" not referred to by Alaric II. Suggested reasons for omission.

[1] See p. 230, footnote 2.

base his ruling on that of Ulpian as on that of Gaius, had he considered it advisable to do so, it appears certain from his adoption of the restrictive part of the *Commentary* of Gaius that the feeling of the jurists of his date was entirely opposed to this form of business contract. Want of evidence as to the cause of this method of dealing with a custom which was, probably, considerably used, and which could have, and possibly had, been developed into a very important branch of business, renders it impossible to formulate any definite explanation thereof. It is suggested that it was due to strong antagonism on the part of some powerful non-business power (such as that of the Church, which, as shown above, exercised great power in the Western Empire during the 5th to 7th centuries A.D.) using its influence in such a way as to damage seriously commercial and military interests. This suggestion is supported by the direct evidence which we have of the opposition displayed by the Church to all financial, though not necessarily commercial, business in the Middle Ages, resulting in the prohibition, *inter alia*, of all forms of contracts or wagers depending for their determination on the death of a human being.[1] In this connection it should be noted that this prohibition in the Middle Ages appears to have been confined to the Latin peoples, whose codes of law were based on Roman Law, and to the Netherlands under the bigoted rule of Philip II of Spain[1]; who, although this would have rendered it more probable that they would have adopted the rulings of Justinian, were probably influenced by the way in which such contracts had been regarded by the Church during the 5th to 12th centuries A.D. This explanation of the action of Alaric II is advanced tentatively, as there is no direct evidence either for or against it.

The Eastern Empire

Eastern Empire.

In the extant portions of the *Corpus Juris Civilis* of the Eastern Empire are found several sections dealing with contracts or stipulations based on death. The first of these in date of publication

[1] See Chapter XIII, pp. 155–7.

is that found in the *Code* of Justinian,[1] and refers obviously to the *Commentary* of Gaius in respect of these stipulations. In this extract it is stated by the Emperor that, having exhaustively considered the careful investigation of the ancients as to whether stipulations based on the formulas "after the death of" or "when he shall die" or "on the day before he shall die" were valid, he ruled that all such contracts, etc., even if based on the formulas "after the death of" or "on the day before the death of," should hold good. From this, the first ruling of Justinian, it is clear that the jurists of his day were disposed to disregard the fine distinctions drawn by Gaius and by other writers whose works have not survived. This tendency to freer and broader treatment of the question is shown more clearly in the later law of Justinian and in that of Basil and Leo.

Code of Justinian.

Broader treatment of formulas.

The next reference to the subject is found in the *Digest*, and consists of the *Responsa* of Ulpian which have been considered above.[2] In the same month Justinian published his *Institutes*,[3] in which the question is dealt with in more detail than in the other passages referred to. The question as to

Digest.

Institutes of Justinian.

[1] *Code*, VIII, xxxviii, 11.
Scrupulosam (veterum) inquisitionem utrum *post mortem* an *cum moreretur* vel *pridie quam moreretur*, stipulatus sit aliquis, vel in testamento legati, vel fidei comissi nomine aliquid dereliquerit, penitus amputantes omnia quæ vel quocunque contractu, vel stipulati, vel pacti sunt contrahentes, vel testator in suo testamento disposuerit etiamsi *post mortem*, vel *pridie quam moreretur*, scripta esse noscuntur; nihilominus pro tenore contractus, vel testamenti valere præcipimus.

[2] See pp. 223 *et seq.*, Chapter XX.

[3] *Inst.*, III, xix, §§ 13, 15, 16, 17.
§ 13. Post mortem suam dari sibi nemo stipulari poterat, non magis quam post mortem ejus a quo stipulabatur. . . . Sed et si quis ita stipuletur, *pridie quam moriar* vel *pridie quam morieris dare spondes?* Inutilis erat stipulatio. Sed cum (ut jam dictum est)* ex consensu contrahentium stipulationes valent, placuit nobis etiam in hunc juris articulum necessariam inducere emendationem,† ut sive *post mortem*, sive *pridie quam morietur stipulator* sive *promissor*, stipulatio concepta est, valeat stipulatio.
§ 15. Ita autem stipulatio concepta, veluti si Titius dicat, *cum moriar dare spondes?* vel *cum morieris* et apud veteres utilis erat et nunc valet.
§ 16. Item *post mortem* alterius recte stipulamur.
§ 17. Si scriptum in instrumento fuerit, promisisse aliquem perinde habetur atque si interrogatione præcedente responsum sit.

* Cf. *Inst.*, III, xv, 1, or xviii, 3.

† *Code*, VIII, xxxviii, 11.

the validity of stipulations based on the formula "the day before {I / you} shall die" is discussed, the rulings of the older jurists as to the invalidity of stipulations thus worded are referred to and revised, the reason for this revision being that stipulations derive their legal validity from the fact that they are based on the mutual consent of the contracting parties and that consequently it pleased Justinian to amend the earlier law. Such stipulations as "if Titius says 'do you promise to pay (give) . . . when I shall die' or 'when you shall die'" are stated to have been valid among the ancients and to be valid now (i.e. December, 533). Also it is ruled that a stipulation which depends on the death of another person can be correctly made.

This passage affords proof that, at the time of Justinian,

(1) the practice of stipulating or making agreements for the payment of money on the death of one of the two parties was of very old standing;
(2) such stipulations could be made on a second or other life, that is to say, on the life of some one other than the person asking or the person replying in the formulas given; and
(3) the decisions bearing on these especial forms of stipulation were important.

Practice of making these contracts of very old standing.

The first of these points is clear, as it is directly stated that the matter had been considered and certain stipulations pronounced valid by the ancients (*apud veteres*): added to which there are the confirmatory extracts from Gaius and Ulpian quoted above [1] which prove that the same questions had been raised and similar verdicts given in (*circa*) A.D. 150 and 225.

Contract depending on death of a third person could be made.

The second point is dealt with definitely in this section. The wording, which is precise and clear, is "Likewise we can stipulate (make stipulations or agreements) correctly (for money to be paid) 'after the death of another [2] person.'" Although, as was shown above, stipulations such as "Do you promise

[1] See pp. 228–9 and 223.

[2] The use of "*alterius*" as equivalent to "*alius*" (genitive of *alius*) was very common. Cf. also XII, Tab. ap. Gell. XX, 1. Si iniuriam faxit alteri.

to pay me after the death of my daughter?" or "Do you promise to pay to my daughter after my death?" were pronounced legally valid by Ulpian,[1] and subsequently confirmed by Justinian[2] and Basil,[3] yet these could only have been considered to be special permissions granted to fathers, had it not been shown in this passage that the general ruling permitted the making of such stipulations on the life of another person. It is of interest to note that this is the only[4] place in the *Corpus Juris Civilis* in which the making of contracts on the death of some one else other than the stipulators is provided for excepting in the special cases of father and daughter.[5] Thirdly, as to the importance of the decisions bearing on such stipulations as were dependent on death for their due performance. The need of such decisions is clearly shown by the fact that they are incorporated in the *Institutes*, which book was compiled by order of Justinian with a view to its serving as a first textbook on Civil Law for the law students of his time; it was not intended to be a comprehensive treatise,[6] but, as is stated by Justinian in his preface, a concise textbook setting out the elements of law and dealing with nothing that was not of practical use or that was superfluous. Consequently the matters dealt with therein are the more important part of the law, with, in some cases, a short statement of the reasons for such laws. This being so, it follows that if the decisions as to the validity of the stipulations under consideration were worthy of being given a place therein, they must have been of considerable practical importance, whence *a fortiori* the practice of making such stipulations must have been general and of such an extent as to render a knowledge of the legal decisions thereon a very necessary part of the training of a young lawyer.

Importance of these contracts.

[1] See Chapter XX, p. 223.
[2] See p. 227.
[3] See p. 237.
[4] But see pp. 237 and 239 below.
[5] See Chapter XX, p. 223, and p. 237.
[6] Proem: Institutionum Justin:
§ 3. . . . specialiter mandavimus ut nostra auctoritate nostrisque suasionibus Institutiones componerent, ut liceat vobis prima legum cunabula non ab antiquis fabulis discere, sed ab imperiali splendore appetere; et tam aures quam animæ vestræ nihil inutile nihilque perperam positum, sed quod in ipsis rerum obtinet argumentis, accipiant.

Basilikôn, Book XXIV, removal of restrictions on contract.

These general and decisive rulings contained in the *Digest* and *Institutes* appear to have met all requirements arising out of such contracts for the succeeding 300 years, as the next allusion to such stipulation is that contained in Book XXIV of the Laws of Basil. This extract may be translated as follows :—

> In ancient times stipulations, legacies and other contracts which matured after deaths were set aside, but we, for the sake of their general utility to mankind, accept them (as valid) : as it has been agreed that that ruling which was in force in ancient days is amended by fixed custom.

From this extract it follows that from the making of such contracts based on death as were permitted under the older laws [1] the great utility of such contracts had been generally recognized, and to such an extent as to cause the legal limitations to be neglected in favour of the broader scope afforded by custom. It is of importance to notice that Basil, in this extract, stated that he considered the opinion of Gaius and other of the earlier jurists that actions could not be begun by, or against, heirs to be based on too subtle reasoning, and that he definitely ruled that actions and obligations could be thus begun in order that the freedom of action of the contracting parties should not be curtailed.

Contracts could have been used for joint lives or survivorship risks.

Further, that these contracts were not, even if they had been prior to the time of Justinian, confined to the death of either of the contracting parties. Again, it is clear that the custom had undergone a further development, since the law here takes cognisance of, and sanctions, the application of the principle of maturing at death to contracts of all kinds.

Basilikôn, Book XLIII, repeating *Responsa* of Ulpian.

There are two more references in later Roman Law to the practice, both of which are also found in the *Basilikôn*. The first is that contained in Book XLIII, and may be translated thus :—

[1] From *circa* A.D. 150.

§ 1. And both he, who is his own master, and also he who is in the power of another, may stipulate (i.e. make a stipulation for a payment of money, etc.) *when he shall die.*

§ 2. I stipulate correctly (i.e. make a valid stipulation) that money shall be paid to my daughter after my death, *or* be paid to me after my daughter's death.

§ 3. The stipulation is equally valid whether he shall have said "if I shall die" or "when I shall die."

The extract endorses the *Responsa* of Ulpian, which had been similarly endorsed by Justinian when incorporated in the *Digest* as shown above.[1] It is clear from this repeated sanction of the stipulation made by fathers in reference to money payments dependent on their own life or that of their daughters that the practice was much in vogue and of great importance.

Another interesting point is the endorsement by both Justinian and Basil of Ulpian's opinion as to the equivalent value of the stipulations *when I shall die* and *if I shall die,* since this second form must refer to a term risk only, as was demonstrated above.

Basilikôn, Book XLIII.

The third ruling on these contracts is also found in Book XLIII of the *Basilikôn* and reads as follows:—

"And as regards him who has stipulated thus *after the death of* or *on the day before he shall die* it is the same thing and the stipulation is similarly valid, since that which is done is valid whether it has been done in a legacy or in another contract."

The first point of interest in this passage is the ruling that the two forms of stipulation *after the death of* or *on the day before he shall die* are of equal value, and contracts based on either formula are valid. It is evident from the context that the jurists had examined the *Responsa* of the earlier writers on the matter and had decided to set aside their opinions as being based on fine-drawn and unnecessary legal quibbles, and as tending to create restrictions which could serve no useful purpose. The second point to be observed is the repetition of the legal sanction given in Book XXIV of the *Basilikôn* to all contracts drawn up on the under-

[1] See pp. 227 and 233.

standing that they were determined directly or indirectly by the time of death of some person or persons, whether such contracts were legacies or any other instruments securing a payment. From these two extensions of the legally authorized practice of the time of Justinian it is evident that, as all the small restrictions and obstructions which limited this class of contracts under the civil law of Rome up to and including the time of Justinian had been removed, the contracting parties, if they wished to do so, were legally able to make any form of contract which they considered suitable. Whence it follows that such contracts could have been made in a form which *mutatis mutandis* would have been a parallel to the modern contract of life assurance. That they did do so is almost certain, since, although their knowledge of the theory of life contingencies, and of the construction of life tables and money values deduced therefrom, must have been very small, yet the fact that they produced the Table of Ulpian shows that they had some appreciation of the effect of mortality and sufficient knowledge to produce a table which appears to follow facts very fairly closely. In any case the probability is that by this time contracts of all kinds were made continually under which the payment of money, etc., at a time depending on the death of some person, was guaranteed, and that such contracts to pay were made in return for a consideration paid or payable. The difference between such contracts and those of modern life assurance would appear to consist chiefly in the value of the consideration as compared with that of the benefit and in, as far as is known, the unscientific way in which premiums were calculated.

Summing up of Parts I, II, and III of Thesis.

To sum up, the evidence in favour of the presumption that a practice involving contracts determined by the failure of life closely resembling in its main features the life assurance of to-day, though, naturally, of much more limited scope, was known to, and in common use by, the Romans, is, briefly, as follows :—

(*a*) That the sale of reversions, etc., was very common from the earliest days of the Empire, if not before.

(*b*) That there are no less than ten direct *Responsa, leges*, etc., in Roman Law from the middle of the 2nd to the 10th century bearing on the validity of contracts which were determined by the death of a specified person whenever it should occur (parallel to a modern contract of whole-life assurance), or by the death of a person or persons within a certain period of time or during the running of a certain risk (a contract similar to the modern one of term assurance or of assurance against death caused by accident or by sickness within the period during which the life is exposed to a stated risk).

(*c*) That these contracts resembled contracts of modern life assurance in that they were made to provide for the payment of a sum of money on the termination of a specified life, (1) whenever it should happen, or (2) if it happened during a certain time or risk.

(*d*) That for the large majority of these contracts valuable consideration was paid, answering to the premium of to-day.

(*e*) That the Romans had a (rough ?) knowledge of the main features of a life table, proved by the fact that they had constructed a table of values of a_x or e_x in or before the 3rd century of our era.

(*f*) That they were continually buying or selling annuities, life and fixed; and had developed a species of tontine which was pronounced illegal by Basil.

(*g*) That they were in the habit of calculating interest and discount, and understood the system of payment by instalments, etc.

Further, there is the evidence that they were acquainted with the advantages of protection against loss in the case of merchandise sent by land or sea, and also, by means of the stipulations described in Chapter VII, could have obtained the equivalent to a contract of insurance against risk of any kind.

PART IV

DEVELOPMENT OF MODERN INSURANCE FROM THE FAMILY-GROUP SYSTEM AS EXEMPLIFIED IN BELGIUM

CHAPTER XXII

DERIVATION OF MODERN INSURANCE

Limitations of methods of insurance in classical times.

IN the preceding sections the methods adopted by the Greeks, Romans, and certain other races of the classical period for protection of the individual against loss arising from certain risks have been investigated. It has been shown that, apart from the mutual life assurance (?) of the *collegia* and the contracts for the payment of money on the death of persons, the only form of insurance[1] of which there is direct evidence that the peoples of antiquity employed it was that against risk arising from transit of property by land or sea. This protection was obtained in various ways—by loans on Bottomry, by a form of wager, by state guarantees containing the essentials of modern insurance and, possibly, by other forms of contract referred to in Novel 110, of the particulars of which, if they existed, there is no record. But, as far as direct evidence is concerned, when this is said, the history of insurance in classical times is finished. There appears to have been no system of providing against loss caused by fire, illness, or other accident.[1] It is probable, therefore, that if the mediæval and modern systems of insurance owe their origin to the classic practice, they do so only in so far as insurance on goods during transit by land or sea is concerned.

Probable derivation of mediæval insurance.

The employment of insurance against other risks may have been handed down as a business practice, but not recorded in any legal system or alluded to by any contemporary writer, or may have been the outcome of a post-classical recognition

[1] As suggested in Chapter VII, the wagers and contracts of indemnification may have been used for risks other than marine, but there is no definite evidence to that effect.

of the value of the practice when applied to risks other than that of safe carriage. There is, however, another possible source, namely, the methods employed by the various *collegia* of traders and merchants, of which there is no evidence in so far as the Roman *collegia* are concerned.

In the records of the Flemings, Menapians and West Germans there is a complete chain of evidence of the growth of mutual insurance against loss arising from fire, shipwreck, misfortune, captivity, damage to live-stock, etc., from the primitive "family-group" system down to the highly developed, businesslike communal systems of the 16th century. There is evidence, also, of the origin and development of non-mutual insurance of the property of merchants, of a widely extended, intricate and highly developed system of non-mutual marine insurance, and of life assurance between the 12th and 16th centuries. When it is remembered how continual and important the commercial intercourse between the Low Countries and England was during the 11th–15th centuries, it is at least reasonable to assume that modern insurance in England is due largely, if not entirely, to the development of the "family-group" system of the inhabitants of Flanders, Menapia and Western Prussia, and in but a small degree, if at all, to the practice of classical races.

Developed from "family groups" and gilds of Flanders and Germany.

The following chart shows the various steps in the development of mutual insurance in the Low Countries and affords a means of comparison of the dates at which the various non-mutual methods of insurance were practised.

DEVELOPMENT OF INSURANCE IN MEMPISC AND FLANDERS FROM 1ST TO 16TH CENTURIES A.D.

Centuries.	Mutual.			Non-mutual.		
	Nature of Group.	Nature of Insurance, etc.	Remarks.	Merchants' Stocks at Fairs, etc.	Marine.	Life.
I–VII	Family Groups of Germans and Flemings	(Assistance generally of members of Group)	—	—	—	—
VIII–X	Gilds–*Geldonia*	Against fire, shipwreck, misfortune	Secret societies—members bound by oath—illegal	—	—	—
XI–XIII	Brotherhoods *Amitié* *Minne* *Confrérie* *Keuren*	Against fire, loss of merchandise, captivity, damage to live-stock, etc.	Granted charters by overlords. Marked change from friendly nature of Brotherhoods to businesslike character of later *Keuren*	Merchants and traders guaranteed against loss by Lords of Manors in return for payment	—	—
XIV–XV	Grouping of *Keuren* in district into one central commune. Cf. Statut du Mont d'Hazebrouck	Against fire	Advantage gained from widening the area of risk and of subscription	—	Company for Marine Insurance established in Bruges, 1310. Insurance by merchants, underwriters, etc.	Life Assurance Life Assurance
XVI	—	—	—	—	—	Life Assurance forbidden, 1571

CHAPTER XXIII

DEVELOPMENT OF COMMUNAL INSURANCE FROM FAMILY-GROUP SYSTEM

(1) The "Family Groups" of Germany and the Low Countries and the Development of Gilds Therefrom

Family group regarded as unit by primitive tribes of Flanders, etc.

THE primitive tribes of Germany and Flanders regarded the family and not the individual as the unit, the tribe being governed by the heads of the family units. Each family was entirely in the power of its head, and through him had its say in the conduct of the religious functions, apportionment of lands, food, etc., of the tribe to which the family belonged. The collective rights and duties of the family over and towards the individual members were generally :—

Mutual rights and duties of members of family group.

(i) Mutual property in land belonging to group.

(ii) Mutual right of succession to property of intestate member.

(iii) Mutual obligation to prosecute murderer of member of group.

(iv) Mutual liability to pay wergeld for murder committed by member of group.

(v) Mutual obligation to assist fellow-members.

(vi) Mutual religious rites and burial.

An important feature of the family régime was the recognition that the rights of the individual members were limited to their shares in the property of the family, the appropriation of which was under the control of the head, and that the welfare of each member was bound up in that of the family. Thus each group formed in itself a small combination for mutual assistance and support. As time went on the gradual centralization of the government in the hands of various large landowners and, later, of the Carlovingian emperors, reduced the power exercised by the heads of the families in the management of the affairs of the tribes, with the result that the families began to lose their power and, consequently, could exercise less direct control over the members. Further, under the increase of civilization and the influx of newer ideas through trade intercourse, etc., the members of the family acquired less localized interests and the families grew larger and less closely knit together by constant intercourse; they also became less cohesive through the various members having gradually acquired special interests mutually inconsistent and requiring closer and more intimate connection between individuals of the various families. The unattached population of the tribal districts gradually increased; slaves and freedmen were added to their numbers; a continually growing number of people became separated from families either by being born in illegal marriage, or by having no living kindred, or by expulsion or voluntary withdrawal from their families; and strangers settled among the descendants of earlier inhabitants with the result that the tie of clan or family gradually changed into that of mutual interest or work.

Gradual change of unit bound by family ties to that bound by mutual interest.

The result of this change was the gradual transformation of a community made up of self-contained family units to one in which the unit was either the natural one of the family or the artificial one of the gild or society containing as members those who, though not related by blood, were bound together by their mutual interests.

Earliest form of gild.

These gilds or societies were in their earliest form merely collections of men who met more or less casually to discuss matters in which they were interested, such as their trade, handicraft, religion, etc.

Opposition of rulers to gilds.

Simultaneously with, and contributory to the change in the form of association of the members of these societies, the government had become more localized and more in the hands of an oligarchy rather than of the representatives of the families and, consequently, instead of being the direct outcome of the wishes of the people as represented by the heads of the families, became antagonistic to them. This led to the next step in the development of the gild, namely, the recognition of the value of the force they could exert in dealing with the government by the pressure they could bring to bear on behalf of their members if they adopted the system of mutual support and assistance as between the members of each such society. Then came the adoption of mutual sharing of loss falling on individuals by all the members of the society, which is, with certain modifications, not only the position taken by each gild and trade union of to-day, but also the root from which sprang the whole system of "Mutual Assurance."

Recognition by gild members of power acquired by combination.

Mutual sharing of loss.

Reasons for keeping internal affairs secret.

In the earliest stages of the development of societies founded on mutual interest, as opposed to the tie of family, membership in such societies must have been made up largely of those who were not bound to their family either because the family from which they had sprung had become so scattered or broken or low in the social scale that it could not afford to the members the support they required, or because they had been expelled from the family for conduct or opinions contrary to those held by the majority of the members; or of those who had no family (such as freedmen or strangers or men of foreign ancestry attracted to the country by trade or other advantages). Such collections of persons who were outside the pale of the older families would be regarded with suspicion both by the members of families still in existence and by the rulers of the land. Whence the societies adopted a certain quasi-secret method of conducting their rites, meetings, etc., which was rendered even more necessary by the gradual transfer of the government to territorial lords, who were naturally antagonistic to any social movement which tended to strengthen the power of the people as opposed to their own. Further, as any disputes or lawsuits arising between members of the gild would afford a *locus ingerendi* for the government, and a consequent weakening of the power of the gild, it was forced upon the members of each gild in such a way to arrange their internal affairs as to retain the power of awarding sanctions for all causes of dispute among members or for any action on the part of one or more individual members which might tend to prejudice the working efficiency of the society.

The means they adopted for this end, as shown by the earliest records of such societies, was the imposition of a binding oath on all members to keep the transactions of the gild absolutely confidential and to obey implicitly the rulings of the executive body.

(2) THE GILDS (*Geldonia*) OF MEMPISC, FLANDERS, ETC.

Gilds providing mutual help in case of misfortune, fire or wreck.

These gilds were the means by which the lower classes of freemen and also slaves endeavoured to protect themselves against oppression by the great territorial lords and also against the losses arising from fire, the loss of a boat or ship by shipwreck, misfortune, etc. They were, in short, clubs or societies for the purpose of the mutual insurance of members. Though little is known of the methods on which they were formed and conducted, yet it is clear that they were originally organized as secret societies and their members were required to take an oath of fealty to the gild and to their fellow-members. They also bound themselves to obey the statutes of the gild. They were obliged to subscribe periodically to the chest of the society, and these subscriptions were accumulated to form a fund from which the claims of members were met. These societies resembled in some ways the *collegia*[1] of the Romans in that each was composed of men of much the same rank of life, generally, if not entirely, belonging to the lower ranks, and interested in the same trade or work. A further point of resemblance is that in both cases periodic subscriptions were payable by the members.[2] Here, however,

Resemblance of gilds to Roman *collegia*.

[1] See Chapters XVI–XIX.
[2] Wauters: *Les Libertés communales*, p. 136.

the points of similarity end. They were dissimilar in their objects. The Roman *collegia* were largely devoted to the cults of the respective patron divinities and, apart from the societies providing *funeraticia* and military societies, provided no form of mutual insurance. The gilds of Flanders, etc., were on the other hand but little interested in religious observances and did not, as far as is known, provide burial expenses for their members; their chief object being the promotion by combination of the mutual welfare of their members and mutual insurance against certain risks. That these gilds were very numerous and that the mutual insurance side of their transactions was generally known and approved by the authorities, is clearly shown by the legislation of the Carlovingian emperors,[1] under which,

Points of difference between gilds and *collegia.*

[1] See *Patrologiæ Cursus Completus*, ed. by Migne (J. P.).

(*a*) CHARLEMAGNE: *Capitulare Francicum*, A.D. 779, s. 16. De sacramentis per gildonia invicem coniurantibus, ut nemo facere præsumat. Alio vero modo de illorum elemosinis, aut de incendio, aut de naufragio, quamvis convenentias faciant, nemo in hoc iurare præsumat.

(*b*) CHARLEMAGNE: *Capitulare Francofurtense*, A.D. 794, s. 31. De coniurationibus et conspirationibus, ne fiant; et ubi sunt inventæ destruantur.

(*c*) HLUDOWICI I: *Capitulare ad Theodonis villam.*, Oct. 821, s. 7. De coniurationibus servorum quæ fiunt in Flandris et Mempisco et in cæteris maritimis locis, volumus ut per missos nostros indicetur dominis servorum illorum, ut constringant eos, ne ultra tales coniurationes facere præsumant. Et ut sciant ipsi eorundem servorum domini quod cuiuscumque servi huiuscemodi coniurationem facere præsumpserint postquam eis hæc nostra iussio fuerit indicata, bannum nostrum, id est sexaginta solidos, ipse dominus persolvere debeat.

(*d*) HLUDOWICI I et HLOTHARII I: *Ansegisi Capitularia*, A.D. 827, III, 9. *De conspirationibus.* Et ut de cætero in regno nostro nulla huiusmodi conspiratio, nec per sacramentum, nec sine sacramento fiat.

And

(*e*) IV, 7. *De coniurationibus servorum in Flandris et in Mempisco et in ceteris maritimis locis.* (Verbatim as (*c*).)

(*f*) HLOTHARI I: *Constitutiones Papienses.* Feb. 832, s. 6. (Quasi-verbatim as (*d*).)

(*g*) HLUDOWICI II: *Imp. Constitutiones. Mantuæ*, 856, s. 12. Similiter et de conspirationibus nocivis iuxta capitulare emendent.

(*h*) *Adnuntiationes domni* HLUDOWICI *regis.* Jun. 860, s. 7. Similiter et de conspirationibus . . . ut nullus hoc in regnis nostris agere præsumat. Et si quis hoc præsumpserit, secundum legem, et sicut in capitularibus progenitorum nostrorum continetur, sic hoc emendare cogatur.

(*i*) *Adnuntiatio* KAROLI II. Jun. 860, s. 6. . . . et de coniurationibus et conspirationibus . . . firmiter banniverunt ut amodo et deinceps nullus præsumat. . . .

(*k*) HLUD. KAR. II and HLOT. II: *Summa Capitulorum quæ apud*

although it is expressly stated that no one should dare to take an oath in respect of membership of such gilds, yet it is clearly indicated that no objection was taken to the gilds themselves, nor to their aims. It is obvious also from the references to the gilds in the Capitularia of the Carlovingians that in the eye of the law the only important features about the gild were the oath which was absolutely forbidden and the mutual insurance which was indirectly regarded with approval.

Laws of Carlovingian Emperors in respect of gilds.

From this it may be gathered that there were in the 8th century A.D. very many groups of men who had voluntarily become members of societies, of which the principal object was the provision of mutual indemnification against loss; that these societies were self-governing and kept their internal proceedings as far as possible from the knowledge and governance of the authorities, and that the law regarded with the sternest disapproval all such societies in which the members bound themselves by oath. The first reference to these gilds is contained in the Capitulare Francicum, dated A.D. 779, which prohibits the combination of people bound together by oaths for the purpose of affording mutual protection against misfortune, fire or shipwreck, but the injunction is against the taking of the oath, not against the mutual insurance. Presumably the reason for the prohibition was the fear that such societies, having a secret membership bound by oath, might acquire a power in politics which could be used to the detriment of the landed proprietors. Whatever the reason was, it was held to be sufficiently important to necessitate further prohibitions in 794, 821, 827, 832, 856, 860, 864, 898, etc. From these continual quotations it is clear that the custom of joining and forming gilds had

Gilds autonomous and secret.

Very numerous and important in 8th and 9th centuries.

confluentes modo accepta sunt . . . Jun. 860, s. 4. . . . a coniurationibus et conspirationibus . . . se omnes caveant. . . .

(*l*) LAMBERTI Imp. *Conventus Ravennas*. Oct. 898, s. 9. Vestræ igitur maiestati non manet incognitum, qualiter illicitas coniunctiones Romani et Longobardi, simul et Franci . . . facere præsumpsere . . . petimus, ut sicut a vestris antecessoribus imperatoribus prohibitum est, ne quoque modo fierent, ita . . . prohibeantur. . . .

become very general and *a fortiori* that they filled a very definite want.

Development of *keuren* from gilds.

These gilds, although not encouraged by the territorial lords, lasted until the 11th century, when gradually a change was introduced into the system of government of the villages which in many cases rendered the gilds unnecessary in so far as mutual insurance was concerned. At that time it became customary for the inhabitants of many of the villages and towns of Flanders, Mempisc, etc., to form themselves into a community obeying their own local laws, which, in the earlier instances at least, were drawn up by the community and were obeyed by the members although they had not received the sanction of the territorial lords; later the overlords ceased to oppose the formation of local communities autonomous in respect of their internal economy, and gradually became favourably disposed towards them. The result of this change was that during the 11th century many of these village communities, for the most part in return for services rendered, received charters from the overlords sanctioning their local customary law, and increasing the authority of these communities by giving them powers of punishment and by the introduction of other law, such as Roman Law, and by the widening of their scope, rendering them more efficient in the pursuit of their various functions. In some of these charters the question of mutual insurance, which had formed an important part of the objects of the gild, was omitted; the mutual benefits provided for being those of mutual support, assistance in business, and the support of the society in disputes with non-members. Among these was the *Amitié d'Aire* [1] or Brotherhood of Aire, of which the charter was sanctioned by Robert II and Clemence his wife, about A.D. 1100. This charter contains a paragraph dealing with the indemnification of a fellow-member whose house was burnt, or who, having fallen into captivity, had paid as ransom the greater part of his property. To such an unfortunate member of the community each of his fellow-members was obliged to pay one piece of silver.

Charter of *Amitié d'Aire.*

[1] Cf. Wauters: *Les Libertés communales en Belgique*, p. 355.

Another form of mutual insurance was provided under *La Charte de la Confrérie de la Charité de Valenciennes,* dated 1070, which provided that if the merchandise of one of the members was seized through no fault of his, all who were there at the time ought to contribute and indemnify him in proportion to the amount which they brought with them.

Other similar charters.

Other village brotherhoods received charters about this time containing similar laws to those of the *Amitié d'Aire.* Such were the charter of Granmont, granted in 1067–1070, and of the *Amitiés* of Gand and Bruges, of which the names still exist in the Minnemeersch and Minnewater respectively (*Minne* being the Flemish equivalent for *Amitié*).[1]

These brotherhoods or communities gradually became more powerful and were, as far as their domestic affairs were concerned, autonomous, being entirely free to act within the powers conferred on them by their charters. These charters became known in the 13th century as *keuren.* These keuren consisted of the laws of each town, granted or confirmed by the Court. They contained the fundamental rules of the public and criminal law of the respective towns and of their judicial organization and procedure; they were mostly confirmations of the old customary laws, as is shown by the continual use of the phrases "*ce sont les usages,*" "*l'usage est tel,*" "*d'après l'usage,*" etc. They also provided for the conduct of the civil administration of the towns.[2]

Fire insurance under *keuren.*

The next step in the development of insurance against fire in Flanders is found in the *keuren,* dating from the first half of the 13th century. In the *keure* of Veurnambacht[3] it is seen that the person whose house is burnt down by a fire was to be indemnified

[1] Cf. Poperinghe, granted in A.D. 1110.
Namur, granted in 1121, confirmed in A.D. 1151.

[2] Cf. Warnkoenig: *Histoire de la Flandre,* etc., Vol. II, pp. 298, etc.; and Poullet, E.: *Histoire politique nationale,* Vol. I, p. 62.

[3] La *Keure* de Veurnambacht, dated 1240. "In quacunque villa combustio facta fuerit occulte, tota villa statim solvat dampnum per illos quos eligent coratores . . ." See Gilliodts v. Severen, *Coutumes, etc., de Furnes,* Tom. III, p. 30.

without delay by the whole village for his loss and was to be paid by the officers elected by the village to serve as *ceurherrs* (or *coratores*). A similar clause is found in the *keure* of Bergues, Bourbourg, and Furnes.[1] These provisions will be found on consideration to be of importance, as they mark a complete change in the procedure. In the case of the early *keuren*, such as the *Amitié d'Aire*, there was no mention as to the cause of the fire; there was also the personal element of each individual bringing a certain fixed contribution to the aid of the impoverished member, and the fact that, in all probability, the sum subscribed was considerably less than the loss incurred. In the later *keuren* these gild-like characteristics had been altered and indemnification was due only if the cause of the fire was unknown and was carried out by the accredited officers of the commune, who, presumably, assessed the damage and also the proportion to be paid by each member of the community. A very good example of the procedure of these village communities in respect of provision against loss from fire is to be found in the Chronicles of the Abbey of St. Nicolas of Furnes, and consists of (*a*) a charter[2] dated 1241 which grants to the abbey the right, subject to the consent and wish of the échevins and *ceurherrs* of Furnes, of being under the same condition and protection against fire as were the lay dwellers in Furnes, provided that the abbey bore its

Fire insurance limited to fires of unknown origin.

Procedure in respect of fire insurance became more businesslike.

[1] La *Keure* de Furnes, Bergues et Bourbourg, dated 1240. "In quacunque villa combustio fuerit facta occulte, tota villa . . ." etc., as in note 3, p. 253. See Conssemaker (I. de), *Annal. du Com. Fl. de France*, Tom. V, p. 188. (A *keure* was granted to Furnes by the Countess Gertrude in 1109. See Warnkœnig, Vol. II, p. 310.)

[2] Summa et confirmacio Thome Comitis et Johanne Comitisse de bonis et libertatibus nostris. "Concessimus preterea eidem ecclesiæ beati Nicolai, de concensu et voluntate scabinorum et coratorum Furnensium, ut sit eiusdem condicionis et protectionis cujus sunt laici in terra Furnensi, quantum ad combustiones occulte contingentes, si tamen ipsa ecclesia pro rata sua et legitima portione bonorum que in villa habuerit in qua continget combustio, voluerit solvere dampna combustionum aliorum. In cuius rei testimonium presentem paginam eidem tradidimus ecclesie sigillorum nostrorum munimine roboratam. Actum anno Domini M°CC°XLI° in vigilia beate Lucie virginis." Charter of Abbey of St. Nicolas of Furnes, p. 97. (See Bibliography, St. Nicolas, etc.)

share *pro rata* in the losses of others caused by fire; (*b*) a letter[1] from the échevins and *ceurherrs* of Furnes, dated December, 1241, stating that the abbey, having obtained the consent of the Count and Countess, would be admitted to a mutual insurance against fire with the lay inhabitants of the district on the understanding that the abbey should contribute *pro rata* in respect of the losses incurred by the lay inhabitants through fires of unknown origin. Similar permission was granted by Count Guido in 1269—in a charter headed "Summa et confirmatio Guidonis comitis de bonis et libertatibus monasterii nostri." [2]

Contributions from persons insured to be *pro rata* with value of their property.

From these extracts it is clear that a well-arranged system of mutual insurance against fire was in force in the district around the Abbey of St. Nicolas of Furnes in 1241, that it was municipal and subject to the control of the échevins and *ceurherrs*; moreover the presumption of its having been of long standing prior to that date is rendered almost a certainty by the fact that it had been in force sufficiently long to have acquired the dignity of being considered a necessary and valuable public institution, that the authorities had learned

[1] Littere Scabinorum et coratorum Furnensis de combustione occulte contingente. "Nos scabini et coratores terre Furnensis, notam facimus universis presentes litteras inspecturis, quod ecclesia beati Nicolai Furnensis de consensu dompni comitis et dompne comitisse et nostro, eiusdem est protectionis cuius sunt laici in terra Furnensi quantum ad combustiones occulte contingentes, hoc notato quod abbas et conventus eiusdem ecclesie nobis promiserunt, quod pro rata sua et legitima portione omnium bonorum que habuerit in villa in qua continget combustio, solvet dampna combustionum aliorum per illos quos eligent coratores. Et quia sigillum proprium non habemus presentes litteras in huius rei testimonium eidem ecclesie tradendas sigillis Wilhelmi de Ostkerka balivi nostri et dompni Riquardi Blavoet militis et Wilhelmi filii dompni Stephani, conscabinorum et concoratorum nostrorum fecimus roborari. Actum anno Domini M°CC°XLI° mense decembri." Cartulaire de l'Abbaye S. Nicolas Furnensis, p. 195.

[2] Summa et confirmatio Guidonis comitis de bonis et libertatibus monasterii nostri. . . . Concessimus etiam eidem ecclesie beati Nicolai, de concensu et voluntate scabinorum et coratorum Furnensium, ut sit eiusdem condicionis et protectionis cuius sunt laici in terra Furnensi, quantum ad combustiones occulte contingentes, si tamen ipsa ecclesia pro rata sua et legitima portione bonorum que in villa habuerit in qua continget combustio, soluere voluerit dampna combustionum aliorum. In cuius rei testimonium et munimen, presentem paginam eidem tradidimus ecclesie sigilli nostri appensione roboratam. Datum anno Domini M°CC°LX nono, feria quarta post Ramos palmarum, mense aprili. Cart. de l'A.S.N. Furn., p. 109.

the necessity of stipulating that only losses arising from fires "occulte contingentes" would be insured against, and that the abbey, if it wished to partake of the benefits of membership, must undertake to subscribe *pro rata* in the case of indemnification of losses borne by others. Thus the old idea of brotherhood and the recognition of the duty of assisting a fellow-member had been dropped and the whole question of mutual insurance had become a part of the municipal or communal system and was as much a matter of business as any other of the municipal duties attaching to the community. The omission of all reference to mutual insurance against poverty, caused by misfortune or payment of ransom, was probably the outcome of this development of business in place of sentiment.

Hamelinghe or the insurance of live-stock.

Another form of mutual insurance, namely, that of live-stock, was also provided by the *keuren*. Section number 24 of the *keure* dated March 5, 1266, granted to the villages of Nord and Zudschoote by their overlord, the Abbess of Messines, reads as follows:—"Ki * autrui beste afole par malisse kon claime hamelinghe, il est a soisante sols et si rent le beste," [1] which means that the person who maliciously *afole* [2] the cattle of another and thus permits him to claim *Hamelinghe*, is to be fined sixty sols in addition to the value of, or replacing, the animal. This "*Hamelinghe*" is the term applied to the indemnification of the loser of cattle, who, on making a claim in the manner prescribed by custom, was entitled to indemnification by his fellow-villagers in a similar way to the person who lost his house by fire. There are several other references to this "Insurance of Live-stock," among which the best found are:—

[1] Cf. A parallel form of mutual insurance against loss of cattle is found in the laws of Athelstane (Schmid: *Gesetze der Angelsachsen*, pp. 165–169, *Judicia civitatis Lundiniæ*, 2), which reads:—

"Diximus, ut unusquisque nostrum ponat unum denarium ad nostrum commune commodum, et persolvamus omne pecus, quod captum est, postquam pecuniam nostram contulimus, et habeamus nobis omnes eam inquisitionem communitur, et conferat omnis homo denarium suum, qui habet pecus xxx denarios valens . . ."

[2] Afoler = to beat, injure, or kill.

* Gilliodts v. Severen, *Coutumes, etc. 'de Furnes*, Tome III, p. 58.

[Note however that the ordonnance referred to on the following page appears to be merely a French version of the above keure.—Edd.]

(1) In an Ordonnance of Margaret, Countess of Flanders, dated 1265.[1] In this Ordonnance direct reference is made to the custom of *Hamelinghe* and it is ordered that the échevins of Messines should themselves settle all the cases for which provision was made (par la présente ordonnance), but that any case which might arise too difficult for them to deal with was to be sent to Furnes to be settled there. In this ordonnance it is noticeable that the custom of *Hamelinghe* at St. Nicolas of Furnes was regarded as well-known and stable and the abbey considered, as it were, a court of appeal on the question.

(2) In the Records of St. Nicolas of Furnes under the date 1292, where there is a letter[2] in which the custom of

[1] Diegerick: Inventaire analyt. et chronol. des chartes etc. de l'ancienne abbaye de Messines, p. 65. Ordonnance by Margaret Ctsse de Flandre. "Pour celui qui blesse méchamment les bêtes d'autrui, ce qu'on appelle Hamelinghe. Pour tous les délits non prévus par la présente ordonnance les échevins suivront ce qui se pratique à Furnes." If the case was difficult they were instructed to go to Furnes, where the practice was thoroughly understood and provided for. Cost of journey was charged to condemned.

[2] Littere scabinorum et coratorum Furnensium de hameling nobis indotate.

Nous Jehans Reifin, Jehans li Noirs, Carens du Bruec, chevalier, Gilles Veize, Lamberts Reinare, David Sporkin, Jehans de Score, Xpelos Bruninc, Jehans Zac de Pervize, et Mickiex li maires, eschevin et courreur dou terroir de Furnes, faisons savoir a tous cheaus qui ces presentes lettres veiront ou ouront, que comme il soit ensy que uns poutreins avoit este naureis et celeirement tues dedens le paroiche de saint Nicolai de Furnes boosterpoort hoirs de le banlieue de le vile de Furnes, li quels apartenoit a monseigneur labei et au convent de S. Nicolas de Furnes, et il soit costume et usaigie dedens le dit tieroir de Furnes ou quel le dite proffie siet et est, que tout chil qui i demorent et apartienent doivent payer hamelingh, communement selonc chou kon les damagies taille qui avienent dedens le dit tieroir et la dite proffe par hamelinghen a chaus qui les damagies aient et a le hamelinghen apartiennent. Et mesires li abbes et li convens de S. Nicolas devant dit soient venu pardevant nous en vierscare bannie et en plaine loy et avoient demandeit et requis par droit et par loy que nous pour chou quil sont et ont este en le hamelinghen de sy loingtains dont il nest memoire, et en ont argent paiet et leveit et en sont bien chartreit de nos trechiers seigneurs contes et contesses de Flandres, et le queil ils ont bien usee par tout si comme corfren dou dit tieroir leur feciessiemes par echevins et courieurs le dite hamelinghen cognoistre se hamelinghen i avoit selonc le loy dou tieroir devant dit et leur fecismes pris et tayer selonc le loy dou dit tieroir leur poutrein devant dit, et que nous sognute le hamelinghen apres chou prissiemes taillieurs en la dite proffie pour taillier et payer a eaus leur poutrain devant nomme. Et faite pardevant nous ceste demande et requeste de monseigneur labei et le convent devant dit ensy comme devant est dit, Estiennes fieux Katerine parrochiens de le dite prochie S. Nicolas bosterport venoit en vierscare bannie et en plaine loy pardevant nous et se mist en encontre et disoit par ampleur et conseil,

Hamelinghe is explained. Under this custom a tax was levied on every one in the territory of Furnes, from the proceeds of which tax the loss of live-stock was made good. In this charter the custom is shown to be of old standing by the statement of the Abbey and the Convent of St. Nicolas of Furnes to the effect that they had both subscribed to and received money from the *Hamelinghe* tax from time immemorial. Allowing for a little natural exaggeration, this statement, combined with the reference to the custom in the Ordonnance of the Countess Margaret, is almost proof that the custom had been in force for many years, the more especially so as the Abbey of St. Nicolas of Furnes had kept careful records of its doings from the date of its foundation, as is shown by the Chronicles, etc., still in existence.

Marine insurance not referred to in *keuren*. Reasons therefor.

It has probably been noticed that no traces of mutual insurance against shipwreck have been found in the *keuren*, although this branch of insurance was provided for in the gilds. This is probably due to (1) the fact that all the above communities were inland and consequently would not have required to insure their members against shipwreck, and (2) the difficulty of mutually insuring ships and freight of greatly varying values, as it is clear that the subscription of one piece of silver would not meet the loss of a large

quil ne doient point estre oy en leur demande et requeste par celle raison quil nestoient point ne avoyent este en le hamelinghen devant dite. Et nous eschevin et corieur devant nomme oyes les demandes requestes et responses del une partye et de lautre, et quant lune partie avoyt eut conseil encontre al autre par le loy del dit tieroir sur leur demandes, resquestes et responses entendu le bonne verite de toutes les chozes devant dites et pour chou que chiex Estienes se trahit arriere, et ne vaut venir avant en iugement rendismes no iugement per coniurement de Jehans Spade no subailiu qui plain poor avoit de nous coniureir ; et dismes par droit iugement que la demande et requeste de monsingneur labei et dou couvent estoit et est loyale souffissance et droituriere, et que les dis Estienenes devoit keir en amende, et que il etoit li parrochien de le dite prochie S. Nicolay boosterport devant dit demorant hors de le banlieue de Furnes doyent payer a monseignieur labei et au couvent desus dit leur poutrain devant nome. Et pour chou que che soyt ferme choze estauble bien tenue et garde, Nous Fransoys Pisson, baillius de Furnes, Jehans Spade, no soubailius, avons mis nos seaux aveuc les seaux des eschevins et courieurs devant nomeis, a ches presentes lettres qui furent faites et donnes en l'an de grace mil CC° quatre vins et douse, le jeusdy apres l'assumption Nostre Dame el mois daoust.—*Cart. de l'A.S.N. Furn.*, p. 195.

trader. In any case, as will be shown, marine insurance was dealt with by merchants who, in most cases, underwrote the amount of risk they were prepared to take. Another necessary form of insurance, namely, that of goods in transit by land and when kept at fairs, was provided by the territorial lords.

Combination of small communities under central authority.

Returning to the *keuren* of the 13th century, and tracing their next development, it is found that by the middle of the 14th century many of the smaller communities joined and merged into larger districts, all the villages in the district being obedient to the statutes of that district. The best-known case of this amalgamated government is that of the *Statut du Mont d'Hazebrouck*, dated 1340.[1] In this Statute provision is made for the indemnification of loss caused by fire, provided that the fire was of external origin and that the demand for indemnification was made in accordance with the law of the country.[2] This again shows a development, as, owing to the increase of the number of houses at risk, and *pari passu* of the number of properties which were liable to contribute in case of a fire, the risks and contributions were spread over a larger area, and, consequently, the liability of having to subscribe large sums in respect of any one fire became less. Another point to be noticed is the change of the condition attaching to the way in which the fire originated. In the early brotherhoods there was no reference to the cause of the fire, then in the *keuren* it was sufficient for the origin of the fire to be unknown, whereas under this Statute the fire must have occurred from without the house. These Statutes and *keuren* remained in force for several centuries.

Statut du Mont d'Hazebrouck.

Fire insurance under *Statut du Mont d'Hazebrouck* limited to fires of external origin.

[1] De Coussemaker (I.): *Annales du Comité Flamand*, Vol. XI, p. 188, defines the Hoop d'Hazebrouck as "une assemblée générale des échevins d'un certain nombre de communes indépendentes les unes des autres, mais liées ou associées entre elles dans un intérêt mutuel ou réciproque."

[2] *Op. cit.*, p. 262. Article 55: "Verborne iemens huus ende tfier came van buten, de meentucht van den dorpe zonden him zine scade ghelden, indien dat hyt bezochte ter wet van den brande."

From the evidence adduced above it is clear that mutual combinations to insure against loss arising from fire, shipwreck, damage to live-stock, seizure of merchandise, and captivity were formed at a very early age in Flanders and that they lasted in an altered form and with more restricted insurance operations until the late Middle Ages. It is proposed now to examine a species of proprietary insurance against damage to goods belonging to merchants visiting the country for purposes of trade.

CHAPTER XXIV

NON-MUTUAL INSURANCE BETWEEN 1227 AND 1310

Insurance of merchants in return for payment of *dorpinghe* or *pertusage*.
1. By Abbess of Messines, 1227.

THE earliest reference to any form of non-mutual guarantee against loss in return for a payment practised in Belgium to be found in the Archives of the Abbeys of Flanders is contained in the Records of the Abbey of Messines,[1] and consists of letters from the échevins of Bruges and Ypres in reference to the *tonlieu* (a species of octroi or duty) to be paid by merchants attending the fair[2] at Messines. In this document, dated A.D. 1227, it is stated that the merchants in general should pay a tax of four deniers, called *dorpinghe* or *pertusage*, except merchants from Bruges, Ypres, etc., who should only pay two deniers. In return for this payment the merchants should not only be permitted to bring their goods to the fair and to deal in them there, but it was also expressly stipulated that " l'Abbesse prendra sous sa protection pendant toute la durée de la foire les merchands et les merchandaises . . ." and " elle fera rendre justice à leurs réclamations." From this agreement it is clear that the Abbess, in effect, insured the safety of the merchants and their goods during the fair and bound herself to meet, or to cause others to meet, their claims for losses, if any. Against regarding this transaction as a type of insurance it may be urged that the undertaking is of too indefinite a character to be so advanced, and that the protection afforded by the Abbess was but the usual protection afforded to visiting merchants by the supreme authority. Granting that this objection is true, there yet

[1] See Bibliography—Diegerick, *Inventaire*, etc., p. 49.
[2] For description of these fairs, see De Coussemaker (I.): *Étude sur les privilèges, lois et coutumes de la ville de Bailleul*, pp. 146, etc.

remains a clear proof that the guarantee of the local authority to shelter and protect the merchants against possible loss or injustice was offered as a part return for the payment of certain fees. Had the matter been arranged so that the merchants paid (say) a moiety of the prescribed fees to the Abbess for enjoying the right to trade and the balance to a capitalist on the understanding that he should hold himself responsible for the safety of the merchants and their merchandise during the fair, the second transaction could be regarded as nothing but an insurance against personal ill-treatment and injustice towards the merchants and against loss, if any, which might arise in so far as the goods were concerned. This being so it is suggested that the undertaking of the Abbess was cognate to an agreement to insure such merchants as came to the fair and paid the prescribed *tonlieu*. Further, this transaction, not being reciprocal, if it can be considered as a form of insurance, is clearly a form of capitalist insurance.

2. By Duke of Limbourg, 1248.

More definite is the statement in the letter,[1] dated January 12, 1248, of the Duke Waleram of Limbourg in reference to the merchants travelling between the rivers Meuse and Rhine, and in doing so crossing his territory. In it are set the various rates to be paid, in return for which permission was given to traverse the territory specified, and in addition the Duke stated: " Ita ut quicquid dampni eisdem mercatoribus sive hominibus, in personis, bonis sive rebus, infra dictos fines sive terminos acciderit, illud eisdem integraliter restituemus et emendari plenarie faciemus."

3. By the Lady de la Wastine and the Lord of Ghistelles, 1298.

A similar undertaking to protect and indemnify against loss those merchants who paid duty was imposed on Bruges by a charter granted to the city by Isabella, Lady de la Wastine, and her son John, Lord of Ghistelles, on December 1, 1298.[2] In this charter the right of levying a duty of two *sols* on each " tonnel de vins rygnois " was granted to the city on the understanding that the city " tuitierent . . . à tous jours plainement chascun en droit de lui."

[1] Eerstenwittenboeck, AA, fol. 46 (see Warnkœnig, Vol. II, p. 443).
[2] G. v. S.: *Ville de Bruges*, Tom. 2, p. 104.

From the consideration of these three different methods of affording or providing indemnification against various risks of loss, it is clear that the country people of Belgium and, consequently, the merchants of Bruges must have been in full possession of a practical knowledge of the advantages and disadvantages of insurance. Whence it would appear probable that some such practice for the insurance of goods was in existence in Bruges during the 12th and 13th centuries. Passing to the consideration of the early capitalist marine insurance of merchandise in Bruges, it is found that there is evidence (which, being of date much posterior to that of the reputed matter to which it refers, if taken by itself, is perhaps not entirely convincing) that a company for the sale of policies of insurance of merchandise against marine or other risks was founded under Ducal Charter at Bruges in 1310. This evidence has been held by M. Pardessus and others to be too unsupported to carry much weight, but, as will be shown below, it is probable that the statement is absolutely correct.

Insurance company founded at Bruges, under Charter, 1310.

CHAPTER XXV

MARINE INSURANCE

Marine insurance general in Western Europe in 14th century

LEAVING the consideration of the evidence as to the foundation of a Chamber of Insurance at Bruges for the present and proceeding to the earliest mention of marine insurance in extant records of date contemporary with the transaction referred to therein, namely, to a judgment of undoubted authenticity of the College of Échevins of the City of Bruges recorded in the Ouden Wittenbouc and dated April 12, 1377,[1] evidence of a trustworthy nature is found of an action based on a contract of marine insurance. This entry in the city records sets out the judgment given by the échevins on an action brought by the insured under a charter "van zecggerscepe" to recover the value of certain parcels of silks and stuffs, "van diverse parcele van ziden, van flourschen gaerne ende van witten ende blaewen lynwade," which had been lost and were covered by the policy of insurance referred to. The judgment of the College was that the insurer be condemned to pay to the insured an indemnity for the loss of the various articles of merchandise set out in the claim. This judgment is recorded as that of an ordinary item of the business of the College and, by the absence of any explanatory phrases, shows clearly that the practice of insurance was understood thoroughly by all parties. From this record it is shown that in 1377 in the City of Bruges (*a*) the practice of insuring against marine risks was of considerable age or at least that it had passed out of the stage of being a novelty in business and legal circles (*b*) the insurance was a true one, i.e. a contract to indemnify the insured against the loss of

Bruges. Judgments given in actions arising from marine insurance, 1377.

[1] G. v. S. *Ville de Bruges*, Tom. 2, p. 104.

certain specified articles and, therefore, not a wager; and (*c*) the contract was not one of mutual insurance, as had it been mutual, the action would not have been between two individuals, unless it be assumed that two individuals had mutually agreed to be responsible for each other's losses, which is much less likely to have been the case than that it was a contract of what has been defined as capitalist insurance. It having thus been proved that capitalist insurance of marine risks was in A.D. 1377 understood thoroughly well in commercial and legal circles and had become so common as to obviate the necessity of any definition of the technical words used and of the form of contract, and that, consequently, it had been in force for some considerable time, the probability that the statement referred to above, as to the foundation of an insurance company in 1310, is based on fact is much enhanced. This statement is found in the *Chronyke van Vlaenderen*, which was published in 1735, and may be translated as follows:—

Insurance company at Bruges, 1310.

Chronyke van Vlaenderen.

"At the request of the inhabitants of Bruges, in the year 1310, he (Count Robert of Flanders) sanctioned the establishment in this town of a Chamber of Insurance wherein merchants might be able to insure their merchandise against risks, marine or otherwise, at a cost of a few deniers per cent., as is the practice to-day. Moreover, lest an undertaking of such value to merchants should be dissolved as soon as it was established he made various laws and forms which both the insurers (i.e. the company) and the merchants (i.e. the insured) were bound to observe."

Arguments adduced by Pardessus against reliability of *Chronyke van Vlaenderen.*

The question as to the truth of this entry in the *Chronyke van Vlaenderen* has been examined in great detail by M. Pardessus,[1] who, in Vol. I, states that he does not consider that reliance can be placed thereon and gives the following reasons for his opinion. 1. That as the Chronicle was not written by an author contemporary with the event it cannot be held unassailable, especially as there is no confirmatory evidence extant by which it may be supported. 2. That if the Chamber of Insurance had been founded in

[1] Pardessus: *Lois Maritimes*, Vol. I, p. 356.

1310 in Bruges, it is improbable that it could have fallen into forgetfulness among people who were, during the 14th century and subsequently, devoted to commerce. 3. That if the practice of insurance was so well known and of such importance then as to require special legislation, some allusion to it should have been found by him in the collections of laws, etc., referring to maritime customs in the Low Countries, examined by him. In Vol. IV, however, he states that he may have expressed himself too strongly in setting aside the idea that insurances were known in Bruges in 1310. Although still insisting that the Chronicle is too modern to deserve full confidence, he admits that there may have been traditions to which the author had access which would justify the statement. Further, after referring to the allusion to insurance in the 14th century, he admits that it is natural to believe that the practice was still more ancient (than the early part of the 14th century) "car ces documents supposent un état des choses connu et existant." Since the date of the writing of this book various other items of evidence have been discovered which enable the objections of M. Pardessus to be met more or less satisfactorily. Objection No. 1 is nullified to a great extent by the proof (shown above) that the practice of mutual insurance against fire, and of subscription to a fund to insure against loss of live-stock, etc., had been in constant use during the 13th century, thus showing that insurance was no new idea in the 14th; and also by the fact that direct reference is made to the foundation of the Chamber of Insurance referred to in the *Jaer-Boecken van Brugge* [1] and in *Brugschen Koophandel.* [2] Were it not that both of the books mentioned are of later date than the *Chronyke van Vlaenderen* and

Reply to Pardessus.

Further evidence.

[1] Custis: *Jaer-Boecken d.s. Brugge,* T. 1, p. 301. 1310. "Ten selven jaere verleende den Graeve aen die van Brugge een Octroy tot het oprechten van eene Kamer van Assurantie ofte versekeringe, aen de selve tot dien eynde verscheyde wetten voorschryvende."

[2] Beaucourt: *Brugschen Koophandel,* p. 23. "Dog om met mender gerustigheyd de commercie te konnen voortzetten, verleende den Grave *Robert van Bethune* aen de Kooplieden ten jaere 1310, een octroy tot oprgeten eene Kamer van Assurance ofte verzekeringe, aen de zelve tot dien eynde verscheyde wetten voorschryvende."

may possibly be indebted thereto for their statements, this evidence alone would appear to be sufficient to establish the point in question. It is, moreover, quite possible that all three derived their information independently from direct evidence which has since been lost sight of or destroyed.

Jaer-Boecken van Brugge and *Brugschen Koophandel.*

The second objection is met by the records of insurance contracts which were made during the 14th and 15th centuries. The mere fact that such undeniably authentic accounts of insurance proceedings were put on record is more than sufficient to show that the practice had fallen into neither oblivion nor desuetude. The third objection raised by M. Pardessus is, perhaps, a little more difficult to meet, but it may be urged that no allusion to the custom was found by him in the collection of maritime laws and writings on maritime usages because the practice of insurance was not essentially for the provision against sea risks, but was general insurance against loss of goods during transit and that, consequently, the question of insurance in Bruges was not regarded as being specially connected with the sea. Again, it may be that the Chamber of Insurance was in a position similar to that of a trading corporation under charter with its own by-laws which would be binding on the company and on its clients but not on outsiders and, consequently, not of sufficient general importance to cause them to be set out in any collection of laws. There is too a strong confirmation of the statement in a letter [1] by the

[1] Ribeiro, J. P.: *Dissertaçoes chronologicas criticas*, No. LXXXV.

Dom Joham pella graça de Deus Rey de Portugal e do Algarve, Avos Gonçalle Anes Carvalho, Juiz por nos na Cidade do Porto, e a outros quaesquer, que esto ouverem de veer, a que esta Carta for mostrada saude. Sabede que o Concelho, e homens boons dessa Çidade nos enviarom dizer, que nos tenpos dos Reys nossos anteçessores ouve na dita Çidade hordinada bolssa de çertos dinheiros, que sse lançavam, e contavam nas avalias do saveres, que sse hi carregavam em Navios pera outras partes, e dos panos que sse hy carregavam de retorno, pera sse pagar delo as despesas, que sse faziam quando envyam per a costeira do mar saber parte deses navios, e averes, se lhe alguum enbargo acontecia: assy como ora em Galiza, e outro ssy em Ingraterra, por costumes, e empossiçoens novas, que lhes demandavam, e por outros eaussos semelhantes, segundo sse senpre custumou de fazer: o qual dito direito sse nom tirou, nem rrecadou, depois que nos ouvemos estes Reignos, per rezom da guerra, e outras neçicydades, e enbargos, que sse seguirrom, e que orra, entendendo por

King of Portugal, dated 1435, in respect of the carrying on of a fund for the indemnification of merchants who might be subjected to taxes and impositions on the goods they wished to import into France and England. In this letter he refers to the existence of the fund in the times of " the Kings our ancestors." If the plural means two kings only it goes back to 1383, and if it includes five, back to 1325.

To sum up, we find that the evidence against the authenticity of the statement that a Chamber of Insurance was established in Bruges in 1310 is entirely negative and such as to have been admitted to be weak by M. Pardessus, whereas that for it consists of three pieces of direct evidence, either of which, if true, would be sufficient to prove the matter, and which may or may not have been obtained independently from original records. We further find that true mutual insurance against fire and loss of live-stock and a species of capitalist insurance had been in continual use in Belgium for very many years, and that, consequently, the value of the practice was known. Also that insurance of goods against loss in transit by land or sea was continually being practised during the 14th century and later by merchants in Bruges, Pisa, Milan, Florence, London, etc. Whence it would appear that the evidence in favour of the statement being correct is so much stronger than that against it, that it is justifiable to accept the statement as

nosso serviço, e por prol e honrra da dita Çidade acordarom de sse renovar, e poer am obra, e que por quanto alghuuns de fora da dita Çidade, que hy carregam, recusam pagar em ello, e que nos pediam por merçee, que lhes ouvessemos a ello remedio. E nos veendo o que nos pediam, teemos por bem, e mandamos-vos, que ffaçades logo chamar todos os desse Conçelho, ou a mayor parte delles per pergom, e sse todos, ou a mayor parte delles diserem, que he bem tirar-se a dito direito da bolsa, como sse sempre em tempo dos outros Reys hussou, e custumou de fazer, que ssem outro enbargo constrangades, e mandedes costranger que paguem em ello esses, que em ello assy recusarem de pagar, e fazedelhes os costrangimentos, que entenderdes, que pera ello conprem, e sobresto nom ponhades outro nenhuum enbargo, em nenhuma maneira que seja. Unde al nom façades. Dante em Santarem XI dias de Julho. El Rey o mandou per Rui Lourenço Dayam de Coymbra, Leçençiado em Degredos, e per Joham Affonsso, Scollar em Leis, sseu Vassallo, anbos do seu Desenbargo. Vasco Anes a ffez. Era de mil CCCCXXXV annos.

Cartor. da Camara do Porto, Liv. das Vereaçoes da Era 1439 fol. 41.
Senhor D. Duarte.

true and to consider that Bruges was the pioneer city to establish under charter and with its own by-laws a Chamber of Insurance—i.e. a corporation for the purpose of carrying on capitalist insurance against risks to goods in transit by land or sea. The growth of the practice during the 14th and 15th centuries is shown by the references to it in the public records. As would be expected the great majority of the cases referred to are based on contracts of marine insurance; this cannot however be considered as an indication that marine insurance was carried on alone and that no other form of insurance was in use. The reason that records of this class of contract are, practically, the only ones extant is probably due to the fact that Bruges was devoted to its mercantile marine and strove in every way to extend its business as a carrier of and dealer in sea-borne goods. Consequently actions arising out of such business would be considered of importance and placed carefully on record, in order that they might form precedents for future and similar actions. It is therefore to the record of the development of marine insurance that we must look for information as to the growth of insurance in Belgium.

Further particulars as to the practice of marine insurance in 15th century in Flanders.

In the 15th century the custom of marine insurance had become so general as to provide matter for continual lawsuits, the records of which have been preserved and serve to show that the practice had reached a state of development which is almost as advanced as that of companies of to-day, dealing with similar risks. The contract of insurance, which might be drawn up so as to guarantee indemnification for the actual loss or might be what was called *de asseurance ghevallen* or *l'assurance commise* covering the merchandise regarded as a whole, and payable in full in the case of the policy becoming a claim, was set out in an instrument known in the 14th century as a *charter van zecggerscepe* and later as a *policie d'assurance* which could be drawn up in any form suitable to an ordinary contract. It could be made in the form of a simple *cédule* or note of hand, that is to say, drawn up between the parties interested under their private seal, or by a public notary or broker (i.e. *ceurherr* or *corator*), and could also be made payable to order or not, as required. It appears, however, that all contracts of insurance were drawn up with the understanding that claims should be paid immediately on proof of loss [1] and that contra-claims for rebate, etc., could only be made subsequently to the payment of the sum payable under the policy in respect of the claim.[2]

The risks provided against under these policies were much

[1] See Reg. des Sent. Civ. in 1469–70, fol. 81, No. 5. In this case the insurer, being sued, demanded that the claim should be made in writing, " begheerde thebbene den heesch jn ghescrifte "; the insured replied that the matter of insurances was " sommaire," and that the payment (or the *nantisement*) of the sum ought to take place without writing according to custom, " dat by niet schuldich en was eeneghen heesch jn geschrifte te ghevene, mids dat zaken van asseurances zyn, maer dat de verweerere schuldich was te betalene of emmer te namptiserene jn scepenen handen van Brugghe, achtervolghende der costume."—G. v. S.: *Ville de Bruges*, II, 107.

Marc Gentil, marchand jenevois, *v.* M. Arnulphian de Luques, C. Lommelin de Jennes and A. Tany de Florence.

" A cause de certaine asseurance faicte de par ledit demandeur aux dessusdis deffendeurs et plusiers autres marchans, sur certains biens pieca chargies . . . sur la neif . . . laquelle neif estoit perie ensemble les biens estant en ycelle : Disant ledit demandeur par ce ladite asseurance estre commise, et requerrant que lesdis deffendeurs lui payassent les sommes par chacun deulx asseurees selon le contenu de la cedule de ladite asseurance par eulx soubsescripte que illec fu exhibe. Sur quoi lesdis deffendeurs respondirent, confessant ladite cedule par eulx estre soubsescripte, et quilz avoient fait ladite asseurance ; mais disoient que selon la coustume entretenue en matiere dasseurance, ledit Marc estoit tenu de ceder et transporter ausdis asseureurs deffendeurs tout le droit qu'il avoit es marchandises chargiez en son nom en le dite neif . . . pour lesdis deffendeurs en estre recouvre ce qui en est ou pourroit estre salve et peschie . . . ledit Marc disant . . . que lesdis deffendeurs lui devoient payer . . . des sommes contenues en la cedule de ladite asseurance, sans en prendre dilay, selon la coustume de tout temps." He further said that if they wished to bring an action against him they could do so " en temps et en lieu sans par ce povoir retarder la solution dicelle asseurance." 2, VI, 1459 (Reg. Sent. Civ. 1453–60, fol. 274, No. 1).—G. v. S.: *Ville de Bruges*, II, 107.

[2] Jehan Boitin, merchant of la Rochelle, *v.* Jehan Jacques Spinola, P. de Auria and G. Lommelin, merchants of Jennes.

Action brought " a cause de certaine assurance que ledit Jehan avait prinse des diz marchans, sur certaines marchandises chargees en la neif de M. Sanses de la Bargena, montant a LX de gros ; laquelle somme ledit Jehan requist avoir desdiz marchans de Jennes, pour ce que ladite neif de M. Sanses estoit en son voyage perye et perdue, selon le contenu de la cedule de ladite asseurance sur ce faite."

The merchants of Jennes were condemned to pay to J. Boitin " les sommes de la dicte asseurance, assavoir chacun deulx la somme par lui soubescripte en la cedule de la dicte asseurance."

Right was reserved to merchants of Jennes, severally and jointly, to bring forward fresh evidence within six weeks. 24, IX, 1444, Groenenbouc, A, fol. 280, No. 2.—G. v. S.: *Ville de Bruges*, II, 104.

the same as those of to-day and comprised capture by enemies or pirates,[1] shipwreck,[2] whether arising from storm at sea, from being driven on shore,[3] from inability to navigate the ship arising from bad weather, fortune of the sea, unseaworthiness of the ship[4] (if not known to the owner of the goods, etc., on which the policy had been taken out), etc. The policies, however, did not cover *fraude de ribaudise*[5] committed by the captain of the ship although the owner of the policy had no share in, or control over, the action of the captain; further, the policies would have been rendered void if the insurer could show that the insured had knowingly placed his merchandise on a ship which was

[1] "La cause et question . . . A. Ferrande, marchand de Portugal, *v.* P. Ambrosani, marchand de Venize, pour lui et ses compaignons asseureurs, deffendeurs . . . a cause de certaine asseurance faicte par ledit Pierre et ses compaignons sur la neif . . . qui avoit este prinse sur mer . . . par aucuns espaignars." 28, III, 1469 (S.C., fol. 52, No. 5).—G. v. S.: *Ville de Bruges*, II, 106.

[2] See note 5.

[3] Jean Vasques had assumed with Jacques Dorie, Merchant of Gênes, and partners "certaines merchandises de sucre chargiez en lisle de Madero en le neif appelée Fortado, dont estoit patron Alfonse Martines, appartenant audit Jean Vasques." The ship was wrecked on the English coast and Vasques claimed the amount of the assurance "qui estoit commise."

The College des Échevins ordered the payment on security being given for the restitution of the whole or part in case the insurers caused "apparoir dans les six mois prochains venans que les biens ou partie diceulx sur lesquels l'assurance fut faite, ont été sauvés et vendus par ledit patron ou maronniers de ladite neif." Dated 13, VIII, 1468.—G. v. S.: *Consulat d'Espagne à Bruges.*

[4] A similar decision was given *in re* Marc Gentil *v.* Estienne Stemmode. The first was ordered to pay the sum of ten "livres de gros" on account of a policy held by the second, wanting the proof that the latter knew at the time of taking out the policy in how bad a state his ship was, "dat scip daer de vorseide asseurance ghenomen hadde, ter tyd als die dede, dedorwen was." Dated 7 Mars 1456. (Sen. Civ. 1453–60, fol. 160, No. 3)—G. v. S.: *Ville de Bruges*, T. 2, p. 105 note.

[5] Gerard Plouvier burgeois de Bruges and Saldonne Ferrier, marchand catalan, had with "la Compagnie de George Spingle" contracted "certaine asseurance sur la nef dont estoit patron Jacques Ribys de Columen, laquelle devoit venir des parties de Catheloigne jusques au port de Lescluse," and demanded payment "selon le contenu des cedules." The defendants said that they were not bound "car le patron avoit en sondit voiage commis et perpetre fraude de ribaudise et selon la coustume sur ce entretenue, ribaudise de patron nest point comprise soubz la generalite des cedules des assurances" and offered to show proof thereof.

The College des Échevins ordered them to pay under surety and with the right to prove "dedens an et jour que le patron a fait ribaudise et fraude oudit voyage," and in this case to return the said sums to the insurers.

Gilliodts van Severen: *Cartulaire de l'ancien consulat d'Espagne à Bruges*, I, p. 76. 20, X, 1456.

unseaworthy,[1] or had made the contract fraudulently.[2] The custom of apportioning losses incurred by the throwing overboard or destroying a portion of the cargo to ensure the safety of the ship, known as " General Average," was understood and, as indicated in a case dated July 15, 1441,[3] had been practised for many years, as it was therein prescribed that the accounts should be computed according to the ancient custom.

When the policy-holder, in the event of his merchandise suffering damage, was entitled under his policy and elected to claim the total sum covered by the insurance policy, he could demand and receive this sum, but if so, was required to transfer his interest in the goods insured to the insurers.[4] Claims for payment of the total sum were granted on proof of the loss, and the insurers were obliged to pay the sum insured before entering a counter-claim for the damaged and remaining goods set out in the policy and covered by it, the insured being obliged to find surety for the delivery of such goods to the insurers, if and when their claim was made good.[5]

In the policy itself was included a schedule setting out all the items of merchandise, etc., insured thereunder, and this schedule, when the policy was signed and the contract of insurance completed, was presumably held to be sufficient evidence as to the merchandise at risk. At least there appears to have been no action brought on this point, and in every record of an action arising out of marine insurance the claim is for the payment of the sum insured " selon le contenu des cédules " or its equivalent.

[1] See note 4, p. 271.

[2] " Lesdiz de Jennes a ce respondans que point nestoient tenus a paier ladite asseurance . . . ledit Jehan avoit fait ladicte asseurance apres ce qu'il savoit que ladicte neif estoit perie . . . et par tant selon la coustume entretenue sur les asseurances, ilz nestoient point tenuz den payer quelquechose, et requerroient estre absolz. Dated 24.IX.1444 (Groenenbouc, A, fol. 280, No. 2). See note 2, p. 270.

[3] " . . . a cause des avaries desdis fers et laines, par la plaine chambre este dit et ordonne, en ensuiant ce que autresfois leur a este en semblable cas enoint que jlz compteront lesdites avaries selon la costume anchienne." 15.VII.1441 (Groenenbouc, A, fol. 264, No. 2). " . . . a cause du fret et avaries de vins." 2.III.1469 (S.C. 69–70, fol. 42, No. 1)—G. v. S.: *Ville de Bruges*, p. 109.

[4] See note 1, p. 270, case of Marc Gentil, marchand jenevois, *v.* M. Arnulphian de Luques, C. Lommelin de Jennes and A. Tany de Florence.

[5] See notes 3 and 5, p. 271.

Insurance was not confined to merchandise only, as it is seen from the action dated March 28, 1469,[1] that it was the practice of merchants to insure their ships also.

Policies of insurance were granted as a rule by merchants,[2] one or more of whom would guarantee or underwrite the policy. When several merchants were the insurers of the merchandise contained in a policy the sum due in case of loss from each individual might be limited to the amount of the risk which he had underwritten, or the signatories to the policy might be severally and jointly liable for the total sum insured.[3] There is, however, a case quoted in which the insurers are cited as the Company of George Spingle,[4] which company may have been one which carried on insurance business only, or may have been a trading company. It is impossible, of course, to draw from this record any definite conclusion of the existence of companies carrying on the business of underwriters, but taken in conjunction with the statement referred to above, that a Chamber of Marine Insurance was founded at Bruges in 1310, and also remembering that in every other case the statement of the claim on which the action rests describes the insurers as merchants, it would appear probable that companies existed in 1450 for the purpose of underwriting marine risks. In this connection a possible solution of the question raised by M. Pardessus as to the total silence in respect of the operations of the Chamber of Insurance may be advanced as follows: (1) Seeing that the only references to insurances against marine risks in the 14th and 15th centuries in Bruges are found in the records of actions arising out of such insurances, and that there are no traces of legal provision dealing with these policies, it is reasonable to assume that in the event of there being any reference to the Chamber of Insurance it

[1] See note 1, p. 270.

[2] "En la cause et question . . . pour et entre Y. Guiole, marchant de Nantes en Bretaigne, demandeur dune part: et P. Baudin, marchand de Florence, et autres marchans asseureurs, deffendeurs." 7.VIII.1469 (Sent. Civ. 1465–69, fol. 220, No. 5)—G. v. S.: *Ville de Bruges*, Tom. 2, 106.

[3] "P. van Aertrike and J. v. Voordeele demeurerent plesges et chacun pour le tout, pour A. Denis, jusques a la somme de cent livres de gros, a cause de certaines pollices dasseurances qui lui sont baillez." 17, VIII, 1468—G. v. S.: *Ville de Bruges*, T. 2, 106.

[4] See note 5, p. 271.

would be found in such records. There is, as stated by M. Pardessus, no such evidence: might this not be due to the fact that the by-laws granted to the Chamber of Insurance by Count Robert de Bethune placed them outside the jurisdiction of the Collége des Échevins and gave them the power of dealing with cases arising from their policies, or of introducing what is known to-day as the "Arbitration Clause"? (2) Assuming that the Chamber of Insurance suffered in the troubled period of the French invasion in aid of Louis of Nevers in A.D. 1328 to the extent, perhaps, of losing its charter and special privileges, it is suggested that the convenience of such a method of insuring and the profit to be derived from such a business at the rates ruling at this date (*circa* A.D. 1400) were such as to foster the formation of companies to carry on the business of underwriters. If these suggested reasons be accepted, there is no difficulty in accounting for the want of reference mentioned by M. Pardessus. Returning to the question of the merchant insurers, it is clear that these insurers were really merchants in the modern sense of the word, since we find the same individual, Marc Gentil by name,[1] appearing in two actions, in one as one of the merchant insurers, in the other as the merchant who had insured his goods. It must be remembered, however, that this form of insurance would not necessarily be in any sense mutual. Clearly if A, B, C, and F join in underwriting a ship or goods belonging to W, it is not mutual unless W is one of the insurers of each of the others, which does not appear to have been the case in any of the records of actions brought in regard to insurance contracts, as there is no allusion to any reciprocity on the part of the insured.

Reinsurances were known at this date (A.D. 1450) and were frequently made, but were usually drawn up in a form by which the reinsurers became guarantors or pledges for the due payment of the insurance money by the merchants who were insuring the goods in the first place.

In the records of the Spanish Consulate at Bruges is found

[1] See note 1, p. 270, and note 4, p. 271.

a decision,[1] dated October 7, 1447, given in an arbitration case, in which it is stated that certain merchandise which was given as security should be insured at the expense of one of the parties. As these goods were to be retained in Bruges it is clear that the insurance would have to cover risks other than marine, probably against fire, accidental damage or theft.

From the above examination of the records of the Abbeys of St. Nicolas Furnensis and Messines, of the Collège des Échevins and of the Consulat d'Espagne at Bruges, it has been shown that the practice of (1) indemnifying merchants against loss, in return for the payment of a tax called *dorpinghe* or *pertusage*, was customary in the early part of the 13th century; (2) forming mutual funds for the indemnification of subscribers against loss arising from shipwreck, captivity, fires caused by accident, and also that known as *Hamelinghe* for mutual insurance of live-stock, was well known before A.D. 1250; (3) that, probably, a Chamber of Marine Insurance had been founded in Bruges in A.D. 1310, and that the practice of underwriting policies of marine insurance had become very common and was thoroughly understood by A.D. 1400; and (4) that non-mutual insurance of goods against risks other than marine was in force not more than fifty years later. Examining again the records quoted it is noticeable that many of the merchants interested either as plaintiffs or defendants were stated to belong to Italian, Spanish and other towns. It is seen also that commercial privileges were granted to Spanish and other merchants.[2] From this it is clear that marine insurance must have been as well known and as much practised among the Latin races as in the Low Countries during the 15th century and later.

[1] Action between Pierre de Sorye and Gonsalve de la Groigne, Spanish merchants, against Jehan Sanses de la Groigne. Sentence . . .
(3°) que les marchandises données en gage seront assurées aux dépens dudit Sanche.
Gilliodts van Severen: *Cartulaire de l'ancien consulat d'Espagne à Bruges*, I, p. 31.

[2] Granted by Count Robert de Bethune under Charter in 1312. This charter was confirmed later in 1367, 1384, etc.
Gilliodts van Severen: *Cartulaire de l'ancien consulat d'Espagne à Bruges*, 7. X. 1447.

CHAPTER XXVI

LIFE ASSURANCE

Practice of life assurance in Belgium.

It will be remembered that in Chapter XIII reference was made to the practice of life assurance in Belgium during the 16th centuries and probably before. Also quotations were given from the Netherlands Ordinance of Philip II [1] and from the Amsterdam Ordinance,[2] and reference was made to the two Rotterdam Ordinances,[3] which prove that contracts of insurance of lives had been very general in Holland during the 16th century. It is clear that the knowledge of a custom in general use in Amsterdam cannot have been kept from the citizens of the neighbouring towns in Belgium. That the inhabitants of Antwerp had long been accustomed to make such contracts is clear from the references to life assurance contained in the records of that city. In those known as *In Antiquis*,[4] Title XXIX, it is stated that it has been the custom from " all old times " to make contracts of insurance on ships, merchandise sent by

And in Holland.

Practice authorized in Antwerp A.D. 1570.

[1] Dated 1570. See Chapter XIII, p. 156 note 1.

[2] Dated 1598. See Chapter XIII, p. 156 note 1.

[3] Dated 1604 and 1635. See Chapter XIII, p. 156 note 1.

[4] Records of the City of Antwerp—*In Antiquis*, Titel XXIX.* Contracten van asseurantien.

Men is, naer costuyme hier van allen ouden tyden geobserveert, gewoonelyck contracten van asseurantien op schepen, coopmanschap ter zee ofte lande gesonden wordende, ende oock leven vande persoonen, te maecken ende aen te gaene, ende op alsulcke contracten doet men recht.

Ende policen van assurantien, soo wanneer het blyckt, volgens onderteeckinge der selver, vande periclitatie vanden schepe, bederven vanden coopmanschap, doot vande persoonen versekert zynde, ende dat partyen van tverlies ende inthimatie to voren gedaen is geweest, staen tot namptisatie, gelyck ander liquide obligatien, soo dat der partyen (de partye) daer jegens gehoort wort, (ende) moet de somme by hem geasseureert namptiseren.

* Longé (G. de) : *Coutumes du pays et duché de Brabant, quartier d'Anvers*, Vol. I, p. 598.

land or sea, and also on the lives of persons, and further that this making of insurances is authorized.

These records were drawn up in the second half of the 16th century, and show that the making of such contracts of insurance must have been general from the beginning of that century, if not before.

Forbidden in A.D. 1571.

In 1571, an ordinance was passed which dealt with insurance, and, although permitting the making of contracts of insurance on merchandise, etc., prohibited life assurance, as stated in Title LIV of the records called *Impressæ*[1] of Antwerp, dated 1581. It is uncertain whether this prohibition of insurances on lives originated in Belgium or was suggested by the Ordinance of Philip II, which had been published the year before. It is certain that in Holland the practice was continued, as is proved by the subsequent Ordinances of Amsterdam and Rotterdam, referred to above.

General movement against life assurance in 16th century A.D.

In this connection it may be noted that there appears to have been a simultaneous movement against assurance of lives throughout all the Catholic countries in or about A.D. 1575. In addition to the restrictive legislation in Holland and Belgium referred to above, there was the equally absolute prohibition of such business contained in *Le Guidon*,[2] which, as Pardessus states, was probably published about that date.[3] Also there was the limitation of the right to make contracts of insurance on lives of eminent persons to those who had obtained permission of the Senate, imposed on the Genoese by their Civil Statute of 1588.[4] As in nearly

[1] Records of the City of Antwerp—*Impressæ*, Titel LIV.* Van contracten van asseurantien, van weddinghe ende spel.

1. Men is nae de costume ende usantie deser stadt gewoonelijck contracten van asseurantien oft versekeringen op schepen oft coopmanschappen ter zee ende te lande te maecken, ende recht daer op te doen.

2. Item hoe wel men voor tijden plochte t'useren asseurantie op d'leven van Persoonen ende op eenighe Reysen, ende daerop recht te doen, sijn de selve asseurancien, obligatien ende weddingen ende diergelijcke inventien ghemaect op d'leven van persoonen, op eenighe reysen oft voyagien, by d'ordinantie vanden twintichsten Januarij int jaer van XV° ende eenenzeventich verboden.

[2] See Chapter XIII, p. 155 note 4.

[3] See Chapter XIII, p. 156 note 5.

[4] See Chapter XIII, p. 156 note 3.

* See p. 276, n. 4; *op. cit.*, Vol. 2, p. 400.

all these and in other countries no restrictions had been placed on this class of business before, it seems impossible that a similar movement against insurance could have arisen in all these countries independently. It is more likely that the Church of Rome brought its influence to bear and forced those governments over which it had control to prohibit life assurance. Be this as it may, there is complete proof that at about 1570 a complete change took place in the legal view of insurance on lives.

Weddinghen on lives of children forbidden in A.D. 1544.

It is further stated in the same Title, Section 3,[1] that in an Ordinance of Charles V, dated December 4, 1544, it had been forbidden to make *weddinghen* (= wager insurances) on little boys or little girls. From the use of the word "*weddinghe,*" which was evidently intended to bear a different meaning from that borne by the word "*asseurantie,*" it is clear that the makers of such contracts in the 15th and 16th centuries had distinguished between insurance and wager insurance. Further, it is of interest to note that the difference between insurances on the lives of adults and that on the lives of children had been appreciated by the people of Antwerp as early as 1544.

[1] *Impressæ,* Titel LIV, p. 400.

3. Ghelijck dat oock volghende der ordinantien vande Keyserlijcke Majesteyt Caroli quinti vanden vierden Decembris des jaers XVᵉxliiij. weddingen op knechtkens oft meyskens sijn verboden.

CHAPTER XXVII

MARINE AND OTHER INSURANCE IN OTHER COUNTRIES[1]

In this chapter is given a very brief description of the various kinds of insurance practised by the mediæval peoples of Europe.

(1) Italy

There are traces of marine insurance in Italy dating from the 14th century, the first of which is the use of the word "siguare" in the *Breve Portus Calleritani*, enacted by the Pisan Republic in 1318 for the port of Cagliari in Sardinia.

Pegalotti in his treatise dated 1350 refers to the insurance contract "a rischio de mare e di genti."

Uzzano, the Florentine merchant, in 1442 quotes rates of insurance for goods during transit from London to Pisa by sea, and also from Bruges to Milan by land, and from Bruges to Pisa by sea and by land. Further, he refers to some regulations issued at Florence on November 22, 1408, forbidding the insurance of foreigners.

(2) Portugal

According to a Chronicle of King Ferdinand (about 1375), reciprocal insurance was well known in Portugal at that date.

There is also a record of the existence at Oporto of a chamber of insurance against charges, etc., on Portuguese shipping in the latter part of the 14th century. This insurance, though not strictly speaking *marine*, as it did not guarantee the insured against the loss of his ship or mer-

[1] I have not been able to add much to this section with regard to insurance of countries other than the Low Countries. For that which follows, I am indebted largely to the writings of M. Pardessus, Mr. Hendriks, and the authors quoted by them.—C. F. T.

chandise, was, nevertheless, a form of insurance against undue charges, etc. It shows that less than half a century after the reputed formation of a Chamber of Marine Insurance at Bruges, a form of insurance was being transacted by a public body at Oporto. This being so, the argument in favour of the statement that the company was formed in Bruges is much strengthened.

In 1436 King Edward of Portugal stated that the merchant vessels of the English which had been chartered . . . had not been insured owing to the fault of their proprietors, whilst those of the Portuguese, even of the Royal Navy, were insured. From this it is clear that the Portuguese in the first half of the 15th century, if not before, had adopted a system of non-mutual marine insurance.

(3) Spain

In Barcelona, as stated by D. Antonio de Capmany, an Ordinance relative to insurance was issued by the magistrates of that city in 1435. Subsequently four other Ordinances dealing with insurance were issued in that city.

(4) England

In England, although there is no direct reference from an English source to insurance in or before the 15th century, it is quite clear, from the fact that rates were quoted by Uzzano in 1442 for the insurance of goods between London and other parts, that the London merchants must have known of the practice. It would appear most probable, therefore, that they were accustomed to insure their merchandise. This is supported by the fact that the greater part of the London banking business was in the hands of Italian bankers, and also that there were many Italian merchants trading in London during the 15th century. From this it is extremely probable that the Italian merchants, at any rate, would have insured the goods they were sending to Italy for which the rates were quoted, as stated above. If this was so, it is practically certain that the custom became general.

In this connection, it may be remembered that Lord

Keeper Bacon in 1558 said: "Doth not a wise merchant in every adventure of danger give part to have the rest assured?"

The first English statute of insurance appeared in 1601. It contains evidence of the antiquity of the custom inasmuch as it refers to it in the following words: "Whereas it hathe bene tyme out of mynde an usage amongste merchants both of this realme and of forraine nacyons. . . ."

In respect of the practice of insurance in England, it should be noted that there is practically no evidence of earlier date than that quoted above, with the exception of a reference to the mutual obligation of the provision of *wergild* in the time of the Anglo-Saxons, and in a reference contained in the laws of Athelstane to a form of mutual insurance against loss of cattle which was practically equivalent to that known as *Hamelinghe*, referred to above, which provided that "each one . . . shall pay one penny into the common fund within twelve months in order to repay the owner for the animal. . . ."

Apart from this instance, there is, as far as I can discover, no trace of the practice of insurance in England before the 16th century, with the exception of the provision made in various gilds for the assistance of members who had fallen into poverty.

Summing up the contents of Part IV of this Thesis, it has been shown there that a direct descent can be traced from the crude idea of mutual responsibility possessed by the family groups composing the Flemish and West-German peoples before the 7th century A.D. through the gradually developing system of mutual indemnity and assistance of the gilds and communal systems down to the businesslike and practical methods of insurance of the Middle Ages, to which must be added the development of the non-mutual and underwritten insurance.

It is not intended, of course, to assert that no similar evolution of insurance took place in England or in any of the Latin nations, but this line of descent is suggested as a possible, if not the most probable, means by which insurance other than life became general in England.

This hypothesis is strengthened by the fact that from the 11th to the 15th century, and later, the merchants of England were in continual trade relationship with those of Bruges and other Flemish towns, with whom they had many trading instincts in common.

NOTE.—When the full title of a work referred to in the notes is not given, it will be found in the bibliography which follows the Appendices.

APPENDIX A

BABYLONIAN CIVILIZATION, COMMERCE, AND TRADE CUSTOMS

THE civilization of Babylonia had already reached a high point in 4500 B.C.,[1] the arts of life were well advanced, and men were able to write down their thoughts and deeds in intelligible language and in permanent form. Even the waters of the rivers were conveyed to fields and cities in artificial canals.[2] Her geographical position in the centre of the trading routes from Persia, India, and China in the East to Phœnicia and Egypt in the West, from Armenia in the North to Arabia in the South made her the junction for traders working along these routes, and banking and the use of money and goods on loan being understood and developed to a high point, and being encouraged by the rulers, as also was the case in Assyria,[3] it is probable that Babylonia became at an early date the clearing house for the financial transactions of Western Asiatic trade.[4] The country was, moreover, intersected by the network of canals referred to above; these canals were so constructed as to be available as waterways [5] bringing produce from all parts of Babylonia to the great cities established on the Tigris and Euphrates. In addition

[1] On the alluvial plain, ordinarily called Babylonia, lived peoples enjoying settled conditions of government and culture as early as 5000 B.C.—see introduction by G. S. Goodspeed to *Babylonian and Assyrian Literature*.

[2] Rogers, W.: *Babylonia and Assyria*, I, p. 350. Hilprecht: *Old Babylonian Inscriptions*, i, part ii, p. 47 and p. 38, footnote 9. Rassam: *Babylonian Cities*, p. 5.

Radau: *Early Babylonian History*, p. 54, gives description of Urukagina, dating from *circa* 4500 B.C. as follows: " For Ninâ her beloved canal . . . he has built."

Of the City of Babylon itself Rogers states (Vol. I, p. 386) that it must have been founded fully 4000 years B.C., and it may have been much earlier. It is named in the omen tablet of Sargon (*circa* 3800 B.C.), but became the capital of Babylonia about 2300 B.C.: " No capital in the world has ever been the centre of so much power, wealth, and culture for a period so vast."

[3] Cf. Herodotus, I, 185 and 193.
Diodorus Siculus, II, 16 and 17.
Strabo, XVI, cap. 1, § 2.

[4] " A land of traffic—a city of merchants." Ezek. xvii. 4.

[5] Duncker: *Hist. Antiq.*, 301.

to the impetus given to trading by this position, a large import trade was imposed on Babylonia by the peculiar character of the country, which produced an over abundance [1] of certain raw products, but at the same time was entirely wanting in others which were absolutely necessary to the support and welfare of a civilized manufacturing country. The raw products for which Babylonia was celebrated were cereals, wheat, barley, rice, etc.; palms; a very wide range of edible vegetables and fruits; in all of which she was exceedingly rich owing to the alluvial soil [2] and the scientific and public-spirited way [3] in which the irrigation system was maintained and worked. Cattle and animal life abounded and the rivers and canals were full of fish. Against this luxuriance of animal and vegetable life must be set the absolute lack of stone [4] or mineral wealth, owing to the nature of the soil; and also of timber. Further, the grape could not be grown there, so that wine was not produced in the country. Hence the Babylonians were forced to import all metals or jewels which they required for their manufactures: stone for building purposes; timber for the manufacture of furniture and also for burning; wine, etc. These imports had to be transported for long distances, and the skill and combined endeavour required for such work tended materially to develop the nation. From a very early date they imported cedars from Lebanon,[5] and stone from Arabia.[6]

The most important manufactures of Babylonia of which we have reliable information were as follows: bricks, which took the place, in many cases, of stone, for building purposes,[7] tiles, or tablets, pottery generally made from the clay everywhere present in the alluvial soil of the country; (remains of these tiles, made nearly 6,000 years ago, are in existence); woven goods of cotton and linen, carpets and rugs (decorated with designs of Indian fabulous animals such as the griffin, etc.), garments generally, and variously coloured cloths. The Babylonians also made glass; worked in metals; cut, polished, engraved, and mounted precious stones and made jewellery. They were especially noted for their cylinder seals made of jade

[1] "A fruitful land." Ezek. xvii. 4.
[2] "Good soil by great waters." Ezek. xvii. 8.
[3] Cf. *Code of Hammurabi*.
[4] Rogers, W.: *History of Babylonia and Assyria*, I, p. 282. *Re* want of stone and consequent use of brick—see Perrot and Chipiez: *Histoire de l'Art dans l'antiquité*, Vol. II, pp. 113–138.
[5] Ur-Ninâ wrote, 4300 B.C., as follows: "From Ma'al the Mountain, all kinds of wood he has brought." Radau: *Early Babylonian History*, p. 63. Cf. Ezek. xxvii. 23 and 24.
[6] Rogers states in his *Babylonia and Assyria* that they procured cedars from Lebanon and stone from Arabia at least 3000 years B.C.
[7] Gen. xi. 3: "They had brick for stone."

and other precious stones or metals.[1] Wood was imported from Syria and Palestine. Ointments and perfumes they used largely, and for the manufacture of these they were widely celebrated. Furniture and leather work too they made both for home use and for export. These various manufactured articles were not merely the production of small makers, but were the outcome of a large and well-organized business. From early times, for instance, large weaving establishments had been erected and were kept steadily working not only in the city of Babylon, but also in the smaller towns on the Euphrates and Tigris.

In order to carry on such varied and extensive manufacturing industries in a country naturally lacking in most, if not all, of the raw products required for such manufactures, an extensive import trade was necessary. This existed, and to such an extent, that the Babylonians attracted to themselves the products of the known world of their day. For their linen and woollen goods they imported cotton from Arabia and Egypt, coarse wool from Arabia and Syria, wool of a finer quality from Carmania, Thibet, and Cashmir, *via* Northern India and Susa. From still farther east they derived their supply of raw silk, penetrating as far as Sera, a town on the river now known as Hoang-ho; and this commerce with China, far from being small, was so great about 2300 B.C., that it has been suggested that China was civilized by a great Eastern movement of the peoples of the Euphrates valley.[2] From India they imported the dyes[3] used for colouring their woven stuffs, clothes, carpets, etc., also from India and Arabia they procured the spices[4] necessary for the manufacture of the ointments and perfumes which they used so freely. Their metal work required gold and silver and iron,[5] which they received from India, and copper and tin which came from the Phœnicians was brought into the country by the Armenians who used to float it down the Euphrates.[6] The precious stones used for their seals, etc., were procured some from India as the lapis lazuli, onyx, jade[7] (which they also imported from Chinese Turkestan),[8] others as emeralds, rubies,

[1] These Babylonian seals have been found on the oldest trade routes to China, see Terrien de Lacouperie: *Western Origin of early Chinese Civilization*, p. 11 and p. 343, note 66.

Cf. Article on *Seals* by Dr. Edkins in *China Review*, 1888, XVI, 372–4.

W. St. Chad Boscawen describes cylinder seal in his possession of date about 2500 B.C.

[2] See Terrien de Lacouperie: *Western Origin, etc., op. cit.*

[3] Ktesias: *Ancient India*, p. 23 (see Bibliog.).

[4] Ptolemy: *Ancient India*, p. 117 (see Bibliog.). Ktesias, p. 64.

[5] Ktesias, pp. 9, 16.

[6] Herod., I, 194.

[7] Ktesias, p. 10. Ptolemy, p. 77.

[8] Terrien de Lacouperie: *Western Origin, etc., op. cit.*, p. 351, note 162, etc.

jaspers, from the Bactrians who inhabited the desert of Gobi or Shanis.[1] Skins came to them from Armenia and Arabia.[2]

In addition to these raw products for the purpose of their manufactures, the Babylonians imported manufactured goods, such as wine and oil from Armenia, etc.; articles of luxury, such as bronze work from Phœnicia,[3] hunting dogs from India.[4] The chief exports of Babylonia were articles of clothing, for which they had acquired a world-wide reputation,[5] a peculiar and rich embroidery which they exported to Phœnicia,[6] perfumes and ointments, furniture, carpets and rugs, engraved stones, jewellery, weapons, etc.; these goods were supplied to the traders either for cash or on the credit system (described below) and by them were hawked in the different marts of Asia and in Egypt. Moreover, the Phœnicians, buying them to sell again, carried them to Crete, and later on to Greece and to the Western Mediterranean. So great was the influence of Babylonian commerce on Syria that the coinage of Babylonia had become general in Syria,[7] as is proved by an inscription found at Karnak showing that in the 16th century B.C. the tribute received from Syria by Thothmes III is reckoned partly in weight by the *mina*, and partly in round sums corresponding to the Babylonian weights. It is known, too, that the trade *mina* of the Syrians was one-sixtieth of the (heavy) Babylonian talent. Babylonian cubic measures were also used by the Syrians. These measures were introduced later by the Phœnicians to the Greeks by whom they were adopted in the 9th century B.C.

It has been shown that Babylonian civilization dates from *circa* 5000 B.C., that from that date to approximately 500 B.C. she was the great manufacturing and trading centre of the world, that she had a large and continual commerce (especially with Phœnicia and India), requiring very extensive caravan journeys through countries in every grade of civilization, and, consequently, involving every kind of danger to caravans, that her control of trade was such as to cause her money, weights, and measures of capacity to be adopted by neighbouring trading states, and finally that through the Phœnicians she had impressed them on Greece.

[1] Theophrastus: *De lapid.*, quoted by Heeren.
[2] Herod., I, 193; Pliny: *Hist. Nat.*, VII, 2; Diodorus Siculus, III, 31.
[3] Sir A. Layard: *Nineveh and Babylon*, pp. 183–187; *Monuments of Nineveh*, 2nd series, 57–67.
[4] Herod., I, 193.
[5] Cf. "A goodly Babylonish garment," Josh. vii. 21.
[6] Cf. "Broidered work," "Chests of rich apparel." Ezek. xxvii. 24.
[7] See Brandis: *Munzswesen*, 5, 93; quoted by Duncker.

APPENDIX B

PHŒNICIAN CIVILIZATION AND COMMERCE, WITH ESPECIAL REFERENCE TO THE EXTENT OF THEIR INFLUENCE ON GREECE

As the geographical position of Babylonia made her the mart of the ancient world prior to the development of sea-borne trade in the Mediterranean, so that of Phœnicia, while rendering it necessary for her to expand as a colonizing and sea-trading nation,[1] gave her the opportunity of doing so. The origin of the Phœnicians is obscure, but it is known that at the time of the Egyptian invasion of Syria under Thothmes III in the 16th century B.C. referred to above, there were in Phœnicia some six or seven towns each carrying on an independent trade. At this date, partly owing to a timely acknowledgment of the power of Egypt, and partly to the fact that Phœnicia was outside the zone of hostilities of the Egyptians, the Phœnicians not only retained their independence, but also acquired great profit by acting as carriers between Asia Minor and Egypt.[2] From this time the power and importance of Sidon rapidly increased, with the result that, until the rise of Tyre in 1000 B.C., that city was predominant in Phœnicia. The constitution of Phœnicia was that of a confederation of quasi-autonomous cities, each of which had complete local control, but was required to combine with the other cities in matters involving the safety and welfare of the state, there having been apparently no autocratic central authority. In other words, Phœnicia was a combination of certain towns inhabited by people of the same blood, speaking the same language, and having like trading interests.[3]

[1] "Enfermé dans un pays qui ne lui permettait pas de devenir une puissance continentale, il devint une puissance maritime et la première en date de l'antiquité." Ducoudray: *Histoire Sommaire de la Civilisation*, Paris, 1886, p. 116.

[2] "Leurs marins pratiquaient le commerce de commission en Égypte pour le compte des étrangers, et à l'étranger pour le compte de l'Égypte." Maspero: *Histoire Ancienne des Peuples de l'Orient*, Paris, 1904, p. 278; Ezek. xxvii. 3–9, 25–27; Herod., I, 1, iii, 47.

[3] Cf. Similar combination of settlements in the Island of Rhodes and the Hanseatic league of the Netherlands' cities in the 13th to 15th centuries.

It has been stated that the Phœnicians by means of their own caravans carried on an extensive land traffic with other Asiatic nations. This does not appear, according to Maspero, to have been the case. They established certain marts or depôts to which the traders of Oriental nations [1] brought their merchandise in order to trade with the Phœnicians. According to Heeren there were three main caravan routes by which foreign traders imported merchandise to Phœnicia, namely (i) that from Arabia, East India, and Egypt; (ii) that from Assyria and Babylonia; (iii) that from Armenia and the Caucasus. For the purpose of this investigation it is necessary to note particularly that there was a large and continual intercourse between Phœnicia and Babylonia and Assyria. In addition to her carrying trade Phœnicia obtained great wealth from her manufactures.[2] It is evident from contemporary evidence, as shown in Heeren's exhaustive work, that the trade of Phœnicia was very great and that between the 16th and 9th centuries B.C. she had practically the whole of the maritime trade of the world in her hands, which, when added to her land trade, made her the connecting link between the three continents of the then known world.[3] It is certain, also, that her ships were to be found in all the known seas, and that her sailors were accustomed to making long voyages [4] and to crossing wide stretches of sea far out of sight of land, to navigating by night, and that the art of navigation was in an advanced state, as is shown by the evidence that they had charts,[5] etc., and were able to calculate the rate of progress of their ships.[6] Seeing that they were in such an advanced state of civilization as regards trade, etc., and were in regular trading communication with the Babylonians and Assyrians, it is probable that they adopted the trading systems, including loans for business purposes, used by the older races. That there is no evidence of Phœnician origin for or against this having been so must be of little weight in guiding our opinion, in so far as there is little or no pre-classical evidence extant of their existence as the great sea-traders of the world other than that afforded by the writers of the Old Testament, who, if they had known of the customs relating to loans, etc., of the Phœnicians

[1] " Toutes les races du monde antique semblent s'être donné rendezvous en Asie Mineure." Maspero: *Histoire Ancienne des Peuples de l'Orient*, p. 283; and compare Ezek. xxvii. 12–24.

[2] Ezek. xxvii. 16.

[3] " Ils ont, par leur commerce, uni les peuples des trois continents de l'ancien monde." Ducoudray, *loc. cit.*, p. 127.
" A Mart of Nations," etc. Isa. xxiii. 3, etc. Cf. Diodorus Siculus, V, 35.

[4] Herod., IV, § 42.

[5] Bérard, V.: *Les Phéniciens et l'Odyssée.*

[6] Strabo: *Geograph.*, XV.

or Babylonians, would have carefully refrained from alluding to them.

As the sea-trade of Phœnicia increased it became necessary for her to colonize and thus acquire depôts for her merchandise and harbours for her ships.[1] This she did in Africa, Spain, and Britain, but was unsuccessful in so far as the Ægean Sea and Greece were concerned. It is, however, a very important point to note that the only permanent settlement made by the Phœnicians in Greek waters was that of Rhodes,[2] which town, as is shown below, exercised during the classic period the position of international law-maker for maritime commerce. Although the Phœnicians did not otherwise succeed in establishing themselves in the Ægean Sea or in Greece, yet many individual traders did so,[3] thus tending to civilize the Greeks in the early years of their history.[4] To the Phœnicians, and through them indirectly to the Babylonians, Greece owed her alphabet, her weights and measures, her knowledge of mathematics, etc.,[5] and, in all probability, her skill in navigation. Whatever may have been the connection between the Phœnicians and the Cretans, the Greek traders of the Heroic age, there is no doubt but that during the 200 or 300 years prior to the regeneration of commercial enterprise in Greece in the historic period "their (i.e. the Phœnician) ships were ever winding in and out of the Ægean Isles from south to north, bearing . . . all manners of luxuries

[1] The Phœnicians also had mining settlements such as those at Laurion (in Attica) (see Ardaillon : *Les Mines du Laurion*), and in Thasos, whence they were driven by the Parians (see Herodotus, II, 44, and VI, 46 and 47 ; and Strabo, X, 5 and 7).

[2] Maspero : *Histoire Ancienne des Peuples de l'Orient*, p. 292. " . . . il n'y eut sur le continent qu'un seul entrepôt phénicien autonome—Astyra, en face de Rhodes. Les Cares y mirent plus de complaisance. Ils laissèrent les Sidoniens débarquer à Rhodes . . . et s'emparer des trois ports, Jalysos, Lindos, et Camyros (Diodore de Sicile, IV, 2, 5, etc. ; Ergias de Rhodes dans Athénée, 1, VIII, p. 360, sqq.)" . . .

[3] Bérard, V. : *De l'Origine des Cultes Arcadiens.* Paris, 1894. Intro., p. 12. " Je croirais donc que . . . les Phéniciens occupèrent . . . tous les postes qui leur semblèrent de quelque utilité. Je crois qu'avant la Méditerranée grecque, il y eu une M. phénicienne, cerclée de possessions et de comptoirs phéniciens."

" En Grèce les Ph. avaient abordé sur toutes les côtes et dans les îles bien avant que les tribus helléniques ne fussent descendues de leurs montagnes du Nord."

[4] Maspero, *loc. cit.* : " L'arrivée et le contact des Phéniciens l'avaient fait naître à la vie civilisée."

[5] Ball, W. W. R. : *A Short History of Mathematics*, p. 2. " The Chaldeans had certainly paid some attention to arithmetic and geometry, as is shown by their astronomical calculations ; and whatever was the extent of their attainments in arithmetic, it is almost certain that the Phœnicians were equally proficient, while it is likely that the knowledge of the latter, such as it was, was communicated to the Greeks."

Strabo, XVI, ii, p. 757.

and ornaments ; and this constant commercial intercourse lasting for two centuries is amply sufficient to account for all the influence that Phœnicia exerted upon Greece." [1] That the Greeks regarded the Phœnicians as noted for their skill and trading, not to mention their piracy and man-stealing, is shown clearly by the references to them in the *Odyssey*.[2]

The influence of the Phœnician skill in seafaring matters on Greece was so great that practically the whole of the maritime commerce of classical Greece was based on the lines laid down by the Phœnicians, to whom they owed *inter alia* their sailing charts,[3] and astronomical knowledge for sailing by night.

[1] Bury : *History of Greece*, p. 77.
[2] *Odyssey*, XIV, 288 ; XIII, 372 *et seq.* ; XV, 415 *et seq.* Gladstone : *Studies on Homer*, pp. 216 *et seq.*
[3] Bérard, V. : *Les Phéniciens et l'Odyssée*, Paris, 1903.

APPENDIX C

LOANS AT INTEREST AMONG THE EGYPTIANS

USURY was in all cases regarded with extreme disfavour by the ancient Egyptians, and is called "a plague"  *sext en uha*, "the plague of usury."[1]

In the early periods of Egyptian history the system of accommodation by loan called by the Greeks ἔρανος, was largely in vogue. It arose from the injunction in the Egyptian moral code to aid one's neighbour, and was entirely limited to religious law, in that this loan, contracted without any written document, could only be proved by administering a solemn oath to the debtor, which he was required to take in a temple.[2]

Money lent or borrowed on usury was known by the Egyptians as *sankh* (=δάνειον); and down to the 24th dynasty the rate of interest was, as in Assyria, fixed by the contracting parties, and from contract tablets we learn that this often reached 33, 50, and even 100 per cent.[3]

In Chaldea compound interest was customary, the creditor being careful to effect, by means of a fresh act made from time to time, the transformation of interest already paid to new capital producing interest itself. In Egypt, on the contrary, *anatocism* was condemned,[4] and it was forbidden to allow the interest to more than double the original sum. For corn, the interest was calculated by the year, and was fixed at a third of the capital, because the measures of capacity were divisible by

[1] Cf. Pierret, *Vocab. hiérogl.*, under the word .

[2] See article in the *Proceedings of Soc. of Bibl. Arch.*, 1895.

[3] Cf. Revillout: *La Créance et le droit commercial dans. l'antiquité*, p. 63.

[4] By Bocchoris, according to Diodorus.

Cf. Revillout, *op. cit.*, II, p. 225. "Pour les dettes de droit civil, nous n'avons non plus jamais rencontré en Égypte l'anatocisme. . . ."

three. That made a little more than the interest allowed on loans of money, viz. 33⅓ per cent., instead of 30 per cent.

Diodorus says that Bocchoris made a law [1] that "if a man borrowed money, and the lender had no writing to show for it, and the other denied it upon oath, he should be quit of the debt; to that end, therefore, in the first place, they were to sacrifice to the gods, as making men's conscience tender and scrupulous in taking of an oath."

The creditors could not seize the debtor's person, their claims and right were confined to the goods in his possession, and such as were really his own, which were comprehended under the produce of his labour, or what he had received from another individual to whom they lawfully belonged. For the person of every citizen was looked upon as the property of the State, and might be required for some public service; and, independent of the injustice of subjecting anyone to the momentary caprice of his creditor, the safety of the country might be endangered through the avarice of a few interested individuals (Diodorus).

This law, which was borrowed by Solon from the Egyptian code, existed also at Athens; and was, as Diodorus observes, much more consistent with justice and common sense than that which allowed the creditor to seize the person, while it forbade him to take the ploughs and other implements of husbandry. For if, continues the historian, it is unjust thus to deprive men of the means of obtaining subsistence, and of providing for their families, how much more unreasonable must it be to imprison those by whom the implements were used. [2]

[1] See Budge: *Hist.*, VI, p. 119; and Wiedemann: *Geschichte*, pp. 578, 579.
See also Mommsen: *Röm. Gesch.*, III, 536; Lombroso: *Economic polit.*, p. 174; and Revillout in the *Revue Egypt.*, II, p. 142.

[2] See the following chapters in *Obligations en droit égyptien* by Revillout: p. 39, Le capital commercial et le prêt à usure; p. 65, Le prêt-créance

ou *Sankh* en droit égyptien.

APPENDIX D

LOANS AT INTEREST AMONG THE GREEKS [1]

FROM the earliest times of which there is a record, lending money and goods at simple interest, payable monthly, yearly, or for the period of the loan, was known to the Greeks. Later the practice of charging interest on unpaid interest [2] became general and a further development, namely, that of discounting [3] the loan by subtraction of the interest when advancing the money, was introduced. The rate of interest charged,[4] although governed by the class of loan and of the security offered, was, generally speaking, very high and varied [5] from 10 per cent. to 36 per cent. per annum for ordinary loans; a very common rate being 33⅓ per cent.[6] Those high rates on loans which were undoubtedly safe as well as those on business and other security were due to the cheapness of slave labour, which permitted land-owners to make large profits by the use of their capital, to the still larger profits made in successful trading and to the deliberate action of the bankers who combined to keep up the rates at which money could be obtained for commercial purposes. The commonest rates appear to have been from 10 per cent. to 16 per cent. on first-class securities, and up to 36 per cent. on loans for trade purposes, other than on a contract of bottomry. The following is a rough classification of the commoner loans and the annual interest payable thereon:—

[1] Authorities consulted:—
Boeckh: *Public Economy of Athens*, I, Ch. 22.
Demosthenes: *Private Orations contra Aphob., pro Phorm.*
Salmasius: *De Fenore Trapezitico, De Usuris.*

[2] Aristophanes: *Nubes*, V, 1140 (*circa* 420 B.C.).
Plat. Legg., 842, D. (*circa* 420 B.C.).

[3] Plutarch: *De vitando ære alieno*, IV.

[4] Excepting when a man delayed in returning the dowry of his lawful wife after separating from her, in which case interest was fixed by law at 18 per cent. (see Demos. *c.* Aphob.), there was no legal restriction on the rate of interest. Boeckh, *op. cit.*, p. 130, quotes *Ex Lege ap. Lys. cont. Theomnest.*, p. 360.

[5] 12 per cent. was considered a very low rate of interest. Cf. Demosthenes *contra* Aphob.

[6] Aristotle: *Rhet.*, 3, 10, 7.

(1) Loans on a person's body, i.e. if debtor could not repay loan plus interest when due he became the slave of the creditor; prohibited from time of Solon.

(2) Mortgages, in which the principal was safe and the interest certain, on which from 10 per cent. upwards was charged.

(3) Loans on moveable property, etc., bearing interest from 12–33⅓ per cent.

(4) Loans to manufacturers, traders, farmers, etc., for use in their business. This class of loan was made very largely by the great banking houses who used the money deposited with them in that way. The interest thereon was high, commonly at 36 per cent.

(5) Loans on bottomry. See Chapter IV.

(6) Loans to bankers, i.e. money placed at the bank on deposit, by persons who had capital but were unable or unwilling to use it or to take the risk of lending it at higher rates of interest, and who could thus obtain a safe investment but at a low rate of interest.

(7) Loans by common usurers and moneylenders on which the interest charged was outrageously high.[1]

(8) Loans made by mutual societies to members at a low rate of interest. See Appendix J.

(9) Loans made to friends bearing no interest.

[1] Theophrastus' mention (Char. VI) of 25 per cent. *per diem*, though doubtless satirically exaggerated, supports this statement: "pro usura drachmae cujusque ternos semiobolos in dies exigit." (A drachma equalled six obols.)

APPENDIX E

COMPARISON OF MODERN METHODS OF CHARTERING SHIPS AND CARRYING MERCHANDISE WITH THOSE PRACTISED BY THE GREEKS IN THE 4TH CENTURY B.C.

WHEN comparing the contract set out in the Oration against Lacritus with that in use at present, it is necessary to recollect that the conditions under which merchandise and ships are dealt with in modern time are very different from those in vogue in the time of Demosthenes. The most important points are, very briefly, as set out below. The modern method of dealing with a ship is :—

I. Either (*a*) that the owners let by an agreement under seal the ship or the major portion thereof for some particular voyage ; in this case the ship is said to be *chartered*, or (*b*) that the owners decide to run a ship to a particular port, and they profess themselves willing to undertake to carry the goods of various persons, who may or may not be connected, to the various ports *en route ;* such a ship is said to be *general.*

II. The owners (practically) never work the ship themselves, but leave it to a master, by whose contracts they are bound.

III. On receipt of goods on board, master gives receipt for them, called a bill of lading, undertaking to deliver them to the party therein named or to his representatives ; a duplicate signed by master is sent by shipper to his consignee, to whom on production thereof the goods must be delivered.

IV. Merchant very rarely goes on voyage—if represented, is usually represented by supercargo.

The parties interested at Athens in a trading voyage during the time of Demosthenes were as follows :—

(1) The owner, who used as a rule to work the ship himself, and was often obliged to borrow money for fitting his ship out and for the expenses incidental to navigation. He used frequently to ship the cargo himself, and to act both as ship owner and as merchant.

(2) The trader, or merchant adventurer, who was usually a person who had small capital and consequently had to borrow money in order to purchase cargo, or, in some cases, to borrow

the actual cargo, and who took it himself to the mart at which he was to dispose of it, and having done so procured another cargo for the return journey.

(3) The capitalist who financed either the owner or the trader or both was generally a banker or wealthy man of rank who could not engage in trade.

At earlier date the capitalist was often a manufacturer, farmer, or producer who supplied the trader with goods on a bond of Respondentia, which class of transaction for convenience may be dealt with under the general term of Contract of Bottomry.

Under Athenian Law loans could only be made on ships trading to or from Athens, not on ships plying between other ports. Cf. Demosthenes, *c.* Lacrit., *c.* Phorm., *c.* Dionysodor. (See Chapter IV.)

APPENDIX F

THE RHODIAN LAWS

It has been generally admitted by all writers on marine law, including Azuni,[1] Boucher,[2] Émérignon,[3] Pardessus,[4] Colquhoun,[5] and others, that the origin of modern legislation on matters dealing with the sea was the maritime law of the inhabitants of the Island of Rhodes. The Laws which were made by them were recognized by the Romans as authoritative in respect of all matters relating to the sea, and were directly confirmed by the Emperor Antoninus in his ruling quoted in the *Digest* by Justinian, who also states that the Emperor Augustus had adopted these laws.[6]

Among other classical authors, Strabo [7] and Cicero [8] speak of the excellence of these laws, which opinion has been confirmed by the later writers quoted above. Some modern writers appear to be of opinion that the influence of the laws of Rhodes was even greater than it was held to be in the Middle Ages, and that not only the laws of the Latin races but the laws of Oleron and the Code of Wisby were more or less remotely traceable to Rhodian origin.[5] In fact, Torr, writing in 1885, says: "Probably much

[1] Azuni, D. A., Vol. I, p. 131.

§ 16. Le Leggi Rodie per consenso universale sono le prime leggi marrittime che siansi vedute.

§ 17. Le Leggi Rodie son dunque le sorgenti della Guirisprudenza marrittima . . .

[2] Boucher: *Consulat de la Mer*, Vol. I, p. 242.

[3] Émérignon: *Traité des Assurances*, etc.

[4] Pardessus: *Us et coutumes de la mer*, pp. 194, 196, 205, etc.

[5] Colquhoun: *Summary of the Roman Civil Law*, Vol. III, p. 137. "It is supposed that the laws of Oleron, and indeed those of all maritime nations, are more or less remotely traceable to a Rhodian origin, if not indeed to the still higher antiquity of the yet more ancient Phœnicians."

Cf. Lindsay: *Merchant Shipping*, Vol. I, p. 184.

[6] *Digest*, XIV, ii, 9. " . . . Id est, deprecatio Eudæmonis Nicomediensis ad Antoninum Imperatorem, Domine imperator Antonine, naufragium in Italia facientes, direpti sumus a publicanis Cyclades insulas habitantibus. Respondit Antoninus Eudæmoni: Ego quidem mundi dominus: lex autem maris, lege id Rhodia quæ de rebus nauticis præscripta est, judicetur: quatenus nulla nostrarum legum adversatur. Hoc idem divus quoque Augustus judicavit."

Michaelis Attaliatæ opus de jure, XLVIII. (See Pardessus, *L.M.*, I, 194.)

Synopseos Basilicorum Minoris, fr. XIV. (See Pardessus, *L.M.*, I, 195.)

[7] Strabo, Book XIV, ii, §§ 4 and 6.

[8] Cicero: *Pro lege Manilia.* "Quorum usque ad nostram memoriam disciplina navalis et gloria remansit."

else of the naval law of to-day has come down from the Rhodians.[1]

It is clear, then, that the influence of the Rhodian Laws on the maritime customs of the Romans and Greeks must have been great; and it also appears likely that the Rhodian Laws dealt with marine insurance since Justinian in dealing with "general average" openly adopts the Rhodian Law.[2] With the exception of this quotation in the Digest (De Lege Rhodia De Jactu)[2] no part of these laws has come down to modern times. There were, however, four fragments of a body of marine law, which although they had been stated in 1559 by Boduin to be "incondita farrago de rebus nauticis" and by Cujacius to be "novissima quidem," were published as genuine fragments of the ancient law of Rhodes by Schard at Basle in 1591. They were also held to be genuine by certain mediæval writers including Godefroi,[3] Vinnius,[4] and Valin.[5]

The authenticity of these fragments was questioned by Heineccius[6] and Schomberg,[7] both of whom considered them to be spurious. Meyer[8] went further and stated that he did not consider that the Rhodian Laws had ever been committed to writing, but were simply the unwritten laws which had grown up from maritime experience.

Pardessus,[9] however, combats this theory, and while recognizing that the fragments are spurious, in so far as they profess to be part of the ancient law of Rhodes, he still considers that there is no evidence to support the theory that the laws of Rhodes were unwritten. With regard to the fragments, he is of opinion that they form portions of a compilation made by a person called Rhodion, dating from about the 9th century.

[1] Torr, C.: *Rhodes in Ancient Times*, p. 52.

[2] *Digest*, XIV, ii, 1 (De Lege Rhodia de Jactu). "Lege Rhodia cavetur, ut si levandæ navis gratia jactus mercium factus est, omnium contributione sarciatur, quod pro omnibus datum est."

Cf. Pardessus: *Us et Coutumes de la Mer*, p. 222. "Mais elle constate . . . une assurance mutuelle entre les armateurs et les chargeurs d'un même navire . . . elle marque un grand pas dans le commerce maritime; elle est l'aurore de l'assurance à prime; elle a dû être d'un grand secours jusqu'au moment où ce dernier contrat, si étonnant dans sa théorie et ses résultats, a fait disparoître et presque oublier celui qui en étoit le précurseur."

[3] Godefroi: *De Imperio Maris*, 1637, Chap. IX.

[4] Vinnius: Preface to Peckius, 1647.

[5] Valin: *Commentaire sur l'ordonnance de* 1681.

[6] Heineccius: *Historia Juris Civilis*, § 296.

[7] Schomberg, A. C.: *Treatise on the Maritime Laws of Rhodes*, Oxford, 1786.

[8] Meyer (E.): *De Historia legum maritimarum medii ævi celeberrimarum*, Göttingen, 1824. "Putaverim ergo illam peritiæ rei navalis Rhodiorum celebritatem ad certa lites in causis maritimis decidendas instituta referendam esse; jus autem eorum navale nunquam scriptum fuisse, sed tantum e consuetudinibus maritimis, tanquam jus universale, agnotis, constitisse.

[9] Pardessus: *Us et Coutumes de la Mer*, pp. 23–32, 209, 230.

Torr [1] is of opinion that nothing remains of the ancient Rhodian Law excepting the Law "De Jactu," quoted in the *Digest*.

From this short description, it will be noted that all the writers on the subject are of opinion that the Rhodians were the pioneers in matters relating to marine legislation, and that in addition to being pioneers, their laws were accepted as being authoritative and were adopted by the most powerful peoples of that time, and also by later Italian Republics.[2]

Granted that these laws were either adopted *in toto*, or used as a basis for similar legislation by the classical peoples, it is clear that the policy of the sea was dictated to other nations by the Rhodians; whence it follows that they were considered to hold the premier place in respect of their knowledge of shipping, seamanship, and all other matters pertaining to the sea.

Carrying the arguments further back, it may be stated that the Phœnicians [3] were the originators of the marine legislation of the Romans and Greeks, inasmuch as the city of Rhodes was the outcome of Phœnician colonization; and although the Rhodian Laws probably do not ante-date as a recognized body of law, 408 B.C., at which time the older towns of the Island of Rhodes joined themselves in a confederation, yet it is certain that the laws themselves are of a much older date. Probably the suggestion put forward by Meyer [4] is correct to this extent—that prior to the confederation of the towns in the island, the laws were more or less unwritten and based on custom, but were codified when the towns formed a confederation. This confederation was possibly based on the system in vogue in Phœnicia where, since the 17th century B.C., the various towns had combined first under the leadership of Sidon, and subsequently, from the time of Hiram, under that of Tyre. This is rendered more probable by the fact that the civilization of Rhodes was the outcome of the Phœnician settlements in that island.[5] As stated by Bérard,[6] the Rhodians owed their civilization to the Phœnicians and the Sidonians who had settled there and intermarried with the natives, and the towns which combined to form the Greek capital of Rhodes were founded by the sailors of the east. There are many allusions to the early history and fame of the Phœnician settlements in Rhodes which it is, perhaps,

[1] Torr: *Rhodes in Ancient Times*, p. 52.
[2] Lindsay: *Merchant Shipping*, Vol. I, p. 502.
[3] See Ch. IV. and Appendix B.
[4] See note 8, p. 298.
[5] See Appendix B.
[6] Bérard (V.): *Les Phéniciens et l'Odyssée*, Vol. I, p. 338. "Il nous a paru de même que les villes antérieures à la capitale grecque Rhodes étaient . . . des fondations de marins orientaux."

unnecessary to quote, but from which it can be learnt that the civilization of the island was advanced in the time of Homer,[1] and that its origin was, as stated above, Phœnician; whence it follows that the argument set forth in Chapters II and IV of this Thesis, that the Babylonian custom was introduced to the Greeks by the Phœnicians, is strengthened by the consideration of the early history of Rhodes. As shown previously, the Phœnicians were famous for their knowledge of seamanship, etc., and, in addition, were the connecting link between the European trading nations and Babylon, the mart of Asia.

If it be admitted that the people of Rhodes had acquired this supremacy in matters relating to the sea from the practice of the Phœnician settlers and traders in that island, it is clear that the other settlements of the Phœnicians on the Greek littoral must have had a certain influence on the inhabitants, especially on such as had trading relations with the Phœnician merchants and traders. It is known that the influence thus exerted by the settlers in Greece was not as complete as that exerted in Rhodes, owing to the fact that the Phœnicians did not colonize Greece in the way in which they colonized Rhodes, but confined themselves practically to the establishment of trading marts, and to developing the native markets, instead of forming actual colonies as was the case in Rhodes. But although the influence thus exerted in Greece was inferior to that exerted in the island, it must be remembered that the persons with whom the Phœnicians came into contact in the island were not generally so receptive as those on the mainland, because in the island they came into contact with persons of all classes, whereas on the mainland the intercourse was limited almost entirely to merchants, shippers, and other persons interested in trading with the Phœnicians. Consequently, the influence they exerted on the persons whom they met must have been greater in the case of the Greeks, although the actual intercourse of the Phœnicians with them was less, because the Greeks being trained and accustomed to business habits were better able to appreciate the advantages of the more highly skilled methods adopted by the Phœnicians.

It seems, therefore, more probable that the Greeks acquired their knowledge of seamanship and of Bottomry and other customs appertaining to sea-borne commerce directly from the Phœnicians at the period stated in the Thesis, than indirectly from the Rhodians, at a later date.

[1] *Iliad*, II, 654 and 656.
Cf. Pindar: *Olymp.*, VII, 131–136.
Also see Selden: *Mare clausum*, I, v, § 5.

APPENDIX G

FINANCE AS KNOWN TO AND PRACTISED BY THE ROMANS BEFORE A.D. 300

THE financial knowledge and practice of the Romans was highly developed and included a thoroughly practical acquaintance with most, if not all, of the branches of what is usually known as the Theory of Finance, including Interest, Banking, Partnership, etc.

Interest.—The question of what was a fair rate of interest to pay for the use of money had been a great cause of dissatisfaction in the earliest period of Roman History, as is shown by the legal limit of 1 per cent. per month fixed by the XII Tables [1]; therefore interest must have been known long before that time. There is no evidence as to whether the practice of adding interest to principal and charging interest on the total (i.e. compound interest) was in vogue at that time, but the fact that it was absolutely forbidden [1] by the Lex Genucia in the 4th century B.C. is strong evidence that it had been generally used for some time prior to that date.[2] In the later days of the Republic and subsequently, compound interest was commonly employed, as is shown in the letter of Cicero to Atticus,[3] wherein he refers to a Decree of the Senate forbidding the use of compound interest; in the extract from Ulpian,[4] in the *Digest*, limiting the amount to which compound interest might accumulate, beyond which amount it could not be stipulated for nor exacted, and, if received,

[1] XII Tables, No. 18, 452 B.C. "Si qui unciario fœnere amplius fœnerâsset quadruplione luito."
Cf. Tacitus. Ann. VI, 16. " . . . nam primum duodecim tabulis sanctum, ne quis unciario fœnere amplius exerceret . . . dein rogatione tribunicia ad semuncias redactum " (344 B.C., see Livy, VII, 27), " postremo vetita versura " (Lex Genucia—341 B.C. Cf. Livy, VII, 42). . . .

[2] For particulars as to use of interest by Babylonians see Chapter II, by Egyptians see Appendix C, and by Greeks see Appendix D.

[3] Cicero ad Att., V, 21, 13. This extract does not state if the prohibition was *ad hoc* or general.

[4] *Digest*, XII, vi, 26, 1. Supra duplum autem usuræ et usurarum usuræ nec in stipulatum deduci nec exigi possunt; et solutæ repetuntur, quemadmodum futurarum usurarum usuræ.

was repayable; and in the *Code* where Justinian,[1] having pointed out that the earlier law-makers had been unsuccessful in their attempts to stop it, absolutely and most definitely (*hac apertissima lege definimus*) forbids it entirely. It was also forbidden in the Basilicon [2] about A.D. 900. It was known to the Greeks, Chaldeans, Egyptians, and Hindus also, but I have been able to find no trace of it in the early writings of the Chinese.

Discount.—From the first of the two extracts from the *Code* [1] it is evident that the practice of anticipating the action of interest is referred to, since a distinction is carefully drawn between the interest for time which has passed and that of the future. This tends to show that the converse of the ordinary action of interest, namely, that of discount, had been evolved by the Romans.

Present Value.—Further, the practice of accepting the discounted value of a sum to be repaid in full, i.e. the Present Value, is referred to incidentally in a section of the *Code* [3] forbidding the evasion of the law as to the maximum rate of interest legally chargeable by means of the loan of money discounted [4] at a higher rate. This extract indicates the frequency of the use of discount and present values by the way in which the custom of advancing a discounted sum is referred to as though it were a usual method; the object of the law being to prevent an ordinary business practice being made a cover for the commission of an illegal act. It appears certain from the two extracts taken together that not only were the Romans cognisant of discount and present value, but that they were able and accustomed to calculate the values at compound interest, and sufficiently skilful in doing so to enable them to perpetrate illegal acts, by the way in which they could manipulate the results of their calculations.

Payments by Instalments.—The use by the Romans of the instalment method of making payments was very general and the custom was developed to a state almost as advanced as that of

[1] *Cod.*, IV, xxxii, 28. Ut nullo modo usuræ usurarum . . . exigantur et veteribus quidem legibus constitutum fuerat, sed non perfectissime cautum. . . . Quapropter hac apertissima lege definimus, nullo modo licere cuiquam usuras preteriti vel futuri temporis, in sortem redigere, et earum iterum usuras stipulari. And *Cod.*, VII, liv, 3. . . . Cum enim jam constituimus usurarum usuras penitus esse delendas, nullum casum relinquimus, ex quo hujusmodi machinatio possit induci.

[2] XXIII, iii, 29.

But see Scholiasts quoted in note to this passage in Heimbach, *Basilicorum Libri*, LX (Leipsic, 1840).

[3] *Cod.*, IV, xxx, 2. Minorem pecuniam te accepisse, et majorem cautionem interposuisse, si apud eum, qui super ea re cogniturus est constiterit, nihil ultra quam accepisti cum usuris in stipulatum deductis restituere te jubebit.

[4] See practice of Greek Moneylenders. Appendix D.

modern times. The contract [1] for the payment of any debt or purchase money, or even of the repayment of a dowry, was drawn up according to a legal form provided for in the *Digest*, consisting of three independent stipulations. In the calculation of the instalments both simple and compound interest [2] were employed, and the prompt payment of each instalment as it became due was enforced by the imposition of a penal rate of interest [3] on such payments as were overdue. There appears to have been a considerable amount of sharp practice in respect of the calculation of the interest chargeable on the transaction, resulting in a law [3] to the effect that interest could be charged on the unpaid (i.e. payable at future dates) instalments only. Also the power to impose a penal rate had been abused, as is shown by the law providing that when a debtor had shown his *bona fide* intention to pay the instalments as they became due by having paid them punctually for some years and was prevented from meeting the instalments when due, the penal rate could not be charged retrospectively, but only in respect of such future payments as were unpunctual. From this it may perhaps be assumed that a person buying a reversion might have paid for it in instalments, at first by a fixed number ($=a_n$) and afterwards by a periodic payment during the life of the person in possession ($=a_x$). Whence it is but a short step to the payment of (annual) premiums in place of a single premium for a payment to be made to a third party on the death of the payer of the premiums, and, subsequently, to the use of periodic premiums generally.

Banking.—In Rome the business of banking was confined (almost) entirely to the receiving by the banks of sums of money on deposit which were lent out on mortgage or used for discounting business. When it is remembered that there were then no Government securities,[4] etc., which could be used as investments by such persons as had money to invest and wished to live on the interest of their investments, but were unwilling to lend their capital first hand to merchants, farmers, etc., it will be understood that the banks supplied a great want, as they offered an investment which, although earning [5] a low rate of interest, was, practically, secure and easily converted into cash if required. The depositors were entitled to a preferential

[1] *Digest*, II, xiv, 75 § 9, 140 § 1. Cf. Ulpian, VI, 8, 13. *Digest*, XXIII, iv, 17, and *Code*, V, 13, 7.

[2] *Digest*, XII, 1, 40; XLV, i, 90, 126 § 2.

[3] *Digest*, XXII, i, 9 § 1; xii, 13, 17; and *Code*, IV, 32, 58.

[4] Open to the public. Certain quasi-government securities existed in the form of loans to the government by the Publicani, etc.

[5] 5 per cent. and 4 per cent., or less, are mentioned as usual rates for loans on good security in certain districts and under certain conditions. It is stated expressly in the *Digest*, XXVI, vii, 7, 10, that the maximum rate of interest allowed by the law was unduly heavy.

charge on all the property, joint and separate, of the partners in the banking concerns. In early times it happened not unfrequently that money was placed on deposit at the bank merely to insure that it would be kept safely, and in such cases no interest was paid by the bank provided that the deposit was returned punctually on the date agreed on, but if any delay occurred, arising from the fault of the bank, a penal rate of interest was payable. It is, however, certain that in the later years of the Republic and during the Empire, interest was contracted for on most, if not all, deposits.

Accounts and Book-keeping.—The system of accounts employed by these bankers and by merchants was very highly developed, and is more than enough to prove that the Romans were perfectly aware of the value of accurate book-keeping and the necessity for valuations, etc. An exhaustive description of their methods is given by Professor Roby.[1]

Joint Trading.—(*a*) Partnerships. In the *Digest* the legal aspect of partnership is dealt with very fully.[2] Partnerships could be formed between any persons legally able to make contracts, etc., and could be made for life, or up to, or from a certain date, or under certain conditions [3]; and were dissolvable by agreement, or death, or diminution of legal status or by poverty.[4] This book deals also with (*b*) the division of profits and, if necessary, the reference of questions arising therefrom to arbitration, and (*c*) the liability of the partners; and shows that in all these matters the Romans had a well-thought-out and very efficient system.

[1] *Roman Private Law.* Appendix to Book V.

[2] Book XVII, Pro Socio., 2, 1, and 2, 4.

[3] I, 1. Societas coiri potest vel in perpetuum, id est dum vivunt, vel ad tempus, vel ex tempore, vel sub conditione.

I, 4. Societatem coire et re et verbis et per nuncium posse. . . .

[4] 2, 4 § 1. Dissociamur renunciatione, morte, capitis minutione et egestate.

2, 6. Si societatem (mecum) coieris, ea conditione, *ut partes societatis constitueres*, ad boni viri arbitrium ea res redigenda est: et conveniens est viri boni arbitrio ut non utique ex æquis partibus socii simus, veluti si alter plus operæ, industriæ, pecuniæ in societatem collaturus sit.

APPENDIX H

THE MATHEMATICAL KNOWLEDGE OF THE ROMANS UNDER THE EMPIRE

In estimating the mathematical knowledge possessed by the Romans at the end of the Republic and during the reigns of the earlier Emperors, we must remember that they had before them all the legal and mathematical discoveries of Greece and Alexandria, and the business methods of the Jews of Egypt, of Phœnicia, and of Babylonia; they were in touch with India and China, etc., and, in addition, the city of Rome being the metropolis of the then civilized world, the greatest business men of all nationalities were attracted thither. Whence it follows that, if the accumulated wisdom of these various nations was in the 2nd century A.D.[1] sufficient to have permitted the construction of tables of annuity values, of single and annual premiums for whole life assurance, or for term insurance, calculated either at simple or compound interest, the Romans would either have been sufficiently far advanced to do so too, or, if not, could have employed skilled mathematicians to make the necessary calculations for them.

The mathematical discoveries of the Pythagorean and later Greek schools were confined, as far as extant references show, to a large extent, to trigonometry and conic sections, and consequently would not have been of much service in the construction of such tables. It is, however, not improbable that the arithmetical side had been developed so as to allow of the calculation of interest and discount values, but that this development, being purely commercial and savouring of trade, was not recorded.

The arithmetical and algebraical side was, however, receiving attention in the Alexandrine school, where, about A.D. 100 Nicomachus[2] published a treatise on arithmetic which Boethius translated in the 6th century, and which remained the standard book on the subject until the 12th century. Some two hundred years or less after Nicomachus, Diophantus[3]

[1] Before which date few, if any, societies were formed for the purpose of providing burial funds for their members and, possibly, for the carrying on of mutual insurance.

[2] Edited by R. Hoche, Leipzig, 1866.

[3] See Bibliography.

produced a work on algebra, in which he dealt with such advanced branches of the subject as the solution of binomial, quadratic, and (in one case) cubic, equations, and also of indeterminate equations of two or three variables. Of this work W. W. R. Ball [1] says: "Broadly speaking, it may be said that European algebra did not advance beyond this stage until the close of the 16th century." This book was followed by the *Aryabhathiya* [2] of Arya-Bhata, published at Patna, in A.D. 476, which treated of trigonometry and algebra, the algebraical portion dealing *inter alia* with the general solution of quadratics, indeterminates of the first degree, decimals, etc. Subsequently to this date, during the early and middle period of the Byzantine or Eastern Empire there flourished many celebrated mathematicians, including among them Isidore of Seville who, in Book III of his *Origines*,[3] treats of arithmetic, geometry, etc., and Alkarismi of Khorassan, in whose work [4] on arithmetic and algebra the decimal system is dealt with. On this work the early mediæval knowledge of decimals was based.

Further, the Romans had from time immemorial, possibly going back to the same source as that from which the Chinese acquired their knowledge of the instrument, been accustomed to carry out complicated calculations with the aid of the abacus.

As it is certain that the study of arithmetic and algebra must have preceded the publication of books dealing with these subjects, it follows that by the 3rd century of our era the Romans were in possession of sufficient arithmetical knowledge to enable them to make the simple calculations necessary for the rough construction of tables of subscriptions (or premiums), etc., for use in the Burial Societies and in ordinary insurance business, if they transacted such business. This view is supported by the existence of the annuity table of Ulpian, which, as stated in Chapter XII, appears to have been based on mortality experience.

[1] *A Short Account of the History of Mathematics*, p. 107.

[2] French Translation by L. Rodet. *Journal Asiatique*, Paris, 1879. Ser. 7, Vol. XIII, pp. 393–434.

[3] Written *circa* A.D. 600. Edited Leipzig, 1883.

[4] Written *circa* A.D. 800. Published with English translation by F. Rosen, 1831, London.

APPENDIX J

THE GREEK RELIGIOUS SOCIETIES

THE Greeks probably derived their practice of combining in societies for the carrying on of certain cults from the Phœnicians.[1] These societies were of three kinds, all of which were primarily intended for the performance of religious duties, but differing in respect of their other objects. They were, however, conducted on very similar lines in so far as the payment of subscriptions by members, method of government, etc., were concerned.

THE THREE KINDS OF SOCIETIES

(1) The Thiasoi, which were strictly religious in their objects.

(2) The Eranoi, which were (*a*) convivial and social, (*b*) religious, and (*c*) for the provision of certain financial benefits for their members.

(3) Those of the Orgeones, who were concerned with the celebration of their special rites.

MEMBERSHIP OF SOCIETIES

The membership of these societies was open to persons[2] of both sexes[3] (some were confined to males, others to females[4]) and of all grades of society, provided that they could pass the necessary examination by the president, secretary, treasurers and syndics as to their moral and religious fitness.[5] All male members of whatever social rank had equal rights, and all, even slaves, were eligible for the highest offices[6]; female[7] members were eligible for some, if not all. Membership was terminated

[1] Marquardt: *Le Culte chez les Romains*.

[2] In some cases foreigners were admitted.
Cf. Foucart: *Revue Archéologique*, 1864, Vol. II, p. 399; and Newton: *Halicarnassus*, Vol. II, p. 756, inscription No. 41.

[3] *Corpus Inscriptionum Græcarum*, 110. List of members contains names of three women.

[4] Foucart: *Des Associations religieuses chez les Grecs*, p. 222, No. 40.

[5] *Corpus Inscriptionum Græcarum*, 126. Heroistes, 11, 31–34.
Cf. reference to examination in society of Orgeones.

[6] Wescher: *Revue Archéologique*, 1865, Vol. I, p. 498.

[7] Foucart: *Des Associations*, etc., pp. 6, 191–198.

by death, withdrawal, or expulsion, the last being the penalty for non-payment of subscriptions [1] and fines, or for brawling, creating a disturbance, or refusal to conform to the rules of the society.[2]

Government of Societies

The government of each society was vested in an assembly [3] elected by the members from among themselves. This assembly was absolute [4] in its power over the society, it could make or alter the laws, controlled the membership, finances, religious observances, etc., and, in addition, appointed the officers of the society. These officers, who were directly responsible to the assembly, were elected annually and were eligible for re-election.[5] They were of two kinds [6]: (*a*) those in charge of the financial and secretarial business, and (*b*) those to whom the performance of the sacrificial and other religious duties was entrusted, but the holding of an office in either class does not seem to have been a bar to the appointment of the holder to an office in the other class in the next year to that in which he held the former appointment. As the functions of the officers entrusted with the performance of the religious objects do not bear on the present inquiry it will be sufficient to describe briefly the duties, etc., of those officers who carried on the business part of the society, who were, generally speaking, two in number, the treasurer and the secretary. The treasurer [5] had charge of the chest, received subscriptions from members and donations from non-members, had control over the property and investments, etc., of the society, and was responsible for its financial position generally. The secretary [5] kept the registers of members, recorded the resolutions of the assembly, did all the secretarial work, and, in conjunction with the treasurer, kept the accounts and made the minor payments.

Legal Position of Societies

These societies enjoyed a very strong legal position in respect of their (domestic) rights of formation, powers of self-government and financial operations. By the law of Solon they could make

[1] Heroistes, 11, 12–15.
Among the Orgeones there appears to have been a partial expulsion, or better a cutting off from the benefits of membership, of members in arrears. Cf. Orgeones. Foucart: *Insc.*, 2, 1, 14.
[2] Heroistes. (Fourmont: *Corpus Insc. Gr.*, 126, 11, 40–42.)
[3] Rieu, F.: *La Coopération ouvrière*, etc., pp. 39 and 40.
[4] Rieu, F.: *La Coopération ouvrière*, etc., p. 40.
[5] Foucart, P.: *Des Associations*, etc., pp. 30–32.
[6] Foucart, P.: *Des Associations*, etc., pp. 33 and 209.

their own regulations provided that in so doing they did not act contrary to the Civil Law.[1] Their powers of owning and dealing with property, whether real or personal, were as full as those of a private citizen;[1] they could own, buy, sell, mortgage land or property of any kind and could advance or borrow money.[1] They had, too, complete control in the matter of the fees, subscriptions, fines, donations, etc., received from their members or others and of the expenditure of such funds in the provision of benefits for their members and of the expenses arising from their religious practices. In respect of their foreign rights, i.e. their rights as against non-members, they came under a special code.

Financial Methods and Position of Societies

The financial methods of these societies, though probably of a very simple nature, consisted of something more complex than the mere keeping of a money-box or chest into which receipts were put and from which the money for payments was taken. It is clear from various references that the societies were accustomed to invest their money on mortgages,[2] etc., and, judging from the knowledge of business, the records of transactions, the book-keeping, etc., of the Greeks, continually referred to by Demosthenes,[3] it is likely that they kept books which, though elementary in the method on which they were kept, would have enabled the secretary to report on the financial position of the society. These books were probably confined to cash "receipts" and "payments" books, books containing a record of the investments, etc., of the society, and to inventories of its property. The "receipts" would have comprised those received (*a*) from members, (*b*) from non-members, and (*c*) from investments; the "payments," those made in respect of (*a*) the sacrifices and other religious ceremonies and the upkeep, etc., of the temple, etc., (*b*) the payments made to and on behalf of members, and (*c*) the expenses of feasts, etc. The financial position of these societies does not appear to have been very satisfactory.[4]

(*a*) *The Subscriptions, etc., of Members.*—The subscriptions of members were (1) entrance fees, (2) periodic (monthly) subscription, (3) subscriptions payable on certain occasions to meet the expenses of sacrifices, etc., the provision of some honour for a

[1] *Digest*, XLVII, 22, 4. His autem potestatem facit lex, pactionem quam velint sibi ferre, dum ne quid ex publica lege corrumpant. Sed hæc lex videtur ex lege Solonis translata esse: nam illic ita est.

[2] Cf. Aristotle: *Œconom.*, II, 2 and 3.

[3] Demosthenes: *Private Orations.*

[4] Foucart: *Des Associations*, etc., p. 47, says: "Ces sociétés étaient le plus souvent embarrassées et qu'elles ne faisaient face aux dépenses que par la générosité des bienfaiteurs."

distinguished person, or to pay some unexpected charges on the society, (4) fines, and (5) donations.

(1) The entrance fee [1] was charged by most, if not all, of the societies. It is worthy of note that this fee was, in the cases of which there is extant evidence, considerably smaller in proportion to the periodic subscription than was the case in similar societies among the Romans. In the society of the Heroistes,[2] for example, the entrance fee was 30 drachmæ, the monthly subscription being 3 drachmæ, whereas in the Roman Society of the "Cultores Dianæ et Antinoi" [3] the entrance fee was 100 sesterces, while the annual subscription (payable monthly) was 15 sesterces. Whence the argument as to the proportion of the subscription, etc., to the benefit, set out on page 191, applies even more strongly to Greek societies.

(2) The periodic subscription was payable in all cases monthly. The prompt payment of these subscriptions was enforced by the imposition of fines [4] on every member who allowed his subscription to fall into arrear, unless he could show that he had been prevented from being present at the monthly meeting and, consequently, from paying his subscription, by illness or by family bereavement. Absence from home was no excuse, as in that event a member was required to have made the necessary arrangements for a friend to make the payment on his behalf. Poverty,[5] and consequently inability to pay, was not accepted as a reason for non-payment. If a member could not or would not pay the subscription in arrear in addition to the fines he was ejected from the society. These monthly subscriptions appear to have been allocated, to a very large extent, to meet the current expenses of the society for maintenance and for the burial of members, as in most cases there were special contributions and subscriptions to meet other demands.

(3) The subscriptions made by the members to meet certain special expenses, such as the provision of sacrifices, the purchase of a crown to be presented to some person whom the society wished to honour,[6] etc. These subscriptions do not as a matter of fact bear on the points under discussion and may, therefore, be dismissed without further examination.

[1] Foucart: *Des Associations*, etc., p. 189, No. 2, 20–23.
[2] Foucart: *Des Associations*, etc., p. 42.
[3] See p. 200, note.
[4] See p. 174.
[5] Wescher: *Revue Archéologique*, 1865, Vol. II, p. 226, states: "L'indigence n'était pas un motif d'exclusion." As, however, poverty was not accepted as an excuse for non-payment of subscriptions, consequently, although poverty *per se* would not cause the exclusion of a member, yet non-payment of subscriptions would, and an indigent man would be excluded.
[6] Foucart.

(4) Fines. Fines were payable by such members as infringed the rules of the society, and were directed especially against those members who were in arrear with their monthly subscription. As shown by the references to the laws of the society of Heroistes, any member who allowed himself to be in arrear was required to pay a fine equal to the amount of his subscription overdue in addition to paying the sum overdue. He was, thus, charged twice the amount which he would have had to pay had he been prompt in payment. Generally speaking, there seems to have been little difficulty in dealing with members who had rendered themselves liable to fines. In the event of the fines not being paid the society not only had the power of expelling the member concerned, but could also recover the fines in the courts, by an action similar to that for any other sum owing.[1]

(5) Donations to the societies.

(*a*) *Receipts from Non-Members.*—Donations to the societies were frequently made by non-members who were interested in the welfare of the society or in the cult carried on by it. These donations, whether made by members or non-members, were, in many cases, added to the fund containing the subscriptions of the members, and the sum thus accumulated was drawn on to meet the various charges on the society, of whatsoever nature they might be. There were, however, many instances in which the donations were ear-marked by the giver for a certain purpose, e.g. charity, etc., in which case the money was kept apart and used for that object.

(*b*) *Interest and Profits on Investments.*—As stated above each society enjoyed a full legal *persona* and could trade, invest or borrow money, etc., and, in fact, did so. The *Eranoi* in addition lent money to members on exceptionally favourable terms.[2]

The payments made by these societies were (1) for the expenses involved in the performance of their religious duties,[3] (2) for the periodic feasts, etc., of the members, (3) for the burial of members and the provision of funeral monuments, (4) for the crowns and other marks of honour bestowed by the society, and (5) charitable gifts, etc., provided by the donations referred to above. In addition to these expenses there were the secretarial and other incidental outgoings arising from the upkeep of the society.

[1] Lycurgus *contra* Leocrat., 22.
[2] See notes 1 and 5, p. 308.
[3] Foucart: *Des Associations*, etc., pp. 44–47.

The Non-Religious Benefits Provided by the Societies

In addition to the carrying on of the religious duties attaching to the cults of the respective societies, these societies undertook the burial of their members. The method of doing so adopted by them is uncertain, but it is most probable that a common burial ground or tomb was provided, as in many of the Roman societies. This right to burial at the expense of the society was common to all members who were not deprived thereof by being in arrears with their subscriptions, irrespective of the length of their membership. As each member paid the same subscription, it follows that, as far as the burial benefit is concerned, the practice was equivalent to a mutual insurance of the burial expenses at a fixed rate of premium for all ages of entry: subject of course to any limitations as to age of entry which the societies may have imposed, of which we have no evidence. In the case of the Eranoi,[1] they provided certain financial benefits, such as the advance of money or goods to members on exceptionally favourable terms. It is of course possible that there may have been societies which were, as Wescher [2] and Joly [3] state, Friendly Societies in the modern sense of the term, but it is extremely unlikely. The only evidence which can be adduced in favour of such a statement is that of one record,[4] which is in a very imperfect state and cannot be considered to be sufficient to warrant the hypothesis that such business was carried on by these societies. Some misunderstanding on this point appears to have arisen from a misconception of the nature of the loans made by the Eranoi to members who were presumably in needy circumstances. These loans were made on very easy terms as to rate of interest and date of re-payment, but were only made on good security, and were in no sense a gift—only and always a loan.[5] As these loans were made from the accumulated funds of the society to members only on easy terms they justify the name of "society for mutual assistance," but only in a limited sense and not in that implied in the modern term of Friendly Society.

[1] Dareste, R.: *La Science du droit en Grèce*, p. 112. "À Athènes, les éranes quand ils étaient faits entre associés, en vertu d'une sorte de contrat d'assurances, donnaient overture à une action."

[2] Wescher: *Revue Archéologique*, 1865, Vol. II, p. 220, says that these societies were "... destinée à fournir des avances aux membres nécessiteux, à leur procurer des secours en cas de maladie. ..."

[3] Joly, E.: *Le passé, le présent, l'avenir de la mutualité*, p. 13. "L'association subvenait, au moyen de cotisations mensuelles, exigées des membres, aux besoins des malades, des infirmes, des veuves, des orphelins, et des nécessiteux."

[4] Foucart: *Des Associations*, etc., pp. 140 *et seq.* Cf. Rieu, F.: *La Coopération ouvrière*, etc., pp. 41 and 42.

[5] Foucart, p. 142.

BIBLIOGRAPHY OF SOME OF THE AUTHORITIES CONSULTED

AESCHINES. Oratio in Timarchum. Recensuit F. Franke. 2nd edition. 8°. *Quedlinburg*, 1846.

ANSALDI (A.). Discursus legales de commercio et mercatura, *etc.* (Cui adjecti sunt B. Stracchæ tractatus duo de assecurantibus et proxenetis atque proxeneticis, *etc.*) Fol. *Geneva*, 1751.

ARDAILLON (E.). Les Mines du Laurion dans l'antiquité, *etc.* (Bibliothèque des Écoles Françaises d'Athènes et de Rome. Fasc. 77.) 8°. *Paris*, 1877.

ARISTOTLE. Aristotelis politica et œconomica ex editione F. Sylburgii cum versione Latina D. Lambini, *etc.* 8°. *Oxford*, 1810.

ARNOULD (A. M.). De la Balance du commerce et des relations commerciales extérieures de la France dans toutes les parties du globe, *etc.* 8°. *Paris*, 1791.

ARNOULD (*Sir* J.). A Treatise on the law of marine insurance and average. 2 parts. 8°. *London*, 1901.

ASCHEN (H. ab). Disputatio juridica inauguralis de assecuratione, vulgo assurantz, *etc.* 4°. *Frankfort-on-the-Oder*, [1693].

AYRER (G. H.). De Vestigiis cambii apud Romanos. 8°. *Leipzig*, 1737.

—— Dissertatio de comparatione eruditionis antiquæ ac recentioris. 8°. *Leipzig*, 1735.
See BLACKWALL (A.).

—— Jurisprudentia vetus ante-Justinianea. Prefatus est G. H. Ayrer. 8°. *Leipzig*, 1737.
See SCHULTINGIUS (A.).

AZUNI (D. A.). Maritime law of Europe. Translated from the French [by W. Johnson.] 8°. *New York*, 1806.

—— Sistema universale dei principi del diritto marittimo dell' Europa. 2 vols. 8°. *Florence*, 1795–96.

BALDUCCI PEGOLOTTI. La Pratica della mercatura. [*Florence*], 1765–66.
See PAGNINI DAL VENTURA (G. F.) — UZZANO (G. di).

BALL (W. W. Rouse). A short account of the history of mathematics. 2nd edition. 8°. *London*, 1893.

BASIL I., *Emperor of the East*. Basilicorum libri lx. 4°. *Leipzig*, 1833–70.

BEAMAN (G. B.). On the Sources of the Dharma Sástras of Manu and Yajnavalkya. 8°. *Leipzig*, 1895.
See MANU.

BEAUCOURT. Brugschen Koophandel. 8°. *Bruges*, 1775.

BENOIT (A.). Du Jus sepulcri à Rome. 8°. *Nancy*, 1890.

BENT (J. T.). Early voyages and travels in the Levant. Edited by J. T. Bent. (*Hakluyt Society*.) 8°. *London*, 1893.

BÉRARD (V.). Essai de méthode en mythologie grecque. De l'origine des cultes arcadiens. 8°. *Paris*, 1894.

—— Les Phéniciens et l'Odyssée. 2 vols. 8°. *Paris*, 1902–3.

BERTIN (G.). Akkadian precepts for the conduct of man and his private life. 8°. *London*, 1884.

BLACKWALL (A.). De Præstantia classicorum auctorum commentatio. Latine vertit atque animadversionibus instruxit G. H. Ayrer. Accedit ejusdem dissertatio de comparatione eruditionis antiquæ ac recentioris, *etc*. 8°. *Leipzig*, 1735.

BOECKH (A.). Public economy of the Athenians. Translated by A. Lamb. 8°. *Boston*, 1857.

—— Corpus Inscriptionum Græcarum. Edited by A. Boeckh. *Berlin*, 1828.
See CORPUS.

BOETHIUS. Arithmetica communis, *etc*. 4°. *Vienna*, 1515.

—— Divi Severini Boetii arithmetica, duobus discreta libris, *etc*. Fol. *Paris*, 1521.

BOISSIER (A.). Recherches sur quelques contrats Babyloniens. 8°. *Paris*, 1890.

BOISSIER (G.). Cicéron et ses amis : étude sur la société romaine du temps de César. 8°. *Paris*, 1865.

—— Promenades archéologiques. Rome et Pompei, *etc*. 8°. *Paris*, 1880.

BONFANTE (P.). Code of Hammurabi. 8°. *Milan*, 1903.
See HAMMURABI.

BORDIER (H. L.). Du Recueil des chartes merovingiennes. 8°. *Paris*, 1850.

BOSCAWEN (W. St. C.). Assyria and Babylonia. (*British Museum Lectures*.) 4 pts. 8°. *London*, [1886].

BOUCHARD (L.). Étude sur l'administration des finances de l'Empire Romain dans les derniers temps de son existence. 8°. *Paris*, [1876].

BOUCHÉ-LECLERCQ (A.). Manuel des institutions romaines. 8°. *Paris*, 1886.

BOUCHER (P. B.). Histoire de l'usure, *etc.* 12°. *Paris*, 1806.
—— Institutions commerciales traitant de la jurisprudence marchande et des usages du négoce, *etc.* 8°. *Paris*, 1801.
—— Institutions du droit maritime : ouvrage complet sur la législation maritime, ayant pour base l'ordonnance de 1681, *etc.* 4°. *Paris*, 1803.
—— Mémoire sur l'intérêt limité et sur l'intérêt illimité de l'argent dans les temps anciens et dans les temps modernes, *etc.* 8°. *St. Petersburg*, 1814.
BRUGES. Inventaire des Archives de la ville de Bruges. Publié sous les auspices de l'Administration Communale. 4°. *Bruges*, 1871, *etc.*
—— *Société d'Émulation de Bruges.* Recueil de chroniques, chartes, et autres documents, concernant l'histoire et les antiquités de la Flandre-Occidentale. Première Série : Chroniques des Monastères de Flandre. Troisième Série : Documents isolés, chartes et keuren. 4°. *Bruges*, 1839, *etc.*
BÜHLER (G.). Laws of Manu. Translated by G. Bühler. (*Sacred Books of the East*, Vol. XXV.) 8°. *Oxford*, 1879. *See* MANU.
BRUSSELS. *Académie Royale des Sciences, etc.* Bulletins de l'Académie Royale des Sciences et Belles-Lettres de Bruxelles. 2nd series. 23 vols. 8°. *Brussels*, 1857, *etc.*
BUNYON (C. J.). The Law of life assurance, *etc.* 3rd edition. 8°. *London*, 1891.
BURY (J. B.). History of Greece. 8°. *London*, 1900.
—— History of the Later Roman Empire from Arcadius to Irene, A.D. 395.–A.D. 800. 2 vols. 8°. *London*, 1889.
—— The History of the decline and fall of the Roman Empire. *London*, 1896. *See* GIBBON (E.).
BYNKERSHOECK (C. van). Questionum juris publici libri duo, quorum primus est de rebus bellicis, secundus, de rebus varii argumenti. 4°. *Leyden*, 1737.
CAGNAT (R.). L'Armée romaine d'Afrique et l'occupation militaire de l'Afrique sous les empereurs. 4°. *Paris*, 1892.
CAILLEMER (E.). Le Contrat de Société à Athènes. 8°. *Paris*, 1872.
—— Le Droit civil dans les provinces anglo-normandes au XIIe siècle. 8°. *Caen*, 1883.
—— Des Intérêts. 8°. *Caen*, 1861.
CAMPBELL (A. C.). Insurance and crime. 8°. *London*, 1902.
CAPMANY Y MONTPALAN (A.). Memorias historicas sobre la marina commercio y artes de la antigua ciudad di Barcelona. 4 vols. 4°. *Madrid*, 1779–92.

CAPMANY Y MONTPALAN (A.) Questiones criticas sobre varios puntos de historia economica, politica, y militar. 8°. *Madrid*, 1807.
CARLI (G. R.). See under Origine.
CASIER (C.). Coutumes du pays et duché de Brabant. Quartier de Bruxelles. Coutumes de la ville d'Aerschot, Neder-Assent et de Caggevinne. (Recueil des anciennes coutumes, *etc.*, publié par la Commission Royale pour la publication des anciennes lois et ordonnances de la Belgique.) 3 vols. 4°. *Brussels*, 1889–94.
—— and CRAHAY (L.). Coutumes du duché de Limbourg et des pays d'Outre-Meuse. (Recueil des anciennes coutumes, *etc.*, publié par la Commission Royale de la Belgique.) 4°. *Brussels*, 1889.
CHWANG TSZE. Divine classic of Nan Hwa with annotations by F. H. Balfour. 8°. *Shanghai*, 1881.
CICERO (M. T.). Epistolæ. Edited by C. G. Schütz. 8°. *Halæ*, 1808.
—— The Letters of Cicero to several of his friends. With remarks by W. Melmoth. 3rd edition. 3 vols. 8°. *London*, 1778.
—— Pro Lege Manilia. Edited by R. Harvey. 8°. *London*, [1897].
CLEIRAC (E.). Us et coutumes de la mer. 4°. *Bordeaux*, 1661.
COOK (S. A.). Laws of Moses and code of Hammurabi. 8°. *London*, 1903.
See HAMMURABI.
CORPUS Inscriptionum Atticarum. *Berlin*, 1873.
—————— Græcarum. Edited by A. Boeckh. Fol. *Berlin*, 1828.
—————— Latinarum. *Berlin*, 1863.
CORVINUS (J. A.). Jurisprudentia Romana, H. Vulteii contracta. 8°. *Amsterdam*, 1658.
COUSSEMAKER (I. de). Un Cartulaire de l'Abbaye de N.—D. de Bourbourg. 3 vols. 8°. *Lille*, 1882–91.
—— Comité Flamand de France. Observations sur l'acte de fondation de l'insigne collégiale du Saint-Pierre de Cassel, suivies de notes biographiques sur les Prévôts qui l'ont gouvernée jusqu'en 1790, *etc.* (Annales du Comité Flamand de France.) 8°. *Dunkirk*, 1891.
CRAKE (A. D.). History of the Church under the Roman Empire, A.D. 30–476. 8°. *London*, 1873.
CTESIAS. Ancient India as described by Ktesias, *etc.*, tr. by J. W. McCrindle. 8°. *Calcutta*, 1882.
CUJACIUS (J.). Observationum et emendationum libri XXVIII . . . Ejusdem de origine juris ad Pomponium commentarius. Vol. IX. 8°. *Cologne*, 1598.
CUMONT (F.). Textes et monuments figurés relatifs aux mystères de Mithra. 4°. *Brussels*, 1894.

CUNNINGHAM (W.). Essay on Western Civilization in its economic aspects. 2 vols. 8°. *Cambridge*, 1898–1900.
—— Growth of English industry and commerce during the early and Middle Ages. 2 vols. 8°. *Cambridge*, 1890.
CURICKE (R.). Jus maritimum Hanseaticum. Accesserunt diatriba de assecurantionibus. 4°. *Hamburg*, 1667.
CUSTIS (C.). Jaer-Boecken der Stadt Brugge, behelsende der gedenckwurdigste Geschiedenissen, *etc.* 3 vols. 8°. *Bruges*, 1765.
D. (N.) and R. (F.). Chronyke van Vlaenderen. Fol. *Bruges*, [1727–1736.]
DARESTE (R.). La Science du droit en Grèce. Platon, Aristote, Théophraste. 8°. *Paris*, 1893.
DARU (P. A. N. B.), *Count*. Histoire de la République de Venise. Quatrième édition, augmentée. 9 vols. 8°. *Paris*, 1853.
DAVIDSON (J. L. S.). Cicero and the fall of the Roman Republic. (*Heroes of the Nations.*) 8°. *London*, 1894.
—— Polybius: [an essay.] (Hellenica: A Collection of Essays on Greek poetry, philosophy, history, and religion, edited by E. Abbot. Pp. 387–424.) 8°. *London*, 1880.
DAVIDSON (T.). Education of the Greek people and its influence on Civilization. 8°. *London*, 1895.
DELMAR (A.). Middle Ages revisited. 8°. *New York*, 1900.
DEMOSTHENES. Orationes. Edited by Dindorf-Blass. 8°. *Leipzig*, 1888.
DEPPING (G. B.). Les Juifs dans le moyen âge. 8°. *Paris*, 1834.
DESLONGCHAMPS (A. L.). Mánava Dharma Sástra. Lois de Manou. 8°. *Paris*, 1833.
See MANU.
DIEGERICK (I. L. A.). Inventaire analytique et chronologique des chartes et documents appartenant aux archives de l'ancienne abbaye de Messines. (Série: *Monasticon Flandriæ.*) 4°. *Bruges*, 1876.
DIOPHANTUS. Diophanti Alexandrini rerum arithmeticarum libri sex, *etc.* Fol. *Basle*, 1575.
DUCOUDRAY (G.). Histoire sommaire de la civilisation depuis l'origine jusqu'à nos jours. 8°. *Paris*, 1886.
DUER (J.). Lecture on the law of representations in marine insurance, *etc.* 8°. *New York*, 1844.
DUNKIRK. *Comité Flamand de France.* Annales. 8°. *Dunkirk*, 1854, *etc.*
DUVIVIER, *Abbé*. Examen du manifeste de la province de Hainaut, *etc.* 8°. *Brussels*, [1790].
EDWARDS (C.). The Hammurabi Code and the Sinaitic Legislation. Translated by C. Edwards. 8°. *London*, 1904.
See HAMMURABI.

ELPHINSTONE (*Hon.* Mountstuart). History of India. 2 vols. 5th edition. 8°. *London*, 1866.

ÉMÉRIGNON (B. M.). Traité des assurances et des contrats, *etc.* 2 vols. 4°. *Marseilles*, 1783.

—— A Treatise on insurances. Translated from the French by S. Meredith. 8°. *London*, 1850.

FINLAY (G.). Greece under the Romans, *etc.* 8°. *Edinburgh*, 1857.

—— History of the Byzantine and Greek Empires. 8°. *London*, 1854.

FINOT (J.). Étude sur les relations commerciales entre la France et la Flandre au moyen âge. 8°. *Paris*, 1894.

FLANDERS. Kronyk van Vlaenderen. *Ghent*, 1840.

FOUCART (P. F.). Des Associations religieuses chez les Grecs—Thiases, Éranes, Orgéons. 8°. *Paris*, 1873.

—— De Collegiis scenicorum artificum apud Græcos, *etc.* 8°. *Paris*, 1873.

FRITSCH (A.). Jus fluviaticum Romano-Germanicum tripartitum, complectens variorum autorum tractatus . . . . de jure fluminum, fontium, piscationum, *etc.* 4°. *Jena*, 1672.

GAIUS, *the Jurist.* Commentaries of Gaius. Translated with notes by J. T. Abdy and B. Walker. New edition. 8°. *Cambridge*, 1876.

—— and ULPIANUS (D.). Commentaries of Gaius and Rules of Ulpian. Translated by J. T. Abdy and B. Walker. 8°. *Cambridge*, 1885.

—— and JUSTINIAN I., *Emperor of the East.* Institutes of Gaius and Justinian, the twelve Tables and the CXVIIIth and CXXVIIth Novels. Translated by T. L. Mears. 8°. *London*, 1882.

GARREAU (L.). L'État social de la France au temps des Croisades. 8°. *Paris*, 1899.

GERMAIN (A. C.). Histoire du commerce de Montpellier, antérieurement à l'ouverture du Port de Cette, *etc.* 8°. *Montpellier*, 1861.

GIBBON (E.). The History of the decline and fall of the Roman Empire. With notes by Dean Milman and M. Guizot. 8°. *London*, 1862, *etc.*

—— Another edition. Edited by J. B. Bury. 8°. *London*, 1896, *etc.*

GILBART (J. W.). Lectures on the history and principles of ancient commerce. 12°. *London*, 1847.

GILLIODTS VAN SEVEREN (L.). Bruges, port de mer, *etc.* (Société d'Émulation de Bruges. Annales). 8°. *Bruges*, 1895.

—— Cartulaire de l'ancien consulat d'Espagne à Bruges. 8°. *Bruges*, 1901–2. (Société d'Émulation de Bruges).

GILLIODTS VAN SEVEREN (L.) Cartulaire de l'ancienne estaple de Bruges. (Société d'Émulation de Bruges. Recueil de chroniques. Série 3.) 4°. *Bruges*, 1904–6.

—— Coutumes des pays et comté de Flandre. Coutume du Bourg de Bruges. (Recueil des anciennes coutumes de la Belgique, *etc.*) 4°. *Brussels*, 1883, *etc.*

—— Coutumes des pays et comté de Flandre. Quartier de Furnes. Coutumes de la ville et châtellenie de Furnes. Vol. I. (Commission Royale pour la publication des anciennes lois de la Belgique.) 4°. *Brussels*, 1897.

—— Coutume de la prévôté de Bruges. Vol. 2. (Commission Royale pour la publication des anciennes lois de la Belgique.) 4°. *Brussels*, 1887, *etc.*

—— Coutumes de la ville de Bruges. 4°. (Commission Royale, *etc.*).

—— Inventaire des Chartes [of Bruges.] (Inventaire des Archives de la ville de Bruges, Sec. I.) 4°. *Bruges*, 1871.

GIRARD (P. F.). Textes de droit romain, publiés et annotés par P. F. Girard. 8°. *Paris*, 1890.

GOBLET (E.), *Count d'Alviella.* Ce que l'Inde doit à la Grèce. Des influences classiques dans la civilisation de l'Inde. 8°. *Paris*, 1897.

GOODSPEED (G. S.). History of the Babylonians and Assyrians. 8°. *London*, 1903.

GREGOROVIUS (F.). History of the city of Rome in the Middle Ages. Translated by A. Hamilton. 8 vols. 8°. *London*, 1894.

GROSS (C.). The Gild Merchant, *etc.* 2 vols. 8°. *Oxford*, 1890.

GROTE (G.). History of Greece. 4th edition. 8°. *London*, 1872.

GUNN (B. G.). The Instruction of Ptah-hotep and the instruction of Ke'gemni: the oldest books in the world. Translated from the Egyptian with an introduction and appendix by B. G. Gunn. 16°. *London*, 1906.

[HALKIN (L.).] Les Collèges de Vétérans. (Revue de l'Instruction Publique en Belgique. Nouvelle Série.) 8°. *Mons, Bruges, and Ghent*, 1895–1906.

HAMMURABI, *King of Babylon.* Code of Hammurabi. Edited by P. Bonfante. 8°. *Milan*, 1903.

—— Code of Hammurabi. Edited by R. F. Harper. 8°. *Chicago*, 1904.

—— Il Codice di Hammurabi e la Bibbia. [By F. Mari.] 8°. *Rome*, 1903.

—— Inscriptions de Hammourabi. Traduites par J. Menant. 8°. *Paris*, 1863.

HAMMURABI, *King of Babylon.* Laws of Moses and Code of Hammurabi. Edited by S. A. Cook. 8°. *London,* 1903.
—— Loi de Hammurabi. Edited by V. Scheil. 8°. *Paris,* 1904.
—— The oldest Code of Laws in the world: laws promulgated by Hammurabi, 2285–2242 B.C. Translated by C. H. W. Johns. 8°. *Edinburgh,* 1903.
HAMON (G.). Cours d'assurances: ou, Abrégé historique et pratique des assurances maritimes, incendie, *etc.* 8°. *Paris,* 1897.
—— Histoire générale de l'assurance en France et à l'étranger. 8°. *Paris,* 1895–96.
HARDWICK (C.). The history, present position and social importance of Friendly Societies. 3rd edition, revised. 8°. *Manchester,* [1893.]
HARLEY (C. de). Yiḥ-King. *Woking,* [1897.]
See YIH-KING.
HARPER (R. F.). Assyrian and Babylonian literature. Selected translations by R. F. Harper. (*The World's Great Books.*) 8°. *London,* 1901.
—— Code of Hammurabi. 8°. *Chicago,* 1904.
See HAMMURABI.
HARPOCRATION (V.). Lexicon decem oratorum. 4°. *Leyden,* 1683.
HAUBOLD (C. G.). Manuale Basilicorum exhibens collationem juris Justinianei cum Græco postjustinianeo, *etc.* 4°. *Leipzig,* 1819.
—— Historia juris Romani. 4°. *Leipzig,* 1820.
HAULLEVILLE (P. de), *Baron.* Histoire des communes Lombardes depuis leur origine jusqu'à la fin du XIIIe siècle. 2 parts. 8°. *Ghent,* 1857, 1858.
HECKETHORN (C. W.). Secret societies of all ages and countries. 2 vols. 8°. *London,* 1897.
HEINDERYCX (P.). Jaerboeken van Veurne en Veurnambacht, uitgegeven door E. Ronse. 8°. *Furnes,* 1853 [–57.]
HEINECCIUS (J. G.). Opera omnia, *etc.* 4°. *Geneva,* 1771.
HERODOTUS. Herodoti historiæ. Edited by H. Stein. 8°. *Berlin,* 1869–72.
—— Herodotus. Translated by G. C. Macaulay. 2 vols. 8°. *London,* 1890.
HEVIA BOLAÑO (J. de). Secunda parte de la curia filipica, donde se trata breve . . . y cõtratacion de tierra, y mar, *etc.* 8°. *Valladolid,* 1623.
HEYD (W.). Histoire du commerce du Levant au moyen-âge. 8°. *Leipzig,* 1885–86.

HIBBERT (F. N.). Influence and development of English Gilds as illustrated by the history of the Craft Gilds of Shrewsbury, *etc.* (*Cambridge Historical Essays.*) 8°. *Cambridge*, 1891.
HODGKIN (T.). Italy and her invaders. 8°. *Oxford*, 1880, *etc.*
HOMER. Iliad. Edited by D. B. Monro. 2 vols. 8°. *Oxford*, 1886.
—— Odyssey. Edited by W. W. Merry. 8°. *Oxford*, 1887.
HOSDEY. Essai sur le Statut du Mont Hazebrouck. 8°. *Dunkirk*, 1854, *etc.*
See DUNKIRK. *Comité Flamand de France.* Annales.
HOW (W. W.) and LEIGH (H. D.). A History of Rome to the death of Cæsar. 8°. *London*, 1896.
HUGO (G.). Histoire du droit Romain, *etc.* 8°. *Paris*, 1822.
HUNTER (W. A.). A systematic and historical exposition of Roman law in the order of a code . . . embodying the Institutes of Gaius, and the Institutes of Justinian. Translated by J. A. Cross. 8°. *London*, 1876.
INSURANCE GUIDE. The Insurance guide and hand-book. By a Fellow of the Society of Arts. 8°. *London*, 1857.
ISIDORE, *Saint. Bishop of Seville.* Origines. Etymologiarum libri XX. 4°. *Leipzig*, 1831, 1832.
JOHNS (C. H. W.). Assyrian deeds and documents recording the transfer of property. 8°. *Cambridge*, 1898, *etc.*
JOLLY (J.). Mánava Dharma Sástra. The Code of Manu. Edited by J. Jolly. 8°. *London*, 1878.
See MANU.
JOLY (E.). Le passé, le présent, l'avenir de la mutualité. 8°. *Saint Etienne*, 1893.
JONES (*Sir* W.). Institutes of Hindi law. 8°. *London*, 1869.
See MANU.
JUSTINIAN (I.), *Emperor of the East.* Les Cinquante livres du Digeste, traduits par M. Hulot, *etc.* 4°. *Paris*, 1805.
—— Corpus Juris Civilis Romani. 2 vols. 4°. *Leipzig*, 1720.
—— Index alphabeticus omnium titulorum qui continentur in corpore Digestorum, Codicis, Novellarum-Constitutionum necnon Institutionum. 8°. *Pisa*, 1852.
—— Institutiones D. Justiniani typis variæ: rubris nucleum exhibentibus. Accesserunt ex Digestis tituli de verborum significatione et regulis juris. [By A. Corvinus a Belderen.] 16°. *Amsterdam*, 1676.
—— Institutes. Translated by T. C. Sandars. 8th edition. 8°. *London*, 1888.
—— Novelles of Justinian. Translated by Bérenger. 8°. *Metz*, 1811.
JUVENAL (D. J.). Satiræ. With a translation by J. D. Lewis. 8°. *London*, 1882.

KANG HE, *Emperor.* The Sacred Edict. Translated by F. W. Baller. 2 vols. 8°. *Shanghai,* 1892.
KING (L. W.). Letters and inscriptions of Hammurabi. (*Luzac's Semitic Text Series.*) 8°. *London,* 1898–1900.
KTESIAS. *See* CTESIAS.
LAMBERT (J. M.). Two thousand pears of gild life. 4°. *Hull,* 1891.
LATTERADE (A.). Le Mutualisme et la question sociale. 8°. *Auch,* 1896.
LE DAIN (A.). L'Inde antique. 8°. *Paris,* 1896.
[LE FEVRE (R.).] Traité de l'usure, avec les réponses au Traité de la pratique des billets et à une dissertation sur les intérêts des derniers pupillaires selon l'usance de Bretagne. 16°. *Rennes,* 1699.
LI-KI. Texte chinois, avec une traduction par S. Couvreur. 2 vols. 8°. *Ho-kien fou,* 1899.
LETOURNEAU (C. J. M.). L'Évolution du mariage et de la famille. 8°. *Paris,* 1888.
LINDSAY (W. S.). History of merchant shipping and ancient commerce. 4 vols. 8°. *London,* 1874–76.
LIVIUS (T.). Historiarum libri qui supersunt. Edited by Weissenborn-Müller. 4 vols. 8°. *Leipzig,* 1829.
LOCCENIUS (J.). De Jure maritimo et navali libri tres. Editio tertia. 8°. *Stockholm,* [1693 ?]
—— and SCHOOCKIUS (M.). Jus et imperium maritimum. 12°. *Amsterdam,* 1669.
LONDON. *British Museum.* Annals of the Kings of Assyria. Cuneiform texts, with translations, etc. Edited by A. W. Budge and L. W. King. 8°. *London,* 1902, *etc.*
LONGÉ (G. de). Coutumes du pays et duché de Brabant. Quartier d'Anvers. (Recueil des anciennes coutumes de la Belgique, publié par la Commission Royale pour la publication des anciennes lois et ordonnances, *etc.*) 3 vols. 4°. *Brussels,* 1870.
—— Coutumes de la ville de Malines. (Recueil des anciennes coutumes de la Belgique, publié par la Commission Royale pour la publication des anciennes lois et ordonnances, *etc.*) 4°. *Brussels,* 1879.
MCCULLOCH (J. R.). Dictionary, practical, theoretical and historical of commerce and commercial navigation. 8°. *London,* 1882.
MACPHERSON (D.). Annals of commerce, manufactures, fisheries, and navigation, *etc.* 4°. *London,* 1805.
MACROBIUS. F. Eyssenhardt recognovit. 8°. *Leipzig,* 1868.
MAINE (*Sir* H. J. S.). Ancient law. 8°. *London,* 1861.
—— Village communities in the east and west. 8°. *London,* 1871.

MANU. Damathat, or the Laws of Menu. Translated from the Burmese by D. Richardson. 2nd edition. 8°. *Rangoon*, 1874.
—— Institutes of Hindu Law, or the Ordinances of Menu according to the gloss of Callúca, verbally translated by Sir W. Jones. 8°. *London*, 1869.
—— Laws of Manu. Translated by G. Bühler. (*Sacred Books of the East.*) 8°. *Oxford*, 1879.
—— The Laws of Manu, or the Mánava Dhárma Sástra. Translated by J. Murdoch. (*Sacred Books of the East.*) 8°. *Oxford*, 1898.
—— Mánava Dharma Sástra. The Code of Manu, edited by J. Jolly. 8°. *London*, 1887.
—— Mánava Dharma Sástra. Lois de Manou. By A. L. Deslongchamps. 8°. *Paris*, 1883.
—— Ordinances of Manu. Translated with an introduction by A. C. Burnell, *etc.* 8°. *London*, 1884.
—— On the Sources of the Dharma Sástra of Manu and Yajnavalkya. By G. B. Beaman. 8°. *Leipzig*, 1895.
[MARI (F.).] Il Codice di Hammurabi e la Bibbia. 8°. *Rome*, 1903.
MARQUARDT (J.). De l'Organisation financière chez les Romains. Traduite par A. Vigie. (T. Mommsen and J. Marquardt: Manuel des antiquités romaines. Vol. 10.) 8°. *Paris*, 1888.
—— De l'Organisation militaire chez les Romains. Traduit par J. Brussaud. (T. Mommsen and J. Marquardt: Manuel des antiquités romaines.) 8°. *Paris*, 1892.
—— Le Culte chez les Romains. (T. Mommsen, *etc.* Vol. 12.) 8°. *Paris*, 1889.
—— La vie privée des Romains. (T. Mommsen and J. Marquardt: Manuel des antiquités romaincs. Vol. 14.) 8°. *Paris*, 1887.
MARQUARDUS (J.). Tractatus politicojuridicus de jure mercatorum et commerciorum singulari. Fol. *Frankfort*, 1662.
MARSHALL (E.). On the early traces of institutions resembling in some particulars the modern hospital, *etc.* 8°. *Oxford and London*, 1876.
MARSHALL (S.). Treatise on the law of insurance. 2nd edition. 2 vols. 8°. *London*, 1808.
MARTIN (F.). History of Lloyd's and of marine insurance in Great Britain. 8°. *London*, 1876.
MARTINET (A.). Les Sociétés de secours mutuels et les assurances ouvrières. 8°. *Paris and Nancy*, 1891.
MASPERO (G.). Dawn of civilization. 8°. *London*, 1901.
—— Histoire ancienne des peuples de l'Orient. 8°. *Paris*, 1904.
—— Life in ancient Egypt and Assyria. Translated by Alice Morton. 8°. *London*, 1892.

MAYNE (J. D.). A Treatise on Hindu law and usage. 4th edition. 8°. *Madras*, 1888.

MEYER (E.). De Historia legum maritimarum medii aevi celeberrimarum. 8°. *Göttingen*, 1824.

MILEY (J.). Rome, as it was under Paganism, and as it became under the Popes. 2 vols. 8°. *London*, 1843.

MISPOULET (J. B.). Les Institutions politiques des Romains ; ou, Exposé historique des règles de la constitution et de l'administration romaines, *etc.* 2 vols. 8°. *Paris*, 1882.

MOMMSEN (T.). De Collegiis et sodaliciis Romanorum. 8°. *Kiel*, 1843.

—— The History of Rome. Translated by W. P. Dickson. 8°. *London*, 1894.

—— and MARQUARDT (J.). Manuel des antiquités romaines. 8°. *Paris*, 1887, *etc.*

MONASTICON FLANDRIÆ. 4°. *Bruges*, 1839–99 [*irregularly*].

MORGAN (L. H.). Ancient Society. 8°. *New York*, 1877.

—— Systems of consanguinity and affinity of the human family. (Smithsonian Institution: *Smithsonian Contributions to Knowledge.* Vol. 17.) 4°. *Washington*, 1871.

MUELLER (F. M.). A History of ancient Sanskrit literature so far as it illustrates the primitive religion of the Brahmans. 8°. *London*, 1859.

MUELLER (J.). Documenti sulle relazioni delle città Toscane coll' Oriente cristiano e coi Turchi fino all' anno 1531, raccolti ed annotati da G. Mueller. 4°. *Florence*, 1879.

NĀRADA. Nâradíya Dharmasástra ; or, the Institutes of Nārada. Translated by Dr. Jolly. 8°. *London*, 1876.

NEVO (Alex. de). Consilia contra Judæos fœnerantes. Fol. *Friedrick Creussner, Nuremberg*, 1479.

NICOMACHUS (G.). Nicomachi Gerasini Pythagorei introductionis arithmeticæ libri II. Recensuit R. Hoche. 8°. *Leipzig*, 1866.

NILAKANTHA MIMAMSAKABHATTA. *Son of Sankara.* Vyavahara Mayukha. 8°. *Bombay*, 1880.

NOODT (G.). De Fœnere et usuris. 4°. *Leyden*, 1698.

OLINGER. Nouveau dictionnaire . . . Flamand-Français et Français-Flamand. Nouvelle édition, augmentée, *etc.* 12°. *Malines*, 1852.

ORIGINE. Dell' Origine e del commercio della moneta e dell' instituzion e delle zecche d'Italia della decadenza dell' Impero sino al secolo decimosettimo. [By G. R. Carli.] 4°. [*Venice*], 1751.

OWEN (D.). Marine insurance notes and clauses, *etc.* 3rd edition. 8°. *London*, 1889.

[Pagnini Dal Ventura (G. F.)]——Balducci Pegolotti (F.) ——Uzzano (G. di). Della Decima e di varie altre gravezze imposte dal commune di Firenze; della moneta e della mercatura de Fiorentini fino al secolo XVI. (Tomo terzo, contenente la Pratica della Mercatura scritta da F. Balducci Pegolotti, *etc.* Tomo quarto, la Pratica della mercatura scritta da G. di Antonio da Uzzano nel 1442.) 4 vols. 4°. [*Florence*], 1765–66.

Pardessus (J. M.). Collection de lois maritimes antérieures au XVIIIe siècle. 4°. *Paris*, 1828–45.

—— Cours de droit commercial. Sixième édition. 3 vols. 8°. *Brussels*, 1833.

—— Us et coutumes de la mer; ou, Collection des usages maritimes des peuples de l'antiquité et du moyen âge. 2 vols. 4°. *Paris*, 1847.

Park (*Sir* J. A.). A system of the law of marine insurance, with three chapters on Bottomry, on insurance on lives, and on insurances against fire. 8th edition. 8°. *London*, 1842.

Periodical Publications. *London*. Journal of Theological Studies, Jan. 1903. 8°. *London*, 1903.

—— *Paris*. Revue Archéologique. Nouvelle Série. (Wescher). 8°. *Paris*, 1865.

Perret (P. M.). Histoire des relations de la France avec Venise du XIIIe siècle à l'avènement de Charles VIII, *etc.* 8°. *Paris*, 1896.

Pertz (G. H.). Monumenta Germaniæ Historica. 4°. *Berlin*, 1877, *etc.*

Petit (E.). Les Sociétés de secours mutuels en France. 8°. *Paris and Nancy*, 1893.

Petitus (S.). Miscellaneorum libri novem. 4°. *Paris*, 1630.

Pied (E.). Les Anciens corps d'arts et métiers de Nantes. 8°. *Nantes*, 1903.

Pierret (P.). Vocabulaire hiéroglyphique, *etc.* 8°. *Paris*, 1875.

Pike (L. O.). History of crime in England, illustrating the changes of all the laws in progress of civilization, *etc.* 2 vols. 8°. *London*, 1873–76.

Piot (G. J. C.). Cartulaire de l'abbaye d'Eename. (Series: *Monasticon Flandriæ.*) 4°. *Bruges*, 1881.

Plinius Secundus (C.). Epistularum ad Trajanum liber. Edited by H. Keil. 8°. *Leipzig*, 1870.

—— Historia. Edited by Jan Mayhoff. 6 vols. 8°. *Leipzig*, 1856–75.

—— Natural history of Pliny. Translated by J. Bostock and H. T. Riley. 6 vols. 8°. *London*, 1848.

POCOCK (L.). A familiar explanation of the nature of assurances upon lives . . . to which are added the principles, seventy London Assurance Offices, *etc.* 12°. *London*, 1842.

POULLET (E.). Histoire politique nationale. Origines, développements et transformations des Institutions dans les anciens Pays-Bas. 8°. *Louvain*, 1882.

PRASANNAKUMĀRA SENA. A Study of ancient law: or, an Analysis of [Sir H. J. S.] Maine's ancient law, *etc.* 8°. *Konnagar*, 1896.

PTOLEMÆUS (C.). Ancient India as described by Ptolemy. Translated, *etc.*, by J. W. McCrindle. 8°. *Calcutta*, 1885.

RADAU (H.). Early Babylonian history down to the end of the Fourth Dynasty of Ur. 8°. *New York*, 1900.

RAGOZIN (Z. A.). Vedic India as embodied principally in the Rig-Veda. 8°. *London*, 1895.

RAMEṢACHANDRA DATTA. A History of civilization in ancient India. 3 vols. 8°. *Calcutta*, 1899.

RAMEṢACHANDRA GHOSHA. History of Hindu civilization as illustrated in the Vedas and their appendages. 8°. [*Calcutta*, 1889.]

RASSAM (H.). Babylonian cities, *etc.* 8°. *London*, [1883].

RAWLINSON (G.). The Five great monarchies of the ancient Eastern World. 8°. *London*, 1871.

REICH (E.). History of civilization. Græco-Roman institutions, from anti-evolutionist points of view, *etc.* 8°. *Oxford*, 1890.

REIFFENBERG (F. de), *Baron*. Memoire: "Quel a été l'état . . . du commerce dans les provinces des Pays-Bas pendant les XVe et XVIe siècles ?" 4°. *Brussels*, 1822.

REVILLOUT (E.). Les Actions publiques et privées en droit égyptien. 4°. *Paris*, 1897.

—— Cours de droit égyptien. 8°. *Paris*, 1884.

—— La Créance et le droit commercial dans l'antiquité. 8°. *Paris*, 1897.

—— Étude complémentaire du cours de droit égyptien. 8°. *Paris*, 1884.

—— Les Obligations en droit égyptien comparé aux autres droits de l'antiquité. 8°. *Paris*, 1886.

—— Précis du droit égyptien. 8°. *Paris*, 1899–1903.

—— La Propriété: ses démembrements; la possession, et leurs transmissions en droit égyptien comparé aux autres droits de l'antiquité. 8°. *Paris*, 1897.

RIBEIRO (J. P.). Dissertaçoes chronologicas e criticas sobre a historia e jurisprudencia ecclesiastica e civil de Portugal. 4°. *Lisbon*, 1810, *etc.*

RIEU (F.). La Coopération ouvrière à travers les âges. 8°. *Paris*, 1898.
ROBERTON (N. S.). Voices of the past from Assyria and Babylonia. 8°. *London*, 1900.
ROBIOU (F.). Les Institutions de la Grèce antique, *etc.* 8°. *Paris*, [1882].
—— and DELAUNAY (D.). Les Institutions de l'ancienne Rome. 3 vols. 16°. *Paris*, 1884–88.
ROBY (H. J.). Roman private law in the times of Cicero and of the Antonines. 2 vols. 8°. *Cambridge*, 1902.
—— Introduction to the study of Justinian's Digest, *etc.* 8°. *Cambridge*, 1884.
ROCCO (F.). De Navibus et naulo. 8°. *Amsterdam*, 1708.
—— Manual of maritime law; consisting of a treatise on ships and freight, and a treatise on insurance. 8°. *Philadelphia*, 1809.
ROGERS (R. W.). History of Babylonia and Assyria. 8°. *London*, 1901.
SACRED EDICT. *See* KANG HE.
SAINT NICOLAS FURNENSIS. Chronicon et cartularium abbatiæ S. Nicolai Furnensis . . . per F. V. et C. C. (Série: *Monasticon Flandriæ.*) 4°. *Bruges*, 1849.
SALMASIUS (C.). De Modo usurarum. 8°. *Leyden*, 1639.
—— De Usuris. 8°. *Leyden*, 1638.
—— Dissertatio de fœnore trapezitico. 8°. *Leyden*, 1640.
SAUPPE (H.). Satura philologa N. Sauppio obtulit amicorum conlegarum decas. 8°. *Berlin*, 1879.
SAYCE (A. H.). The Archæology of the cuneiform inscriptions. 8°. *London*, 1907.
—— Babylonians and Assyrians: Life and Customs. (*Semitic* Series No. 6.) 8°. *London*, 1900.
—— Hittites: The Story of a forgotten Empire. 8°. *London*, [1883].
—— Social life among the Assyrians and Babylonians. (*By-Paths of Bible Knowledge*, No. 18.) 8°. *London*, [1883, *etc.*].
SCHEIL (V.). Loi de Hammurabi. 8°. *Paris*, 1904.
SCHLEGEL (G.). T'oung Pao. (Archives pour servir à l'étude d'histoire des langues, redigées par G. Schlegel.) 8°. *Leyden*, 1890.
SCHERER (H.). Histoire du commerce de toutes les nations. Traduit par H. Richelot et C. Vogel. 2 vols. 8°. *Paris*, 1857.
SCHIESS (T.). Die römischen Collegia Funeraticia nach den Inschriften. 8°. *Munich*, 1888.
SCHMID (R.). Die Gesetze der Angelsachsen. 8°. *Leipzig*, 1858.

SCHOMBERG (A.). A Treatise on the maritime laws of Rhodes. 8°. *Oxford*, 1786.

SCHRIJVER (P.). Veteres de re militari scriptores quotquot extant, nunc prima vice in unum redacti corpus [by P. Schrijver]. Accedunt (i) G. Stewechii in F. Vegetium commentarius. (ii) Ejusdem conjectanea, et F. Modii notæ in S. J. Frontinum. (iii) P. Scriverii in F. Vegetium et S. J. Frontinum animadversiones. 3 parts. 8°. *Wesel*, 1670.

SCHULTINGIUS (A.). Jurisprudentia vetus ante-Justinianea ex recensione et cum notis A. Schultingii. Prefatus est G. H. Ayrer. 4°. *Leipzig*, 1737.

SERRURE (C. P.) and BLOMMAERT (P.). Kronyk van Vlaenderen van 500 tot 1467. Edited by C. P. Serrure and P. Blommaert. 8°. *Ghent*, 1839, *etc.*

SHEPPARD (J. G.). Fall of Rome and the rise of the new nationalities. 8°. *London*, 1892.

[SIRET (A.)]. Bulletins de l'Académie Royale des Sciences et Belles-Lettres de Bruxelles. (Brussels. Académie des Sciences.) 8°. *Brussels*, 1857.

SMITH (J. Toulmin). English Gilds. 8°. *London*, 1870.

SMITH (W.). A Concise Dictionary of Greek and Roman antiquities. 8°. *London*, 1898.

SPANO (G.). Testo ed illustrazioni di un codice cartaceo del secolo XV contenente le leggi doganali e marittime del Porto di Castel Genovese, e la fondazione e storia dell' antica città di Plubium pel Can. G. Spano. 8°. *Cagliari*, 1859.

STARCKE (C. N.). The primitive family in its origin and development. 8°. *London*, 1889.

STEWECHIUS (G.). *See* SCHRIJVER (P.).
See VEGETIUS RENATUS (F.).

STRACCHA (B.). Discursus legales de commercio et mercatura. *Geneva*, 1751.
See ANSALDI (A.).

SUETONIUS TRANQUILLUS (C.). De Vita Cæsarum. Edited by C. L. Roth. 8°. *Leipzig*, 1858.

SYMMACHUS (Q. A.). Lettere fatte di Latine volgari dal canonico G. A. Tedeschi, *etc.* 4°. *Rome*, 1724.

SZE SHOO. The Four Books, or the Chinese classics in English. 8°. *Hongkong*, 1898.

TACITUS. (*Oxford Pocket Classics Series.*) 8°. *Oxford and London*, 1860.

TALMUD. Le Talmud de Babylone, traduit en langue française par L. Chiarini. 2 vols. 8°. *Leipzig*, 1831.

—— New Edition of the Babylonian Talmud. English Translation by M. L. Rodkinson. 8°. *New York*, 1900, *etc.*

TAYLOR (M.). Students' manual of the history of India from the earliest period to the present. New edition. 8°. *London*, 1896.

TERRIEN DE LACOUPERIE (A. E. J. B.). Babylonia and China. 4°. [*London*, 1887].

—— Oldest book of the Chinese, the Yih-King and its authors. 8°. *London*, 1892.

—— Western origin of early Chinese civilization from 2300 B.C. to A.D. 200. 8°. *London*, 1894.

THEODOSIUS II. *Emperor of the East.* Codex Theodosianus.

THEOPHRASTUS. Characteres, emendavit F. Dübner. 8°. *Paris*, 1840.

THIERRY (A. S. D.). Histoire des Gaulois depuis les temps les plus reculés jusqu'à l'entière soumission de la Gaule à la domination romaine. 3rd edition. 8°. *Paris*, 1844.

—— Récits des temps Mérovingiens. 2 vols. 8°. *Paris*, 1838.

THORPE (B.). Diplomatarium anglicum ævi saxonici. A Collection of English Charters, *etc.* 8°. *London*, 1865.

TORR (C.). Rhodes in ancient times. 8°. *Cambridge*, 1885.

UZZANO (G. de). Della decima e di varie altre gravezze imposte dal commune di Firenze, *etc.* 4°. [*Florence*], 1765–66.

VEGETIUS RENATUS (F.). De la milice Romaine, traduict de J. Jaques de Wallhausen, *etc.* Fol. *Frankfort on the Main*, 1616.

—— De re militari libri quinque ex recensione N. Schwebellii, cum integris ejusdem, et selectis G. Stewechii, P. Scriverii, *etc.* 8°. *Strassburg*, 1806.

—— De re militari scriptores, *etc.* 8°. *Wesel*, 1670.
See SCHRIJVER (P.).

—— Institutorum rei militaris libri quinque. [Edited by J. Valert.] 12°. *Paris*, 1762.

VILLANI (F.). Liber de civitatis Florentiæ famosis civibus ex codice Mediceo Laurentiano, *etc.* 4°. *Florence*, 1847.

VINCENT (W.). The Periplus of the Erythrean Sea. 4°. *London*, 1800.

—— Voyage of Nearchus from the Indus to the Euphrates, *etc.* 4°. *London*, 1797.

VIREY (P.). Études sur le Papyrus Prisse. Le Livre de Kaquimma et des Leçons de Ptah-Hotep. 8°. *Paris*, 1887.

WALFORD (C.). Gilds: their origin, constitution, objects and later history. New and enlarged edition. 8°. *London*, 1888.

—— The Insurance Cyclopædia. 8°. *London*, 1871, *etc.*

WALTZING (J. P.). Étude historique sur les corporations professionelles chez les Romains depuis les origines jusqu'à la chute de l'Empire Occident. (Académie Royale des Sciences, des Lettres et des Beaux Arts de Belgique. Vol. 50.) 4 vols. 8°. *Brussels*, 1895–1900.

WARNKOENIG (L. A.). Histoire de la Flandre et de ses institutions civiles et politiques jusqu'à l'année 1305. Translated by Gheldolf. 2 vols. 8°. *Brussels*, 1835–36.
WAUTERS (A.). Inventaire de la ville de Bruxelles. 8°. *Brussels*, 1888, *etc.*
—— Les Libertés communales. 8°. *Brussels*, 1878.
WESCHER (C.). Revue Archéologique. 8°. *Paris*, 1865.
WHISTON (R.). Fœnus Nauticum.
WILDA (E.). Das Gildenwesen im Mittelalter. 8°. *Halle*, 1831.
WILKINSON (*Sir* J. G.). Manners and customs of the ancient Egyptians. New edition, revised by S. Birch. 8°. *London*, 1878.
WILLEMS (P.). Le droit public romain depuis l'origine de Rome jusqu'à Constantin le Grand. Cinquième édition. 8°. *Louvain*, 1883.
WILLIAMS (F. W.). Chinese and mediæval gilds. 8°. *Boston*, 1902.
WOEPCKE (F.). Récherches sur l'histoire des sciences mathématiques chez les Romains. 8°. *Paris*, 1860.
YIH-KING: A new translation from the original Chinese by C. de Harlez, *etc.* 8°. *Woking*, [1897].
ZIMMERN (H.). The Hansa Towns. 8°. *London*, 1889.

ADDENDA TO BIBLIOGRAPHY

BREASTED (J. H.). A History of Egypt. 8°. *London*, 1906.
BUDGE (E. A. W.). A History of Egypt. 8°. *London*, 1902.
ERMAN (A.). Life in Ancient Egypt. 8°. *London*, 1894.
GRIFFITH (F. L.). The Petrie papyri. Hieratic papyri from Kahun and Gunrob. 8°. *London*, 1898.
LONDON. *Egypt Exploration Fund. Græco-Roman Branch.* [Memoirs].
I, II and V. The Oxyrhynchus papyri. Edited with translations and notes by B. P. Grenfell and A. S. Hunt. 8°. *London*, 1898–1903.
III. The Fayum towns and their papyri. By B. P. Grenfell, A. S. Hunt, and D. G. Hogarth. 8°. *London*, 1900.
IV. The Tebtunis papyri. Edited by B. P. Grenfell, A. S. Hunt, and J. G. Smyly. 8°. *London*, 1902.
Issued conjointly with the University of California.
MAHAFFY (J. P.). Egypt under the Ptolemaic Dynasty. 8°. *London*, 1899.
MILNE (J. Grafton). Egypt under Roman Rule. 8°. *London*, 1898.
WILLIAMS (*Sir* Monier). Indian Wisdom. 8°. *London*, 1893.

Printed in Great Britain by Butler & Tanner Ltd., Frome and London

www.ingramcontent.com/pod-product-compliance
Ingram Content Group UK Ltd.
Pitfield, Milton Keynes, MK11 3LW, UK
UKHW041131071026
15587UKWH00009B/412